Germans, Jews, and Antisemites
Trials in Emancipation

The ferocity of the Nazi attack on the Jews took many by surprise. This book tries to explain why. Volkov argues that a new look at both the nature of antisemitism and the complexity of modern Jewish life in Germany is required in order to provide an explanation. While antisemitism had a number of functions in pre-Nazi German society, it most particularly served as a cultural code, a sign of belonging to a particular political and cultural milieu. Surprisingly, it had only a limited effect on the lives of the Jews themselves. Theirs was a remarkable success story. By the end of the nineteenth century, their integration was well advanced. Many of them enjoyed prosperity, prestige, and the pleasures of metropolitan life. This did not necessarily entail an abandonment of Judaism. This book stresses the dialectical nature of assimilation, the lead of the Jews in the processes of modernization, and, finally, their continuous efforts to "invent" a modern Judaism that would fit their new social and cultural positions.

Shulamit Volkov is the Konrad Adenauer Chair for Comparative European History and Professor of Modern European History at Tel Aviv University. She was a Fellow at St. Anthony's College, Oxford; The Wissenschaftskolleg in Berlin; and the Historisches Kolleg in Munich. Volkov is the author of *The Origins of Popular Antimodernism in Germany: The Urban Master Artisans, 1873–1896* (1978), *Die Juden in Deutschland 1780–1918* (2000), and two volumes of essays: *Antisemitismus als Kultureller Code* (2000) and *Das Jüdische Projekt der Moderne* (2001). She is the editor of *Deutsche Juden und die Moderne* (1994) and *Being Different: Minorities, Aliens, and Outsiders in History* (in Hebrew, 2000).

Germans, Jews, and Antisemites

Trials in Emancipation

SHULAMIT VOLKOV

Tel Aviv University

CAMBRIDGE
UNIVERSITY PRESS

32 Avenue of the Americas, New York NY 10013-2473, USA

Cambridge University Press is part of the University of Cambridge.

It furthers the University's mission by disseminating knowledge in the pursuit of
education, learning and research at the highest international levels of excellence.

www.cambridge.org
Information on this title: www.cambridge.org/9780521609593

© Shulamit Volkov 2006

First published 2006

A catalogue record for this publication is available from the British Library

Library of Congress Cataloguing in Publication data

Volkov, Shulamit, 1942–
[Ba-ma'agal ha-mekhushaf. English]
Germans, Jews, and antisemites : trials in emancipation / Shulamit Volkov.
    p.   cm.
Includes bibliographical references and index.
ISBN 0-521-84688-9 (hardback) – ISBN 0-521-60959-3 (pbk.)
1. Antisemitism – Germany – History – 20th century.   2. Germany – Ethnic relations.
3. Jews – Germany – History – 1789–1945.   4. Jews – Germany – Social
conditions – 20th century.   5. Jews – Germany – Identity.   6. Jews – Cultural
assimilation – Germany.   I. Title.
DS146.G4V6513   2005
305.892'4043'09–dc22   2005018817

ISBN 978-0-521-84688-2 Hardback
ISBN 978-0-521-60959-3 Paperback

It is like a miracle! I have experienced it a thousand times and it remains forever new to me. One blames me for being a Jew, the other forgives me for it; the third even praises me on this account; but they all think of it. As if they were caged in that magical Jewish circle, no one can get out.

Ludwig Börne, in a letter from Paris, February 7, 1832

Contents

Preface

This book addresses the great hope for equality, citizenship, and a life of partnership that had uplifted German Jews during the Era of Emancipation. It treats the various factors that caused the shattering of this hope. It also treats the Jews' extraordinary achievements – sometimes indeed against all odds – during that period. It is the story of success on the brink of destruction. However, I do not intend to tell it in full nor in a perfect chronological order. My purpose is to dwell upon some of the questions this story has raised for me, from my own, personal point of view. Yet this is not a private matter. My personal perspective is, in a sense, the perspective of an entire generation, a generation of Jews, in particular Israeli Jews, who seem to be still contemplating the strange life-experiences of their parents and grandparents, sometimes even their great grandparents, in Germany before Nazism. Mine, I believe, is likewise the perspective of a generation of historians, endeavoring to rethink what has traditionally been presented to them as a closed, reasoned, and sealed story. The questions I pose reflect my place in the generational chain of German Jewry as well as my position in the historiographical chain of writing about them. They also reflect, as always, the uneasy times in which we live. They reflect, or so I hope, something of the search for identity by those who were brought up, as I was, on Zionism without doubts, or, in any case, on Zionism that felt unable to openly discuss doubts; of those who were brought up while the extent of the catastrophe in Europe was being revealed but also while Jewish life was being reconstructed within the confines of a new world, with different and changing parameters.

The history of the Jews in Germany has all too often been regarded as a mirror of Jewish fate in general. Zionists on the one hand, and non-Zionists, or even anti-Zionists, on the other, have repeatedly made ideological use of it. Even today historians continue to find themselves grappling with issues that were controversial among German Jews as long as a hundred years ago. Telling this story, historians find themselves all too often participating in debates belonging to past generations. We seem to be still entangled in that Jewish "magical circle," referred to by Ludwig Börne in the epigraph of this book. Equally complex and many-sided is the discourse about antisemitism, particularly in Germany, saturated by current political attitudes and dictated by positions taken on various current affairs. While I have not refrained from occasionally taking on explicit positions in this book, I tried to make at least some use of the relatively long historical distance now at our disposal. Even in dealing with such delicate issues, distance permits us, at long last, to detach ourselves from the circumstances of past debates and rethink them from our own angle. As a historian, I am committed to applying the full range of historical sources, concepts, and methodological tools. I am committed to the effort of searching truth about the past. However, I am well aware of my limitations. This history continues to bear upon my life. It touches my personal roots and the issues I am concerned with – not only as a historian. I have tried not to ignore this fact.

For more than two decades I have been preoccupied with the history of antisemitism in Germany and the life of the Jews in that country. Some of the essays I wrote in the process, such as my work on "Antisemitism as a Cultural Code," have had a modest influence on this field. Nevertheless, when I first began to compile these essays, I realized that they seem to form chapters of a single book and that the arguments in them stand out much better when presented together. The structure of the book, then, partially reconstructs the path I trod during the years of research and partly reflects my present understanding of the theme as a whole. It begins with the question that had initially driven me to work in this field: Why was it so hard to see the approaching disaster? What caused the "blindness" that afflicted so many Jews and non-Jews, in Germany and abroad? The premise underlying my answer to this question is that the difficulty was a result of the true complexity of the situation. Contemporaries did not suffer from a rare case of blindness or insensitivity. Matters were indeed so obscure and so multidimensional that it was practically impossible, even for many clear-sighted men and women, to see through and extract the ominous signs.

In the first part of the book I therefore attempt to reconstruct what men and women living in that era saw, to tell their story by getting closer to their own world of vision and associations from a variety of perspectives. Only then do I proceed to form my own interpretation of what I believe was the essence of their experience, discuss the external forces that influenced them, their individual and collective motivations, and above all, the various dilemmas they were forced to confront. I open with a re-evaluation of the history of modern antisemitism in Germany. This is the focus of Part II of the book. Considering the tragic end of this story and my insistence on keeping alive today's point of departure, discussion of this question could not be deferred. Here I mainly address the antisemitism of the second half of the nineteenth century, while exploring the role it then fulfilled in the functioning of German society and its connections with a variety of other, related issues at the time. This part is intended as a contribution to German, not only to German-Jewish, history. Again, the underlying assumption may not be entirely self-evident: Coping with antisemitism, I would argue, was no doubt an integral part of the life of German Jews. It was central to their lives even in that "semi-neutral society," to use historian Jacob Katz's fitting term, within which they then learned to move and act. Undoubtedly, in order to properly appreciate their experience, we must understand its history. But the story of antisemitism, despite its paramount importance for Jews, despite the giant shadow it casts on every aspect of their life, is mainly the story of the non-Jews, in this case the other Germans, including but not exclusively the antisemites among them. It is the peculiarities of German society and culture that inform the arguments in this part of the book.

As for the Jews, antisemitism in this period was not really the focus of their existence. Part III of the book turns to tell their story. It often dwells, indeed, upon that seam connecting Jews with other Germans, but its focal point lies in issues that concerned Jews alone. As the discussion develops, I try to show that modern German Jewish history revolved around neither antisemitism nor Jewish efforts to be accepted, "Germanized" or assimilated. Jews were busy doing many other things at that time. Following an excursion into the problem of minorities in the modern nation-state, Part III describes first Jewish efforts to climb up the socio-economic ladder and then some aspects of their acculturation. It then turns to deal with the process of Jewish modernization and explain its tactics of exploiting old advantages and devising new ones. After taking a closer look at one area in which Jewish success was, indeed, phenomenal, namely in the natural sciences, Part III moves on to observe the limits of assimilation. By the late nineteenth century, "entry" could still be only partially achieved, but by then Jews were once again preoccupied with other matters, now mainly with the debates among themselves concerning the ways in which to reshape their identity under the new circumstances. This had to be done within a complicated context, within a society that simultaneously accepted and rejected them, that appreciated and resented them at the same time, that opened some gates for them and locked, partially or fully, some others. Thus, the story gets more intricate as we move along. The questions raised get thornier; the answers become, alas, less conclusive.

There is a broad historiography on German Jewry. In much of it German history merely serves as a background. In this book I tried to present Germany and its Jews within a single perspective. Jews, antisemites, and "ordinary" Germans formed a whole that could not be untangled. Theirs is a single history. In addition, I reject the historiographic convention according to which various historical genres must never be truly mixed. This book is conceived as both a cultural and a social history. In writing it I used sources considered characteristic of intellectual history, such as the works of philosophers, literary figures, and a variety of social observers. I also used sources deemed typical of social history, such as newspapers, memoirs, and some quantitative, statistical data. I maintain that historians must utilize all the sources at their disposal and that only by doing so can they begin to offset their major professional "drawback," namely their inability to interrogate and poll contemporaries, to fully decipher their symbolic and associative world. Moreover, within the book I have placed together findings based on extensive reading of the secondary literature with results based on my own primary investigations. These investigations, such as the one constructing a demographic profile of one particular Jewish community in Germany, that of the city of Altona, or the one concerning a small yet important group of outstanding Jews in the natural sciences, were conceived in an effort to explore and expound very concrete questions raised in the course of my work. Although such studies may also be read separately, I try to place them in their proper context, within an overall framework. Hopefully they enrich the story.

An earlier version of this book was published in Hebrew by Am Oved Publishing House in Tel Aviv, 2002. Orit Friedland has prepared a full English translation of this version with much care and sensitivity. I am deeply grateful to her. The final text, however, has undergone numerous stylistic reformulations, as well as some changes in structure and organization. A warm thank-you goes to Aya Lahav, too, who rewrote the notes with extreme care, rendering them more useful for the English reader, and in the process corrected and improved them considerably. I have also attempted to update my bibliography, but despite the continuing stream of works on German Jews, some of which are of the highest standard, I decided to make only slight revisions and a few sporadic additions to my own text in response to these works. I hope my arguments hold within this rich and ever-changing historiographical context, too.

I cannot possibly mention here all the people who have contributed to my work along the way – teachers, colleagues, friends, and students, in Israel and abroad. But I cannot conclude this preface without invoking the memory of my parents, both of whom have passed away during the years I was working on this project. They both followed with some amazement my interest in the history of Germany in general and its Jews in particular. I, on my part, never understood why they were amazed. After all, it was my father who had epitomized for me all the generosity and dignity typical of the German Jews, and it was my mother who had taught me, in her own way, to think critically even about those I loved. This book is indeed related to my parents and interwoven in their lives by many strings, both obvious and subtle. But finally, it was only Alik Volkov, who shared with me the journey itself, the years of research, writing, and rewriting. He always believed, even when I had my grave doubts, that this was a worthwhile effort. It grieves me immeasurably that he will not be able to see the finished product. This book is dedicated to his memory with love.

Prologue

My Father Leaves His German Homeland

The story that I intend to tell in this book, the story of the Jews of Germany, can only be told backwards. It is a story that must begin at the end. And the end is that singular event in which European Jewry, millions of men, women, and children, were led to their death, gassed, and massacred in all manners of unnatural death. Hitler and his followers may have indeed known all too well how they were going to "solve" the "Jewish question"; or perhaps the "final solution" was crystallized only gradually, out of partial, local action, taking on its true proportions at some later stage. We shall probably never know for sure. But outside the small circle of Nazi leaders and a number of staunch, ruthless antisemites, hardly anyone could imagine that *this* would be their policy – simple, and total. Many of the Jews in Germany regarded the transformation that their country was undergoing as the Nazis took over the government on January 30, 1933, as a transient affair, disturbing but temporary. But even among those who *did* understand that "their" Germany would never be the same again, only a few, fewer than it seems in retrospect, anticipated the force of the blow that awaited them.

Signs were abundant. Once the Nazis gained control of the central government in Germany they promptly began imposing restrictions on Jews. Emergency orders and legislation concerning German citizens of the "Jewish Race" began pouring in from the various official authorities of the Third Reich, even during the early months of its existence. The boycott on Jewish businesses was scheduled for April 1, and its limited success did nothing to dampen the enthusiasm of the new regime. On April 7, the law excluding officials of Jewish origins from public service was pronounced, followed by decrees restricting the employment of Jewish lawyers and medical personnel. A strict *numerus clausus* (restricted number or quota) designed to prevent what was seen by the Nazis as the flooding of Germany's universities by Jewish students was announced. And while the rate of excluding and isolating Jews slowed slightly during 1934 and 1935, the pressure put on them continued unmercilessly. Restricting regulations issued by the bureaucracy came in quick succession, and supposedly peace-loving citizens found ways of their own to abuse and harass their Jewish neighbors. The Nuremberg Laws, which were put into effect in September 1935, at first seemed to be aimed at the completion and consolidation of that ongoing process of exclusion. But economic prohibitions and the various manifestations of social ostracism were becoming ever more severe. Those who refused to acknowledge the gravity of the situation up to that point were finally shaken out of their illusions when violence was given free rein across Germany during the so-called *Reichskristallnacht*, the landslide pogrom that occurred on and immediately after November 9, 1938.

Yet even at that time it was difficult to grasp the dimensions of the impending horror. Although the majority of German Jews had by then realized that it was pointless to expect things to improve, surely not in the foreseeable future, many still failed to anticipate the true scope of the Nazi threat. Understandably, those who were observing the events in Germany from afar could not grasp the scale of the imminent catastrophe. It remained beyond the capacity of human imagination.

From our vantage point some seventy years later, this combination of hopefulness and tenacity with which so many Jews hung onto their German identity and the evaporating reality of their past existence seems disconcerting. People of my generation, in the relative shelter of Israel at the time, during the 1950s and 1960s, had often encountered German Jews in their little shops and coffee houses in Tel Aviv, in the streets of the northern town of Nahariya, or on the shaded paths of some of Jerusalem's new Jewish neighborhoods. Although we could not understand what was being said in these immigrants' living rooms, which were crowded with old furniture and rugs that somehow had found their way across the Mediterraniean, we knew they were often preoccupied with the affairs of the world they had left behind. Even more so – they were involved in issues related to that highbrow, wondrous, and for us unattainable culture that they brought with them from that world. Its fruits decorated every naked corner on their walls with fine paintings and elegantly bound volumes. They were busy with poetry, literature, and music, cultivating the treasures of their lost homes. On their part, they seemed to regard us forgivingly, somewhat suspiciously, and with apparent reservations. It seemed as if they were judging us from afar or from within that strange bubble in which they lived among us, under the scorching sun of their new land. Those were the days during which the scope of the atrocities perpetrated on the Jews in Europe were only beginning to dawn upon us.

Even as a young girl, the peculiar combination that Jews of German origin had projected – an enduring admiration for German culture on the one hand, and a burning hatred for this modern-day oppressor on the other – was a constant source of discomfort for me. My father immigrated to Palestine from Germany in the summer of 1933. Our apartment contained the familiar German bookshelf, including ornamented editions of the writings of Goethe and Heine, first editions of Thomas Mann's novels, some Schiller and Nietzsche, and even Bismarck's memoirs in three gold-trimmed volumes. However, at home we spoke only Hebrew. On Saturday nights, when Pinchas Rosen, Israel's first Minister of Justice, would come up from his next-door apartment to smoke a cigar with my father and attempt one of those uneasy conversations in German, my father would always respond in Hebrew. Of course he retained the unmistakable German-Jewish, the so-called Yeke accent, but he was proud of his eloquent, fluent Hebrew. *His* story, we have always believed, was the Zionist story at its best: Dad was "there" when Nazi students raised their flag on the central building of the Kaiser Wilhelm University in Berlin. He immediately realized that there was no place for him there anymore. The preparations took a few months, as several matters had to be taken care of, but he had no doubts about the right course. Going to *Eretz Israel* was clearly the only solution. In any case, that is what the family story always implied, though others did not always see it that way. It was always understood that "the parents," that is, my grandparents, would not hear of it. Their elegant villa, adjacent to the multistory sanitarium that they owned on the wooded slopes of Baden-Baden, a lively resort town in Southern Germany, was their only home. Their children were raised there as genuine Germans. The desert town to which their young son had sailed away to them seemed menacing and alien. They could not fathom what this offspring of a typical Jewish bourgeois family – of successful bankers and businessmen, scientists, physicians, and lawyers – a family that had been rooted in German soil for generations, would be doing in the dunes of that remote country. We did not discuss the matter too often at home, but we were always proud of our father, the only Zionist in his assimilated family – our kind of man.

And we had never questioned this story. The first cracks appeared unexpectedly. One morning, my father was rushed straight from his office in the Ministry of Justice in East Jerusalem to the Sha'are Tzedek Hospital in a coma. The next morning, as he began to recover, I was at his bedside when a young doctor interviewed him, trying to assess the damage. The patient was not sure of his whereabouts, nor could he give his name, his date of birth, or any other personal information. Then the doctor, in a seemingly offhand manner, asked him when he had immigrated to Israel. "Nineteen-thirty-three," my father promptly replied, and I suddenly grasped how central this date must have been for him. This indeed was the watershed in his life. It was a watershed even for those German Jews who had not yet sensed the magnitude of the imminent catastrophe at the time. It was a moment of great inner shock that would sooner or later require each and every one of them to perform a complete reassessment of their existence. The basis of their self-image had been completely shaken. Their personal and collective expectations were shattered. They were now forced to reexamine all the assumptions – social, cultural, and ideological – underlying their daily lives, their personal connections, their past experiences, and all of their economic and professional plans for the future.

Though my father's condition slowly improved, he never recovered completely. Interestingly, his relationship with the treasures of German culture, which he had apparently relinquished on immigration, became more accentuated now, in the twilight of his life. I noticed, too, that he was getting slightly softer on the use of the German language. It seemed that he was even pleased to help me in my first steps as a student of German history, though he was apparently rather perplexed at my new interest. He spoke German more often now with his old friends, and the connections with other members of his family, the ones who had opted for immigration to the United States, their children and grandchildren, grew warmer and more genial. Father passed away on November 29, 1985. During the week of mourning, in search of old photos, we found in the attic a wooden box containing an entire archive, of which we had had no inkling: hundreds of letters written to him by his parents and friends after he left Germany. Among them, one packet, held together by an old rubber band, immediately captured my attention. The packet contained thirty-seven letters my father had written to his future wife, my mother, between April and June of 1933. He was still in Germany then, while she, a "Palestinian" who had come to Germany as a student a few years earlier, was already back at her parents' home in Tel Aviv. When the Nazis came to power, my mother had just managed to obtain her physician's diploma, and by the end of March she was sailing back to Jaffa. With a clear and steady hand and in fine German prose, this young man of twenty-five tried to tell his sweetheart what he was going through during those days. When we found the letters, my mother was as curious as I. Yet when she glanced through them, she seemed upset. "Had I been less certain that he actually wrote them," she pointed to the meticulously numbered pile, "I would not have believed it." She could not cope with the pain. That night I tightened the old rubber band around the letters again and placed them back in the wooden box, now temporarily shoved under one of the beds. My mother never asked what happened to them.

It was only after her death that I went back to the wooden box and fished out my father's letters again. The more I read, the more I understood my mother's displeasure. Surprisingly, the letters did not support the story we had been telling ourselves all those years. Only the basic "dry" facts matched. Mother had gone to Germany to study physics in Berlin, the science capital of Europe in those days, and later switched to medicine. Her father was a pioneering Zionist. This enlightened autodidact had been a Hebrew teacher even back there in Berditschev, and his mastery of Hebrew grammar served him well when he immigrated in 1912, along with a pregnant wife and seven young children. Shmuel-Chaym Berkus soon became a teacher at the first Hebrew Gymnasium in the by-then barely established town of Tel Aviv. The children grew up there and were naturally staunch Zionists. From my mother's point of view, there were indeed no doubts: Nazi Germany left only a single alternative to Jews. She promptly returned home. In his letters to this energetic and clear-sighted woman, young Otto Rudolph Heinsheimer could probably express just a fraction of his conflicting emotions. Nevertheless, the shock he had suffered was clearly reflected in his writing: the pain, the confusion, the imminent depression, the disorientation, and, finally, the hesitant decision to sail after her to Palestine forthwith.

During the first days of the Nazi regime, Berlin must have been a very disconcerting place for this young man. On April 25, despite his dark mood, so he wrote, he decided to go to the opera: "In the intermission – foyer: the public of a new Germany – completely uniform. Income between 250 and 1000 marks per month. Social position between chief clerk and government counselor. Not more than one percent Jews. I was dumbfounded as I have not been in a long time: because of the complete transformation, because of the incredible uniformity. . . ."[1] A few days later he had a similar experience when he heard – and he must have made a special effort to hear – "a particularly weak speech" by Berlin University's new rector, anthropologist and race scientist, Professor Eugen Fischer. "It became clear to me, that in this new university [sic!] there was no room for us Jews," the young Heinsheimer dryly wrote, "no, no room at all." And on a more personal note he added: "Do you remember how I always used to go to the university and how I used to come back?"[2] How he must have loved to go there and how he loved the city opera!

In the atmosphere of those days, Heinsheimer found it difficult to write: "Not a thought is being formed," he complained, "not a word. Inside me – a kind of dark, powerful, strangely exciting vibration, unrest and silent agitation."[3] The words most commonly repeated in his letters from these days were "wilderness," "a dead-end desert," "darkness," and "uncertain darkness." "Inside me – utter darkness," he wrote to his beloved, "and thoughts, sensations, feelings and everything else scramble in confusion like ghosts. It all seems like a play of shadows on a half-lit wall, one cannot recognize the people responsible for it, nor grasp them." "Not yet," he adds with a sudden gust of youthful hope, "but soon it will all be fine."[4]

The depth of despair of this young man was finally fully revealed in his letter of May 2, written after hearing on the radio the speech that Hitler gave the previous day at the Tempelhoferfeld in Berlin. The letter is brimming with enthusiasm, even a sense of exultation vis-à-vis the slightest, albeit far and vague possibility, one that would soon slip away forever: a glimmer of hope that maybe, just maybe, he could still be a part of Germany again. The personal context of Heinsheimer's life in Berlin only serves to highlight the message of this letter. At the time, many of his close friends were hard-core Zionists. My mother, too, surely had no doubts. Here was a man who was just one step away from a decision to join her and her friends and draw all the necessary consequeces. Indeed, he probably was then, as he had always been, a slightly introverted, withdrawn person, strictly rational, and very hard to impress. And this was only days after the passage of the *Arierparagraph*, which virtually destroyed any chance

---

[1] Here and throughout the Prologue I am quoting from a collection of my father's personal letters in my possession, all numbered chronologically by him. The passage quoted here is from letter number 4.
[2] Letter number 9.
[3] Letter number 3.
[4] Letter number 4.

for him to advance a professional career in Germany. Yet Hitler's speech had an immense impact on him. It was not the text itself that so deeply moved him, but primarily that sparkle of new hope, the hope of joining a course that had seemed totally obstructed before. But then, soon enough, came another wave of confusion, paralyzing indecision, and finally, again, just "darkness."

According to his own testimony, Heinsheimer listened to Hitler's speech in a somewhat reserved and generally unsympathetic milieu, at a friend's home. Yet it was an overwhelming experience: "The shocking, crushing – yet at the same time uplifting – thing about the speech . . . was certainly not the details of the program; not the elegant, organic structure, the flawless eloquence, but the sheer expression of a gigantic force of nature, a brilliant testimony of an unshakable belief, a direct communication with a visionary and the thunderous call of a colossal personality."[5] From these heights, Heinsheimer was once again thrown into the existential abyss in which he found himself: "Is there really no possibility at all for a Jew to take part in this thing here? Or, if not now, when would it be possible again? Can one perhaps wait through this time of transition? Should one?" Then came the unavoidable disillusionment. He was engulfed by doubts and rhetorically addressing himself he wrote: "And what exactly are you giving up here? What awaits you outside? Where do you belong? How and where can you set yourself up? What do you look for, after all? What is really important for you? Where and what are your values, your talents, your aims, your ideals? Where, who, how, what?" "At times it seems to me," he concludes in despair, "that I can no longer live nor die."[6]

There is surely a measure of general malaise in these lines, an expression of the existential agony of a young man. But it is also the voice of a person whose world was shattered, undergoing a deep crisis, seeking a way out of a real catastrophe. Heinsheimer was twenty-five years old then, gifted, hardworking, and energetic. Within a couple of months he gathered his strength and left for Palestine. "As much as it seems attractive – in theory – to participate in this new and wonderful project that is apparently being built here . . . " he writes, "so it seems inexorably certain – in practice – that our cooperation is unwanted, prohibited and rejected; and so the conclusion that we should turn our back to this country is inevitable."[7] His friends, who as in many other cases were mostly

---

[5] Letter number 8.
[6] Letter number 8.
[7] Letter number 9.

of Jewish origin, went each their own way: During those very days one of them married a non-Jewish woman, moved to Hamburg, and later on made his way to the shores of the Pacific Ocean and the suburbs of San Francisco. Another always had a liking for all things English, and that summer he sailed off to England without much reservation or sentimentality. A third was determined to stay. Eventually he even joined the *verband Nationaldeutcher Juden*, the organization of German-Jewish nationalists. But he too managed to escape the inferno in time. They were all in their late twenties, from well-to-do and highly cultured families, dynamic and resourceful – exceptional in that atmosphere of general "lethargy" among Jews, of which Heinsheimer reported in his letters. Yet how difficult this extraction must have been for them! One had to be freed, my father wrote in another letter, from so many ties that were "unshakable and unquestionable.... From the country and your sense of belonging to it – something that was taken for granted; from the language and the culture – which are still your natural foundations; from the profession of German law and its surroundings" – and here he stresses his own personal experience – "in which I grew up and which has been my legacy," and also from the "urban milieu of Central Europe, the practices and lifestyle of the intellectual petit bourgeois, from the climate and the seasons of the temperate zone, etc." After all, he comments elsewhere, one should never forget nor underestimate that self-evident certainty with which, despite everything, "I had been a German – even if it were a thousand times an error."[8]

The depth of disillusionment cries out from every sentence. It was a personal tragedy. Moreover, this tragedy must be viewed in contrast to that sense of success and satisfaction that had inspired so many Jews in Germany in previous years. In a 1988 article, historian Jacob Toury reminded us of the "sense of security of being German" that prevailed among the leadership of most Jewish organizations during the Weimar Republic.[9] This sentiment was not limited to the fully assimilated, negligible margins; it was the sweeping sense of an entire community, even of those who maintained their Jewishness openly and explicitly, who developed close ties almost exclusively among themselves and held themselves responsible for sustaining the uniqueness of their separate social world.

[8] Letter number 15.
[9] See Jacob Toury, "Gab es ein Krisenbewusstsein unter den Juden während der 'Guten Jahre' der Weimarer Republik 1924–1929?" *Tel Aviver Jahrbuch für Deutsche Geschichte* 17, 1988, 145–68.

In that difficult hour, even they were faced with a crucial choice. "I am speaking here about the good German bourgeois Jews," my father wrote on the eve of his departure from Germany, already looking at them as if from outside, "not only about the loss of everything, about the new exile. No, this is a real collapse. A hard and terrible fall. People who have been moving safely on a wobbly scaffold are now realizing that everything is falling apart. And into what? Into nothingness..." As my father saw it, these Jews found themselves, suddenly and without warning, "sailing on a ghost ship which can no longer be saved from drowning."[10]

He himself arrived in Jaffa in July 1933. With surprising agility he adopted a new identity – Jewish, national, and eventually Israeli. Perhaps his young age, and maybe his wife's loving family, which immediately embraced him, facilitated this transition. After all, a new national community was being built here as well. Here, too, it was possible to take part in a great, exciting nation-building project. And my father ardently joined in. When he went to Germany to visit his parents two years later, he was already writing home long letters in high, standard Hebrew. After some searching, he found his way back to the law, passed the bar examination in its British version, and began to work in his profession, both in the private and in the public sectors of the Jewish *Yeshuv*. When the State of Israel was declared, my father was among the founders of the Ministry of Justice. He was among those who drafted the various versions of the Charter of Independence, the Law of Return, and other fundamental laws needed by the emergimg State – he was one of the forefathers of Israel's corpus of civic law. Our family story about his road from Berlin to Jerusalem perfectly suited this new identity. The days of "darkness," the shame, the indecision concerning emmigration – all of these were suppressed. His memory – and ours – has been adapted to the new reality.

[10] Letter number 33.

PART I

INTERPRETING THE DANGER SIGNS

I

Views from East and West

a. The Eastern Perspective

In his autobiography, *From Berlin To Jerusalem,* Gershom Scholem described how he had found himself isolated among his Jewish friends when he began to take interest in the antisemitic literature of the time. Twenty years before Hitler's accession to power, he recalled, he had discovered in this literature "clearly and unmistakably . . . everything that the Nazis later translated into action."[1] And this was how he tried to account for the blindness that gripped his co-religionists: Jews in Germany had never bothered to familiarize themselves with this literature, just as later on hardly anyone bothered to read Hitler's *Mein Kampf.* They failed to appreciate the gravity of the situation although the writing had been clearly on the wall. They kept repressing that one single truth, already upheld and propagated by Zionism then and there: that Jews cannot live safely amongst the nations. No amount of tolerance and liberalism would do. No emancipation could ever eradicate the eternal enmity toward them.

From this point of view, blindness seemed to have been a chronic condition. It did not begin with the Nazis' rise to power. Of paradigmatic importance was Jewish reaction to the manifestations of antisemitism that surfaced during the decade after the completion of their legal emancipation, in the early years of Bismarck's New Reich. Historians usually regard anti-Jewish activities during that time as manifestations of

---

[1] Gershom Scholem, *From Berlin to Jerusalem: Memories of My Youth*, New York, Schocken Books, 1980, p. 45 (originally in German, 1977).

"modern antisemitism." While its precise nature will be dealt with later on in this book, I want to begin by focusing on Jewish reactions to this presumably new phenomenon, on their apparent refusal to acknowledge its true scope, and on their inability to observe the danger signs attached to it.

Surprisingly, that new wave of antisemitism had a particularly critical impact on Jews *outside* Germany. To be sure, only a small minority of educated or well-traveled Jews in Eastern Europe was truly familiar with events in Germany. However, occurrences in the West seem to have played a major role in their self-consciousness. They have almost dimmed the effect of what was happening in their more immediate environment at the same time. During the early 1880s, violent pogroms took place in various locations in southwestern Russia. These at least partially premeditated attacks made a lasting impression on the intellectual elite of Russian Jewry. Indeed, one would expect these events to leave a much stronger imprint on them than would the mere war of words waged in faraway Germany. The pogroms in the Russian Empire were, after all, a matter of life and death; they represented a real battle – with bloodshed and arson. But while the basic motivation of Eastern Europe's Jewish leadership and the psychological makeup of its members were indeed shaped by the experience of these pogroms, it was in the context of what was happening in Germany that their theoretical and ideological arguments were being formulated.

Leo Pinsker was the first to react in his path-breaking *Auto-Emancipation* (1882).[2] Still under the immediate impact of the pogroms, the example of "enlightened Germany" explicitly played only a minor role, yet it clearly had deep implications. It is evident from Pinsker's text that he was fully aware of the situation in Germany and that the German case provided him with important insights for discussing his main theme, namely, the failure of emancipation. According to Pinsker, such insights could not be derived from the Russian experience alone. The pogroms did confirm the existence of a deep-rooted anti-Jewish sentiment among the Russian mob and at least the ill will of the authorities. Yet these could not throw much light on the possible success or failure of emancipation as such. After all, Russian Jews had never attained emancipation under the Tsar. Based on the experience of pogroms alone, it would have been reasonable to pursue its attainment, not to reject it. What became clear in Russia, as Pinsker endeavored to explain to his enlightened readership,

[2] Leo Pinsker, *Auto-Emancipation*, New York, Masada, 1935 (originally in German, 1882).

including many in Western Europe, was the true nature of antisemitism, that obsessive and instinctive kind of "Judophobia," as he termed it, the incontrollable fear of the "ghost-like" existence of Jews in the midst of non-Jewish society. But only the German case could illuminate the nature of emancipation. It was the re-appearance of antisemitism in modern-day Germany that proved emancipation, so eagerly sought by Russian Jews, an inadequate solution to their plight, he argued. Despite its inherent values, emancipation could not overcome the prevailing hatred of Jews among gentiles. Emancipation was a noble cause, indeed, Pinsker agreed, but it could not be obtained from the powers that be. Genuine emancipation could only come from within, through the development of an independent Jewish collective will and a full-fledged national revival movement. Emancipation had failed; from now on *auto*-emancipation alone ought to be the goal. Interestingly, while so keenly aware of the tragedy of Jewish life in the diaspora, Pinsker expressed no moral rage. Seeing antisemitism as a kind of hereditary psychosis allowed him to regard it as one regards a disease or a natural disaster. When the volcano erupts, it is best to move away, and, better still, to stay away.

Nahum Sokolow published another view of the history of antisemitism, in awkward, old-fashioned Hebrew at the same time.[3] This had little of the spirit that animated Pinsker's presentation. Nevertheless, its message was equally illuminating. For Sokolow, too, the main lesson to be learned from the current outburst of antisemitism in Europe was the failure of emancipation. It failed, in his opinion, because it had never been granted whole-heartedly. Emancipation was an act of reason, stemming from the inner logic of the French Revolution, and it was granted without true passion. As such, it could never combat antisemitism effectively. Europeans everywhere were only waiting for the first pretext to renew their attacks on the Jews. Significantly, runs Sokolow's argument, the first explicit sign of this dismal failure came from Germany, the birthplace of that glorious bourgeois *Bildung*, the epitome of the Age of Enlightenment. It was against the antisemitic wave that hit the German capital in 1879 that faith in the Enlightenment's healing power was finally shattered. For Sokolow, the German antisemites,, lashing out at the Jews of Germany, provided the final proof of the bankruptcy of emancipation.[4]

Sokolow's analysis initially appears to be very different from Pinsker's. For him antisemitism was nothing but the other side of an authentic

[3] Nahum Sokolow, *Eternal Hatred for an Eternal People* [Hebrew], Warsaw, 1882.
[4] Ibid., Introduction and pp. 54, 202.

national self-interest; not a disease, but a natural and understandable force, the inevitable psychological counterpart of what he considered "a healthy national egotism." With great pathos he applied to the problem of antisemitism tools borrowed from nascent social psychology, whose reverberations must have reached Warsaw, too. A physician by profession, Pinsker preferred to borrow pathological terms, while Sokolow ventured to take his cues from a newer and to him more relevant conceptual world. For both, however, antisemitism did not represent a *moral* problem, but an all-too-human response to inherent forces – psychological, cultural, or both. Pinsker and Sokolow both indicated other sources for the new antisemitism, too. These were derived from social conditions, economic rivalries, and a variety of political conflicts. They seemed to be able to address these factors in the same temperate tone of open-eyed moderate realism. And this tone was striking indeed in comparison to the indignant moral reproach that was so characteristic of German Jews at that time. Despite the fact that the grievances they had to endure would but pale against the "Storms in the South," as the Russian pogroms were later named, the reactions of German Jews seemed far more emotional. The Russians were less taken by surprise. They were perhaps more in need but seemed more capable of drawing practical conclusions.

A particularly interesting example is that of Moshe Leib Lilienblum. From the 1860s onward, Lilienblum regarded himself as a typical Russian-Jewish *maskil* (Hebrew for a "disciple of the Enlightenment"). Like many devoted liberals in Western Europe, too, he believed that antisemitism was a passing ailment, a relic from earlier times. It could not and should not be allowed to cloud the sunny skies of Mother Russia. If only the Jews were to seek self-improvement, he argued, nothing would prevent their full integration in their beloved land of residence. The Odessa pogrom of 1871, however, made the first dent in Lilienblum's ideological armor. Despite his natural optimism, by 1881 this veteran idealist found himself thrown into a deep personal crisis. Lilienblum touchingly describes his five months of depression and soul-searching as he was trying to accommodate the new facts into his worldview. He finally emerged on the other side of that crisis a new man: a Jewish Nationalist, a zealous Zionist.[5] Clearly, the initial impulse came from his own experience of the pogroms. But by 1884, when he finally published (in Hebrew) what would eventually become a classic of *Hibbat Zion* (the Love of Zion) movement, "On the Rejuvenation of

[5] The process is described in his book: Moshe L. Lilienblum, *The Way of Return* [Hebrew], Warsaw, 1899.

Israel in the Land of Its Fathers," German antisemitism seemed to assume a central role for him, too.[6] Lilienblum exhibited mastery of the debate between Heinrich von Treitschke and Theodor Mommsen on the question of the Jews in Germany, and his socio-economic analysis of antisemitism repeatedly referred to the German case, addressing Russian events only implicitly. It was the German merchant, the German scholar, the German pauper, and the unemployed who feared, and therefore hated, "their" real or imagined Jew, he wrote. "It was the German national egotism" that apparently could not tolerate the existence of the foreigner, and it was therefore the German case, first and foremost, that made it necessary to review Jewish history. It was there – and not in Russia – that the utter failure of emancipation and the inadequacy of the policy of integration could be best perceived.

Like Pinsker and Sokolow, Lilienblum too never blamed the non-Jews for antisemitism, directly or indirectly. He found it natural and understandable that they all wished to eject the stranger from their midst. Civilization, he wrote, could protect the Jews against religious discrimination and prejudice, but it could not force the insider to love the outsider. It was precisely within the framework of "the culture of emancipation," which in Lilienblum's terminology was identical to civilization, that antisemitism was an understandable impulse. Within this civilization it could even be considered inevitable. At least until the rise of pan-Slavism in Eastern Europe, this disillusioned Russian Jew now argued, nationalism had been a true expression of human progress, providing the basis for world peace and life improvement for all, though at the same time, indeed, this very nationalism was also the source of antisemitism. In Lilienblum's poetic phrasing, antisemitism was nothing but the shadow of civilization, the dark side of an essentially positive force, an inevitable result of the nature of the *galut* (life in exile). Western culture had done its best to foster emancipation, he believed, but it was a solution that ultimately went against the grain. Like Sokolow, Lilienblum saw antisemitism as the necessary counterpart of essentially positive and progressive forces.

Many of the central questions preoccupying the Zionists were already being suggested here: What was the meaning of antisemitism and what was its significance for the Jews? Was it a tractable illness or a chronic,

---

[6] For the following see: Moshe L. Lilienblum, *On the Rejuvenation of Israel in the Land of Its Fathers* [Hebrew], Jerusalem, 1953 [1884], especially pp. 59, 90, 100–17. For a partial translation see Arthur Hertzberg (ed.), *The Zionist Idea: A Historical Analysis and Reader*, New York, Atheneum, 1971 [1959], pp. 166–77. See also David Vital, *The Origins of Zionism*, Oxford, Clarendon Press, 1975, Ch. V.

incurable disease? Was it in contradiction to the values of emancipation or
merely its inevitable counterpart? Finally, it was Ahad Ha'am, who sought
and seemed to have found a middle-of-the-road solution to these questions.[7] We, the Jews of the East, he proclaimed, have suffered poverty,
ignorance, and humiliation. But they, the Jews of the West, were now
struggling under the yoke of something much worse – a spiritual servitude.
The events surrounding the new wave of antisemitism in the enlightened
German Reich and later in Republican France during the Dreyfus affair
have become constitutive for his thinkung, too. The Jews in the West,
Ahad Ha'am argued in one of those essays that were soon to become Zionist classics, "Slavery in Freedom," had become slaves to their own rights,
to their yearned-for emancipation. The efforts they invested in assimilation had been so great that they were now incapable of adequately coping
with the antisemitic menace forced upon them. They therefore attempted
to repress or deny it, to minimize its true significance. Thus, it was now
the task of the Jewish national movement to force them confront the
true nature of antisemitism and the inherent limitations of emancipation.
Ahad Ha'am, like Sokolow, believed that emancipation had been granted
in the West as a derivative of the inner logic of the Liberal political tradition and not out of any genuine sense of partnership or solidarity with
the Jews. And thus, while antisemitism was allegedly incompatible with
emancipation, the two continued to coexist side by side. The capacity of
society to preserve pockets of reaction and barbarism in an age of reason
and progress made such a paradox possible: "It is not impossible," he
wrote in his distinctive Hebrew prose, "that with time 'humanism' would
spread and would indeed include all mankind; white, black, gray, etc.,
until it spreads its wings over even the greatest sinners, as famous 'criminologists' would wish, and the world will be filled with justice, honesty,
compassion and mercy for every creature, extending even to the bird's
nest – only 'except for the Jews.'"[8]

Of course, it was not only the Zionists in Eastern Europe who reacted
so energetically to the outbreak of antisemitism in Germany, but it was
in the East that its implications echoed most powerfully. By 1890, Simon
Dubnow, the Jewish-Lithuanian historian, undertook the labor of writing

[7] Ahad Ha'am, "Slavery in Freedom," in *Selected Essays*, Philadelphia: Jewish Publication
Society of America, 1912, 171–94 (originally in Hebrew, 1891), and on him see especially
Steven J. Zipperstein, *Elusive Prophet: Ahad Ha'am and the Origins of Zionism*, Berkeley,
CA, University of California Press, 1993.
[8] Simon Dubnow, *Weltgeschichte des jüdischen Volkes*, 10 vols., Berlin, Jüdischer Verlag,
1925–1929.

his monumental history of the Jewish people. This immense historiographical project was to be published in its entirety only between 1925 and 1929, but parts of it were already in print before World War I.[9] Ever since the days he spent in Odessa in the 1890s, Dubnow became the voice of non-Zionist Jewish nationalism. Today it is indeed difficult to determine whether his interpretation of Jewish history as a story of shifting geographical centers was a result of his comprehensive historical research or its original driving force. But in any case his "History" later served him well as a detailed cachet for his worldview. Accordingly, antisemitism had a very distinct function: It was the force that compelled Jews, in varying but repeated intervals, to abandon one center of their life and replace it with another. Like Lilienblum, but perhaps especially like Ahad Ha'am, Dubnow perceived antisemitism as a challenge. Its power and influence were insufficient for wiping the glorious Jewish diaspora out of existence, he believed. It could only bring about a shift of its gravitational center. This was Dubnow's way of coming to terms with antisemitism. He saw it as part of an all-inclusive, progressive historical force that finally promised a better future for Jews, even against all odds. Like his great predecessor, Heinrich Graetz, and despite their differences, Dubnow also emphasized the persistent European pattern of Jew-hating, its relentlessness, and the repetition of familiar motifs in its various manifestations.[10] Antisemitism remained for him a permanent factor in Jewish history, valuable despite its ugly face. Even later on, in viewing the rise of the Nazis and shortly before his violent death at their hands, antisemitism did not seem to him reason enough to abandon the diaspora and give up its civilizatory achievements.

Zionists at the time differed from Dubnow-style nationalists mainly in their emphasis on the "negation of the *Galut*" (life in exile); in *their* ideological arsenal, this was the most effective tool for dealing with antisemitism. The core of their approach was a shift from focusing attention on Jew-hatred, which was to be found among non-Jews after all, to stressing self-criticism, which was practiced by Jews themselves. This was a central tactic in their attempt to persuade Jews to abandon their places of residence and migrate to the mythical land of their fathers, but it had the added value of helping to consolidate Zionist historiography

[9] Ibid., Vols. 9 and 10.
[10] Salo Baron argued against this approach in his essay "Ghetto and Emancipation: Shall We Revise the Traditional View?" *Menorah Journal* 14, 1928, 515–26. See also his essay on antisemitism: "Changing Patterns of Antisemitism: A Survey," *Jewish Social Studies* 38, 1976, 5–38.

and explain its rationale. In a way, closest to Dubnow among the Zionists was his apparent rival, Ben Zion Dinur, who later became Israel's first Minister of Education. Dinur saw himself as a fierce opponent of Dubnow. Like Dubnow, he too discerned in Jewish history a story of changing political and cultural centers. But contrary to Dubnow, he wished to get rid, once and for all, of this unstable cycle of existence, its cultural and social implications and its political consequences. Dinur loathed the Jewish existence in the diaspora and dreamed about eliminating it through the one, last move of the center of Jewish life – this time to *Eretz Israel* (Land of Israel). Unlike Dubnow, he viewed all previous moves as a chain of calamities that had to be broken once and for all.[11] Because Jew-hatred was chronic and impossible to overcome, there was no point in trying to preserve Jewish life in the diaspora, according to him. Thus, contrary to all shades of non-Zionist nationalism, as well as to the so-called Cultural Zionism, led by Ahad Ha'am, political and practical Zionism made the negation of the *galut* in whatever form or shape its main tenet.

It is not difficult to imagine the horror of ordinary assimilating Jews upon reading the articles of yet another Zionist thinker, Jacob Klatzkin.[12] Editor of the leading Zionist organ *Die Welt* from 1909 to 1911 and renowned as a sharp-tongued publicist, Klatzkin gave the most radical expression to Zionism's anti-*galut* stance. Contrary to many others, his point of departure was not antisemitism or the impossibility of Jewish assimilation. Instead, Klatzkin always believed that full integration was not only possible but inevitable. With the decline of institutional and theological religious links, there was nothing to unite the Jewish people and preserve them as a community, he felt. In fact, even antisemitism could no longer do the job. Klatzkin did admit that antisemitism had done much for a renewed sense of Jewish solidarity, but he thought that this would not hold up against the rapid blurring of all features of Jewish uniqueness and the collapse of the traditional bonds among them. The source of evil for him was not antisemitism but the abnormality and decadence of *galut* life, not the curse of the Gentiles but the deterioration of the Jews. A hint of this bitter overtone could indeed be traced to the early writings of many other Zionists, but this "Germanized" Russian Jew was now relentlessly focusing on this theme. Klatzkin conceded that the most brutal manifestations of antisemitism had to be resisted, but an ideological

---

[11] See Ben-Zion Dinur, "Diasporas and their Ruin" [Hebrew], *Knesset* 8, 1943/4, 46–60.
[12] See Klatzkin's book: *Krisis und Entscheidung im Judentum*, Berlin, Jüdischer Verlag, 1921. For a partial translation see Hertzberg, *The Zionist Idea*, 316–27.

stand against it was illogical, he claimed. "If we deny this antagonism all its justification, we also deny our own identity as a *Volk*," he wrote.[13] In any case, he added, antisemites should be more acceptable to Zionists than the so-called philosemites, since the former acknowledge the existence of a separate Jewish identity, whereas the latter only seek to eradicate it. Klatzkin insisted on exposing the links between antisemitism and Jewish nationalism. The *galut*, he repeatedly asserted, had totally destroyed the character of the Jews and filled the world with sick and spiritually deformed people. Indeed, it was not only the *galut* as a historical phenomenon that he rejected, but the "*galut* Jews" themselves, human beings who for him were no more than its unfortunate products. From his point of view, then, antisemitic attacks on Jews were at least understandable, if not altogether justifiable.

Klatzkin's viewpoint was surely extreme, yet the sentiment he expressed was not uncommon. One only needs to glance at the writings of Yosef Haym Brenner or Micha Yosef Berdichevski to find more descriptions of those loathsome products of *galut* life. One may even turn to Mendele Mocher Sefarim for that type of Jew, though here he is depicted in a somewhat different tone, perhaps more forgiving, even more generous. In any case, that total negation of the *galut* had been an essential part of Zionist ideology – and to a certain extent, a substitute for what had been considered a futile war against antisemitism. Zionists of other varieties, those who would not have the *galut* Jew so totally abused, such as Yehezkel Kaufmann, nevertheless remained adamant in their rejection of the *galut* as such.[14] For Kaufmann, too, the source of Judaism's predicament was the abnormality of existence in the *galut* – not antisemitism. Writing in a different time, but still augmenting Lilienblum's or Ahad-ha'am's arguments, Kaufmann wished to demonstrate that even democracy could show its darker side to the Jews. Fascism, he argued, was indeed a wild growth, yet the source of its antisemitism was not its reactionary policies, nor the particular social basis of its popular support, but the popular, "democratic" nature of the regime it gave rise to. In any case, Kaufmann was quick to generalize, every phase of human progress was bound to bring only calamities upon the Jews in the Diaspora.[15]

---

[13] Klatzkin, *Krisis und Entscheidung*, 92

[14] Yehezkel Kaufmann, *Diaspora and Foreign Lands* [Hebrew], 2 vols., Tel Aviv, Dvir, 1929–1931, especially Vol. 2.

[15] Yehezekel Kaufmann, "The Destruction of the Soul," in his *In the Throes of Time* [Hebrew], Tel Aviv, Dvir, 1936, pp. 254–74, 293–307.

b. Loyalty and Complacency

While Russian Jews, or at least their intellectual elite, were devoting much attention to events in Central Europe, especially in Germany, the Jews in the West were reluctant to draw conclusions from the pogroms taking place in Russia. The organized communities and the international philanthropic Jewish organizations did raise an outcry and made special efforts to aid the refugees fleeing from the East, but they did not feel the need to go into the details of what was actually happening there. They assumed they had a sufficient grasp of the situation and that it bore no consequences for them. Their view of their own past and of their own present surely seemed clear and coherent to them, and it seemed to require no immediate adjustment. The Western countries had for some time now led the emancipatory campaign, moving from the center to the periphery, and it was easy enough to regard the surge of violence against the Jews in the East as but another manifestation of long-standing prejudice, further evidence of that proverbial backwardness of the Czarist Empire. Hence, the national revival among Russian Jews failed at first to raise the interest of their presumably more sophisticated and enlightened brethren in the metropolitan centers of Central and Western Europe.

But events in their own backyard could not be so easily ignored. The wave of open antisemitism that swept Germany, especially Berlin, toward the late 1870s came as a surprise and seemed contrary to all expectations. It was indeed so venomous that not much seemed to remain of the comfortable atmosphere enjoyed by Jews in the early days of the new *Reich*. The presumably *new* antisemitism had a strong political face and was driven by a powerful popular movement, seemingly relentless and uncompromising. Moreover, the Jews, especially those in Berlin, were stunned by the support that the new movement was winning and particularly by the occasional sympathy manifested toward it in the most unexpected circles. Heinrich von Treitschke's public statements on the matter seemed astounding. Jews could comfortably continue to ascribe the old-fashioned Jew-hatred on street corners and by the vulgar mob to ignorance and the rabble-rousing agitation by fanatic, irresponsible leaders. It was but a reminder of what was then termed "medieval barbarism," a phenomenon bound to disappear with time. But the pronouncements of this renowned scholar could not be placed in that same category. Treitschke was by then at the peak of his fame, already the most prominent historian of the so-called Prussian School and an influential political figure within the moderate Liberal camp. He was an enthusiastic supporter of Bismarck and a popular lecturer on various political issues. When Treitschke proclaimed from the pages of the prestigious *Prussian Yearbooks* that "The Jews are our calamity," the effect was shattering.[16] Berthold Auerbach, for instance, a Jewish author enjoying respectable fame in educated circles, spent the rest of his life under the shadow of that unexpected eruption of antisemitism. He had devoted a lifetime to telling the story of the South German peasantry and, like Treitschke, had for decades participated in formulating the tenets of German liberal-nationalism. In November 1880, writing to a close relative, Auerbach conveyed his distress: "When I am gone, then tell them all: B. Auerbach [*sic*] died from shame in deep pain."[17] Young Hermann Cohen, then a budding philosopher full of confidence in that spiritual and deep-rooted connection between Judaism and "Germanism," composed a detailed public reply to Treitschke: "We, the younger generation," he concluded, "were allowed to hope that we would gradually succeed in joining in with the nation of Kant ... This confidence has now been shattered. The old anxiety is reawakened."[18]

Even more typical was Harry Bresslau's reaction. Like Treitschke, Bresslau was a historian, teaching at the University of Berlin, though not as an *Ordinarius* (a full professor) but as an *Extraordinarius* (an adjunct professor). Like Treitschke, he was a declared and active Liberal. Thus, Bresslau naturally attempted to respond to Treitschke in a moderate fashion. His senior colleague's onslaught and the venomous atmosphere in the streets of Berlin did not shake his confidence in the possibility of total Jewish integration in Germany. As he set out to refute Treitschke's assumptions regarding the "healthy popular nature" of the new antisemitism, he nevertheless found himself, like many others before and after him, appealing for nothing but some extra time. Confident of Jewish desire and ability to fully adopt German culture, Bresslau was equally convinced of the need to grant them a respite to complete this task. The Liberals, he believed,

---

[16] Heinrich von Treitschke, "Unsere Aussichten," in *Preußische Jahrbücher*, November 1879. Here I used a later printing, in: Heinrich von Treitschke, *Deutsche Kämpfe: Schriften zur Tagespolitik*, Leipzig, S. Hirzel, 1896, pp. 1–28.

[17] Berthold Auerbach, *Briefe an seinem Freund Jakob Auerbach*, Vol. 2, Frankfurt a.M., 1884, p. 438; quoted in: Ismar Schorsch, *Jewish Reactions to German Anti-Semitism 1870–1914*, New York, Columbia University Press, 1972, p. 56.

[18] Hermann Cohen, *Ein Bekenntnis in der Judenfrage*, Berlin, 1880. Reprinted in: Walter Boehlich (ed.), *Der Berliner Antisemitismusstreit*, Frankfurt a.M., Insel-Verlag, 1965, pp. 124–5.

ought to make sure that this would in fact be granted. Gradually, as he phrased what was to him the prevalent belief among Liberals, Jews would shed their singularity and the residues of their "dual nationality."[19] No amount of antisemitic poison could ever rob them of their German-ness, he insisted.

Above all, it was Heinrich Graetz, who between 1853 and 1876 had published his monumental eleven-volume *History of the Jews* and was singled out for attack by Treitschke in the above-mentioned article, that found himself on the defensive. Graetz denied any intention to ever define or defend the existence of a separate Jewish national life in Germany or within the political framework of contemporary Europe in general.[20] Nevertheless, like Hermann Cohen but not like Bresslau, he now felt obliged to rethink the Jews' place within this framework and even ponder anew the nature of their Judaism. Indeed, Jewish response to this first wave of post-emancipation antisemitism may be regarded as the beginning of their return to a more conscious search for ways to preserve their Judaism. Total devotion to the project of assimilation was apparently no longer enough. But at this stage, no radically new answers were forthcoming. Jews were not yet looking for ways to react jointly or publicly to their attackers. They did not yet seek to apply any organizational or legal measures in an attempt to defend their reputation. Antisemitism upset and troubled them, but it was not enough to spoil their sense of loyalty to what was for them a beloved fatherland, or their satisfaction at their entry into its social fabric. The new manifestations of prejudice and discrimination could not shake their pride in the numerous signs of their success within it.

In Austria's thriving capital, Theodor Herzl too was forced to confront the reality of antisemitism. He first addressed the subject early in 1882, apparently unaware of the recent pogroms in Russia. But he was deeply distressed by the literary expressions of a "new" antisemitism in nearby Germany. It was primarily a book by Eugen Dühring that had just been published in Berlin that most deeply upset him. Dühring was considered a serious though somewhat eccentric scholar, and Herzl's astonishment at reading his text echoed the bewilderment of Eastern Jews at

---

[19] Harry Bresslau, "Zur Judenfrage. Sendschrieben an Herrn Prof. Dr. Heinrich v. Treitschke," in Boehlich, *Antisemitismusstreit*, 52–76.

[20] For Treitschke's attack on Graetz, see also: "Herr Graetz und sein Judentum," published in the *Preußische Jahrbücher,* December 1879, and Boehlich, *Antisemitismusstreit*, 31–45. Graetz's response, first published in the *Schlesischen Presse* on December 7 and 28, 1879, is also reprinted in Boehlich, *Antisemitismusstreit*, 25–31, 45–52.

the expressions of antisemitism in Germany as a whole.[21] Like them, he was agonized and consternated. How should one respond?

Herzl first struggled to formulate a straightforward reply to Dühring's indictments. He tried to evaluate the author's accusations "objectively," as he then put it, but soon found himself clinging to old, often-repeated arguments. Like most educated Jews in and out of the German-speaking region of Central Europe, he too thought the book was nothing but a catalog of medieval prejudices in modern, seemingly scientific, guise. Young Herzl was still able to dismiss antisemitic charges as a relic of the past, a passing childhood ailment of bourgeois society. The reality of his own life, however, soon forced him to reconsider his position. As a student he had occasionally encountered the antisemitism prevalent among his fellow students at the University of Vienna, and in the liberal literary salons of the Habsburg capital, too, he was treated with suspicion, primarily because of his Jewish origins, he felt. Finally, the experience of reporting the Dreyfus affair from Paris may have provided him at least an added impetus to the formulation of his Zionist utopia.[22] Integration and assimilation, which had earlier been the obvious goals of Jewish life in the old and the new German Reich, were now exposed as a much more difficult, maybe even an impossible task. From this standpoint, he now believed, more radical conclusions were called for. Indeed, in his opening speech at the First Zionist Congress in Basel, on August 28, 1897, Herzl did not conceal the underlining bitterness of his vision: "In these times, so progressive in most respects, we know ourselves to be surrounded by the old, old hatred," he exclaimed. "That very part of Jewry which is modern and cultured, and which has outgrown the ghetto and lost the habit of petty trading," he so typically continued, "that part was pierced to the heart."[23] Yet hatred from the outside must become a force for renewal from the inside. If not for that hatred, European Jewry would have been assimilated to oblivion within two generations. It was this hatred that

---

[21] Herzl's impressions of this book are recorded in his early notebooks, which are now at the Central Zionist Archives in Jerusalem and are reconstructed in: Amos Elon, *Herzl* [Hebrew], Tel Aviv, Am Oved, 1975, pp. 71–5 (also in English, New York. Holt, 1975).

[22] Herzl himself is the source of the widespread notion that the Dreyfus affair was of major importance for the emergence of his Zionist vision. This has now been reevaluated and accorded a much less prominent role in his actual intellectual development. See Jacque Kornberg, "Herzl, the Zionist Movement, and the Dreyfus Affair," in Roselyne Koren and Dan Michman (eds.), *Les Intellectuels face a l'affaire Dreyfus*, Paris, L'Harmattan, 1998, pp. 107–19, and the introduction (in Hebrew) by Shlomo Avineri to the Hebrew edition of Herzl's diary, Vol. 1, Jerusalem, Mosad Bialik, 1997.

[23] Quoted in: Hertzberg, *The Zionist Idea*, 226–7.

had repeatedly made them strangers in their own lands, and it alone had shaped them into a modern nation.

In the present context, the question of whether Herzl's diagnosis was accurate is beside the point. Significant is his basic understanding of the role of antisemitism in the regeneration of that Judaism that he was rather suddenly seeking to lead. Unlike most of the spokesmen for German Jewry at the time, and unlike his own position only a few years earlier, Herzl now basically refrained from addressing the old-style, traditional hatred of the Jews. As a modern Jewish nationalist he considered only the new, contemporary antisemitism a relevant phenomenon; it was not another chapter in the chronicles of an "eternal people," but a basically different phenomenon, a direct result of the social, economic, and political conditions of Europe at that time. Like his predecessors in Eastern Europe, and, as we have seen, based on the same historical reasoning, Herzl now believed that antisemitism was but the dark side of emancipation, not a passing failure of the world's nations, but a healthy, even "reasonable" reaction on their part. Contemporary antisemitism was for him above all a response of the educated middle class in German-speaking Central Europe to the overproliferation of Jewish intellectuals. It was, more than anything else, his own personal experience that formed the basis of this assessment, but there was enough in it to fire his imagination.[24]

Herzl's uniqueness was thus not in providing a better or more comprehensive analysis of the situation at hand. What characterized him, and what ultimately made him the only effective leader among the figures mentioned above, was his determination to find a new solution to a new problem. Herzl realized that a preoccupation with the deeper roots of antisemitism might jeopardize his basic optimism about western civilization, a necessary precondition for his Zionism. He was by no measn ready to give up this civilization. Instead, he offered a detailed plan for an independent Jewish state to be established outside Europe, to be sure, but unequivocally within its cultural orbit. It was designed to solve not only the problem pressed on the Jews by non-Jews, but also the problem pressed on non-Jews by the Jews. Accordingly, Jews who experienced the new sense of national solidarity expressed in Zionism and responded to the national revival it spawned could emigrate to their own homeland, while those wishing to continue to assimilate in the European environment

[24] For Herzl's position on antisemitism, see *Der Judenstaat: Versuch einer modernen Lösung der Judenfrage*, Berlin, Jüdischer Verlag, 1934 [1896]. An English translation is in Hertzberg, *The Zionist Idea*, 204–25.

would now enjoy better treatment and an improved chance of success.
Europe, too, had something to gain from the new arrangement. It would
be rid once and for all of its "Jewish Problem." As historian Jacob Talmon
wrote, "Herzl apparently believed in the possibility of a deal with the
antisemites.... We shall take out the excess Jews from your countries,
and you will help us find them a refuge and establish their own state."[25]
In other words: You will help us solve the Jewish Problem, and we shall
release you from your own painful dilemma. We shall remove the obstacle, which has been standing in the way of the onward march of human
progress, and you shall reward us by cooperating with our grandiose plan.
Herzl was indeed prepared to negotiate with even the worst antisemites,
as evidenced by his meeting in 1903 with the Russian Minister of Internal
Affairs, von Plehve. But above all, it was the representatives of enlightened Europe whose good will Herzl wished to stir; it was in their hands
that he decided to entrust the fate of Zionism. He based his thought on
the existence of permanent and perpetual antisemitism in Europe, and yet
he never gave up his faith in the liberal and emancipatory forces in that
same Europe.

In fact, it was not only Herzl who remained so powerfully attached
to the liberal principles of a Europe that had repeatedly proven itself
unreliable. Other Zionist leaders also held on to this dialectical position.
Max Nordau, for instance, a man who by the mid-1890s was already
a well-known critic of the European enlightened tradition, also wished,
as a last resort, to remain loyal to it.[26] In his pre-Zionist phase, Nordau
could be classified as a "cultural pessimist" of the type that was often
attracted to antisemitism. As a Jew, however, even if totally assimilated,
Nordau could not possibly apply his overall vision to the Jewish issue
in the way of other contemporary critics. Instead, he merely used it as
an indisputable proof of Europe's moral decay. Like other anti-modern
thinkers, Nordau resented the entire rational basis of the liberal creed. No
one equaled him in formulating the Zionist position against that rational,

[25] Jacob Talmon, "Herzl's *Judenstaat* – 70 Years After," in his *The Age of Violence* [Hebrew], Tel Aviv, Am Oved, 1974, p. 173.
[26] On Nordau (1849–1923), see the biography by his wife and daughter: Anna and Maxa Nordau, *Max Nordau: A Biography*, New York, The Nordau Committee, 1943. For his pre-Zionist phase, see especially his *Paradoxes*, London, William Heinemann, 1906 (originally in German, 1885); *The Conventional Lies of our Civilization*, Chicago, Laird & Lee, 1895 (originally in German, 1883); and *Degeneration*, Lincoln, NE, University of Nebraska Press, 1993 (originally in German, 1892/93) with an interesting introduction by George L. Mosse.

and hence, flimsy basis of emancipation. Emancipation ought to have been first accomplished in "the world of the sentiment," he claimed, before it was made into law. Since its true values were never really internalized, it was bound to remain a dead letter.[27] Nordau saw the Jews as a separate race, accepted the impossibility of assimilation, and concluded that immediate action must be taken to set Europe free of the dilemma posed by them. At the same time, he believed, Jews would finally be liberated of their humiliating existence. But following the first spell of ideological enthusiasm, as he began working within the framework of the Zionist movement, Nordau began to sense unease when attacked as an enemy of progress, a traitor to the ideals of liberty, equality, and fraternity. When criticism from the liberal anti-Zionist Jewish camp grew sharper in the summer of 1899, he set out to defend himself. From the open letter he first published in the French *Le Siècle* and later in the German *Die Welt*, it appears that he had upheld little of his earlier radicalism.[28] Basically, Nordau was now arguing that the future Jewish state should above all serve as a haven for refugees from the East. The return to Zion was not a return to "barbarism" but an escape from the ghetto. Moreover, was it not possible to finally mobilize the Jews, this long-suffering people, for yet another effort on behalf of genuine human progress, he asked. In a speech at the Third Zionist Congress, Nordau clearly stated his trust in Europe:

I openly declare that I do not believe that the catastrophes of our past will be reenacted in the future ... Today there is a European conscience, a conscience of humanity, limited indeed, but requiring at least the appearance of a degree of honesty, and it could hardly tolerate preposterous mob crimes.[29]

Thus, even he, perhaps the most outspoken anti-liberal among the West European Zionists at the time, a man whose Zionism was unquestionably based on confronting the reality of antisemitism, did not lose faith in the basic decency of modern Europe. Both he and Herzl, along with the great majority of Zionist leaders of that first generation, kept clinging to the values that made Europe enlightened in their eyes, regarding these very values as the basis as well as the ultimate goals of their own "separatist" movement.

[27] See Nordau's speech before the First Zionist Congress in Basel, 1897, in his *Max Nordau to His People*, New York, Scopus, 1941, pp. 63–74, especially 65.

[28] *Die Welt*, August 8, 1899.

[29] Max Nordau, *Zionist Writings* [Hebrew], Jerusalem, Hasifria Hazionit, 1956–1962, Vol. 1, p. 156.

If Herzl and Nordau felt hard pressed to reconcile their faith in European enlightenment with their budding Zionist impulse, such a reconciliation must have been all the more painful for one who viewed himself a critic of European enlightenment not from the right or the center but from the left. Bernard Lazare was a French radical, a revolutionary with a streak of anarchism.[30] His book on antisemitism was published well before he had become a dedicated Jewish nationalist. In it he placed the main cause of antisemitism not on the intolerance of non-Jews, but on the inflexibility of the Jews; not on the non-Jews' wish to exclude the Jews, but on their own stubborn refusal to assimilate. Still, he too did not lose hope:

In every way I am led to believe that antisemitism must ultimately perish . . . because the Jew is undergoing a process of change; because religious, social and economic conditions are changing; but above all because antisemitism is one of the last, though most long-lived manifestations of that old spirit of reaction and narrow conservatism, which is vainly trying to arrest the onward movement of the Revolution.[31]

It was Maurice Barrès who pushed Lazare, as well as others of his generation, to look deeper into the hidden roots of their own self, extending both their personal and their political consciousness. As a result, Lazare grew increasingly more interested in his Jewishness, though it was only later on, during the Dreyfus affair, in his case, as in that of Nordau, that he was given the final push in this direction. He was now ready to abandon his efforts at assimilation and declare himself a Zionist. An inner transformation – reminiscent of what Martin Buber later described in terms that were likewise borrowed from Barrès – gave the first impetus to his change of course and the experience of the Dreyfus affair completed the process.[32]

[30] On Lazare's life and ideas (1865–1903) in the context of French and Jewish history, see Michael R. Marrus, *The Politics of Assimilation: A Study of the French Jewish Community at the Time of the Dreyfus Affair*, Oxford, Clarendon Press, 1971, pp. 164–95. See also Shlomo Sand, "Bernard Lazare: From Symbolistic Poetry to Poetic Nationalism," *ha-Zionut* [Hebrew] 19, 1995, 369–83. As to the effects of the affair on Nordau, see Robert Wistrich, "Max Nordau and the Dreyfus Affair," *Journal of Israeli History* 16(1), 1995, 1–18, and Christoph Schulte, "Fin de siécle, Dreyfus, Zionismus: Max Nordau als Beobachter der III. Republik," in Christopher Miething (ed.), *Jüdischer Republikanismus in Frankreich*, Tübingen, M. Niemeyer, 1998, pp.50–60.
[31] Bernard Lazare, *Antisemitism. Its History and Causes*, New York, International Library, 1903, pp. 375 (originally in French, 1894).
[32] For Martin Buber's version of the search for roots, see his early speeches, and especially "Das Judentum und die Juden," in his *Reden über das Judentum*, Frankfurt a.M., Literarische Anstalt Rutten & Loening, 1923, pp. 1–16.

A clear sense of Jewish identity, even Jewish pride, was thus engendered in the heart of this ardent international revolutionary. And while Lazare later qualified his declarations about the near demise of antisemitism in the modern world and sharpened his criticism of the so-called assimilationists, he never discarded his leftist radicalism, even as he was forced to admit the failure of emancipation and as he grew increasingly more loyal to his newly discovered Jewish national identity. Like most Zionists in Western Europe, Lazare did not consider his newfound insight into the Jewish predicament a just cause for abandoning his former ideals. Like Herzl or Nordau, indeed, antisemitism had deeply shocked him, but it did not make him reject his former spiritual assets.

If this was true for ardent, leading Zionists, it was of course all the more so for other, less radical Jews. Even those who did acknowledge the importance of the "new antisemitism" and internalized its significance did not feel the need to formulate a completely uncompromising response. In the eyes of most Central and Western European Jews, their home countries continued to be worthy places of residence; they were hostile at times, no doubt, but never – unlike the countries where actual pogroms were taking place – were they truly dangerous.

Jews reacted to the waves of antisemitism in the last quarter of the nineteenth and early twentieth centuries in four major ways. Many reasserted their faith in the values of universal liberalism and emancipation while usually adhering to the dominant nationalism of the society in which they lived. Others, feeling as strangers indeed within that liberal Europe that so repeatedly disappointed them, were loath to adopt any nationalism, including the Jewish one. Many of them opted for the international, Socialist solution. Yet another group, accepting the need to uphold a national distinction as Jews, still looked for ways to do so within the existing European frameworks. And finally, there were those who transferred their hopes to what could then be considered "the Jewish utopia," to Zionism. Groups representing different combinations of these diverse positions were fighting among themselves for the hearts of the Jews across Europe.

It is noteworthy that, in those years between the end of the nineteenth century and the beginning of World War I, the line dividing Jewish Nationalists from Jewish Liberals did not run parallel to the line separating German or French Liberals from German or French Nationalists. For Jews, the central issues were not republicanism, parliamentarism, or the feasibility of social equality. The struggle among them was about the divergent interpretations and the possible conclusions to be drawn from the brief experience of emancipation and the recent resurgence of anti-semitism. Since only few were willing to relinquish the liberal dream and unequivocally embrace the nationalistic discourse, most were faced with a difficult dilemma. Their reactions covered a wide political-ideological spectrum. The Liberals, on the one end, wished to obscure the gravity of antisemitism as much as possible and continue to regard it as an embar-rassing but passing aliment, no more than an unfortunate discomfort. Nationalists, on the other end, and Zionists in particular, saw in the resur-gent antisemitism a major, formative event, but still no cause to abandon their faith in enlightenment. German Jews in particular were often devoted liberals. Most of them were proponents of integration and assimilation, bona fide "assimilationists," as it were, to the very end. But even Jewish Nationalists and Zionists, while seeing in antisemitism a grave moral dis-grace, often underestimated its magnitude and importance. It was some-thing that must not be allowed to raise its head, but it was not enough to force them to modify their overall worldviews, and surely it was not enough to force them to any kind of radical action.

Useful in diverting attention from antisemitism was the apparent suc-cess of so many Jews in Germany, their role in its artistic life, its science, literature, and even politics. From the 1890s onward, the Jewish press repeatedly stressed the manifestations of this success and the Jewish pub-lic seemed deeply gratified. Later historiography also repeatedly dwelt on these feats: It wasn't assimilation and its hardships that lay at the center of attention, but success and its sweet fruits. "The contribution of German Jews" is a recurrent and popular motif in much of the writings about German Jewry. The exact nature of the link between personal achieve-ments and ethnic or religious origins is rarely explored. But in the midst of the intoxication with success few seemed to question the relevance of Jewishness to the triumphs of individual Jews. The Nazis were quick to refer to it, while the Jews themselves were never capable of forgetting it. Einstein, Kafka, Freud – we keep reminding ourselves of the glorious landmarks in the course of German Jewish history; and for the "initiated" – a longer and no less glorious list can easily be added.

Their achievements have been extraordinary, no doubt. The vast major-ity of these Jews were often members of the second or third generation of acculturation only. These were people whose parents had come from small towns in Prussia's eastern provinces, from Galicia, or from remote villages set at the margin of German metropolitan culture. It was not unusual for them to improve their economic status, augment their education, and penetrate the professions or a particular sphere of intellectual and artistic activity within a single generation. The halo of success impressed Jews around the globe. It was in fact an international success story. The unpleasant, occasionally menacing attacks of antisemitism seemed at the time rather insignificant in comparison.

2

Excursus on Self-Hatred and Self-Criticism

Only a small minority remained unimpressed by this success. It was, indeed, easier to see its pitfalls from the outside. As early as 1891, Ahad Ha'am, who later became the leading light of "Cultural Zionism," published in *Ha-Melitz*, a Hebrew journal that was edited in Odessa, an essay entitled "Slavery in Freedom." This was a raging attack on the Jews of the West who were, according to him, boasting their successful emancipation while disregarding their "spiritual slavery." A few years later, indeed, Zionism was slowly emerging in Germany, too, relying on the same assumptions concerning the crisis of emancipation and focusing on its implications. But the vast majority of German Jews in *fin de siècle* Germany had lovingly accepted the combination of legal emancipation and economic cum cultural success. Only the minority, consisting of Zionists and non-Zionists alike, was not ready to compromise. It was this minority that continued to harshly criticize the position of the Jews, their life, and their ideals. While most chose to be content with their personal and collective success, the minority, at the margin, continued to view the situation anxiously, with their ears and eyes wide open. They were the ones who heard the voices of the antisemites, read their writings, listened to the sounds of hostility, and became acutely conscious of the dangers.

Herzl's Zionism clearly indicated a turn to the inner Jewish sphere to seek a solution to antisemitism. At the same time, since he never abandoned the values of the surrounding world, he was now suggesting their implementation within the framework of a separate Jewish sphere – political and geographical. His own critique of Jewish life in the Diaspora was yet another motivation for this radical solution. Among some of his younger followers, such a critique was also often manifested in a resolve to match the moral and physical standards applied by their non-Jewish contemporaries. They organized in separate associations; for instance, to be worthy of a true duel, they emphasized the development of their physical prowess, they endeavored to return to a healthy life in nature, and so on. This may not have been a line that was acceptable to all. Such activities sometimes enraged other Zionists, especially those in Eastern Europe who were looking for more specifically Jewish solutions to their plight. But worries about the physical and mental health among Jews were not uncommon among them, too. In Germany, in any case, Jewish and non-Jewish medical men were then debating the special tendency of Jews to particular diseases or asocial behavior, and a streak of self-critique, sometimes no doubt echoing antisemitic parlance, went through the generally smug mood that was characteristic of German Jewry at the time.[1]

This, to be sure, was not merely a Jewish phenomenon. Concern about health, particularly about mental health, was widespread in German society as a whole.[2] It was also a major theme in the critical public discourse in Austria. And it is in this context that the common accusation of Jewish self-hatred ought to be examined. The historian of German "nervousness," Joachim Radkau, claims that expressions of group inferiority among Germans at the time were both numerous and "amazingly vehement." Among those who provide written evidence of this sentiment he counts not only Richard Wagner and Hermann Bahr, the Austrian author and playwright, but also the Kaiser's closest friend, Philipp von Eulenburg, and the younger Moltke, head of the General Staff from 1906.[3] Pronouncements of self-hatred among Jews, however, were noted especially among Jewish intellectuals, who were often marginal men indeed, and were only later made to appear, erroneously, I believe, as a trademark of German Jewry.[4]

---

[1] For a detailed analysis of this discourse, see John M. Efron, *Medicine and the German Jews. A History*, New Haven and London, Yale University Press, 2001, chs. 4 and 5, pp. 103–85, and the bibliography cited there.

[2] See especially Joachim Radkau, *Das Zeitalter der Nervosität. Deutschland zwischen Bismarck und Hitler*, Munich, Hanser, 1998.

[3] Ibid., 337–38.

[4] See Sander L. Gilman, *Jewish Self-Hatred: Anti-Semitism and the Hidden Language of the Jews*, Baltimore, MD, Johns Hopkins University Press, 1986; Allan Janik, "Viennese Culture and the Jewish Self-Hatred Hypothesis: A Critique," in Ivar Oxaal et al. (eds.), *Jews, Antisemitism and Culture in Vienna,* London, Routledge & Kegan Paul, 1987, pp. 75–88; Peter Gay, "Hermann Levi: A Study in Service and Self-Hatred," in his *Freud, Jews and Other Germans: Masters and Victims in Modernist Culture*, Oxford, Oxford University Press, 1978, pp. 189–230. From the older literature, see Kurt Levin, "Self-Hatred among Jews," in his *Resolving Social Conflicts: Selected Papers on Group Dynamics,*

Accusations of self-hatred have a long tradition of being applied by one Jew to another, often as a part of some political dispute. Present-day Israelis encounter the term all too often in public discourse, where it is used indistinctly and often demagogically, mainly to avoid coping with criticism from within. It is, in fact, no less commonly applied in contemporary Germany and has often been heard in discussions concerning the legitimation of nationalism in that country. There, too, self-hatred is often confused with self-criticism, and it is this tendency, rather than the vague meaning of the term itself, or its linguistic components, that has repeatedly contributed to its misuse.[5] It has also blurred matters with regard to antisemitism and the ways in which it was conceived and interpreted. From its inception, indeed, the discussion of modern antisemitism in Germany has been intertwined with the issue of Jewish "self-hatred."

On March 6, 1897, Walther Rathenau published one of his first articles in Maximilian Harden's journal, *Die Zukunft,* under the title "Shema Israel" ("Hear, O Israel"). The article, appearing under a pseudonym, was a passionate call to Jews to talk properly, to walk properly, and to at least try to behave like "Jews brought up and educated as Germans." Initially it generally met with indifference. Five years later, however, when it was republished under the author's name, the Jewish press mounted an all-out attack on the author, who was by then still a little-known figure in German public life.[6] Only in the most aggressive antisemitic literature, the critics asserted, could one find such a hateful description of Jewish physiognomy, such sanctimonious preaching, and such outspoken admiration for the "Aryan" type. But a few months later, this time in Vienna, another book came out, written by a young, recently converted Jew, Otto Weininger, entitled *Geschlecht und Charakter* (Sex and Character).[7] Its general sentiment on the matter of Jewish life was not unlike that expressed by Rathenau. While the book mainly dealt with the tension and the dualism between the sexes and attempted an elucidation of the fundamental inferiority of women, one very long and apparently central chapter was dedicated to Jews. Weininger made a comprehensive analogy

---

New York, Harper, 1948, pp. 186–200, and from the literature that stresses cases outside Germany: Nancy A. Harrowitz, *Antisemitism, Misogyny, and the Logic of Cultural Difference. Cesare Lombroso and Matilde Serao,* Lincoln, NE, University of Nebraska Press, 1994.

[5] Stress on blurred defitions is central to the discussion in Paul Marcus and Alan Rosenberg, "Another Look at Jewish Self-Hatred," *Journal of Reform Judaism* 36, 1989, 37–59.

[6] Walther Rathenau, *Impressionen. Gesammelte Aufsätze,* Leipzig, S. Hirzel, 1902.

[7] First published in Vienna in May 1903.

between femininity and Jewishness and restated, perhaps on the basis of his rudimentary familiarity with Freud's early writings, that a certain feminine element was to be found in the personality of every male, but most particularly in the personality of every Jewish male. Antisemites, he explained, are in fact fighting the feminine-Jewish side in themselves, and every self-conscious Jew ought to wage the same intractable war against himself, too.[8] "Jewish antisemitism," denoting a position taken by some Jews in the public sphere, and "Jewish self-hatred," a term applied to the individual's spiritual, mental, and psychological state of mind, were drawn nearer and the confusion surrounding them kept escalating.

Evidence of the extent to which Jews were indeed preoccupied with the issue at that time can also be found in Arthur Schnitzler's novel, *Der Weg ins Freie* (The Road to the Open), written between 1905 and 1907.[9] The Jews in this novel keep hurling the charge of self-hatred at each other, and the noble Baron, naturally not a Jew but a friend to some of them, is constantly contemplating the meaning of this phenomenon. Significantly, the scene is set in Vienna once more, not only Weininger's hometown but also the home of Karl Kraus, Egon Friedel, and other Jewish authors known for their "self-hatred." The Austrian capital presented a particularly complex ethnic situation and was distinguished at the time by its rabid popular antisemitism and by its antisemitic establishment. Between 1897 and 1910 it was headed continuously by Mayor Karl Lueger.[10] But examples of the sense of disgust with Judaism and especially the despair at the impossibility of ever getting rid of it abound not only in literary fiction and surely not only in *fin de siècle* Vienna. Expressions of such attitudes can be found in the writings of very real Jewish figures at least since the first half of the nineteenth century. One can begin by mentioning Rahel Varnhagen, Heinrich Heine, and Ludwig Börne. Rahel, the famous salon lady in the first decade of nineteenth-century Berlin, experienced her Jewishness throughout as a humiliation, a stain that could not be cleansed.[11] Heine,

---

[8] On the link between antisemitism and anti-feminism, see Chapter 6, Section B.

[9] First published in installments in *Die Neue Rundschau*, between January and June 1908, and later the same year it was reissued in one volume in Berlin.

[10] On Austrian antisemitism see Peter G. J. Pulzer, *The Rise of Political Anti-Semitism in Germany and Austria*, New York, Wiley, 1964, especially pp. 162–88, and the interesting presentation in Carl E. Schorske, "Politics in a New Key: An Austrian Trio," in his *Fin de Siècle Vienna. Politics and Culture*, New York, Vintage Books, 1981, pp. 116–80.

[11] See especially Hannah Arendt, *Rahel Varnhagen: The Life of a Jewess*, London, East and West Library, 1957 (now available in a completely new edition with an illuminating introduction by Liliane Weissberg, Baltimore, MD, and London, Johns Hopkins University Press, 1997).

who was baptized yet remained loyal to a kind of personal Jewish identity throughout his life, regarded it intermittently as a blessing and a curse; and Börne, another convert, struggled under the yoke of his Jewishness yet found in it the essence of his personality and the source of his love of freedom.[12] Still, self-hating Jews seemed to have proliferated especially at the beginning of the twentieth century. The prevalent use of the term by Jews and non-Jews alike was typical of a certain particular phase in the history of German Jews, following the completion of their formal emancipation, especially during the years immediately preceding World War I.

When Theodor Lessing's book about Jewish self-hatred was published in 1930, it was already slightly dated.[13] The men used by him as illustrations were active mainly in the pre-war years, and, in any case, the scope and importance that the book ascribed to the entire issue seemed no longer relevant in view of the Nazis' raging antisemitism at the time. Soon enough, those supposedly Jewish antisemites were to be found in the same camp as those they apparently so despised. Earlier, they were the men representing the attitude of only a small minority of German Jews, I would argue – those who sought to seriously address the problem of Jewish life in the context of both assimilation and antisemitism, and of both complacency and self-hatred.

In one of the major studies on Jewish self-hatred, Hans Ditter Hellige offered a comprehensive review of that figure of a Jew – one who is artistically inclined, a member of the second generation of emancipation who is in deep conflict with his father and therefore apparently prey to a permanent, tantalizing self-hatred.[14] His list of examples is long, indeed. In Berlin, the Reich's capital, Hellige counts Expressionist playwright Karl Sternheim; Ludwig Jacobovski, author of *The Jewish Werther*, a book that enjoyed a considerable readership at the time; theater critic Alfred Kerr; and of course Walther Rathenau, a man of letters, industrialist, and statesman, all in one. To these he adds Rudolph Borchardt, Karl Wolfskehl, Jakob Wassermann, Fritz Mauthner and Franz Kafka, Franz Werfel and

[12] There is a huge literature on Heinrich Heine. For his complex link with Judaism, see especially, Siegbert S. Prawer, *Heine's Jewish Comedy: A Study of his Portrait of Jews and Judaism*, Oxford, Clarendon Press, 1983. Secondary sources on Börne are scarce, but see Lothar Kahn, "Ludwig Börne: First Jewish Champion of Democracy," *Judaism* 25, 1976, 420–34.
[13] Theodor Lessing, *Der Jüdische Selbsthass*, Berlin, Jüdischer Verlag, 1930.
[14] Hans D. Hellige, "Generationskonflikt, Selbsthaß und die Entstehung antikapitalistischer Positionen im Judentum," *Geschichte und Gesellschaft* 5, 1979, 476–518.

Stephan Zweig, Karl Kraus, and Egon Friedel – all representatives of the Jewish or once-Jewish intelligentsia of Munich, Vienna, and Prague, and all presumably clear-cut cases of self-hating individuals. It suddenly seemed that their varied activities and divergent positions all boiled down to a single issue: the mental processing of a certain psychological complex that was uniquely their own but somehow also characteristic of an entire community.

Presenting the issue in this light forces us to view matters from a psychological, or psychoanalytical perspective, attempting a kind of psychohistory. But while on a personal level, indeed, explanations using such approaches may be legitimate within the framework of social history, focusing on the Jewish collectivity they seem rather inappropriate. Such a group therapy leaves us with nothing but a collection of skeletons, no longer flesh and blood. By studying self-hatred on the personal level we may learn that it is a sign of excessive aggression, ultimately turned against the self; that it is the result of a unique combination of inferiority complex and/or a sense of superiority, a manifestation of an unresolved Oedipal complex or of a latent, persistent fear of castration; that it suggests homoerotic, sadomasochist needs, and so on. The diagnosis is partly based on incidental comments by Sigmund Freud, or on bits and pieces from the work of Anna Freud, Erik Erikson, and Wilhelm Reich. Finally, it is well to remember that none of the figures discussed have ever been subjected to a comprehensive analysis, and it is no longer possible to have them lie on the psychiatrist's couch today. Incidentally, Weininger, Lessing, and Kafka were vehemently opposed to the idea of being psychoanalyzed. All three felt that such therapy would have them resign to a situation they refused to accept, considering their position, the outcome of a conscious decision, not of some hidden needs or repressed desires.

Freud himself was in fact much more of a representative of the German-speaking Jewish majority than one of those others, the wandering "self-haters."[15] He usually regarded his Judaism not as a burden but as an

---

[15] The most useful biography of Freud now is Peter Gay, *Freud: A Life for Our Time*, New York, Norton, 1988. However, it does not contain a full treatment of the various aspects of Freud's Jewishness. Most illuminating in this respect are Marthe Robert, *From Oedipus to Moses: Freud's Jewish Identity*, London, Routledge & Kegan Paul, 1977 (originally in French, 1974), and Yosef Hayim Yerushalmi, *Freud's Moses: Judaism Terminable and Interminable*, New Haven, CT, Yale University Press, 1991. Comparre also Robert S. Wistrich, "The Last Testament of Siegmund Freud," *Leo Baeck Institute Yearbook* XLIX, 2004, 87–104.

advantage. A member of the first generation of emancipation, Freud apparently felt more comfortable among Jews than among non-Jews. He chose to marry a woman from an Orthodox family, and Jews were prominent among his acquaintances, colleagues, and disciples. Throughout his life, Freud had been a member of only one public organization, namely *Bnei Brith*, and he had never wavered in his loyalty to Judaism. But beyond that, Freud had internalized to perfection the most important trait of contemporary Jewry, especially in German-speaking Central Europe: ambition. The analysis of his own dreams in *The Interpretation of Dreams*, first published in 1900, reveals an energetic drive, a desire to succeed at any price, to make his mark, to overcome death by way of eternal fame. From the dreams he did not publish, but of which he told his friend Wilhelm Fliess during the late 1890s, emerges a man who craved such fame and success – perhaps in the hope of finally penetrating that "good society" of which he wrote, but ultimately, even without that hope.[16] Freud apparently gave up on assimilation early in his career, but success preoccupied him for the rest of his life. His mental life, as he himself interpreted it with rare candor, unfolds the conflict so typical of his generation, the conflict between old loyalty to Judaism and a fervent ambition to succeed among non-Jews. In his self-psychoanalysis, Freud gradually became aware of this conflict and learned to accept it with a measure of dignity and resignation.

Other members of this tortured group of Jews, a minority-within-a-minority, were unable to follow the same route. Kafka, for instance, saw the therapeutic aspect of psychoanalysis as "a hopeless mistake," preferring instead the confusion, the doubt, and even the "sweetness of disease."[17] It seemed as though the members of this group at the margin were intent on defending their peculiar position as outsiders. Indeed, their marginality offered them an important advantage and seemed to some to be in itself a spiritual virtue. As outsiders, they could look at both the general and the Jewish societies from a distance and in proximity, in identification and alienation, in partnership and criticism. And the criticism was fierce, radical, and sharp-tongued. Nevertheless, as I see it, it was usually *not* merely an expression of self-hatred, *not* an inwardly directed

---

[16] Siegmund Freud, *The Origins of Psycho-Analysis: Letters to Wilhelm Fliess, Drafts and Notes, 1897–1902*, Marie Bonaparte, Anna Freud, and Ernst Kris (eds.), New York and London, Imago, 1954, 246. See also Robert, *From Oedipus to Moses*, 61–82.

[17] See Frederic V. Grunfeld, *Prophets Without Honor: A Background to Freud, Kafka, Einstein and Their World*, New York, Holt, Rinehart and Winston, 1979, p. 200.

hatred that could turn into a source of pathology. At times this was a criticism launched from the outside, directed at a group from which these men had fully dissociated themselves. At times the rage was pointed at a particular Jewish subgroup to which they did not, and did not care to, belong. Only rarely does one find in their writings a hatred that is truly directed inward, and even then it seems to have miraculously turned into a source of inspiration: a starting point for creativity on the individual level and world-reforming on the public one.

Let us look briefly at three particular cases: Franz Kafka, Theodor Lessing, and Jakob Wassermann. With the first, a deep and authentic self-hatred turned into an enormously powerful, creative force; with the second, it was transformed into a great public sensitivity and became a positive and original reformatory power; while with the third, it was finally revealed as the expression of an agonizing soul, but also of great love, concern, and a deep sense of responsibility.

Only Franz Kafka's case is pertinent as an example of true, inwardly directed self-hatred. Of the entire gallery of writers, journalists, and thinkers often seen as representatives of that typical Jewish self-hatred, only one really contemplated himself in shame and at times in genuine loathing. In his letter to his father, while expounding on his resentment toward him and everything he stood for, Kafka describes himself in his youth as a weak, scared, hesitant, and restless boy, and later on as a sickly adult, mentally exhausted, incapable of raising a family, engulfed by his ailments, and haunted by fear. With repressed abhorrence Kafka depicts his father, his violence and insensitivity, his intellectual tyranny, and his ominous physical superiority: "My writing was all about you," Kafka writes to his father, "all I did there, after all, was to bemoan what I could not bemoan upon your breast. It was an intentionally long drawn out leave-taking from you...."[18] Yet even this long and heartfelt letter ends not in insolent hatred for the father, but in a catalog of self-criticism. Above all, Kafka judges harshly his own literary pursuit – the center and content of his life. His very use of the German language, he felt, was nothing but a sham. The language is not ours, he argues, and we shall never be able to use it without self-consciousness. Our Jewish intuition cannot be repressed and our literature is but pretense. In Kafka's moral dictionary, there was no deadlier sin. In a letter to Max Brod he describes the situation of the Jewish-German intellectual: "Stuck by his

[18] Franz Kafka, *Letter to his Father: Brief an den Vater*, New York, Schocken Books, 1966 (originally in German, 1919), p. 87.

little hind legs in his forefathers' faith, and with his front legs groping for, but never finding new ground."[19] Instead of the privileged onlooker or the advantaged outsider, he prefers the image of the bridge: "I had been tough and cold; I had been a bridge, hanging over the abyss, my toes pinned into one side, my hands over the other; my teeth biting into the dirt and the lapels of my coat flying aside. In the depth of the stream of trout clamored, cold as ice..."[20] Yes, Kafka concedes, the Jews of the West were greedy, domineering, and possessive. In a letter to Milena he gives expression to his distaste and horror: "At times I would wish to take them, precisely because they are Jews (me included) and shove them – let's say – into a linen drawer, then wait a while, and then open the drawer just enough to peek inside and make sure they have all suffocated by now – and if not – close the drawer again and continue this to the end..."[21] Kafka is always careful to ensure that there is not the slightest doubt: He always counts himself among the Jews he so heartily despises.

This becomes even clearer when juxtaposed with his admiration for the Jews of the East. On his deathbed he wrote, in another letter to Milena: "Had I been given freedom to choose what I wanted to be, then I would have chosen to be a little Eastern European boy."[22] And in a moment of self-forgiveness he said to an audience of wealthy Jews in Prague who had come to a reading performance by a Yiddish theater actor from Poland: "Ladies and gentlemen, before the Polish Jew begins the show, I'd like to assure you that you all understand Yiddish much better than you imagine."[23] Coming from a Rathenau, a Lessing, or a Wassermann, this could be construed as subtle rebuke, but coming from Kafka, it sounded like an expression of hope. In view of the cruel and inexorable trial that Kafka daily and hourly held against himself, the alleged expressions of self-hatred by people like Mauthner, Werfel, and Zweig appear meek indeed, mere lip service, not self-torture but coquetry, not a judgment but at most a confession. And yet their pain too was real.

---

[19] Franz Kafka, *Briefe 1902–1924*, in Max Brod (ed.), *Franz Kafka: Gesammelte Werke*, Frankfurt a. M., Fischer Taschenbuch Verlag, 1975, pp. 337–8.

[20] Franz Kafka, "Die Brücke," in his *Beschreibung eines Kampfes, Novellen, Skizzen, Aphorismen aus dem Nachlaß, Gesammelte Werke*, edited by Max Brod, Frankfurt a. M., Fischer Verlag, 1969, pp. 84–8.

[21] Franz Kafka, *Briefe an Milena*, Frankfurt a. M., Fischer Verlag, 1966 [1920–23], p. 43. (also available in English: *Letters to Milena*, New York, Schocken Books, 1990).

[22] Ibid., 168.

[23] Max Brod, *Über Franz Kafka*, Frankfurt a. M., Fischer Taschenbuch Verlag, 1974, p. 101.

Like the young Franz Kafka, Theodor Lessing had also struggled under the yoke of a strict and ruthless father.[24] A sickly child, pale and weak, he suffered cruel beatings at home and countless insults outside it for years. Throughout his life, Lessing begrudged his father and anything related to him power, money, and success. As a child, his only solace had been his friendship with Ludwig Klages. Already as an adolescent, he had developed, together with Klages, a radically dualist worldview in the philosophical tradition of Schopenhauer, Nietzsche, and Kirkegaard. For these two youngsters the world revolved around the contrast between nature and spirit. In later years they both wrote philosophical essays, containing a "vitalist" critique of the new industrial Germany. According to the philosophical tradition of the time, and under the influence of Houston Stewart Chamberlain's writings, the Aryan-Judeo contrast was then incorporated into the web of contradictions that preoccupied them. Accordingly, the Jew represented the kingdom of the mind, the intellect, and paralyzing morality. The Aryan represented nature, the senses, the mystical, and the will. Lessing stayed true to these distinctions all his life, and this always remained the theoretical, as opposed to psychological, basis of his negative view of Judaism. He was repelled by the Jewish religion and by the Jew as a type alike.

Some of the supposedly self-hating Jews that Lessing himself later described in his book of 1930 adhered to a polar, dualistic worldview much like his own. The specific nature of this dualism may have been different in each case, yet for all those represented in this collection the Jew stood for the negative side of the equation. Otto Weininger and Max Steiner, two eccentric youngsters, have each built their own world of contrasts in a metaphysical language. Arthur Trebitsch and Walther Calè built a similar pattern in a social and political mode. No wonder they all found it extremely difficult to function within the boundaries of everyday reality. Suicide, as in some of these cases, was an expression of their despair at attaining perfection, overcoming the tension between the contradictory elements of their worldview, reaching harmony in death against all odds. The Judeo-Aryan dichotomy was but one of many contradictions

---

[24] Lessing's autobiography was published in Prague in 1935. Here I used a later edition: Theodor Lessing, *Einmal und nie wieder*, Gütersloh, Bertelsmann-Sachbuchverlag, 1969. See also Lawrence Baron, "Theodor Lessing: Between Jewish Self-Hatred and Zionism," *Leo Baeck Institute Yearbook* XXVI, 1981, 323–40, and now also Yotam Hotam, "Modern Gnosticism and the 'Jew': The Crisis of Culture, Life Philosophy and Zionist Thought" [Hebrew], Diss. the Hebrew University of Jerusalem, 2003, with extensive chapters on Ludwig Klages, Theodor Lessing, and Jacob Klatzkin.

in the dualistic conceptual system of these people, and not necessarily the central one. They rejected an abstract Judaism that was the figment of their imagination and that each of them, in his own terms, refused to be identified with. As he finally decided to take up a new faith, Weininger claimed that "a Jew who converts to Christianity has the superior right to be considered Aryan." And the others, like him, insisted on placing themselves on the positive pole in their scheme of things: on the side of life, nature, and creative imagination. Lessing himself, having identified the Jew with the moral and spiritual world that is directly opposite to that of nature and dream, in his language, reached a particularly comfortable solution: In his later years he learned to place the Jews not at one of the poles in his insoluble equation, but at an intermediate position, as a bridge between two worlds. Yet unlike Kafka's bridge, this one was not doomed to collapse; it was a bridge that signified security and hope, the beginning of the road to salvation.

Despite his agonized childhood, and the crisis following the separation from Ludwig Klages, who grew to be a staunch antisemite and disowned his old friend, Lessing's hatred was not finally directed simply toward himself. Indeed, as he matured, he increasingly managed to place the objects of his hate and criticism outside of himself. To begin with, his attacks focused on Eastern European Jews. If he ever felt some affiliation with Judaism at this point in his life, he certainly did not feel any with these foreigners. In 1909 Lessing published a series of articles in the *Allgemeine Zeitung des Judentums* entitled "Impressions from Galicia" and containing an appalling account of Jewish life in this province. Despite his preference for "life" over "intellect," Lessing was shocked at what he saw. In a synagogue in a small town he suddenly found himself amidst loud crying, mad gestures, general excitement, and restlessness: "I was practically shaking with fear at this prayer," he recounted. "I got sick. I forced my way out and fled away."[25] Lessing's articles provoked sharp criticism. His unabashed nausea at the sight of his brethren was shocking even for some of the regular, often similarly disposed readers of the *Allgemeine Zeitung des Judentums*. Nevertheless, they were published in full in this respectable journal and were apparently not entirely unacceptable to the Jewish readership at that time. The criticism of Eastern European Jewry by people like Lessing was not *self*-hatred in this milieu; it was a critique from the outside, from a position of aloofness and distance.

---

[25] Quoted in Grunfeld, *Prophets Without Honor*, 84.

Eventually Lessing was able to overcome his initial critique of Judaism and develop practical solutions to alleviate what for him seemed the most debilitating social ills. He became an active social reformer. This was no doubt proof of the seriousness of his intentions and the authenticity of his pain. On the eve of World War I, Lessing became a firm pacifist, and he later moved from a mild Socialism to an outspoken Communist position. He tried his hand in an adult education enterprise and worked in various types of social institutions. Finally, when he was murdered by local Nazis in the resort town of Marienbad in August 1933, he had behind him years of activity as a supporter of the women's rights movement, an organizer of a large-scale public campaign for the prevention of noise and environmental pollution, a steadfast opponent of every nationalistic faction in the Weimar Republic, and a Zionist. Lessing's energy sources, which at first seemed to be directed into futile rage and vindictiveness, were later channeled into extensive public activity. From his harshly critical position against Jews and non-Jews alike, he had reached the total negation of bourgeois life and found a new existence of positive, creative action.

Beyond the special case of Kafka and the unpredictable course of Lessing's life, let us now consider the personality of Jakob Wassermann. Despite a difficult childhood and growing up in what may be considered a prolonged period of economic and mental distress, Wassermann did not start out by negating his Judaism. On the contrary, his first novel, *The Jews of Zindorff*, published in 1897, dealt explicitly and sympathetically with Jewish content. Many of his other earlier works also handled a variety of Jewish themes. Personally, the young Wassermann encountered antisemitism only rarely, but problems of identity seem to have plagued him repeatedly since his Munich days. Upon arriving in Vienna, the Jewish circles in which he moved turned out to be a heavy burden on him. In a later autobiographical work, *Mein Leben als Deutscher und Jude* (My Life as German and Jew), Wassermann explained his feelings with great candor. In Vienna, he recounts, "I never got rid of a certain amount of shame. I was ashamed of [the Jews'] behavior and ashamed of their manners... at times my shame overcame me until it turned into despair and nausea"[26] We have somehow learned to name this shame, felt by the parvenu in facing his relatives, "self-hatred." In fact, and despite

[26] Jakob Wassermann, *Mein Weg als Deutscher und Jude*, Berlin, S. Fischer, 1921, p. 103 (also available in English: *My Life as German and Jew*, New York, Coward-McCann, 1933). See Gershon Shaked, "The Wassermann Affair (an Appendix that is an Introduction)," in his *If You Ever Forget: Reviews of Jewish American Literature with an Appendix on a Jewish German Novelist* [Hebrew], Tel Aviv, Akkad, 1971.

the despair and disgust expressed in these words, there is no hate here, but a typical combination of love, embarrassment, and a sense of responsibility. In this sentiment, Wassermann is the true representative of the group of intellectuals discussed here, and he is perhaps more characteristic of this group than either Kafka or Lessing.

The focus of embarrassment for the acculturated Jew in the context of late nineteenth- and early twentieth-century Germany was the behavior of the newly arrived. Since these "new" Jews, immigrants from Eastern European villages and small towns, were a permanent fixture of the Jewish environment of Central Europe, the embarrassment associated with their strangeness had likewise become a permanent sentiment and the cause for much anxiety for local Jews. The majority of the content Jewish bourgeoisie, proud of their successes, and preoccupied with their own daily affairs, suffered little from the contacts with the "new" Jews. In fact, the immigration from the East had ultimately strengthened existing Jewish institutions and infused them with new vitality. It was the small intelligentsia at the margin, those Jews who endeavored to achieve not only personal success but also a complete assimilation, who found themselves so resentful of these "foreigners." They refused to identify with them, but they could not manage to dissociate themselves from them. After all, these were often their own parents; in other cases, they were their family members, close or remote relatives, and usually, just plain ordinary, "other" Jews.

From his patrician position as son of a successful and well-to-do father, we saw Rathenau called on the "Tiergarten Jews," mostly newcomers from the East, to behave and beware of becoming a laughingstock. It was often their peculiar use of the German language that aroused resentment. Fritz Mauthner, a philosopher and a linguist, particularly despised the language of the new immigrants, their accent, and what he saw as their "Jewish tactlessness": "That bunch," he wrote, "is simply not fit for contact with Europeans."[27] Even Martin Buber diagnosed the sources of tension in the relationships between Jews and non-Jews in similar terms. He too considered the Easterners' use of language and their social manners problematic.[28] Freud and Schnitzler repeatedly addressed these issues. Both refer in this context to the same Jewish joke: A Jew from Galicia

---

[27] Quoted in a private letter from May 17, 1906, in Gershon Weiler, "Fritz Mauthner: A Study in Jewish Self-Rejection," *Leo Baeck Institute Yearbook* VIII, 1963, 147.
[28] Martin Buber, "Die Hebräische Sprache," in his *Die Jüdische Bewegung. Gesammelte Aufsätze und Ansprachen, 1900–1914*, Berlin, Jüdischer Verlag, 1920, pp. 174–94.

is leisurely reclining in a train coach. When a properly dressed gentleman enters the cabin, he straightens out, but when the strange gentleman approaches him as a Jew to his fellow Jew, asking when is Yom Kippur this year, the 'Galicianer' lets out a sigh of relief and puts his feet back on the opposite seat.[29] The superficiality of manners – perhaps of civilization as such – so central to the life of the Central European bourgeoisie was repeatedly the focus of insecurity among the highly educated, ambitious German Jews. This apparent superficiality kept thrusting them anew into the Jewish space – away from the non-Jewish sphere where they wished to find permanent abode.

Heinrich Bermann, Schintzler's main Jewish protagonist in *Der Weg ins Frei*, complained of his weariness vis-à-vis that apparent necessity "to always feel responsible for the shortcomings of others," and the "need to atone for every crime, for every act of tastelessness and recklessness on the part of any Jew wherever they are around the globe."[30] Above all, Bermann felt responsible. A sense of "genuine responsibility," Wassermann wrote in his autobiography, engulfed him, "like a contract sealed in blood."[31] In a moment of truth, Bermann bared his soul to the young Miss Elsa behind the piano in her elegant salon: "Those we love," he explained to her, "we know better than others, yet we always love them out of shame, bitterness and fear. . . . Love means a chronic fear that others might discover in us the same inferiority that we have discovered in our own beloved." Bermann refused to join the Zionist ranks, but in a conversation with a Zionist friend, the affinity between the two is evident. For this kind of people, Jewish life in Germany had remained problematic and fraught with danger. They had never felt that sense of self-satisfaction and smugness so prevalent among their Jewish contemporaries. Their heightened sensitivity had to find artistic expressions or turned them into reformers, revolutionaries, and ideologues of sorts. Such Jews, open-eyed and incisive, may have even been able to sense the impending disaster, as did Heine in his own time. But in the flourishing and smug Wilhelmine Germany, such Jews were very rare, indeed.

[29] Sigmund Freud, *Jokes and their Relations to the Unconscious*, New York, Norton, 1960, pp. 80–1.
[30] Here and below, from Arthur Schnitzler, *Der Weg ins Freie*, Frankfurt a. M., Fischer Verlag, 1964 [1908] (also available in English: *The Road to the Open*, New York, A.A. Knopf, 1923).
[31] Wassermann, *Mein Weg als Deutscher und Jude*, 103.

3

Past Shadows, Present Needs

a. The *Kristallnacht* and Other Pogroms

Despite past experience, when the Nazis came to power, the blindness of Jews and non-Jews alike seemed almost complete. It was this total distortion in perceiving reality that manifested itself most dramatically, indeed most tragically, at that final moment, when all hope for a respectable Jewish existence in Germany was lost, at the time of the *Kristallnacht*. By then, one could assume, the threat of further violence against the Jews could no longer be ignored. In those days, so it seemed, no particular insight and no long-term historical perspective were needed to understand that 1938 had been a fateful year. In fact, this was generally acknowledged well before the year was over. Historians, too, readily accept this diagnosis.[1] By the end of 1938, the Nazis' intentions were easily apparent. Their determination to find a "solution" to the Jewish question could no longer be doubted. Their blatant disregard of world opinion was clearer than ever, and if it had still been possible to read "mixed signs" during earlier years, as historian Peter Gay passionately argued in his autobiography, the *Kristallnacht* finally brought home to the Jews the hopelessness of their situation.[2] Approximately 150,000 Jews had left Germany between

---

[1] See the attempt by Avraham Barkai to challenge this view, at least with regard to the economic fate of the Jews in Germany, in his "The Fateful Year 1938: The Continuation and Acceleration of Plunder," in Walter H. Pehle (ed.), *November 1938: From 'Reichskristallnacht' to Genocide*, New York, Berg, 1991, pp. 95–122 (originally in German, 1988).

[2] Peter Gay, *My German Question. Growing Up in Nazi Germany*, New Haven, CT, and London, Yale University Press, 1998.

the Nazis' ascent to power on January 30, 1933, and November 1938, with almost one-quarter of them leaving during 1933 alone.[3] In the aftermath of the *Kristallnacht*, emigration took on new proportions. Nearly 120,000 Jews left Germany in 1938–39 alone. Thousands of "unaccompanied children" were sent away; families were forced to split, and at this stage many who hesitated before were finally ready to leave behind whatever business or property they still possessed.

Various historical studies correctly stress that in terms of the ongoing anti-Jewish policy of the Nazis, the *Kristallnacht* did not constitute a particularly significant point of departure. The restricting decrees imposed on the Jews in its aftermath were by then only a continuation of previous measures.[4] After all, by November 1938, physical attacks on individual Jews and the destruction of their communal and personal property was no longer a novelty. Especially indicative of things to come were – if at all – the events in Vienna following the *Anschluß* in March of the same year.[5] There, a new "style" seemed to be applied from the outset, and the Nazis made special efforts to find more effective ways of expropriating the Jews and expelling them. Similar actions inside the old Reich soon followed suit. The Munich *Hauptsynagoge* was burnt down on June 9, 1938, and those in close-by Nuremberg and in faraway Dortmund followed soon afterward. The *Kristallnacht* finally brought about the ultimate disillusion. At this point the Nazis had given up any attempt at pretence and removed the thin veil of legality that they had used before. It was clear that the authorities were now openly and actively participating in the anti-Jewish campaign, inciting the presumably authentic, yet highly orchestrated "popular rage." From then on, pretence was no longer necessary. Previous efforts to avoid foreign pressure and to keep up a minimum of public order seemed redundant.

It is important to remember that the Nazis had tried this tactic, of occasionally breaking up all legality at carefully chosen moments, previously too. The so-called Night of the Long Knives, on June 30, 1934, could be considered an earlier case in point. It left in shambles the legal façade

---

[3] Precise data are unavailable, but for reliable estimates see Herbert A. Strauss, "Jewish Emigration from Germany: Nazi Policies and Jewish Responses (I)," *Leo Baeck Institute Yearbook* XXV, 1980, 326.

[4] See in addition to Barkai, "The Fateful Year 1938," Shaul Esh, "Between Discrimination and Extermination: 1938 – The Fateful Year," *Yad Vashem Studies* 2, 1958, 79–93. See also Herbert A. Strauss, "The Drive for War and the Pogroms of 1938 – Testing Explanatory Models," *Leo Baeck Institute Yearbook* XXXV, 1990, 267–78.

[5] For this and the following, see Leni Yahil, *The Holocaust: The Fate of European Jewry 1932–1945*, New York, Oxford University Press, 1990, pp. 104–106 (originally in Hebrew, 1987).

of the recent Nazi seizure of power. The hierarchy of leadership in the Third Reich was now made crystal clear, as was the certainty that the government would tolerate no opposition – real or imagined. The events surrounding the *Kristallnacht* in their turn clarified the earnestness of the Nazis' intentions, this time regarding the Jews. The "Jewish Question" was to remain a major item on their agenda, and it was going to be solved, one way or another, in a combination of pressures from below and disciplined planning from above. Germans of all walks of life witnessed the *Novemberpogrom* and its aftermath. Their willingness to take part in it, or at least to remain indifferent to it, corroborated the expectations of the regime.[6]

And yet ambiguity was sustained, at least for those who did not directly experience the events of that late autumn in 1938. It is interesting to follow the reactions of Jews outside Germany, most particularly in Palestine, to the occurrences. From their perspective it was apparently easy enough to misjudge the situation. Paradoxically, it was precisely the overt violence that seemed to have strengthened the already existing tendency to perceive the Nazis as yet another bunch of Jew-haters of the old, familiar type. On one level, the events of November 9 shocked all outside observers and certainly every Jew around the world; on another, these same events helped to obliterate the novel character of Nazism and belittle the real dimensions of the looming threat. While the consistent policy of isolating and ostracizing the Jews via explicit legal means had astounded Jews around the world by its radicalism and thoroughness, the pogrom allowed the discussion to use, yet again, old categories and concepts. It was now possible to regard the Nazis as murderous, violent, and dangerous, but nothing out of the ordinary. Here, presumably, was another chapter in the long chronicles of Jewish persecution.

The previous experience of German Jewry with the reality of pogroms occurred during the 1848 Revolution, romantically known as "The Spring of Nations."[7] But while an earlier wave of pogroms three decades before that received considerable attention from historians, both contemporaries

---

[6] The best description of the events is now in Saul Friedlaender, *Nazi Germany and the Jews: The Years of Persecution, 1933–1939*, New York, Harper Collins, 1997, ch. 9.

[7] See Jacob Toury, *Turmoil and Confusion in the Revolution of 1848: The Anti-Jewish Riots in the "Year of Freedom" and their Influence on Modern Antisemitism* [Hebrew], Tel Aviv, Moreshet, 1968, especially pp. 24–62. Compare, Stefan Rohrbacher, *Gewalt in Biedermeier. Antijüdische Ausschreitungen in Vormärz und Revolution (1815–1848/49)*, Frankfurt/New York, Campus, 1993, and see Werner Bergmann, Christhard Hoffmann, and Helmut Walser Smith (eds.), *Exclusionary Violence: Antisemitic Riots in Modern German History*, Ann Arbor, MI, University of Michigan Press, 2002.

and later observers conceived of the events of 1848 as marginal, even
negligible. It was in the summer of 1819 that the so-called Hep-Hep riots
spread from Würzburg in Bavaria to Frankfurt am Main, and from there
northward and eastward, even into Prussia. As it was the first instance of
violent attacks on Jewish communities in Germany during the new "Era of
Emancipation," it seemed an important and extraordinary event that must
be weighted and analyzed.[8] In contrast, the pogroms of 1848, despite the
fact that instances of violence occurred in dozens of locations, from Baden
in the south to Upper Silesia, Posen, Bohemia, Moravia, and Hungary in
the north and the east, were usually passed over. Jews preferred to see
them as mere "wild weeds of freedom," as the Jewish weekly the *Orient*
put it, or just "outbursts of a raging mob," to quote Leopold Zunz, who
was by then one of the prominent spiritual leaders of German Jewry. Jacob
Ettlinger, Rabbi of the Jewish community of Altona, referred to the events
in his Orthodox publication as German liberty "consecrated in blood,"
and Ludwig Philippson, editor in chief of the liberal *Allgemeine Zeitung
des Judentums*, seized the opportunity to preach once more about the
need for "productivization." This would be the best antidote for the rage
of Germany's rural population, he believed.[9] The fact of Jewish participation in the revolutionary movement seemed infinitely more important
to all these men than the riots attached to it. In that heroic "Year of Freedom" Jews were able to demonstrate their faith in everything German and
received the first real promise of complete equality. The ongoing process
of emancipation seemed much more crucial to them than the transient
conflicts with the local peasantry – an ignorant public who would ultimately also be touched by the light of European enlightenment and its
gospel of universal brotherhood.

 Later historiography also did not attribute any particular significance
to the violent attacks on Jews during the revolution. Jewish historians
who were part of the social milieu of German Jewry – such as Heinrich
Graetz, Martin Philippson, and Ismar Elbogen – all shared the enthusiasm
for the Revolution of 1848, choosing to ignore its less pleasant aspects.
Even Simon Dubnow refrained from mentioning the pogroms during the
"Spring of Nations." He too mainly addressed the political aspects of the
revolution; the discussions held in the National Assembly, known as the

---

[8] Eleonore Sterling, "Anti-Jewish Riots in Germany in 1819: A Displacement of Social
   Protest," *Historia Judaica* XII(2), 1950, 105–142, and Jacob Katz, *Die Hep-Hep-
   Verfolgungen des Jahres 1819*, Berlin, Metropol, 1994 (first in Hebrew, 1973).
[9] For these and other reactions, see Toury, *Turmoil and Confusion*, 62–73.

Frankfurt parliament; and those Jewish key figures that made their first appearance on the political center stage during the revolution. The story of the pogroms that swept Germany at the same time remained untold. Later on, even Jacob Katz, the leading modern historian of German Jewry, in his major work on this period, referred to the 1848 Revolution only in its overall European context, ignoring the violent manifestations of antisemitism in its midst. Even his book on antisemitism in modern times contains but a passing reference to these events.[10]

For reasons of its own, German historiography also addresses only the issue of granting equal rights to the Jews during 1848, refraining almost entirely from alluding to the pogroms. Not only did conservative historians, who traditionally focused on the revolution's political events and write its history "from above," ignore them. Social historians also did not see fit to mention them. In fact, the entire German historiography after 1945 passed over the antisemitic events during the revolution. Even Thomas Nipperdey, one of the major German historians of our time, a man deeply interested in the history of German Jews, only mentioned in this context the Jewish money-lenders who were, among others, the butt of peasants' attacks in March 1848. The full history of the pogroms was first told by Jacob Toury in a little Hebrew book entitled *Turmoil and Confusion in the Revolution of 1848: The Anti-Jewish Riots in the "Year of Freedom" and Their Influence on Modern Antisemitism*. Only a shorter version of this book appeared in German, while neither this book nor a more recent and in some ways more complete analysis of the events by Stefan Rohrbacher have been translated into English.[11]

The memory of the 1848 pogroms was thus repressed and forgotten. In the aftermath of the *Kristallnacht*, it could hardly be used for comparison. Historical analogies were therefore drawn from other times and places: the Crusades attacking Jewish communities en route to the Holy Land, for instance, or events outside Germany, in far away Tsarist Russia. In fact, many among the rank and file, as well as the leadership of all major Jewish communities and organizations everywhere in the world at that time, were equipped with more or less vivid personal memories of pogroms they had experienced first-hand before leaving Russia for the shores of London,

---

[10] See Jacob Katz, *Out of the Ghetto: the Social Background of Jewish Emancipation*, Cambridge, MA, Harvard University Press, 1973, and *From Prejudice to Destruction: Anti-Semitism, 1700–1933*, Cambridge, MA, Harvard University Press, 1980.

[11] For a somewhat fuller treatment of this issue and some bibliographical details, see Shulamit Volkov, "Reflections on German-Jewish Historiography: Dead End or New Beginning?" *Leo Baeck Institute Yearbook* XLI, 1996, 309–320.

New York, Buenos Aires, or Jaffa.[12] In order to understand their reaction to the atrocities in Germany, it is essential to try to reconstruct the world of their historical associations. A brief summary will do here for our purpose.

The history of the pogroms in Eastern Europe goes back at least to the Cossack raids in the mid-seventeenth century and the infamous Ukrainian Haidamacks' slaughter in the mid-eighteenth century.[13] In modern times reference was usually made to the events immediately following the murder of Tsar Alexander II, in March 1881.[14] Hundreds of communities, especially in the southern parts of Western Russia, were then hit. Sporadic attacks continued until 1884, and many communities suffered near extinction. The second wave came in conjunction with the revolutionary turmoil that finally erupted in 1905, beginning as early as 1903 in Kishinev and spreading everywhere in southwestern Russia. These pogroms must have left an indelible mark on both local Jews, many of whom then fled Russia to settle elsewhere, and on the Jewish leadership of all political and ideological convictions. Later, too, many of the immigrants to *Eretz Israel*, especially those arriving as part of the so-called Third *Aliyah* (the third wave of immigration) immediately after World War I, carried fresh memories of recent anti-Jewish violence.[15] Hundreds of pogroms were counted in the Ukraine alone between December 1918 and April 1921. The local population and the various competing armies ferociously attacked more than 500 communities in the vicinity of Kiev, Wohlin, and Podolya. Estimates of the number killed vary between 60,000 (Dubnow)

---

[12] See, e.g., the opening pages of Golda Meir's *My Life*, London, Weidenfeld and Nicolson, 1975, pp. 1–2. Chaim Weizmann indicated in his memoirs that he never experienced actual pogroms in his youth, but their effects on the Jewish community in Tsarist Russia were nevertheless formative experiences of great significance for him. See his *Trial and Error: The Autobiography of Chaim Weizmann*, London, H. Hamilton, 1949, pp. 28–30.

[13] For these early pogroms see the detailed description given by Simon Dubnow, *Weltgeschichte des jüdischen Volkes*, 10 vols., Berlin, Jüdischer Verlag, 1925–1929, vol. 7, sects. 3, 4, and 17.

[14] In addition to Dubnow, *Weltgeschichte*, vols. 9 and 10, I have also relied on Benjamin Pinkus, *Russian and Soviet Jews: Annals of a National Minority* [Hebrew], Be'er-Sheva, Ben-Gurion University, 1986, pp. 105–24. For a partial translation see Benjamin Pinkus, *The Jews of the Soviet Union: the History of a National Minority*, Cambridge, Cambridge University Press, 1988, pp. 22–33.

[15] In 1940, Dubnow's eleventh volume of his *Weltgeschichte des jüdischen Volkes* was published, taking the narrative up to 1938. I have used the Hebrew edition of this volume. See section 2. On Jewish reaction in the west see William M. Hagen, "Mord im Osten. Die polnische und andere osteuropäische Pogrome von 1918–1919 im Verständnis der zeitgenössischen deutshcen Juden," in Dietrich Papenfuß and Wolfgang Schieder (eds.), *Deutsche Umbrüche im 20. Jahrhundert*, Cologne, Bohlau, 2000, pp. 135–46.

and as many as 200,000 (in official Soviet publications).[16] A major and vibrant center of Jewish life in the heart of Europe was almost extinguished during those years.

The term "pogrom" presumably applies to a spontaneous and sudden popular action, and, as such, it was deemed by some inapplicable to the *Kristallnacht*. But for Russian Jews, the myth of "popular rage" lost its meaning much earlier. By the beginning of 1881, it was already common knowledge that there was not much spontaneity about the violent action of the mob against the Jews, and this was indeed cause for much bitterness and protest. The Tsarist government to be sure did not have at its disposal the means for fully controlling the masses, or even its own garrisons, but the involvement of the central government in Moscow, as well as the incitement of the populace by local authorities, did not remain a secret for long. A look at the events on November 1938 promptly reveals that the Nazis, too, did not have a complete grip on the situation. But the sudden inertia, the lethargy of the law enforcement agencies, and their later unexpected efficiency in calming the situation all provided ample evidence of the scale of planning and control that had ultimately dictated the scope of the pogroms and brought them to a halt.[17]

Furthermore, in Russia, too, the pogroms were only a prelude to further anti-Jewish activities. Immediately after the first wave of hostilities in 1881, the Russian government issued orders restricting (once again) the area of Jewish settlement, prohibiting the purchase of land by them, and imposing strict police control on their personal movements and choice of occupation. In early 1890 most Jewish inhabitants of Moscow were expelled. Their rights of participation in national and local politics were severely curtailed, and they were now explicitly excluded from higher army ranks and from all public administrative positions, the attainment of which had been in any case always most difficult. An intricate *numerus clausus* system intended to limit the Jews' entry into the various schools of higher learning was institutionalized. Finally, a system of orders and provisions brought about Jewish expulsion from many regions of the Empire. During World War I, this policy was given a particularly drastic

---

[16] The latter figures are quoted in Bernard D. Weinryb, "Antisemitism in Soviet Russia," in Lionel Kochan (ed.), *The Jews in Soviet Russia Since 1917*, Oxford, Oxford University Press, 1978, p. 310. For some literary evidence, see especially Isaak Babel, *The Red Cavalry*, London, A.A. Knopf, 1928 (originally in Russian, 1926).

[17] As for the "spontaneity" of the *Novemberpogrom*, see in addition to Freidländer, *Nazi Germany and the Jews*, chap. 9, Uwe D. Adam, "How Spontaneous Was the Pogrom?" in Pehle, *November 1938*, 73–94.

twist, when over 600,000 people, mostly though not only Jews, were expelled from large areas in Western Russia, often with only twenty-four hours' notice. An estimated five percent managed to salvage their property, and about one-quarter fled empty-handed.

In addition, it should be remembered that blood-libel suits often preceded pogroms in the various parts of Europe.[18] In these cases, an accusation of murder perpetrated by Jews against a Christian, often a Christian child, was used for inciting the mob. Although the case of Herschel Grynspan, the Jewish youth who assassinated Ernst vom Rath in Paris, and whose act had been used as a pretext for the *Kristallnacht*, did not exactly fit this pattern, the manner in which the Nazis exploited the incident was clearly reminiscent of previous events. They too were apparently quick to realize the potential of the situation; and they too may have been unconsciously reconstructing old historical patterns.[19] In any case, this chain of events could not but seem familiar to those Jewish refugees from other pogroms and persecutions. It was therefore, paradoxically, the *Novemberpogrom*, internally seen as the worst Nazi transgression to date, that was perceived by many Jews abroad as just another episode in a drama foretold. It was precisely this uncommon event that helped to impair their understanding of the novelty and misjudge the gravity of the situation in Germany. It was this set of historical references that further impaired their ability to discern the nature of the impending catastrophe.

b. A View from Eretz Israel

Let us take as an example the ways in which Jewish men and women living under the British mandate in Palestine at the time viewed the situation in Germany.[20] The *Yishuv* (the Jewish collective settlement in *Eretz Israel*)

[18] Most famous in modern times is the blood-libel case in Damascus, 1840. See Jonathan Frankel, *The Damascus Affair: "Ritual Murder," Politics, and the Jews in 1840*, Cambridge, Cambridge University Press, 1997.
[19] In view of the attempts to present certain Soviet policies as actual precursors of the Nazis' actions (e.g., by Ernst Nolte), I wish to be absolutely clear on this point: My argument here does not concern Nazi policies as such, but their perception and interpretation, particularly by Jewish victims in Germany and elsewhere.
[20] The following Hebrew newspapers were used here: *Ha'Aretz* (The Land), a liberal paper founded in 1920 (the first Hebrew daily in Palestine); *Davar* (Speech/Word), the daily paper of the *Histadrut* (General Workers' Federation), founded in 1925; and the *Palestine Post*, an English language daily, appearing from 1932.

naturally followed with great interest and much unease the events in this country. But while various voices were heard in the discussion of Nazam prior to the *Kristallnacht,* the old-style pogrom analogy dominated public discourse from that point onward. *Ha'Aretz,* the main middle-class daily published in Tel Aviv, first chose to open its reporting on events in Germany by denouncing that "miserable boy" who murdered vom Rath in Paris, and by dissociating the Jews in Germany and elsewhere from his criminal act. But by November 11, it emphatically reported on a "pogrom" in Germany. "The Nazi government," ran the text, "has learnt well the methods of the Tsarist regimes." Moreover, despite the fact that the paper clearly stressed the orchestrated nature of the violence against German Jews, it was primarily preoccupied with "the rage of the mob" and its "uncontrolled barbarism." In this manner, the events in Germany were made to fit the presumably known pattern of Jewish history, "in which horrors repeat themselves in awful frequency." In *Davar,* the mouthpiece of the moderate Labor Movement, a direct lineage of Grynspan's predecessors was exposed in a long letter to the editor, signed "a refugee"[21]: Pinhas Dashevski, Shalom Schwarzbard, and David Frankfurter were all mentioned, thus sketching the basic historical framework within which the present events were to be conceived.[22] On November 17, *Davar* explicitly correlated the riots in Germany with previous Russian pogroms. It quoted a selection of Russian antisemitic publications, comparing them to the National-Socialist *Der Stürmer,* and called for an international reaction to recapture the "storm of indignation and protest" that the world had witnessed in the aftermath of the Kishinev pogrom in 1903. On November 18, the London *Jewish Chronicle* also published a detailed description of the "Nazi Pogroms," and an article entitled "Hitler as Tsar" offered a systematic comparison between the Tsarist policies against the Jews in the early twentieth century and the Nazi transgressions.

Jews everywhere were touched and excited at this time by what appeared to them to be the depth of public sympathy in the West, and the memories of these days only bolstered the basic optimism that seemed

[21] This and the following appeared in *Davar,* November 11, 1938.
[22] Pinhas Dashevski attempted to assassinate a well-known Russian journalist, the alleged instigator of the Kishinev pogrom, in 1903; Shalom Schwarzbard, a Ukrainian Jew, assassinated Petlyura, the Nationalist Ukrainian leader, in Paris in May 1926, several years after the Ukrainian pogroms of the Russian Civil War period; David Frankfurter, a student, killed Wilhelm Gustloff, a Nazi official, in an act of revenge in Davos, Switzerland, in February 1936.

to characterize the tone of Jewish reaction in the wake of the *November-pogrom*. The public protests of Tolstoy and Korolenko, who had been outspoken in denouncing the Russian slaughter, were repeatedly recalled, and despite the deep disagreements with British policies in Palestine, the *Yishuv* stressed with open gratitude the massive public rallies in London and the shocked reaction of the respectable London *Times* to events in Germany.[23] Above all, however, the Jewish press everywhere in the world based its hopes on what it regarded as the ever-regenerating survival instinct of the Jewish people. The *Palestine Post* reported a meeting of the Anglo-Jewish Association in London, where it was confidently argued that, "schooled in adversity, the Jews know that they would outlive the Nazi tyranny, destined to break under the weight of its own follies and iniquities."[24] The *Jewish Chronicle* in London was likewise hopeful, even if perhaps somewhat more skeptical: "We always came out stronger from the pogroms, and perhaps we will this time too."[25] In a public protest rally organized in Tel-Aviv by the Association of Hebrew Writers, Eliezer Steinmann, a well-known Hebrew author and leading intellectual of the time, chose words of encouragement, too. He gave a sanguine speech about the coming fight with the "new Amalek." The Nazis should know, he warned, that an ancient people, 17 millions strong, was at war with them, and with the support of the whole civilized world "we shall still see victories." "In an elated mood," the reporter concluded his brief account of the Tel Aviv meeting, "the crowd joined in singing the Zionist national hymn, *Hatikva*."[26]

Thus, despite the gloomy diagnosis characterizing the Zionists' view of Jewish existence among the nations, they had managed to preserve a hopeful stance vis-à-vis the unfolding events in Germany. A number of years earlier, at the nineteenth Zionist Congress in 1935, Nahum Sokolow, who was among the founding fathers of the movement and prominent among its ideologues, had argued that that same history of Jewish suffering and persecutions was also a story of great faith, endurance, heroism, and magnanimity: "The Jewish people is suffering, but it is living today with greater intensity than ever; it is today more inspired and more

[23] See, for example, the reports on speeches at the assembly called by the Association of Hebrew Writers in Tel Aviv, *Davar*, November 25 and 28, 1938. See also sporadic comments at the 21st Zionist Congress in August 1939, e.g., in Wetizmann's speech (see the Hebrew language Protocols, Jerusalem, n.d., 2).
[24] *Palestine Post*, November 22, 1938.
[25] *Jewish Chronicle*, November 18, 1938.
[26] *Davar*, November 25, 1938.

active than ever," he declared.[27] And a generally more astute observer, Berl Katznelson, who was certainly one of the most respected spiritual leaders of the Zionist Labor Movement in *Eretz Israel*, sensed with satisfaction, as he said, the confident mood of the *Yishuv* even at a later date. Speaking at a meeting of the Central Committee of the *Mapai*, the main political branch of the labor movement at that time, on December 7, 1938, Katznelson, while highly apprehensive, still found consolation in "the single encouraging aspect of the situation," namely the optimism of the men and women in *Eretz Israel*.[28] A great part of the *Yishuv*, he claimed, shared "faith in victory and in the possibility of victory." At a time when the international working class had succumbed to Fascism, he added, when both democracy and the greatest empires had capitulated before it, "we are the people who must not give in!"

This fundamental optimism no doubt relied on a deep national pride and faith in the effectiveness of Zionism. The internal strength manifested in those harrowing days stemmed from the hopes for the eventual success of the Zionist undertaking in *Eretz Israel*. In his closing address to the Zionist Executive of the Labor Movement in London, in November 1938, Yosef Sprinzak, another prominent Labor leader, declared that, despite all objective difficulties, the only salvation for German Jewry was in *Eretz Israel*: "'The rescue project' of German Jewry must find its path now, the rescue path leading to *Eretz Israel*."[29] This was to be more than a physical rescue. It was generally understood as an opportunity for spiritual regeneration. Enemies were all around Berl Katznelson noted at the same meeting; Hitler was not only torturing German Jews but also humiliating and denigrating all and every Jew wherever they might be. Yet at the same time, "*Eretz Israel* saves and lifts them."[30] The truth has never been so apparent, he concluded: "The Land of Israel elevates the dignity of the People of Israel." In an open appeal to German Jews, the Zionist Executive finally called on them not to despair: "Your sorrow is our sorrow and our hope is your hope," ran the text of the official resolution. "The Jewish

---

[27] See the printed Hebrew Protocols of the 19th Congress, 70.

[28] Mapai is the Hebrew acronym for the main Workers' Party in Eretz Israel, the dominant party in the *Yishuv*, and from 1933 it was the dominant party in the Zionist Organization as well. The protocols of the party's Central Committee meetings are at the Labor Party Archives at Beit Berl. Katznelson's speech is reported in the protocols of the meeting held on December 7 (hereafter "*Protocol BB*"), 34–40.

[29] The protocols are available at the Central Zionist Archives in Jerusalem. For the above quotes see Files S25/2708 (hereinafter "*Protocols*").

[30] This speech has been reprinted in Berl Katznelson's collected writings, *Ktavim* [Hebrew], Tel Aviv, Mifleget Poalei Eretz-Israel, 1948, vol. 9, pp. 18–19.

people laboring at the rebuilding of its national home is with you, and the eternal forces of humanity support you. Demonstrations of sympathy throughout the world, torch lights in the darkness of these days, prove that the conscience of mankind is still awake and that hatred shall not forever reign. The victims of today shall form the vanguard of reconstruction in the land of freedom."

The public reaction in *Eretz Israel* to the *Kristallnacht* was a faithful reflection of this basic attitude. The Zionists did conceive the events in Germany as a cause for serious alarm, but at the same time these same events served as confirmation of their fundamental historical view. Nazism was the final and irrefutable proof of the chronic presence and permanent nature of antisemitism. Once again, and this time loudly and clearly, Nazism had proven the futility and hopelessness of sustaining Jewish life in the *Galut*. The reaction of the Zionist public in Palestine to the intensifying persecutions in Germany was, accordingly, unequivocal: In addition to the spontaneous and essentially private sense of anxiety, and on the basis of the Zionists' analysis of the situation, which saw in Nazi antisemitism nothing but yet another, this time overwhelming, proof of its own position, there was no alternative but to double the efforts to build the National Homeland for the Jews in *Eretz Israel*. This much, after all, was clear at the outset. The eighteenth Zionist Congress in Prague, in late August 1933, gave full expression to this position. On this occasion Nahum Sokolow proclaimed the dawning of a new era: "The foundations of emancipation are now shattered and destroyed as if by an earthquake," he announced. "The entire façade of our civilization is collapsing. . . . We are facing the ruins of Jewish emancipation in one of the greatest states in the world." The only way to confront the crisis, he continued, was by squarely facing the truth and fighting the lie, "that lie within us – the lie of assimilation."[31] A bitter reckoning with German Jewry then followed. Sokolow reproached them for their overenthusiasm to gain the sympathy and trust of their fellow Germans, and for scoffing at the Zionists. "Yes, we were the dreamers indeed," he admitted, using his most effective rhetoric, "but the others were sleep-walkers."[32]

The Zionist leadership thus had no qualms about using the harsh conditions in Germany to settle old accounts with the reviled "assimilationists."

[31] Like many of the speeches in the Zionist Congresses, this one was also given in German. See *The Protocols of the 18th Zionist Congress*, Prague, August 21 – September 4, 1933, Vienna, 1934, p. 29.

[32] Ibid., 30.

It was unable to forgive them their contempt for the Zionist version of Jewish history, their rejection of a collective Jewish memory, and, finally, their "perennial passivity" that repeatedly precluded any fitting response to adversity. Although it must have been more than merely embarrassing to feel vindicated in the face of so much suffering, the urge to express a measure of satisfaction in view of the age-old Zionist predictions could not be completely suppressed. As early as mid-January 1933, while observing the critical situation in Europe, David Ben-Gurion commented that, under the present circumstances, it was no longer necessary to use Zionist propaganda among the Jews there. "From a Zionist point of view," he said, "there is no need at present [to carry on] propaganda... for *Eretz Israel.* The life of the Jews in the *Golah (place of exile)* now operates as the most powerful propaganda of all. It produces such a propaganda in the language of extinction... [by destroying] all means of existence for the masses... Jews are now storming *Eretz Israel.*"[33] Yitzhak Grünbaum, a leader of Polish Jewry who was by then active in Palestine, recaptured this tone at a meeting of the Zionist Executive in London immediately after the *Kristallnacht.* Even at that late date, he could not refrain from noticing that it was "no longer necessary to try to convince the Jews to come to Palestine. They will now be sufficiently convinced by the arguments of blood, restrictions and persecution."[34]

Indeed, throughout the late 1930s, the European crisis had often been conceived by the Zionist leadership as a source of renewal.[35] This was the line taken by Ben-Gurion, whose pragmatism and calculating, shrewd attitude stood out in the ideological discourse of his peers. As early as January 1933, speaking at a *Mapai* party convention, Ben-Gurion formulated what was to be for him a central question in the years to come, namely, how to exploit the "Great Jewish anguish"? Here is what he had to say about it in 1939: "The role of a leader and a statesman is to turn every failure into a lever." And occasionally he was even more outspoken: "We wish to see Hitler destroyed," he argued, "but for as long as he exists – we wish to use that for the building of *Eretz*

[33] Quoted in Shabtai Teveth, *Kin'at David: The Life of Ben-Gurion* [Hebrew], Jerusalem and Tel Aviv, Schocken, 1987, vol. 3, p. 284 (from a speech on January 1, 1933, at the Mapai Party Conference).
[34] Quoted from the *Protocols.*
[35] For much of this discussion I have relied on Arik Kochavi, "The Jewish Agency Executive and the Plight of German and Austrian Jews from the *Anschluß* to the Outbreak of the Second World War" [Hebrew], *Dapim* (A Journal for the Study of the Holocaust) 3, 1984, 97–121.

Israel."[36] When contemplating such statements, it is important to remember that the times were particularly trying in Palestine, too. The Arab Revolt that had kept the country in its grip since 1936 was at its peak. During the summer months of 1938 alone, over 200 Jews were killed in British-Mandate Palestine. These were years of economic depression and unemployment, and the struggle with the Mandate authorities reached new heights. The government in London was clearly in the midst of changing its policy, and the plan to divide Palestine, propounded by the 1937 "Peel Commission," was now abandoned in favor of the principles of a more recent "White Paper," practically retracting the promise of the Balfour Declaration and drastically restricting Jewish immigration. The Jewish *Yishuv* was facing a grave crisis.

It is against this background that the position of the Zionist leadership during the second half of 1938 must be seen. Most Zionist leaders focused their attention and efforts on the events and developments in Palestine. Even on the eve of the Evian Conference, as the refugees' problem in Europe began to take on threatening proportions, the immediate concern of the Zionists was the fear that the new solutions would jeopardize the project of immigration to *Eretz Israel*.[37] Menachem Ussishkin went so far as to demand that the Zionist delegation to Evian only participate in discussions related to Palestine, since, according to the protocol, "all the other countries of immigration are of no interest to us."[38] Ben-Gurion opted for a more sophisticated line. While sharing the suspicion that the Palestine project might lose its centrality in the planned conference, he demanded that the Zionist delegation not lose touch with other Jewish delegations at the conference, making sure not to appear to place obstacles to massive emigration out of fascist Europe. Still the tenor of the Zionist position remained firm and clear: There was only one solution to the Jewish plight – *Eretz Israel*, and every effort was to be made never to lose sight of that maxim.

This remained the essential position of the leadership in the immediate aftermath of the *Kristallnacht,* too. Most telling is the often-quoted protocol of the meeting of the *Mapai* Central Committee on December 7,

---

[36] The quotes in this paragraph are from Teveth, *The Life of Ben-Gurion*, 284.

[37] For this matter see the extensive, critical, though not always balanced discussion in Shabtai B. Beit-Zvi, *Post-Ugandan Zionism on Trial: A Study of the Factors that Caused the Mistakes Made by the Zionist Movement during the Holocaust*, Tel Aviv, 1991 (originally in Hebrew, 1977). In the following I have relied more eavily on Kochavi, "The Jewish Agency Executive," especially 100–5.

[38] Quoted in Kochavi, "The Jewish Agency Executive," 103.

1938. At the time, the Zionist leadership had to formulate its position on the British preparations for what would later be known as the Round Table Conference at St. James' Palace. Moshe Shertok set the tone of that meeting in an extensive opening report, arguing that the British government had been systematically exploiting the refugees' plight to diminish the significance of Palestine and in the meantime carry out its hostile policy toward the Jews there.[39] Sprinzak, who only a few weeks earlier had passionately urged the Zionist movement to concern itself more effectively with the fate of the refugees, was now more worried instead about the effects of possible international "territorial" solutions. Pushing for a practical approach, he chose a rather mundane line: "Should the Jews find it impossible to immigrate to *Eretz Israel*, it could cease to be a cause for fundraising and contributions, and the Jews would find refuge elsewhere, in England, etc."[40]

The mood at the meeting was tense and anxious. Some demanded that the Zionists stay away from the planned conference, or that the granting of certificates for the 10,000 children from Germany, which were just denied by the British cabinet, would be made a precondition for any kind of cooperation with the Mandate government. At this stage of the discussion, speaking confidentially among his party colleagues, Ben-Gurion did not even try to pretend that the children were uppermost in his mind. At that time he was solely preoccupied with breaking the prohibitions imposed by the Mandate authorities on Jewish immigration to *Eretz Israel* and fighting the stubborn anti-Zionist line reflected in the British government's general policy. Here is what he had to say:[41]

The demand to bring children from Germany to *Eretz Israel* does not spring here only from compassion for these children. Had I known that it were possible to save all the children of Germany by bringing them over to England, or save only half of them by transferring them to *Eretz Israel*, I would have chosen the latter – because we have to consider not just these children, but the total historic account of the People of Israel . . .

This is no doubt a particularly shocking quote, even when its precise context is taken into consideration. Neither did it reflect a consensus on these matters. Some of Ben-Gurion's colleagues at the time were

---

[39] All references are to *Protocol BB*. For Shertok's speech, see 17–23.
[40] Sprinzak's earlier pronouncements were made at the 4th Mapai party convention in early May 1938. Quoted by Kochavi, "The Jewish Agency Executive," 100. Sprinzak's speech at the December 7 meeting is in *Protocol BB*, 44–48. The quote above is from 47.
[41] *Protocol BB*, 30.

notably more distraught and tormented by the fate awaiting European Jewry. A good example was Berl Katznelson, for whom immigration now became the single most critical issue. In a heated correspondence with Ben-Gurion during March 1938, Katznelson tenaciously insisted on the difference between them: Ben-Gurion, he believed, had placed the Zionist struggle for a Jewish state above all, whereas Katznelson's top priority now was the fight for free Jewish immigration to Palestine.[42] By September of that year, Katznelson undertook work for illegal immigration to *Eretz Israel*. He was weary of rational arguments. His appeals became increasingly passionate. At the twenty-first Zionist Congress, in a key address that swept the delegates to their feet in stormy applause and left the less radical leaders worried and annoyed, Katznelson openly called on the Zionist movement to concentrate all its efforts on the great rescue project, openly defying the restrictions of the British government. Despite the impending international crisis, Katznelson was ready to declare "war" on the Mandate authorities. In his opinion, they had lost all remnants of legitimacy by preventing the *Yishuv* from doing anything to salvage what could still be salvaged of European Jewry.[43]

Berl Katznelson's fervent attitude grew from a dreadful vision of the catastrophe ahead. In November 1938, immediately after the *Kristallnacht*, foreseeing the nature of the imminent war, he described the following scenario: "Here the reckoning seems very simple to me. The Jews in all of the enemy's lands are doomed to extermination. They will be the first to be sent to the fire. No trace will be left of them."[44] Ben-Gurion's vision was not less tragic. At the *Mapai* party convention in May 1938, he shared his colleagues' bleak prophecies, painting the future in even gloomier colors. In a speech at the *Mapai* Convention in May 1938, he reiterated that "the war of annihilation against the Jews" was imminent, adding that what faced them now was not "a denial of rights as it had been in Russia, nor the pogroms as in the days of the Tsar... [but] a centralized policy aimed at dispossession, destruction and expulsion on a massive scale, using totalitarian, absolutist means." Ben-Gurion talked about "this terrible situation of millions of Jews targeted for extermination," and on

---

[42] See Anita Shapira, *Berl Katznelson: A Biography* [Hebrew], Tel Aviv: Am Oved, 1980, vol. 2, p. 568 (there is an abridged English translation: Anita Shapira, *Berl: the Biography of a Socialist Zionist, Berl Katznelson, 1887–1944*, Cambridge, Cambridge University Press, 1984).

[43] Katznelson's speech at the Zionist Executive in London was reprinted in his *Ktavim*, 17–29. The quote above is from p. 29.

[44] See his speech in the *Protocol BB*, 34–35.

November 9, in a meeting of the Zionist Executive in London, he argued that "the innermost desire of [Hitler's] sadistic and fanatic soul is the destruction of Jewry throughout the entire world."[45] In a closed session a month later, here is what he had to say of the approaching disaster:[46]

The month of November 1938 marks a new chapter, a chapter probably unprecedented in the chronicles of our people's persecution. This is not merely an organized physical extermination accompanied by a sadistic abuse of a community of 600,000 Jews. This is a warning sign for the annihilation of the entire Jewish people. I wish this prophecy would prove false, but I fear this is only the beginning . . . until now not even the devil has ever dared to play such tricks. Now that evil has been unleashed, there's no limit to what can be done to the Jews.

Yet despite all this, at the December 1938 meeting of the Party Executive, he opened his speech with an affected apology: "I must mention my sins," he said. "In these horrible days, [while] the beginning of destruction hovers over the Jews of Europe, and perhaps on the eve of the Mandate's demise, I am worried about the election in our Tel Aviv party branch."[47] He rejected the moralizing tone of his party comrades and urged them to contemplate the situation in a clear-headed manner, without overemotionality or naiveté. Ben-Gurion was preparing for a struggle under new, unfamiliar circumstances and was pragmatically seeking the most suitable course, with unwavering equanimity.

Ultimately, even Ben-Gurion, despite his clear-sightedness, could not have imagined the proportions of the future horror. The entire *Yishuv* was anguished by the events in Germany and genuinely concerned with the fate of the Jews there. Yet what characterized the local Zionists at the time was their preoccupation with the immediate political issues and the fate of the Zionist project in *Eretz Israel*. The tension and the uncertainty, along with fears of the moment and memories of the past, all combined to obscure the picture. In addition, it was the nature of modern antisemitism and its unique function in Germany at the turn of the nineteenth century that made matters worse and contributed to the confusion. It is to this aspect of the problem that the second part of this book is dedicated.

---

[45] Teveth, *The Life of Ben-Gurion*, 247.
[46] Yizhak Ben-Zvi (ed.), *Book of Documents of the National Committee of the Israeli Parliament* [Hebrew], 2nd enlarged edition, Jerusalem, Defus Rephael Haim Ha-Cohen 1963, p. 278.
[47] *Protocol BB*, 41.

PART II

ANTISEMITISM AS A CULTURAL CODE

4

Antisemitism Old and New

a. Origins and "Complete Explanations"

The history of antisemitism in Nazi Germany tends to be written from the perspective of antisemitism in the nineteenth century and vice versa: The history of nineteenth-century antisemitism has been normally written, and can perhaps only be written, from the perspective of the Nazi era. It is thus usually presented as a "dress rehearsal" for the National Socialist "final solution."[1] It is, no doubt, easy enough to list the various manifestations of antisemitism throughout the history of modern Germany, leading eventually to destruction. Even concrete plans to get rid of the Jews can be found in this catalog. It seems to be generally agreed that, although there have never been antisemites more fanatical, dangerous, and murderous than the Nazis, there was nothing particularly novel about their antisemitism. It is considered a phenomenon whose origins are well known and patently familiar.

Historians, after all, are always concerned with the tension between continuity and break, and their answers to the apparent dilemma created by this tension usually reconstruct the same pattern: In the last resort, the two are always intertwined, only mixed in varying degrees. Clearly, from a historical point of view, every event is rooted in the past, but at the same time, every phenomenon is at least in some way new and unique. The ongoing debate on break and continuity is thus only about the correct proportions. One cannot hope to decide between the

---

[1] This was first acknowledged in Paul W. Massing, *Rehearsal for Destruction: A Study of Political Anti-Semitism in Imperial Germany*, New York, 1949.

two; one can only judge their relative importance. And this, indeed, has been a matter that has never been absent from the agenda of German history. Anyone who refuses to regard National Socialism as a historical "accident," a mere aberration, regrettable but of limited consequences, cannot avoid reviewing the more or less prolonged historical origins of Nazism when trying to explain its nature. Anyone who believes this is an especially important historical chapter within a larger context, must nevertheless seek to demonstrate its uniqueness.

Now, the task of balancing continuity and break is especially complex in deciding the role of the so-called Second Reich in bringing about the Third, and one would normally expect that the history of antisemitism between 1871 and 1918 ought to play a major part in linking the two periods. Yet despite the centrality of this issue, it is only rarely the subject of serious study. Historians dealing with German history discuss it in passing, while scholars of Jewish history tend to treat it as self-evident, a familiar and quite predictable story. The former usually limit themselves to a few pertinent, sometimes illuminating, but always hasty and unsystematic observations.[2] The latter, sharing a consensus regarding both the scope of antisemitism in Germany and its deadly continuity, are likewise only marginally interested in its in-depth examination. Finally, the specialists, those whose focus of research is the history of antisemitism itself, are all too often in disagreement over most issues – just as specialists in general are prone to be.[3]

The tendency to emphasize the continuous aspect of antisemitism is particularly characteristic of Jewish historiography.[4] Ben Zion Dinur's essay mentioned above, is a good example. Dinur offered a circular

---

[2] See, for instance, the illuminating comments in Hans Rosenberg, *Grosse Depression und Bismarckzeit. Wirtschaftsablauf, Gesellschaft und Politik in Mitteleuropa*, Berlin, W. de Gruyter, 1967, pp. 88–117, and Hans-Ulrich Wehler, *The German Empire 1871–1918*, Leamington Spa, U.K., Berg, 1985(originally in German, 1973), pp. 105–13. In the third volume of Wehler's later, monumental *Deutsche Gesellschaftsgeschichte*, Munich, C.H. Beck, 1995, the issue is treated schematically on pp. 924–34.

[3] But lately there have been quite a few new works on antisemitism in general and on its history in Germany, in particular. Among them see, for exmaple, two collections of essays: Wolfgang Michalka and Martin Vogt (eds.), *Judenemanzipation und Antisemitismus in Deutschland im 19. und 20. Jahrhundert*, Egginger, Edition Isele, 2003, and Christhard Hoffmann, Werner Bergmann, and Helmut Walser Smith (eds.), *Exclusionary Violence: Antisemitic Riots in Modern German History*, Ann Arbor, MI, University of Michigan Press, 2002.

[4] See Shmuel Almog (ed.), *Antisemitism through the Ages*, Oxford, Pergamon Press, 1988 (originally in Hebrew, 1980), especially the article by Yisrael Gutman, "On the Character of Nazi Antisemitism," pp. 349–80.

conception of Jewish history in which European Jewry was perpetually forced to establish new cultural centers and witness their destruction.[5] Like a phoenix, such centers kept rising anew, only to be destroyed; an endless chain of creation and annihilation to be finally broken only with a return to the historical homeland of the Jews in *Eretz Israel*. Though Dinur's essay was written as early as 1943 and does not address the Nazis at all, their work of destruction could have been easily integrated in it as yet another chapter in this tragic tale; a particularly appalling chapter, to be sure, but still no more than just another station on that familiar Via Dolorosa. According to Shmuel Ettinger, to take another prominent representative of Jewish historiography in Israel, the roots of "eternal antisemitism" lay in the continuous transformations of the negative Jewish stereotype that is deeply ingrained in Western culture.[6] Again and again, especially in times of crisis, the memory of that stereotype seems to arise, and the latent, repressed hatred is activated and turns destructive.

In contrast to these two historians, both committed Zionists, Salo Baron, the leading Jewish historian in the second half of the twentieth century outside of Israel, developed an approach to Jewish history that is less concerned with the analysis of antisemitism and more with the position taken by Jews among the various nations and the precise social and economic contexts of their life in changing locations and in different periods. He too, however, regarded antisemitism as a permanent fixture of European history, an expression of the near-instinctive hatred of the other that could be found in each and every society.[7] He too considered the antisemitic policies of National Socialism as yet another chapter in the history of that "eternal hatred for an eternal people,"[8] a modern manifestation of those same pogroms, persecutions, oppression, and destruction of times immemorial.

Other historians preferred a more dynamic picture, allowing for development through change and not merely for the repetition of a constant pattern. Jacob Talmon, for instance, did not regard Nazi antisemitism as yet another episode in one and the same drama, but as the culmination of

---

[5] Ben-Zion Dinur, "Diasporas and their Ruin," [Hebrew], *Knesset* 8, 1943/4, 46–60.

[6] Shmuel Ettinger, *Modern Antisemitism: Studies and Essays* [Hebrew], Tel Aviv, Moreshet, 1978.

[7] Salo Baron, "Changing Patterns of Antisemitism: A Survey," *Jewish Social Studies* 38(1), 1976, 5–38.

[8] This was the title of Nahum Sokolov's book on antisemitism, published 1882. Compare this with note 3 in Chapter 1.

a prolonged process of acceleration. He was not content with observing the similarities between the opinions of Richard Wagner or the theories of Huston Stewart Chamberlain on the one hand, and those promoted by Adolf Hitler or Alfred Rosenberg, the Nazis' racist ideologue half a century later, on the other. Instead he was concerned with presenting the gradual exacerbation of antisemitism in the passage from the world of Wagner and Chamberlain to that of Hitler and Rosenberg. He wished to present a process of "ripening," so to speak. According to Talmon, earlier racist thought grew to provide the systematic basis for Nazi antisemitism and served as the anchor for their policy of annihilation. It was the basis for later events, the source of later evil. In his last book, however, Talmon slightly modified his position. The developmental element in his history seemed to be somewhat marginalized, and he too regarded antisemitism now as a permanent neurosis, always the same illness, expectedly culminating in "murderous madness."[9]

George Mosse, never concentrating on Jewish history alone, also regarded National Socialism as the final stage in a continual process of aggravation. His view of the history of antisemitism was conspicuously broader than that of Talmon, as he extended his research beyond the ideological positions of prominent thinkers to more popular forms of anti-Jewish sentiments. But for him, too, antisemitism was always at the center of the so-called German Ideology, a constructed and established part of the *völkisch* movement and thus finally a major component of Nazism, too. Nazi antisemitism accordingly turns out to be the keeping of an ancient promise, the fulfillment of a long-standing wish.[10] Even Jacob Katz, a historian of striking originality, reached similar conclusions. The racist theory has not been "a primal and primary cause" for the hatred of Jews, Katz explained, since it did not *create* the "conflict between the Jews and their environment." Nevertheless, under the particular historical circumstances in the aftermath of emancipation, and considering the "Nazi mentality," racism was instrumental in formulating some rather

[9] See in particular his essay "Mission and Testimony – The Universal Significance of Modern Anti-Semitism," in Jacob Talmon, *The Unique and the Universal. Some Historical Reflections*, London, Secker & Warburg, 1965, pp. 119–64. Compare his position in this essay with Part IX of his book, *Myth of the Nation and Vision of Revolution: Ideological Polarization in the Twentieth Century*, New Brunswick, NJ, and London, Transaction Publications, 1991 (originally in Hebrew, 1981), pp. 507–34. The quote is from page 522.
[10] George L. Mosse, *The Crisis of German Ideology: Intellectual Origins of the Third Reich*, New York, Grosset & Dunlap, 1964, especially pp. 294–311; and his "Culture, Civilization and German Anti-Semitism," *Judaism* 7, 1958, 1–11.

vague plans for the removal of the Jews, which finally materialized in their extermination by the Nazis.[11]

In the immediate post-war years, this dominant paradigm lost some of its hegemony. Philosopher and historian Hannah Arendt, was the first to accentuate the relevant dilemmas arising from the continuity thesis.[12] As early as 1951, in the first chapter of her book on totalitarianism, Arendt had already warned against conceiving modern antisemitism in general and Nazi antisemitism in particular as only further manifestations of that ill-famed "eternal hatred." The annihilation, she argued, was by no means a mere continuation of a long-standing tradition, rooted in the ancient world; a mere link in a chain of eternal animosity. It was, moreover, this very ignorance of the nature of past antisemitism and the misguided assumption regarding its continuity that has been responsible, in her opinion, for the miscomprehension of Nazism by so many of its contemporary observers. Such misapprehension had fatal consequences. It contributed to the confusion among Jews and may have even endangered their life.But while Arendt drew a sharp distinction between old and modern antisemitism, she did perceive a clear line of continuity between *modern* antisemitism and the murderous acts of the Nazis. The "new antisemitism," according to her, emerged with the birth of the nation-state, as a response to the unique role of the Jews within this state, and ended in "Auschwitz."[13] Its history did not begin in ancient times, but toward the end of the eighteenth century. It should be regarded as a new phenomenon, unique to the era of emancipation, a by-product of modernity. The distinction between this antisemitism and what preceded it was not based on a change in the antisemites' conduct, nor was it based on some change in the ideology of Jew-haters, runs Arendt's argument, but on the fundamental structural changes, typical of the modern era, affecting Jews and non-Jews alike. The novelty of "modern antisemitism," accordingly, lies in the "objective" changed situation of the Jews, not in the "subjective" attitude of their oppressors. Throughout this period, antisemitism was a reflection, albeit a distorted one, of the unique role of Jews in the social and political fabric of Europe. Arendt wished to cut off "modern

[11] Jacob Katz, *From Prejudice to Destruction: Anti-Semitism, 1700–1933*, Cambridge, MA, Harvard University Press, 1980, p. 325.

[12] Hannah Arendt, *The Burden of Our Time*, London, Secker & Warburg, 1951, p. 8 (in its American edition, the book appeared as *The Origins of Totalitarianism*, New York, Harcourt, Brace, 1951). See also her *Eichmann in Jerusalem: A Report on the Banality of Evil*, London, Faber and Faber, 1963.

[13] Compare Chapter 8.

antisemitism" from the past to stress its uniqueness, yet she continued to link the latter to Nazism. According to her, modern antisemitism was the beginning of a large-scale change that was eventually completed by the Nazis.

At about the same time, while Arendt's book challenged old conceptions, other historians were also trying to explain what came to be known as "modern antisemitism." At the center of this effort, according to Arendt's own guidelines, was the attempt to provide new parameters for dealing with the familiar events, and dating the onset of the new antisemitism then seemed paramount to the discussion. Both Paul Massing, in the late 1940s, and Peter G. J. Pulzer, in a book published in the early 1960s, while stressing the uniqueness of the new antisemitism and reaffirming the link between it and Nazism, disagreed with Arendt on periodization.[14] Both suggested that the years following the establishment of the Bismarckian Reich, during the late 1870s, and not the early nineteenth century, were a point of departure. For the two of them, it was the emergence of new, openly antisemitic political parties in Germany that signaled the new beginning. The similarities between Adolf Stöcker, the energetic Protestant priest who in the autumn of 1879 tried to infect Berliners with his antisemitic zeal, and Adolf Hitler, who half a century later exploited the crisis atmosphere in the Weimar Republic to his electoral ends, seemed crucial to them. "Modern Political Antisemitism," accordingly, was a "rehearsal for destruction," as Massing's title aptly announced. It became the banner of a continued struggle against all those liberal principles on which pre-Nazi Germany had been built. For despite all its shortcomings, Germany was at that time a bona fide *Rechtsstaat*, a member of that unwritten covenant of the civilized nations of Europe.

In 1975, in a book entitled *The Downfall of the Anti-Semitic Political Parties in Imperial Germany*, Richard Levy, for the first time, openly challenged this often-assumed link between pre–World War I antisemitism and that of the Nazis and their immediate predecessors. He did so by stressing the complete failure of the antisemitic parties during the *Kaiserreich*.[15] Levy describes the various antisemitic organizations in Germany from the 1890s until the "Great War" as helpless, even ludicrous. According to him, their paramount characteristic had been their incessant internal

[14] Massing, *Rehearsal for Destruction*; Peter G. J. Pulzer, *The Rise of Political Anti-Semitism in Germany and Austria 1867–1914*, New York, J. Wiley, 1964.
[15] Richard S. Levy, *The Downfall of the Anti-Semitic Political Parties in Imperial Germany*, New Haven, CT, and London, Yale University Press, 1975.

conflicts, the clashes of personalities within them, their amateur working methods, and the ongoing recruitment and fund-raising problems they experienced. Finally, on the eve of the war, these parties indeed suffered a total defeat. Levy never explicitly refers to the issue of continuity in the history of antisemitism, but his analysis clearly suggests that the dynamic movement led by Hitler could not be regarded as an heir to these earlier incompetent parties. Their legacy, he argues, was one of internal discord and unfounded political ambition. Even before the war they had lost their public support – in the Reichstag; in the parliaments of the German confederate states; and in the regional, municipal, and local councils. Any new political party with an antisemitic platform would have had to disassociate itself from that tradition and make a fresh start.

In fact, even before Levy, Peter Pulzer had described the decline of the antisemitic political parties during the last pre-war decade. But as he broadened his canvas in a series of short chapters at the end of his book, he managed to shift the emphasis by showing how "political antisemitism" had infiltrated beyond politics in Imperial Germany and into the various layers of its society. On the eve of World War I, the antisemitic parties were clearly a negligible phenomenon in Germany, Pulzer claimed, but at the same time, social and semi-political organizations had adopted their creed and were using it for their own purposes. The momentum that fed the antisemitic parties in the beginning was indeed slackened, but antisemitism itself remained pervasive, penetrating public life in a variety of other ways.

Pulzer's thesis was reinforced by the work of another historian, Werner Jochmann, who contributed two extensive essays to this discussion, taking us on a tour of Wilhelmine Germany with all its political, semi-political, and nonpolitical organizations.[16] Jochmann examined the degree to which antisemitism penetrated into each of the various public bodies at the time and the function that it served for them. He found Jew-hating to be ubiquitous. According to him, opponents of the antisemitic movement tended to underestimate its significance due to the fragmentation that characterized it, so that it was freely allowed to spread into student organizations, teachers' associations, and even the respectable professional bodies of judges and bureaucrats. It found its way into the ranks of the Protestant as well as the Catholic clergy; it gained ground in the smallest *Bürgervereine* and *Heimatsvereine*, those patriotic groupings that worked to preserve local

---

[16] Werner Jochmann's essays are collected in his book *Gesellschaftskrise und Judenfeindschaft in Deutschland 1870–1945*, Hamburg, H. Christians, 1988.

traditions, and in a variety of other local groups. Jochmann claims that, at the time, antisemitism in German society was practically endemic. It was to be found in trade and vocational interest groups, political pressure groups, local authorities, and central government agencies. And these bodies, even when they did not officially adopt antisemitic policies or initiate actions against the Jews, were generally responsive to public sentiment and the hostile mood in the streets. Even in the Social Democratic camp, particularly in some of the trade unions, antisemitic views could be discerned. The weakness of the antisemitic political parties, runs the argument, should not cover up the real strength of antisemitism in Imperial Germany. Indeed, it was precisely this weakness that made possible the wide-scale infiltration of anti-Jewish sentiment into the heart of pre-war German society, preparing it for the assiduous attack against the Jews mounted in its aftermath.

Thus, though one cannot point to any direct link between the ephemeral antisemitic parties of Imperial Germany and the Nazi party, one can trace the link between the antisemitism-saturated society of the *Kaiserreich* and the smooth reception of the principles of National Socialism later on. In another essay covering the years 1916–1923, Jochmann provids the material needed for establishing this continuity, suggesting that there had never been an appreciable slackening of antisemitism in Germany, even during the war itself and during the revolutionary intermezzo immediately following it. Certain antisemitic organizations did disintegrate, indeed, but others took their place in rapid succession. Nazi antisemitism, in fact, took new forms and exhibited unparalleled intensity and violence, but it grew directly on the institutional and ideological structures provided by Wilhelmine society.

The decline of the antisemitic parties in the *Kaiserreich* may thus no longer be considered an indicator for the overall decline of antisemitism in Germany, but as a sign of an ongoing shift in its character and formation. Antisemitism thus spread from radical groups of "true believers" into various organizations that were normally engaged with other issues, but it is doubtful whether it had been truly weakened in the process. Be this as it may, the importance attributed to the antisemitic parties of the *Kaiserreich*, both to their dramatic rise and to their apparent fall, has surely been exaggerated. Even the argument that they were to be viewed as "pioneering" bodies, the first to utilize antisemitism for direct politicization, is not very convincing. After all, the political use of antisemitism, albeit not in an organized partisan framework, was by no means a novelty. In Germany, as elsewhere, it did not begin in the 1870s. Jacob Toury has shown the political usage of antisemitism in 1848, during the "Springtime of Nations."[17] And although he argues that the antisemitism of those days grew rather spontaneously from a general, popular protest and was not an outgrowth of a planned political action, its political objectives and functions could not have been doubted.

To be sure, it was only in the last third of the nineteenth century that antisemitism first emerged as an element on the platforms of organized political parties. But even as the effectiveness of this political model began to be recognized, only a few of these parties managed to establish themselves as national bodies with a coherent message and a stable structure. Even in their heyday, between 1893 and 1907, these parties never carried more than 2 percent of the votes. In addition to their explicit opposition to Jews, they were always involved in a series of different issues, often entirely unrelated to their antisemitism. In any case, they were never even close to implementing their program. From the days of Adolf Stöcker in Berlin and throughout the 1880s and 1890s, their leaders campaigned for a variety of social reforms using their antisemitic propaganda mainly to link the disparate components of their platforms.[18] Antisemitism often had a subsidiary role in these parties, and their leaders frequently blamed each other for employing it for mere "tactical" gains. In fact, different motivations were always intermixed here. True belief and cynicism were intertwined in the rhetoric of these parties, and historians tended to attribute so much significance to them mainly because of the constant commotion they raised and their leaders' often-scandalous conduct. They grew "bigger than life" simply because we have become accustomed to always examining them in retrospect, from the perspective of National Socialism.

To regard the racist worldview that was sometimes embraced by the antisemites during the *Kaiserreich* as a fundamental innovation is also questionable. No doubt, racism as a theory claiming to rely on the natural sciences in general and on biology in particular had been an important innovation in those days, but its role in shaping "modern" antisemitism

---

[17] Jacob Toury, *Turmoil and Confusion in the Revolution of 1848: The Anti-Jewish Riots in the "Year of Freedom" and their Influence on Modern Antisemitism* [Hebrew], Tel Aviv, Moreshet, 1968. See also Eleonore Sterling, *Judenhass: Die Anfänge des politischen Antisemitismus in Deutschland (1815–1850)*, Frankfurt a. M., Europäische Verlagsanstalt, 1969.

[18] See Dieter Fricke, *Die Bürgerlichen Parteien in Deutschland: Handbuch der Geschichte der bürgerlichen Parteien und anderer bürgerlicher Interessenorganisationen, vom Vormärz bis zum Jahre 1914*, Vol. 1, (East) Berlin, Das Europäische Buch, 1968, pp. 36–40, 245–55, 429–31, 754–6, 759–62.

was less than crucial. It is true that the antisemitic discourse had been transformed during the second half of the nineteenth century. Its vocabulary grew and its slogans were reformulated, but these changes had only a marginal impact.[19] Marc Bloch argued that "men fail to change their vocabulary every time they change their customs."[20] But the opposite is also valid: When men – and women – change their vocabulary, it does not necessarily mean that they will also change their customs, or even their views. Richard Wagner is an interesting example in this context. Wagner's writings, and probably his speaking style, too, were full of antisemitic expressions of the most acerbic nationalistic and racist kinds, yet it can be persuasively argued that Wagner was not a true racist, although he certainly was a staunch antisemite.[21] After all, Wagner was willing to tolerate Jews whom he regarded as fully assimilated into German culture, and he even acknowledged the fact that some of them succeeded in achieving such full assimilation. According to Jacob Katz, it was this belief that separated Wagner from the genuine modern racists, who insist on the inborn and immutable inferiority of Jews. Like other antisemitic propagandists at the time, Wagner was not a systematic theorist. He used the terms of "scientific" racism when they seemed to fit his argument, and he deserted them when they were no longer useful. Other antisemites have likewise used the terminology provided by racism, employing it as an additional weapon in their arsenal; it was an efficient, though not always vital tool in converting traditional Jew hatred into a secular, modern ideology. Their main motivation was their hatred of Jews, not their racism.

Among the radical antisemitic publicists of the time, there were even those who opposed and despised racism. It was Paul de Lagarde who

---

[19] Despite the emphasis on the shift toward racism, old reliance on the religious, socio-economic, and cultural roots of antisemitism was quite evident even in the late nineteenth century. See Uriel Tal, *Christians and Jews in Germany: Religion, Politics and Ideology in the Second Reich, 1870–1914*, Ithaca, NY, Cornell University Press, 1975 (originally in Hebrew, 1969), and Katz, *From Prejudice to Destruction*, chap. 25. Particularly on Catholicism see Olaf Blaschke, *Katholizismus und Antisemitismus im Deutschen Kaiserreich*, Göttingen, Vandenhoeck & Ruprecht, 1997. A special issue of *Central European History* 27(3), 1994, was dedicated to various aspects of religious antisemitism and included a number of illuminating, original essays on this topic.

[20] Marc Bloch, *The Historian's Craft*, New York, A.A. Knopf, 1953 (originally in French, Paris, 1949), p. 34.

[21] See Katz, *From Prejudice to Destruction*, chap. 14, as well as his book, *The Darker Side of Genius: Richard Wagner's Anti-Semitism*, Hanover, NH, University Press of New England, 1986. There is a great deal of literature on the antisemitism of Wagner and his circle. See especially Saul Friedländer, *Nazi Germany and the Jews: The Years of Persecution, 1933–1939*, New York, Harper Collins, 1997, chap. 3, pp. 73–112.

dubbed it "a crude form of Materialism, scientifically meaningless."[22] But there were others who were quick to emphasize the moral and cultural aspects of their antisemitic theory over its biological-racist aspect. Even Eugen Dühring, who promised to address the Jewish question as a race issue in the opening pages of his major antisemitic work, used this term in an uncommitted manner. In his text, the terms "people," "nation," and "culture" were used interchangeably with "race," and his frequent use of the term *Judenhaftigkeit*, referring to the characteristics of non-Jews behaving like Jews, made it impossible for him to adhere to strictly racist arguments. Dühring hated anyone and anything seeming Jewish. Even those who were "Jewish" in style only, in conduct, and not necessarily by blood and race – were an abomination to him.[23] Wilhelm Marr and Otto Glagau, leading formulators of the supposedly "new antisemitism," also vehemently attacked any manifestation of *Verjudung* ("Judaization"). Their aggression against such trends equaled the zeal of their campaign against "genuinely Jewish" cases.[24] Finally, the following is an excerpt from the most popular antisemitic book of its time, Theodor Fritsch's *Antisemitic Catechism* from 1910, which is generally regarded as the ultimate text of contemporary antisemitism:[25]

The claim that presents opposition to Judaism as a result of stupid religious or racial hatred is nothing but a wrong and superficial claim, since it is in fact nothing but an unselfish kind of defense, carried along by the most sublime idealism, against an enemy of humanity, decency and culture.

As I mentioned before, for a long time, most historians tended to highlight the existence of a "new" or "modern" antisemitism, usually referring to events in Germany from the last third of the nineteenth century to the National-Socialist era and beyond. The modernity of such antisemitism was usually marked by two elements: the establishment of political parties with distinct antisemitic platforms – a novelty on the political map of the

---

[22] Quoted in Fritz R. Stern, *The Politics of Cultural Despair: A Study of the Rise of the Germanic Ideology*, Berkeley, CA, University of California Press, 1961 (quoted here from the 1965 edition), pp. 91–2.

[23] See Eugen K. Dühring, *Die Judenfrage als Rassen-, Sitten- und Kulturfrage*, Kralsruhe: Reuther, 1880, and the comments in Christoph Cobet, *Der Wortschatz des Antisemitismus in der Bismarckzeit*, Munich, Fink, 1973, pp. 82–94.

[24] Wilhelm Marr, *Der Sieg des Judentums über das Germanentum: Vom nichtconfessionellen Standpunkt aus betrachtet*, 8. Aufl. Berlin, Costenoble, 1879; Otto Glagau, *Der Bankrott des Nationalliberalismus und die Reaktion*, 6th edition, Berlin, Luckhardt, 1878, passim.

[25] Theodor Fritsch, *Antisemiten-Katechismus*, Leipzig, T. Fritsch, 1887. The quote is from the 1910 edition of the book, p. 20.

times; and the formulation of a new racial antisemitic ideology of a secular, modern shade. In the political and parliamentary activity of such people as Stöcker, Otto Böckel, Hermann Ahlwardt, and later Oswald Zimmermann and Bernard Förster, who were among the leading antisemitic agitators and organizers in Imperial Germany, historians saw an attempt to rejuvenate traditional antisemitism and turn it into a powerful motivating force in German politics. In addition, as it was generally argued, the racial theories of Gobineau and Chamberlain, along with the racist interpretations of some research in the natural sciences, provided new justification for antisemitism that was free from the image of unfounded prejudice and its distinctly Christian orientation. On this supposedly modern and scientific basis, it was now possible to draw from antisemitism practical conclusions and demand changes in legislation and a whole catalog of social and political reforms. A closer look, however, exposes the weakness of these arguments. Antisemitism had been put to political use long before antisemitic parties were established in the Second Reich, and in any case, these parties were not very significant at the time. Antisemitism had flourished in different places in Imperial Germany and wielded much influence without the dubious political support from the short-lived parties that were mushrooming on the fringes of German parliamentary life. At that time, racism also played only a secondary role. Although the theoretical means for what would later become the firm basis of Nazi ideology had already been formulated, they were only a supplement to the existing antisemitism during the pre–World War I years, which were exploited or discarded at will.

This conclusion has far-reaching consequences. As we shift the focus of our discussion from the organized antisemitic parties to the less established associations; when we examine sporadic antisemitic expressions in other frameworks, too, even among socialists during the Second Reich; when we reexamine the general phenomenon of antisemitism in all its aspects, emphasizing its broad social base, its implacable nature, and not necessarily its ideological constructs – we are actually reaffirming, albeit inadvertently, the "eternal hate" concept. If all the familiar characteristics of antisemitism are present again, and if what seemed a novelty has turned out to be but a repetition of familiar patterns, what, then, is that "new" or "modern" antisemitism with which all seem to be concerned? Could it really be nothing but yet another repetition of the same old scenario? Does it have any distinctly new elements at all? Did a new type of antisemitism indeed emerge in the 1870s, as the experts claim, or must we readopt the principally ahistoric notion of "eternal hatred" and consider antisemitism to be a kind of metaphysical, permanent feature that keeps reappearing in its old mode even in the dynamic and changing modern world?

Indeed, the theme of "eternal hatred" was powerfully renewed by Daniel Goldhagen, in a book that caused much controversy in the mid-1990s.[26] Interest in Holocaust-related issues seems to enjoy strange sorts of revival in the wake of some extraordinary political or cultural events. This was the case when U.S. President Ronald Reagan chose to address his hosts at a memorial ceremony in a small-town cemetery in Germany in 1985, for instance, after the screening of a new, moving film like *Schindler's List* or the publishing of an especially important book like the diary of the forgotten linguist and literary scholar Victor Klemperer, recounting his life in the shadow of the Nazi regime.[27] Voluminous scholarly works on the subject rarely leave such a public impression. They are read by experts who debate matters among themselves and are occasionally mentioned in the literary columns of the respectable press before vanishing without a trace from the public arena. In this respect, Goldhagen's book was for a time a remarkable exception. The public commotion around the book began in the United States and spilled over to Germany even before its translation had been completed. Even in Israel it received a great deal of attention, although there, for reasons that we will discuss later, it eventually raised only a passing and limited interest.

Throughout the book, Goldhagen claims to be a true innovator, offering his basic thesis as an academic and conceptual breakthrough. He explains that his view of German history is anthropological, not merely historical, since the Germans, he claims, have always had a special, essentially magical way of thinking that is fundamentally different from anything familiar to "us," the proper citizens of the Western world. Their campaign for Jewish extermination can thus be explained only through studying the Germans' unique cognitive structure, their "mindset," in Goldhagen's terms. Individuals in German society have been unable to set themselves free from this dominant "cultural model" that eventually dictated the extermination "project" to an entire nation, a joint "project" in which everyone participated, usually with a great deal of enthusiasm. In this framework, antisemitism had been a central and constant component.

[26] Daniel J. Goldhagen, *Hitler's Willing Executioner. Ordinary Germans and the Holocaust*, New York, A.A. Knopf, 1996.
[27] Victor Klemperer, *I Will Bear Witness: A Diary of the Nazi Years, 1933–1945*, 2 vols., New York, Random House, 1998 (originally in German, 1995).

Long before the Age of Enlightenment, Goldhagen argues, German society had been deeply antisemitic. Later, throughout the modern era, and despite the typically liberal rhetoric of that time, it had continued to regard "the extermination of Jewishness" as an unequivocal objective. With time, this peculiarly German "Exterminatory Antisemitism" grew more blatant, and once the Nazi regime made it into an official ideology, it was gladly accepted by the population. Goldhagen argues that Germans in general believed that Jews should be exterminated and have therefore obeyed from the outset all laws and regulations that prepared the ground for the Final Solution. They readily volunteered to implement it, and finally executed it, not only in exemplary meticulousness but also with energy and dedication. This uniquely German antisemitism, Goldhagen insists, was the necessary and sufficient cause of the Holocaust. It was this antisemitism that motivated not only the Nazis but also all of German society. Hitler's goals and the not-so-secret yearnings of the Germans as a national collective were the same, and the symbiosis between them provided the momentum needed for their realization. The Germans, who were strangely lacking any sense of compassion or human empathy, rapidly turned into "willing executioners." In fact, Goldhagen claims, no learned explanations are needed here. This is the only way that extermination could have taken place, and this is, finally, the only way to explain it.

Goldhagen's book need not concern us here but for the fact that it did contain a full and renewed formulation of a widespread attitude. If we were to present this thesis to the Israeli "man on the street" who was raised on the principles of Jewish historiography, he would shrug his shoulders in apathy. Is there anyone who does not know who and what the Germans are? Is there anyone who has not heard of their ruthless antisemitism? Is there anyone who has not encountered this explanation of the Holocaust in one form or another? What is new about the notion that German antisemitism, a permanent and eternal matter to begin with, had been aggravated in time until it finally became the central doctrine of the Nazis? As is widely known, and as might be expected from such consistent, obedient, and efficient types, the Germans drew the necessary conclusions from their antisemitism and set out to implement them, often willingly and, in any case, with no special qualms.

There is of course some truth in this argument, as there is in other, more moderate formulations of the continuity thesis. Most historians have always accepted the "origins thesis" with regard to the study of Nazism in general and to Nazi antisemitism in particular. Some look for deeper roots while others are content with a shorter course of events. But without underestimating the importance of this line of historical thinking, I would like to point out some of its limitations and attempt to outline a different approach.

The criticism of the "continuity thesis" may aptly begin with a quote from Marc Bloch's book, *Métier d'historien*:[28]

> The explanation of the very recent in terms of the remotest past, naturally attractive to men who have made of this past their chief subject of research, has sometimes dominated our studies to the point of hypnosis. In its most characteristic aspect, this idol of the historian tribe may be called the obsession with origins... However, the "origins" is disturbing, because it is ambiguous. Does it mean simply "beginnings"? That would be relatively clear – except that for most historical realities the very notion of a starting-point remains singularly elusive... On the other hand, is "origins" taken to mean the causes? In that case, there will be no difficulties other than those which are inherent in the nature of casual inquiry (and even more so, no doubt, in the sciences of man). But there is a frequent cross-contamination of the two meanings, the more formidable in that it is seldom very clearly recognized. In popular usage, an origin is a beginning which explains. Worse still, a beginning which is a complete explanation. There lies the ambiguity, and there the danger!

Indeed, in the historiography written after 1945, German antisemitism before 1914 had become just this kind of "beginning which explains," and often a "beginning which explains all." Accordingly, antisemitism was a necessary prerequisite for Nazism in general and surely a necessary prerequisite for the Final Solution. Although it is not usually made explicit, antisemitism is taken to be a necessary and *sufficient* condition for it, or better, in Bloch's words, "a complete explanation." For the purpose of our discussion, there is no need to go back to the roots of antisemitism in the Ancient World. The heart of the problem is the connection between "modern antisemitism," whether its beginning coincides with early modernity or only occurs in the last third of the nineteenth century, and Nazi antisemitism. I would argue that it is precisely the distinction between this older antisemitism and its murderous version adopted by the Nazis that could help us to reinterpret the events. As in the study of history in general, in this case, too, it is the differences that count, not the similarities; it is the shift, the new phrasing, and the change, not the repetition of the same structures nor the inertia.

---

[28] Bloch, *The Historian's Craft*, 29–30.

b. The Language of Antisemitism

Wilhelm Marr has been identified as the man who coined the term "anti-semitism."[29] Although this fact has been contested, since both the date specified in this context (1879) and Marr's original use of the term are dubious, his role in popularizing the term is assured. Clearly, at a certain historical moment and within a particular cultural atmosphere, "anti-semitism" became stock-in-trade almost overnight. It spread rapidly and soon supplanted other, age-old familiar terms. Within a few months it also acquired a complex meaning, probably far exceeding Marr's intentions and surpassing his and his "co-inventors'" anticipations. It soon turned out to be an element in the formulation of a unique worldview. Up to this point, Marr and his associates had managed quite well with the old termi-nology. Venomous anti-Jewish literature had been published in Germany throughout the nineteenth century, apparently not wanting for pertinent concepts. The older ones, *Judenhass*, *Judenfeindlichkeit*, and *Judenverfol-gung* seemed quite sufficient. Nevertheless, in Berlin in the late 1870s, in an atmosphere of economic and political crisis, the need arose to replace them.

Significantly, the term "antisemitism" did not refer directly to Jews or to Judaism. It spelled a rather vague opposition to "semitism," that is, to everything related to the existence of some obscure semitic race. According to all contemporary authorities, the Jews, who were known and familiar to the European nations from time immemorial, constituted only one segment of this race, whereas no one could precisely identify the others. Still, the new term created a larger semantic space as a vessel for a variety of desired contents. It had a scientific aura and could be placed on a par with such terms as "liberalism" or "conservatism," thus entering respectable linguistic company, no doubt.

Early in his political career, as a member of the left-liberal wing of the legislative body of the free city of Hamburg during and after the

---

[29] See Alex Bein, "Der Moderne Antisemitismus und seine Bedeutung für die Judenfrage," *Vierteljahreshefte für Zeitgeschichte* 6, 1958, 340–60; Reinhard Rürup und Thomas Nipperdey, "Antisemitismus," in Otto Brunner, Werner Conze, and Reinhart Koselleck (eds.), *Geschichtliche Grundbegriffe: Historisches Lexikon zur politisch-sozialen Sprache in Deutschland*, Stuttgart, E. Klett, 1972–1997, vol. 1, p. 129. On Marr, see Moshe Zim-mermann, *Wilhelm Marr: The Patriarch of Antisemitism*, New York, Oxford University Press, 1986 (originally in Hebrew, 1982), and his "Two Generations in the History of German Antisemitism: The Letters of Theodor Fritsch to Wilhelm Marr," *Leo Baeck Institute Yearbook* XXIII, 1978, 89–99.

Revolution of 1848, Marr was known as an agitator against the Jews. During his later years as a journalist and social commentator, and afterwards, when he published in 1879 what was to become his major work, entitled *Der Sieg des Judenthums über das Germanenthum* (The Victory of Jewishness over "German-ness"), he was still applying the old familiar language. But since the 1870s, his attempts to abstract his object of hate from any concrete content, to remove it from any criticism based on genuine experience and concrete situations, to turn it into the cornerstone of an overall worldview, were repeatedly evident: "There is no Jew hatred in my heart," he writes, "even less some hatred towards the Jews on a religious basis; not even a 'hatred of this nation' or a 'hatred of this race'...Indeed in the past I have sharply polemicized against the Jews, but I plead guilty of the charge...my politics has been nothing but an anachronism."[30]

Regardless of the way we choose to explain the psychological makeup of a Wilhelm Marr, his repeated assertions at the time that he did not bear "even the slightest grudge against the Jews" is not merely ludicrous.[31] It is indicative, above all, of the social atmosphere and the prevalent discourse within which he was forced to operate. Direct attacks on Jews, as individuals or as a community, had repeatedly been proven ineffective in the fight to prevent their emancipation. In a society that professed an open and liberal attitude, such "medieval superstitions" were bound to arouse contempt and opposition. Marr sought to launch a new kind of anti-Jewish campaign by offering a new term for the old hatred, one that fit the rhetoric of the period and invested it with a new content, according to modern parlance and modern style. Finally, by changing the name, the phenomenon itself took on a new meaning, so that the new name provided the budding movement with a powerful impetus.

In fact, efforts to overcome the anachronism attached to explicit anti-Jewish attitudes began much earlier. For a while, earlier in the century, Judaism replaced Jews as the declared object of hostility. Even in the debate over emancipation in Germany, beginning as early as the 1780s, tendencies to focus on Judaism and not necessarily on Jews were clearly noticeable. Judaism was perceived as dated and archaic, the religion of an ancient barbaric law, an anathema for enlightened men. From Kant to Karl Marx, Judaism – rather than Jews – had been the target of attack;

---

[30] Marr, *Der Sieg des Judentums*, 38–9.
[31] Ibid., 40.

the ancient religion, rather than its believers.[32] The shift, though never complete, enabled even the staunchest supporters of Enlightenment to set out against an anachronistic faith, which they regarded as greedy and money-worshipping, a relic from an era of violent tribalism. For Marr's purposes, however, this tactic was no longer useful and he was quick to distance himself from it. The world in which he operated, at the height of Bismarck's *Kulturkampf,* during the 1870s, tended to stress the social and political implications of upholding a particular religion and disregarded what now seemed to be outdated theological debates. To avoid confusion, Marr was quick to declare his "non-confessional point of view." Judaism for him was not merely a religion, he stressed, but a collective name for the Jews. It stood for everything he abhorred: the absolute opposite of what he wished to revere – *Deutschthum* ("German-ness"). In any case, Judaism was too specific for Marr's purposes. Its link to real living Jews, then and there, in the streets of Hamburg or Berlin, was too direct and therefore of little practical use. In a biography of Wilhelm Marr, the historian Moshe Zimmermann suggested that Marr was too concerned to deflect any counterattack by the Jews, whose power and influence he greatly overestimated.[33] But clearly the application of the terms "semitism" or "antisemitism" served him on a wider front, too. It suited both his tactics and his aims. Although the intention to harass Jews had not been lost, the new term enabled Marr to point the new popular movement he was then busy founding in a different direction. By using the new term, reminiscent of other ideological positions associated with scientific progress and presumably compatible with modernity, he wished to outgrow the old, anachronistic meaning of Jew-hatred. And, in any case, from then on antisemitism was to signify more than that. It pretended to connote an entire corpus of social and political opinions, a cohesive worldview, an ideology.

The first stage then was name giving. The next was the formulation and dissemination of new slogans. This was achieved by other publicists. Otto Glagau, like Marr, had been a local journalist with liberal preferences. His

[32] From the vast literature on these issues see, e.g., Nathan Rotenstreich, *Jews and German Philosophy: The Polemics of Emancipation,* New York, Schocken Books, 1984; Hans Liebeschütz, *Das Judentum im deutschen Geschichtsbild von Hegel bis Max Weber,* Tübingen, 1967; Yirmiahu Yovel, *Dark Riddle: Hegel, Nietzsche, and the Jews,* University Park, PA, Pennsylvania State University Press, 1998. And see, of course, Karl Marx, "Zur Judenfrage," in Karl Marx and Friedrich Engels, *Marx, Engels: Werke,* Berlin, Dietz Verlag, 1959 [1843/4], vol. 1, pp. 347–77; also see Chapter 6.
[33] Zimmermann, *Wilhelm Marr,* 88–91.

personal reasons for deserting the liberal camp and developing a passionate hatred of Jews are not known,[34] but by 1876, as he began a career of an independent pamphleteer, this was already his main inspiration. In that year, Glagau reprinted in a book form a series of articles that had previously been published by the *Gartenlaube*, a popular periodical, sounding the cultural preferences of the German middle class. The book was entitled *Der Börsen- und Grundungsschwindel in Berlin* (The Stock Exchange and the Swindle of the Foundation Era). He followed it in 1878 with *Der Bankerott des Nationalliberalismus und die 'Reaktion'* (The Bankruptcy of National-Liberalism and the 'Reaction'), blaming the Jews, in both essays, for the collapse of the European stock exchange markets in 1873. The catastrophe was a result of their devious manipulations of capitalism and of the German banking system. As Glagau was apparently more interested and involved in current social and economic affairs than Marr, he soon succeeded in giving his ferocious hatred of the Jews a distinctly social character that was present but only marginal in Marr's analysis. By linking Jews with the hated "Manchesterism," a radically liberal economic theory associated with the ideas of Manchester's renowned economist and politician Richard Cobden, Glagau managed to posit the Jewish question at the center of a far more urgent question than the "Jewish Question" – the "Social Question." Glagau then turned these two into one, creating a powerful identification between them, a volatile mixture that spread rapidly through German society.

The "Social Question" had by then been turned into a familiar label in German public discourse, indicating a variety of controversial social issues. While the focus of attention had shifted from one issue to another, according to the current circumstances, an abstract, overriding "question" seemed to remain the focus of attention for generations. In the second quarter of the nineteenth century, for instance, the main problem was the so-called pauperism. Following the 1848 Revolution, it was the emergence of a new industrial proletariat, or alternatively the fate of the lower middle classes, who were the presumed victims of rapid industrialization. With the onset of a relative economic slump after 1873, the middle class was hit even harder. Most concerned and disappointed were

---

[34] On Otto Glagau, see Pulzer, *The Rise of Political Anti-Semitism*, 88–90; Massing, *Rehearsal for Destruction*, 10–4; and Levy, *The Downfall of the Anti-Semitic Political Parties*, 13–6. See also Shulamit Volkov, *The Rise of Popular Antimodernism in Germany: The Urban Master Artisans, 1873–1896*, Princeton, NJ, Princeton University Press, 1978, pp. 173–8, and Henry Wassermann, "Jews and Judaism in the Gartenlaube," *Leo Baeck Institute Yearbook* XXIII, 1978, 47–60.

those who previously enjoyed, despite their misgivings, the fruits of liberal capitalism in its prime. They were now disillusioned by what seemed to be its failure, and while they would not readily go back to their previous conservative position, they were now unable to accept either the old-style liberalism nor the up-and-coming socialism. After decades of supporting liberalism, albeit one of a very specific kind, a wide stratum of the lower middle class now lacked a clear political and ideological home. The present "Social Question" was thus associated not only with specific and concrete issues but also with specific and concrete social groups. In 1879, Glagau's third pamphlet dealt directly with their complaints. It was entitled *Deutsches Handwerk und historisches Bürgertum* (German Artisanship and the Historical Bourgeoisie), and for the first time included a slogan that contributed more than anything else to Glagau's reputation as an antisemite.[35] The pamphlet, which dealt with the history and future role of master artisans in German society, ended with a call to all working men to unite against exploitation and the degradation of human labor, particularly against the hateful domination of "a foreign race." "*Die soziale Frage ist die Judenfrage*" Glagau concluded his essay. He thus supplied the "right" phrase at the "right" time and in the "right" place. By using it, he linked a general, rather defused attitude toward some of the most pressing issues of the day with a pronounced hatred of Jews. The link was not new, but it was the slogan that turned it from a vague sentiment into a cornerstone of a new ideology, hoping to lead to concrete action.

The link between antisemitism and anti-liberalism, familiar from the first half of the nineteenth century, though much less important in later years, grew more significant again as a result of the economic crisis of the late 1870s. It was claimed that Jews and "Jew-like Germans" were the culprits for the severe hardship. It was at best a result of their reckless conduct and, at worst, an outcome of their sinister scheming. The alliance between antisemitism and anti-liberalism became central to the petit bourgeoisie attitudes in German towns both small and large. Despite the radical leaning of a significant segment of this population prior to 1848 and immediately afterward, hostility toward Jews was clearly discernible during that time, too. Especially in times of economic decline, these people tended to hark back to the principles of the old economic order that had presumably offered them better protection in the past. They detested the

---

[35] Otto Glagau, *Deutsches Handwerk und historisches Bürgertum*, 5th edition, Osnabrück, Wehberg, 1879.

rapid changes brought about by modernization and found it "natural" to associate its evils with the Jews.

An interesting case in point is the position taken by Germany's small independent handicraft masters.[36] While explicit antisemitic expressions are hard to find in the proceedings of their public gatherings during 1848, there is enough evidence to show the prevalence of anti-Jewish senti-ments among them. Thus, for example, a group of master-artisans from Leipzig sent out a letter to all guild members in Germany late in 1848, spewing a tirade of anti-liberal rhetoric against the intention to revoke the guilds and the privileges attached to them with an attack on the emancipa-tion of the Jews. The Jews, according to this dispatch, are the archenemies of the honest German *Bürgertum*, of the hard working men and of soci-ety at large. They are "the hated strangers, who are nowhere at home and lack all compassion for the *Volk*, where [sic] they live."[37] Later on, in the immediate aftermath of the Revolution, masters often continued to associate their difficulties with the activities of the Jews, although in times of prosperity such claims were considerably less audible. After all, in their daily life, master craftsmen only rarely encountered Jews as direct competitors. In the old territories of the Reich, Jews were barred from the practice of most handicrafts, and in Prussia of 1817, only 4.6 per-cent of the Jews were handicraftsmen, while more than 90 percent were employed in various commercial, mostly small enterprises.[38] The number of Jewish craftsmen may have increased during the nineteenth century, first under the influence of the French occupation and then through the effects of liberal state legislations. However, centuries-old customs, among both Jews and Christians, slowed the rate of change. Despite the constant immigration of Jews from the East and a population flow from Prussia's annexed territories in Poland, where craftsmanship among Jews was much more common, even by the end of the nineteenth century less than one-fifth of the Jewish working population in Germany was engaged in crafts and industry. Moreover, while in the general population the majority of

---

[36] See my book, *The Rise of Popular Antimodernism in Germany* as well as my article, "Popular Anti-Modernism: Ideology and Sentiment among Master-Artisans during the 1890s," *Jahrbuch des Instituts für Deutsche Geschichte*, Tel Aviv University III, 1974, 203–25.

[37] *Offener Brief an alle Innungsgenossen Deutschlands so wie zugleich an alle Bürger und Hausväter von Zweiundzwanzig Innungen zu Leipzig*, Leipzig, B.G. Teubner, 1848, pp. 21–2.

[38] Mark Wischnitzer, *A History of Jewish Crafts and Guilds*, New York, J. David, 1965, pp. 197–205.

those employed in this sector were wage laborers, close to one-half of the Jews were self-employed businessmen and employers. In addition, Jewish craftsmen tended to concentrate in a limited number of trades only and were mostly tailors, shoemakers, butchers, and bakers.[39] Thus significant competition between Jews and non-Jews in most crafts was very rare. A similar situation prevailed in the small retailing and peddling sectors, although these were pet subjects of the antisemitic rhetoric. Despite its vehemence, Jews never held a monopoly over them, and their share of such activities was constantly on the decline. By mid-century, Jewish peddlers constituted less than one-quarter of all peddlers in Germany, and by the end of the nineteenth century they amounted to barely 5 percent. Despite these facts, and perhaps as a result, Jews were, indeed, very clearly felt in varied other economic sectors, especially in the fast-growing urban centers. In the cities, peasant immigrants encountered a far larger proportion of Jews than in their previous rural communities, and that minority was often uncommonly high-profiled.[40] The Jews' energy, skills, and ambition have often attracted public attention to their activities, providing various demagogues with obvious grounds for agitation. Among the immigrants into cities such as Berlin and Vienna, who were struggling under conditions of difficult economic, social, and cultural adaptation, antisemitic slogans found eager ears.

When Glagau sounded off "the Social Question is the Jewish Question" call, he produced above all a powerful analogy, a new metaphor. As in poetry, so too in the language of politics, it is the "wrong metaphor" that can prove to be most potent.[41] Clearly, the Social Question in German public life was not and had never been *identical* to the Jewish Question. If Otto Glagau himself was not aware of his "mistake," artisans, retailers, and other lower middle-class men certainly knew better. Nevertheless, the slogan worked. It was endlessly repeated and eventually helped to achieve, perhpas by a process that Kenneth Burke called an "associative merger," a

---

39 See Jakob Segall, *Die beruflichen und sozialen Verhältnisse der Juden in Deutschland*, Berlin, M. Schildberger, 1912, and P. Voigt, "Das Tischlergewerbe in Berlin," *Schriften des Vereins für Sozialpolitik* 65, 1895, 377.

40 Urbanization proceeded faster among Jews than among non-Jews. For further details see Chapter 10.

41 See Clifford Geertz, "Ideology as a Cultural System," in his *The Interpretation of Cultures. Selected Essays*, New York, Basic Books, 1993 [1975], pp. 193–233, especially 210–11. See also Walker Percey, "Metaphor as Mistake," *Sewanee Review* 66, 1958, 79–99.

conceptual link between the social critique prevalent in *Mittelstand* circles and antisemitism.[42] Writing of another metaphor in a different social situation, American anthropologist Clifford Geertz has commented:[43]

The power of metaphor derives precisely from the interplay between the discordant meaning it symbolically coerces into a unitary conceptual framework and from the degree to which that coercion is successful in overcoming the psychic resistance such semantic tension inevitably generates in anyone in a position to perceive it. When it works, a metaphor transforms a false identification . . . into an apt analogy; when it misfires it is a mere extravagance.

For many in Glagau's Germany, his metaphor was clearly a misguided extravagance, a "demagogy" in the language of the time. But for segments of the *Mittelstand* and for others who were in search of a conceptual framework within which to comprehend unwanted transformations, it provided a much sought-after clue. For them, overcoming the "psychic resistance" created by Glagau's patently false metaphor was amply rewarded by a relaxation of other tensions, by the offer of what they saw as a concrete solution to far more pressing needs.

In his memoirs, Hellmut von Gerlach, who began his political career in the conservative right and ended up in the radical left, recalled Glagau's influence on his intellectual development:[44]

His catchphrase was: "The Social Question is the Jewish Question." For me, the Social Question stood at the foreground of my interest. Glagau had invented a miracle cure for its solution: Get rid of the Jews and the Social Question is solved! So, I went over to him in order to drink this social wisdom from the source.

Glagau's slogan was simple, elegant, and extremely suggestive. It was the very stuff of propaganda, and it was effective. A measure of its success may be gained from an interview given by the aged Adolph Wagner to Hermann Bahr, a progressive journalist and politician, in 1893.[45] Wagner, who was among the leading theorists of social conservatism in mid–nineteenth-century Germany and himself among the first to link antisemitism with social conservatism, repeatedly sought to dissociate himself from the popular identification of the Social Question with the Jewish

[42] Kenneth Burke, "The Rhetoric of Hitler's Battle," in *The Philosophy of Literary Form*, Berkeley, CA, University of California Press, 1973 [1957], pp. 200–7.

[43] Geertz, *The Interpretation*, 211.

[44] Hellmut von Gerlach, *Von Rechts nach Links*, Zürich, Europa Verlag, 1937, pp. 110–1.

[45] Hermann Bahr, *Der Antisemitismus. Ein internationales Interview*, Berlin, S. Fischer, 1893, p. 76.

Question, à la Glagau. He thought it necessary to stress over and over again that he saw danger in the confusion of the two and that the slogan combining them was false. Yet, by then, through endless repetition, its truthfulness was taken for granted by too many in his own camp, and Wagner's efforts to enlighten them had no chance of success. Virulent attacks on both capitalism and socialism, and the demand for social reforms along corporatist lines, were by the end of the century invariably associated with antisemitism. In the eyes of many the slogan replaced reality. The link was made as a matter of course. It became part of the prevailing culture.

5

Functions and Meaning

a. National Consciousness: The Jew as the Other

Despite the importance of the precise social context for the crystallization of modern antisemitism, it was no less dependent on that ongoing effort by Germans in the course of the nineteenth century to construct their collective self and define their national identity. Among the great nations of modern times, the case of Germany readily exemplifies the pattern according to which nationality has been consolidated before the formation of a nation-state. The contrasting pattern is the one that is typical of England or France, where presumably a modern centralized state preceded the emergence of national consciousness. Although historians often stress this distinction, it is only partially convincing.[1] The study of nationalism has made considerable progress during the last two or three decades, and new approaches that set the historical research free of its long-standing ideological dependence on the presuppositions of nationalism itself now allow for a fresh look at the events. In Germany, solid nationalism coupled with a significant degree of social cohesion based on an explicit national awareness became in fact a reality only in the years following the establishment of the Imperial Reich by Bismarck. Despite Germany's "lagging behind" in this respect, nation building in Germany too had been a long and complicated process. While certain aspects of it were concurrent and unusually rapid, others were completed only gradually. We have recently learned to accept the fact that, even in the more

---

[1] Significant examples are Friedrich Meinecke, *Cosmopolitanism and the National State*, Princeton, NJ, Princeton University Press, 1963 (originally in German, 1908), and Elie Kedourie, *Nationalism*, London, Hutchinson, 1960.

established nation-states west of Germany, such national-social integration had not been completed much earlier. There, too, only with the help
provided by a well-oiled political apparatus did the birth of the modern nation occur, involving a long, drawn-out, and painful labor. Turning the peasants in rural France into nationally conscious citizens, for
instance, had been a protracted and complex process that took the entire
nineteenth century to complete.[2] In England, too, a clear national consciousness had not fully emerged before the mid-nineteenth century; and
the simultaneous attempt to integrate such consciousness into a broader
and somewhat vague "British" identity had greatly complicated matters.[3]
Germany's starting point was admittedly especially problematic, but the
creation of a national society based on inner cohesion has never been a
trifling matter anywhere.

Indeed, up until the establishment of the Bismarckian Reich in 1871,
there had been no single country in central Europe that could be considered a German nation-state. The Holy Roman Empire that served as
the political backbone of the region for centuries had been based on feudal principles, emerging finally after the Peace of Westphalia (1648) as a
confederative structure headed by a Habsburg emperor who reigned over
hundreds of separate, often combatant political units. Some of these grew
during the eighteenth century into more or less independent, absolute
monarchies, although most remained dependent on the Kaiser's protective rule. In the new centralized states, a more or less efficient bureaucracy
gradually began to run the government, operating the taxation system and
controlling many aspects of its subjects' life. The most powerful of these
was Prussia, which had successfully waged a series of wars against the
Habsburgs themselves during the eighteenth century and on the eve of
the French Revolution was already a bona fide European power, albeit
not of the first order. *De jure*, the Kaiser's authority had been retained
and the Holy Roman Empire was still in existence, but *de facto*, no one
could really control this complex, disintegrating system.

It was finally Napoleon who brought on the disintegration of the
Reich, dismantling many of its smaller political units and giving new
leases on life to the mid-sized ones. As a result of his complete reorganization of the territories east of the Rhine, not only were the church

---

[2] Eugen Weber, *Peasants into Frenchmen: The Modernization of Rural France, 1870–1914*,
Stanford, CA, Stanford University Press, 1976.
[3] See mainly Linda Colley, *Britons: Forging the Nation 1707–1837*, New Haven, CT, Yale
University Press, 1992.

territories in southern and southwestern Germany liquidated, but so were many of the tiny princedoms whose existence had been dependent on the Kaiser's protection. These were annexed to the mid-sized states, mainly to Bavaria, Würtemberg, and Baden, which were now zealously eager to protect their sovereignty. The *Rheinbund*, a regional federation established by Napoleon and fully subordinated to him, was later disintegrated on his defeat, and a new German confederation was established, headed by Austria under the uncontested leadership of Prince Clemens von Metternich. Up to the Prussian victory over Austria in the summer of 1866 and the establishment of the North-German federation as a precursor to the Bismarckian *Kaiserreich*, no country ever aspired to give political expression to the German nation.

Pre-unification "Germany" suffered fragmentation in a number of other respects, too: It was notorious for its winding inner borders, excessive taxes and tolls, and fragile transportation system. Moreover, it was already abundantly clear by the eighteenth century that the attempt made during the Reformation to prevent religious pluralism within the individual German states of the old Empire had failed. More than any other political structure in Europe, the religious wars left Germany torn between Catholics and Protestants. In addition, deep class divisions and considerable cultural rifts between the north and south, east and west, as well as within each of these regions, characterized the German-speaking society of central Europe.

Nevertheless, a budding conception of nationality can be discerned in Germany even prior to the French Revolution. The champions of this conception were here as elsewhere members of a small stratum of educated men who maintained close communication among themselves, despite all objective obstacles. They managed to create and maintain a dynamic public sphere in which current affairs were energetically debated, and which surmounted formal borders as well as a host of legal and governmental restrictions. Only later, following the conquests of the French revolutionary army and Napoleon's reign, did the national idea gradually permeate broader social strata. During a prolonged period of social and economic change, the propertied bourgeoisie also discovered the advantages of a unified, larger, and less restricted market that was free of traditional bureaucratic shackles, and the prospect of linking economic progress with national unity began to appeal to the lower strata of German society, too. Already in this initial state it was clear that nationalism – whether as the focus of an as-yet-obscure collective identity or a roughly formulated political ideology – needed some additional props, and in an era when it became a major social and political force, it found itself closely allied with liberalism. Following the example of the French Revolution, nationalism and liberalism were considered to be two sides of the same coin. In revolutionary France, nationalism was in fact the main manifestation of the demand for popular sovereignty. But even in Germany, where it did not develop within a revolutionary context, nationalism maintained its bond with liberalism. Finally, when German nationalism took on an ever-more pronounced romantic character, and even as the national discourse increasingly focused on ethnic issues, echoes of the liberal creed still reverberated within it for a long time. Concurrently, however, the option of combining nationalism with conservatism, social and even political, became increasingly attractive. In the quest for the nation's ancient roots, German nationalism came to sanctify the same aspects of the past, that German conservatism, also a product of the first half of the nineteenth century, set high on its agenda. Surprisingly, Germany's medieval past, which had captivated the Conservatives' imagination, enthralled the architects of nationalism, too. The historical approach cultivated by the new nationalism was a perfect fit for the one cherished by conservatism. Thus it became gradually apparent that nationalism – and not only in Germany – could mesh well both with liberalism and with its ideological opposite. Its "rightist connection" turned out to be as powerful as its "leftist connection."

At the same time, other aspects of the Nationalist syndrome gradually became apparent. By the early nineteenth century, for instance, it was clearly and ubiquitously associated with xenophobia. In the case of Germany, indeed, it was always simpler to define the foreigner and agitate to exclude him rather than to determine the borders of the nation and provide it with common, positive characteristics. It was easier to point at those who did not belong than to define criteria for national affiliation. Under the circumstances in this fragmented country – a socially fissured conglomerate of confessions, subcultures, and dialects – antisemitism soon became a familiar and welcome companion in nationalistic circles. And later, when inner strife in Germany did not cease, antisemitism would always have a vital role to play.

It is intriguing that this simple fact is rarely mentioned in modern historiography. Reviewing historian Thomas Nipperdey's by now already classic text on nineteenth-century Germany, one finds that in an extensive chapter on nationalism, while he meticulously sketches its social and intellectual origins, categorizes its various types and accounts for its emergence in Germany prior to 1848, antisemitism does not feature at all.

Even in a separate article about "Romantic Nationalism" in Germany, antisemitism is not mentioned.[4] Nipperdey finds the first usage of anti-semitic argumentation only in the late 1870s, a hallmark of what he labels "radical Nationalism." This, accordingly, developed only toward the end of the century, stressing the attack on the "enemy within" – above all the Socialists – while applying a spirited rhetoric against a variety of national minorities in Germany, most particularly the Polish. Even at this late stage, according to Nipperdey, antisemitism did not occupy a major place in the worldview of the "national camp."

This may be yet another attempt – conscious or unconscious – to clear the name of the German national movement and legitimate its mani-festations, both in the past and in the present. Astonishingly, another book, the monumental work of Hans-Ulrich Wehler on the modern his-tory of German society, paints a similar picture.[5] But while by the 1990s Nipperdey openly defended the revival of a "healthy" German national consciousness, Wehler, Germany's leading social historian, could not be suspected of defending German nationalism. He is among its most promi-nent critics and staunchest opponents. In the first volume of his book, Wehler dedicates an entire chapter to the beginning of the national move-ment in Germany, seen as a reaction to the crises of modernization, revolu-tion, and foreign rule. He explains that, at the time, a socio-psychological mechanism for reinforcing social ties was operated by emphasizing hos-tility toward various enemies, real or imaginary. He goes on to exten-sively discuss the anti-French campaign accompanying the emergence of German nationalism in the Napoleonic era and the years of its imme-diate aftermath but leaves out entirely discussion of contemporary anti-Jewish sentiments. In a later article, written in 1994, at a time of mount-ing xenophobic sentiment in post-reunification Germany, Wehler once again avoided any reference to antisemitism. He repeated his old thesis about nationalism in the Bismarckian Reich, relying on enmity toward Russia and England from without, and especially the ongoing conflict with Catholics and Social Democrats from within. Both cases, he argued, were instances of deliberately utilizing the familiar tactics of achieving

---

[4] Thomas Nipperdey, *Germany from Napoleon to Bismarck, 1800–1866*, Princeton, NJ, Princeton University Press,1996 (originally in German, 1983), chap. 7. See also his article, "Auf der Suche nach der Identität: Romantischer Nationalismus," in his *Nachdenken über die deutsche Geschichte*, Munich, C.H. Beck, 1986, pp. 110–25.

[5] Hans-Ulrich Wehler, *Deutsche Gesllschaftsgeschichte*, 4 vols., Munich, C.H.Beck, 1987–2004. See especially vol. 1, pp. 506–30, and his article, "Nationalismus und Fremdenhaß," in his *Die Gegenwart als Geschichte*, Munich, C.H. Beck, 1995, pp. 144–58.

solidarity through hatred. But this approach is abruptly discarded when he addresses antisemitism. Wehler makes no attempt to integrate its manifestations within his overall view of the period. For him, antisemitism remains an important, but isolated matter.

The difficulty of integrating it into the history of the *Kaiserreich* is understandable. After all, the Jews were a very small minority in Germany. The war against France in the beginning of the nineteenth century and the struggle against the socialists near its end were undoubtedly more important matters. It is understandable therefore that a historian such as Friedrich Meinecke, whose book on the German nation-state was first published in 1908, ignored the "Jewish Question," apparently considering it negligible. After all, in his day and age, the integration of Jews into German society seemed secure, and their situation rarely engaged the attention of men of his social standing and cultural milieu. But for historians writing today who are surely aware of the importance of antisemitism in German history, ignoring it seems distinctly less comprehensible. Had things gone differently, perhaps it would have been possible to pass over Fichte's offensive statements about Jews or the critique cast against him in this context by Saul Ascher, the Jewish radical who regarded him as "a second Eisenmenger,"during the first decade of the nineteenth century. The prose of Father Jahn or the poetry of Ernst Moritz Arndt could still be regarded as nothing more than "the heralding signs of political reaction" or typical manifestations of "Germany's social backwardness."[6] But from today's perspective, Ascher's critique certainly deserves to be treated as more than a case of paranoia and there is hardly a justification for disregarding the rampant hatred for Jews among the zealous members of the new *Burschenschaften* in the pre-March years nor the distinctly antisemitic atmosphere surrounding the emergence of German nationalism at the time. Historian Leonora Sterling has amassed plenty of relevant material on this issue and addressed it in her book on antisemitism in the 1960s.[7] The late Uriel Tal treated this theme extensively in a pioneereing essay of 1974.[8] The simple facts may be common knowledge, indeed, but

---

[6] Walter Grab, "Ein jüdisch-deutscher Spätaufklärer zwischen Revolution und Restauration," *Jahrbuch des Instituts für Deutsche Geschichte*, Tel Aviv University VI, 1977, pp. 131–79. The quote is from pp. 165–6.

[7] Eleonore Sterling, *Judenhass: Die Anfänge des politischen Antisemitismus in Deutschland (1815–1850)*, Frankfurt a. M., Europäische Verlagsanstalt, 1969.

[8] Uriel Tal, "Young German Intellectuals on Romanticism and Judaism – Spiritual Turbulence in the Early Nineteenth Century," in *Salo Wittmayer Baron: Jubilee Volume*, Jerusalem, American Academy for Jewish Research, 1974, pp. 919–38.

why should they go unnoticed? Likewise, is it justified to ignore the early signs of political antisemitism during the 1848 Revolution? Is there no significance in the fact that, in that most heroic moment of liberal nationalism in Germany, its other, dangerous face had been exposed, too? Is there no need to discuss the ambiguous attitude toward the question of Jewish equality that was so common in revolutionary circles at the time?

In any case, it was during the difficult days following the establishment of a unified German state under the leadership of Otto von Bismarck that the "usefulness" of antisemitism was rediscovered. A veritable civil war, border shifts, and changes of sovereignty in the various German states gave special urgency to efforts at social integration. Antisemitism contributed its share. The *Kulturkampf*, pitting Bismarck and his Liberal allies against the Catholics, in effect worked to exclude a minority of some 40 percent of the population from the national community. Despite the need to achieve an unchallenged statehood, the onslaught against such an influential sector was surely incongruous with integration. Neither was the ongoing war against the Socialists and the emerging Social Democratic Party (SPD) conducive to national cohesion. Presenting the working class as "the enemy within" could have perhaps facilitated the closing of the *Mittelstand*'s ranks, but it could not help to cement that yearned-for overall national unity. Attacking the Jewish minority, however, amounting to little more than 1 percent of the German population, proved more effective. While Bismarck and the Kaiser were repelled by the style of the antisemitic politicians in Berlin and feared their agitation, the anti-Jewish campaign had too many advantages for anyone in the upper echelons to take action against it.

The Bismarckian Reich was inflicted not only with internal splits and divisions but also with a range of other problems, and antisemitism soon proved a simple means of handling at least some of them. It seemed an effective tool in diverse contexts. Antisemitism thus played a major role in channeling the general sense of dissatisfaction resulting from the economic distress and mounting social tension caused by the rapid and thorough industrialization during the third quarter of the nineteenth century. This process was generally equated with the Liberal-Capitalist economic system, which then enjoyed a period of unprecedented flourishing. But, starting from the crash of the European stock exchanges in 1873 and continuing through the period of economic instability that lasted until the mid-1890s, this system came to be conceived of as crumbling. By attributing the responsibility for this situation to the Jews, it was possible to attack the system without fearing revolution or inciting class war. It was the Jews who distorted capitalism, or so it was claimed; they were the destructive force behind liberalism. A variety of public figures and politicians were then quick to exploit the difficult atmosphere in the streets. Primarily through their astute intuition, these people managed to manipulate the crisis for their own purposes.

We have seen that the roles played by Marr and Glagau were in constructing the vocabulary of antisemitism and its arsenal of slogans and catchphrases. But it was Heinrich von Treitschke who first achieved the integration of all these elements into one influential text. Historians have often noted the significance of Treitschke's writings on the "Jewish Question." It has been rightly claimed that he made antisemitism *salonfähig*, that is, worthy of the elegant salons of the affluent and the educated in German bourgeois society. In fact, he made it "politically correct." Above all, Treitschke let antisemitism in the front door of the German universities. In his monumental *History of the German People in the Nineteenth Century*, his famous lecture course on politics, and his articles in the *Preußische Jahrbücher*, Treitschke built up a complex of ideas that later came to constitute the essence of a unique German national ideology.[9] His popularity derived from his unfailing ability to always sense the mood of his audience and his talent for providing them with adequate materials, bringing together the different issues that were uppermost in their minds. Treitschke, indeed, gave the best available expression to a cluster of attitudes that was gradually crystallizing into a nationalistic worldview. He finally succeeded in indicating the intellectual, political, and moral boundaries of the new ideology and in sketching the contours of a unique culture within which it could flourish. Unlike most of the publicists who had arrived at a similar position by the late 1870s, Treitschke had the intellectual stature needed to link the German idealist and historicist tradition with the new radical nationalism, applying a philosophy of history and a unique ethical system in an attempt to provide a suitable interpretation of German history, outline a political program for the present, and offer an inspiring vision of the future.

Treitschke's first article dealing with Jews and antisemitism also gives an excellent exposition of his overall social, political, and cultural

---

[9] For the controversy over Treitschke's essay on the Jews, see Walter Boehlich (ed.), *Der Berliner Antisemitismusstreit*, Frankfurt a. M., Insel-Verlag, 1965. For the development of Treitschke's historical and political approach, see Andreas Dorpalen, *Heinrich von Treitschke*, New Haven, CT, Yale University Press, 1957, and Georg Iggers, "Heinrich von Treitschke," in Hans-Ulrich Wehler (ed.), *Deutsche Historiker*, Göttingen, Vandenhoeck & Ruprecht, 1971, vol. 2, pp. 66–80.

position. Dated November 15, 1879, it opens with an analysis of world affairs.[10] Treitschke reiterates the familiar theme of German isolation in world politics and denounces the suspiciousness and hostility of other nations. This state of international affairs, Treitschke believed, made the need for a strong state – a state based on a "true harmony between the Crown and the *Volk*"– particularly urgent. A free, debating parliament, exposing any inner controversy, was not only an unnecessary luxury, it was entirely foreign to "true Germans," arousing only contempt, even nausea, among them. Instead of democratic demagoguery, Treitschke offered a therapy in the form of a rising consciousness of the *Volk*. It alone, he claimed, could withstand the tide of "feminine philanthropy" and the devastating contemporary cosmopolitanism. Continuing in the same vein, Treitschke turned to the "genuine" mass antagonism toward Jews, characterizing it as an encouraging "symptom of the time." Praising the "healthy instincts of the masses" that he so often derided, Treitschke himself was finally made aware of the potential of anti-Jewish propaganda and its imminent link with the other components of his worldview. The Jews, he explained, were a danger to the emerging "new form of German life." They were the opposite of everything German, and their very presence was a danger to German culture. Jews stood for "*Lug und Trug*" (lying and cheating), for unscrupulous materialism, in blatant opposition to the "industrious spirit of our *Volk*." The entire intellectual community in Germany, Treitschke declared, had finally arrived at the unavoidable conclusion: "*Die Juden sind unser Unglück*" (The Jews are our misfortune).

Treitschke not only achieved the "associate merger" necessary for creating the link between antisemitism and his special brand of nationalism, he also applied the familiar propaganda technique of the "wrong metaphor." The "Jewish Question" was not one problem among others, but the essence of all evil. A quick turn of the pen made a single problem stand for all others. The Jews were equated with every negative aspect of German life, everything that Treitschke and his readers detested. Their equation with an entire syndrome of ills – social, political, and cultural – was a stroke of genius. By using a simple rhetorical technique, an unsatisfactory situation was suddenly made comprehensible. A strong

[10] Heinrich von Treitschke, "Unsere Aussichten," in *Preußische Jahrbücher*, November 1879. Here I used a later printing, in Heinrich von Treitschke, *Deutsche Kämpfe: Schriften zur Tagespolitik*, Leipzig, S. Hirzel, 1896, pp. 1–28. All of the following quotes are from this article.

opposition to government policies could now be coupled with an idolizing of the state. The responsibility for weakness of character, for folly and failure, was placed where it hurt the least – at the margin, on the outcast, on the Jews.

The effect of Treitschke's writing on the *Judenfrage* was all the more striking because he had not been previously known as an antisemite. During the 1860s, he even complained in his letters of the blatant intolerance toward Jews that he had encountered in academic and student circles and, like his liberal colleagues, objected to coarse anti-Jewish propaganda. Later, the anti-Bismarck anti-Jewish campaign of the mid-1870s appeared dangerously unpatriotic to him. But with his overall turn to the right in 1878/79, Treitschke too began to "see the light." During the economic crisis of these years, he left the National Liberal Party, supported Bismarck's anti-Socialist legislation, and adopted an openly antisemitic stand. It was not an anti-Jewish passion that made him defend antisemitism in his polemical articles, but the realization of the link between it and his general stand. He perceived the affinity and in turn helped to make it more "natural" and self-evident. Treitschke managed to combine his uncompromising brand of nationalism with antisemitism, and as he was joining the two, he seemed to discover the tactical potential of this merger along with its intrinsic logic. This anti-Socialist, anti-democratic, anti-emancipatory ideology of Germany's leading historian during the late 1870s could not be complete without antisemitism.

b. The Political Function of Antisemitism in the *Kaiserreich*

The central role of antisemitism in the new German nation-state was not limited to the ideological sphere; it was highly instrumental in the daily political practice of the "Second Reich." By the 1870s, antisemitic agitators of various shadings began to align themselves with the existing political forces in the country. Some of them sought to link their fate with the conservative parties, despite the fact that at that early date most of the established leaders of these parties were quick to disown them. In contrast, others had developed different allegiances. These men, often coming from the left, did not intend to abandon this camp. Wilhelm Marr, as we saw earlier, fought in the Revolution of 1848, while Otto Glagau had once been the economic correspondent of one of Germany's leading liberal dailys, the *Nationalzeitung*. These people expressed the sentiment of a considerable sector of German society, mostly of the lower middle classes, who by the late 1870s felt not only rejected by their opponents, but also – and more importantly – deserted by their former allies.[11]

It was during the 1848 Revolution that the Liberal movement in Germany finally seemed to have conquered the hearts of the masses. In those turbulent days, Liberals fought not only for individual civil and political rights or for a free economy, but they also championed nationalism, demanding a strong, unified, and constitutionally based Germany. During the 1840s, the national-liberal associations, mostly comprised of students and free professionals, gradually grew into a mass movement. While small farmers and peasants in Germany's rural regions and day laborers in the towns were still excluded from the political sphere, the majority of Germany's urban population – craftsmen, small traders, local officials, and teachers – were already politically aware and active. They were usually committed to one of the factions in the Liberal camp. Despite their inner struggles, and although a large proportion of this lower middle class had always had reservations concerning the Liberals' economic line, liberalism seemed to represent them, at least from mid-century onward, against autocratic monarchy and the still omnipresent, powerful nobility. It was the rapid economic growth in the third quarter of the century and the relative prosperity it produced that brought together – if only temporarily – the established German *Bürgertum* and what was then called the German *Mittelstand* – the traditional lower middle class. While a fundamental inconsistency was always characteristic of this alliance, especially with regard to economic policy, social tensions raging under the surface were now camouflaged by grandiose rhetoric, stressing shared interests and that yearned-for national unity.

For as long as the economic upward trend continued, inner tensions could be overlooked. During the 1860s, the Liberals managed to implement many of the economic and social reforms on their agenda, and with the establishment of the new Reich in 1871, it seemed that their main objectives had been realized, indeed. Germany's effective industrialization seemed to improve the economic situation of the lower middle classes, too, and their opposition to a free market policy weakened in the face of what seemed to be the Liberals' ultimate triumph. Even the apparent weakening of Liberalism, under pressure from Bismarck's reign, was dwarfed by its previous achievements. It was only later on that the sharp economic

---

[11] For a more extended version of the discussion on artisans, see Shulamit Volkov, *The Rise of Popular Antimodernism in Germany: The Urban Master Artisans, 1873–1896*, Princeton, NJ, Princeton University Press, 1978.

reversal heralded by the 1873 stock-exchange crisis reached a peak in 1879 and finally brought about the breakup of the Liberal camp. In times of rampant bankruptcies and plummeting market prices, while industrialization continued under changing and worse conditions, traditional craftsmen, for instance, and small businessmen in general, felt that they were no longer able to support the free market economy. The weaker elements within the lower bourgeoisie now clamored for state protection, and, along with most agricultural and some industrial sectors, they began to turn their back on Liberalism. After all, the nationally oriented platform of the two major Liberal parties in the *Kaiserreich* – the Progressive and the National-Liberal – was by now also embraced, if not always wholeheartedly, by the Conservatives. They quickly developed into an alternative political force and were attempting to enlist at least some segments of the *Mittelstand*, both urban and rural alike.

At the same time, the new Social-Democratic Party had proclaimed itself a working-class party, and its radical platform was deeply disturbing, even alarming, for precisely these lower middle-class elements. They feared sinking deeper into the proletariat, along with losing their relatively higher social status, and dreaded the destructive consequences of any revolutionary act on their property and lifestyle. Although the Socialists often aimed their propaganda at the *Mittelstand* in Germany's towns and villages whose life experiences were not very different from those of the blue-collar workers, their success in enlisting these men was limited. Social Democracy was usually not a real political option for the *Mittelstand*. Neither could the Conservatives, despite their efforts, offer them a comfortable political home. After all, the old rightwing parties represented above all the aristocracy and fought for its political and economic interests. It was difficult to regard them as an alternative from the perspective of the lower middle class. When voters from among its ranks deserted their Liberal anchor, only the new "Reform" parties, headed by some of Germany's most vocal antisemites, seemed to fill the political vacuum. While they lacked parliamentary experience and social prestige, they could and did offer, at least temporarily, a roof for the politically homeless elements of the new Reich.

The history of the handicraft masters in Germany provides yet another example of the manner in which political antisemitism was intertwined with the protest reaction of the lower middle classes during the last quarter of the nineteenth century. This group, still relying on traditional forms of production and on the corporate organizational structure attached to it, was easily attracted by antisemitism. Glagau's anti-liberalism, for

instance, was based on a consistent opposition to liberal economic policies, and other antisemitic spokesmen also harked on their sympathy
for the hard-presssed, even impoverished lower middle classes. Accustomed to guild protection and vocational restrictions, this population
now found itself in a world where its age-old advantages were revoked,
and the protective walls on which it had traditionally relied were finally
torn down. For as long as Germany's economy flourished and its industrial growth benefitted everyone, it was possible to agree to the changed
rules of the game brought about by liberalism. But when the rapid growth
came to a halt and economic hardship followed in succession, the political
alliance between artisans and Liberals was broken. A former Liberal himself, Glagau's brand of antisemitism provided these people with a palatable explanation for the degeneration of German liberalism. And while
it was initially difficult for them to openly assail their previous allies, it
was made much easier by attacking not the basic weakness of the liberal
movement, but its progressive *Verjudung*. Thus it was possible to attack
not capitalism itself, but its Jewish version; not genuine Liberalism, but
"Manchesterism," that is, its presumably distorted Jewish version; not
the truly "national" government, but its Jewish advisers. Frank Perrot, a
senior publicist in the *Kreuzzeitung*, the reactionary organ of the Prussian
conservative aristocracy, attacked the government's Liberal policy with
hardly any anti-Jewish overtones, but former Liberal Glagau, like many
of his readers, could not. They needed the props of antisemitism. It served
them as a stage of transition, from the open support of liberalism into an
endorsement of conservatism, a bridge from the left to the right.

During the 1870s, many master artisans severed their former ties with
the Liberals, while no other political power held any attraction for them.
Some of their leaders attempted to fill the vacuum by establishing a separate artisans' party. They tried to prevent a full-scale shift of the artisans' votes into the Conservative camp. Not surprisingly, however, none
of these organizations survived the planning stage, and by the time of
the election campaign of 1879, they were all long forgotten. Instead,
the existing parties vied for these floating votes, and while explicit antisemitism was rare in public assemblies of the various artisans' organizations at the time, many of them began to support the parties that led
an uncompromising offensive against the Jews: The *Soziale Reichspartei*,
home of the formerly "progressive" liberal Ernst Henrici in Berlin; the
Deutsche Volksverein, led by the Conservative politician Max Liebermann
von Sonnenberg; the Saxonian *Deutsche Reformpartei;* and various other
antisemitic leagues and associations. These all wished to appear as allies

of the small handicraft masters in their struggle against the liberal state and the "unfair" competition of big capital and modern industry. Each in its peculiar style supported the master artisans' demands for compulsory guild membership, the reintroduction of masters' qualifying examinations, restrictions on the competition of prison workshops, the reorganization of the bidding system, and the like. They clearly felt the potential for massive support along these lines.

There is no way to assess the number of handicraft masters among the 46,000 antisemitic votes cast in Berlin during the election of 1881.[12] We know that in Dresden, another center of handicraft production, a building master won the Reichstag seat on the antisemitic *Deutsche Reformpartei* ticket. In May 1880, the two most prominent leaders of the Berlin master artisans' movement took part in a campaign rally organized by Adolph Stöcker, the leader of the antisemitic Social Conservative Party in the Prussian capital. They had indeed traveled a long way from their days of political activism on behalf of the leftwing Progressives in Berlin to their campaign for the antisemitic court priest.

As early as the spring of 1878, Stöcker was attempting to dissociate Berlin's workers from the grip of Social Democracy and bring them back, so to speak, under the banner of "Church and Crown." By the beginning of the 1880s, he had to admit defeat. By that time, his real target audience was not the proletariat, but the *Mittelstand*; not the workers but the middle classes – primarily artisans and small retailers.[13] In a March 1880 speech about the "Artisans' Question" in Breslau, Stöcker urged his audience to desert liberalism, which had betrayed them, and stand united to protect their rights.[14] The protocol of the event revealed that the audience was not entirely at ease with this attitude. In response to interjections from the crowd, the speaker was forced to adopt a defensive stance. He reiterated that he was not attacking liberalism as such, but its "rotten branch." He was not against the "system," only against its destroyers. Here Stöcker was not facing the enthusiastic crowd of his Berlin rallies, but instead people whose political background was radically different from his own. They came to hear him because they were no longer sure

[12] Peter G. J. Pulzer, *The Rise of Political Anti-Semitism in Germany and Austria*, New York, WIley, 1964, p. 99.

[13] Siegfried Kaehler, "Stöckers Versuch, eine Christlichsoziale Arbeiterpartei in Berlin zu begründen," in Paul Wentzke (ed.), *Deutscher Staat und Deutsche Parteien*, Munich, R. Oldenbourg, 1922, pp. 227–65, and Hellmut von Gerlach, *Von Rechts nach Links*, Zürich, Europa Verlag, 1937, p. 104.

[14] Adolf Stöcker, *Christlich-Soziale Reden und Aufsätze*, Bielefeld, Velhagen & Klasing, 1885, pp. 338–53.

that their prior political choices were consistent with their needs. Their old ties with Liberalism, ideological as well as emotional, were not yet completely severed. They were still not ready for the full ideological about-face that support for Stöcker indicated. And it was encounters such as this that made him aware of the need to supply his potential supporters with an additional battle cry. Antisemitism, which by then had already proven successful in the streets of Berlin, seemed the obvious choice, and Stöcker enthusiastically seized on it. He was now operating in the spirit of the Conservative Liebermann von Sonnenberg, who had shocked even his staunchest supporters in a street-side café in Berlin by remarking: "First we want to become a political power; then we shall seek the scientific evidence for antisemitism."[15]

In the same way that a militant social-conservative, antisemitic movement was needed in Protestant Berlin and in some other parts of Prussia and Saxony to sever the ties of the *Mittelstand* with liberalism, so was it needed in the mixed Protestant-Catholic areas of Western Germany, too. The small master artisans in the Rhine area and in Westphalia were the first to join the liberal fight against the conservative establishment on the eve of the 1848 Revolution. They were also the first to demand the repeal of the hated *Gewerbefreiheit* (freedom of occupation) and the reinstatement of the guild system. Their support of liberalism never extended to this movements' economic creed. By the 1870s they were losing faith in its other principles, too. Still, they needed a transition through militant social-conservatism and antisemitism before they could finally join the more established conservative forces. They seem to have had a hard time finding political allies in the volatile situation in Germany of those days.

Freiherr Friedrich Carl von Fechenbach was a Catholic landowner from Hesse who began his political career as a National Liberal and supported Bismarck and German unification. Later he evolved his own political agenda and was, for several years, stormily engaged in attempting to give it an organizational backbone. Living in a mixed Catholic-Protestant area, he too toyed with the idea of a social conservative force that would bridge confessional differences to withstand "the tide of Socialism."[16] He campaigned for the implementation of strong anti-capitalist

---

[15] Gerlach, *Von Rechts nach Links*, 112.
[16] On Fechenbach, giving him exaggerated importance and disregarding his antisemitism, see Hans-Joachim Schoeps, "CDU vor 75 Jahren. Die sozialpolitischen Bestrebungen des Reichsfreiherrn F. von Fechenbach 1836–1907," *Zeitschrift für Religions- und Geistesgeschichte* 9, 1957, 266–77. My thanks to Margaret L. Anderson, who set me straight on the details of this man's rather dubious character. See her *Windthosrt: A Political Biography*, Oxford, Clarendon Press, 1981, pp. 252–55, 257–59, 311–13, 391–93.

social measures, and his agitation was invariably antisemitic. Fechenbach
seemed to be driven by strong personal ambition and was apparently,
not unlike other publicly active antisemites, fickle and rather untrustworthy. Early in 1880 he attempted to reach an agreement with Stöcker,
Perrot, and a number of other social conservatives. When this failed,
he decided to carry on alone. He then established the *Verein für kon-
servative Sozialreform* (the Association for Conservative Social Reform),
declaring war on "free capital" and "unfair competition," a return to the
joint silver-gold standard, a "healthy" colonial policy, an expulsion of
non-Christians from all German legislative bodies, and the establishment
of a corporatist parliamentary system.[17] In striking parallelism with the
development of Stöcker's career in Berlin, Fechenbach sought to create a
grass-roots movement based on *Mittelstand* supporters, especially master artisans and small shopkeepers. Because he mainly operated in rural
areas, he also attempted to reach the peasantry. Fechenbach sought to
combine a strong anti-liberal campaign with fervent antisemitism, lacing
it all with familiar nostalgia for the pre-modern age. It was a mixture
specifically designed to appeal to the small ex-liberal master artisans in
the rapidly industrializing regions of Western Germany who were clinging
to the old economic structures and its social concomitants as a remedy
for the present hardships.

Like his colleagues in the Prussian capital, Fechenbach too seemed to
be initially successful. By 1881, he had established some fifty branches
of his *Verein zum Schutze des Handwerks* (Association for the Protection of Handicrafts), proof of the resonance he sought and apparently
found among them. Concurrently, he had managed to publish for some
years a special bi-monthly artisans' journal, *Die Innung*, subtitled *"Organ
der Sozialkonservativen Vereinigung für das deutsche Handwerk"* (the
Organ of the Social Conservative Craftsmen Association), while run-
ning a carefully orchestrated campaign among his potential supporters.
But Fechenbach's projects were all short-lived. For a while, the tireless
Freiherr entertained the prospects of a national antisemitic movement
and attempted to cooperate with like-minded men, this time mainly in
Dresden, but he finally abandoned this course of action, too, and by
1885 he had joined the Catholic Center Party. Presumably his former
supporters, perhaps not as numerous as he had himself claimed, followed
suit.

---

[17] *Die Post*, November 13, 1880.

In any case, the Center Party had been a more comfortable political home for Catholic lower middle-class voters than the Conservatives ever were for the Protestants. But here, too, at least for a minority, an antisemitic interlude enabled the shift from Liberalism to the right. Thus, toward the end of the nineteenth century, many supporters of the various small, antisemitic parties exhibited a tendency to join forces with the established conservative camp, which was by then apparently ready to absorb not only their membership but some of their ideas and ideals as well. In Protestant Germany, this was mainly sustained by the new style adopted by the Conservative Party, which made real efforts to restrain its aristocratic preferences. Gradually, it appeared, the party was capable of internalizing the demands of a new political era, and where it was only partially successful, the *Bund der Landwirte* (the Farmers' League), operating under its auspices, quickly filled in the gap. Applying aggressive propaganda methods, the leadership of both the party and especially the *Bund* was not loath to exploit antisemitism. The link between the unyielding monarchism and the forceful nationalism, between the adulation of the old Prussian traditions mixed with modern Imperialism, and between all of these and antisemitism proved a powerful concoction. The "New Right" that emerged in Germany during that period was finally capable of sweeping large segments of Germany's *Mittelstand* while adopting part of their vision. Many of those who had formerly placed their faith in liberalism now crossed over to the Conservative camp when it donned a more dynamic image and set out to represent their interests. Within a couple of decades it became clear, indeed, that modern nationalism, too, was no longer championed by Germany's liberals alone but was propagated most effectively by the right as well. Simultaneously, and despite the Conservatives' overt opposition to democratization, this camp now concerted all its energy on recruiting new voters precisely from those sectors formerly repelled by their elitism. In this general shift, antisemitism played a central role. Following an interim of supporting small popular parties that preached antisemitism cum regressive social reforms, many *Mittelstand* voters finally moved their allegiance all the way to the right, embracing its principles and lending it social legitimacy of a new kind.

c. The Cultural Meaning of Antisemitism

In addition to its role in the social and political discourse of late–nineteenth-century Germany, antisemitism also played a unique role in the crystallization of its culture. In a pioneering 1974 article on the so-called Jewish Question, Reinhard Rürup, a leading historian of German antisemitism, after noting its novel character since the 1870s, reasserting its uses as a political tool, and indicating its new theoretical groundings, suggested yet another line of approach:[18]

> In the age of Emancipation, expressions of Jew-hating . . . were concretely related to the Jews and their position in bourgeois society . . . But since the second half of the seventies [of the nineteenth century], radical Antisemitism turned into a "*Weltanschauung*", and even the moderate Antisemitism of the Conservatives clearly showed a tendency to become one.

Cautiously placing *Weltanschauung* in quotation marks, Rürup goes on to define it as an "explanatory model" for comprehending a rapidly changing world, combining an analysis of the existing circumstances with a blueprint for the solution of all pressing problems.

But while in Rürup's view antisemitism is a *Weltanschauung* in its own right, other authors usually prefer to see it as a distinct aspect of a larger, more inclusive one. In the post–World War II years, many historians – at least among those who were not Marxist in orientation – tended to emphasize the inner relationship between the ideas associated with antisemitism and an array of other constitutive values in modern Germany. George Mosse regarded the "new" hatred of Jews as one of the motifs in what he termed the "German ideology."[19] In a book carrying this title, first published in 1964, Mosse has shown the intellectual links between antisemitism and racism, a variety of *völkisch* ideas and the aggressive nationalism that was rapidly taking root in Germany at that time. He repeatedly warned against treating antisemitism in isolation and asserted that it was no less than "a part of German intellectual history" in that period. In *The Politics of Cultural Despair*, Fritz Stern enlarged our conception of the intellectual milieu relevant to antisemitism. Not only were racism and *völkisch* Nationalism related to it, he claimed, but the whole complex that he chose to name "cultural pessimism."[20] Like Mosse's,

---

[18] Reinhard Rürup, "Die 'Judenfrage' der bürgerlichen Gesellschaft und die Enstehung des modernen Antisemitismus," in *Emanziaption und Antisemitismus: Studien zur 'Judenfrage' der bürgerlichen Gesellschaft*, Göttingen, Vandenhoeck & Ruprecht, 1975, pp. 74–94. The quote is from p. 91.

[19] See George L. Mosse, *The Crisis of German Ideology: Intellectual Origins of the Third Reich*, New York, Grosset & Dunlap, 1964. Also by Mosse, see "Culture, Civilization and German Anti-Semitism," *Judaism, a Quarterly Journal of Jewish Life and Thought* 7, 1958, 11.

[20] Fritz R. Stern, *The Politics of Cultural Despair: A Study in the Rise of the Germanic Ideology*, Berkeley, CA, University of California Press, 1961. A more detailed discussion

Stern's sources too were those of intellectual history, but his book is a kind of *histoire de mentalité*. His analysis portrays not a rational, orderly system of ideas but a general worldview stemming from complex emotional sources and rooted in an overall mental set, a genuine *Weltanschauung*.

As already mentioned, Werner Jochmann also sought to anchor antisemitism in a broader social and cultural context. With time, he argued, the hatred of Jews had become an element of the overall creed of nationalism, an integral part of a new Imperialist drive that was bound together with conservatism and *Kulturpessimismus*. Earlier still, in a study of the myth of the "Elders of Zion," Norman Cohn suggested that, during the course of the nineteenth century, Jews became a "symbol of the modern world" and antisemitism an immediate companion to a variety of anti-modern attitudes that were woven into nostalgia for a lost pre-industrial past. For German conservatism, one of its chief historians, Hans-Jürgen Puhle, claimed that antisemitism served as an element of a wider "ideational common ground" that was typical of the Prussian agrarian elite, while Andrew Whiteside, who dealt with the history of the Pan-Germanic movement in Austria, diagnosed it as a component of an intellectual syndrome that was characteristic of the Viennese student movement, a "working form," to use his language, for absorbing and assimilating a variety of motley ideas.[21]

Since the 1950s, following the work of Theodor W. Adorno and his California collaborators, we have come to associate antisemitism not only with a certain type of worldview, but also with a certain psychological type, the so-called "authoritarian personality."[22] The debate on

---

of antisemitism in the Bismarckian era is available in Stern's biography of Bismarck's private banker: *Gold and Iron: Bismarck, Bleichröder, and the Building of the German Empire*, New York, A.A. Knopf, 1977, especially pp. 461–541.

[21] See Werner Jochmann, *Gesellschaftskrise und Judenfeindschaft in Deutschland 1870–1945*, Hamburg, H. Christians, 1988, pp. 30–98; Norman Cohn, *Warrant for Genocide: The Myth of the Jewish World Conspiracy and the Protocols of the Elders of Zion*, London, Eyre & Spottiswoode, 1967, pp. 23–4, 164–79; Hans-Jürgen Puhle, *Agrarische Interessenpolitik und Preussischer Konservatismus im Wilhelminischen Reich (1893–1914)*, Hannover, Verlag für Literatur und Zeitgeschehen, 1966, p. 133; and Andrew G. Whiteside, *The Socialism of Fools: Georg Ritter von Schönerer and Austrian Pan-Germanism*, Berkeley, CA, University of California Press, 1975, pp. 84–5.

[22] Theodor W. Adorno, *The Authoritarian Personality*, New York, Harper & Row, 1950. For a good summary of the discussion, see Nevitt Sanford, "The Roots of Prejudice: Emotional Dynamics," in Peter Watson, (ed.), *Psychology and Race*, Harmondsworth, Penguin Education, 1973, pp. 57–75 (including references) or, for a later summary, John Levi Martin, "The Authoritarian Personality, 50 Years Later: What Lessons are there for Political Psychology," *Political Psychology* 22(1), 2001, 1–26.

the precise makeup of the authoritarian personality continues, and efforts to find a way to diagnose and perhaps eventually even treat it are bound to remain controversial. But the existence of a unique authoritarian psychological syndrome is accepted even by many of Adorno's critics.[23] The literature reveals two levels at which this syndrome operates: the level of intellectual choice, ideas, and ideology, on the one hand, and that of the individual's personality, behavior pattern, automatic responses, and associate meaning, on the other hand.[24]

The term *Weltanschauung* seems to fit only the first of these two levels. But toward the turn of the nineteenth century, while a segment of German society showed symptoms that may be considered analogous to the ones typical of an authoritarian personality, it was clearly operating, in society as well as in individuals, both on the intellectual-rational level and on that of implicit values, norms, lifestyle and thought, common ambitions, and emotions. The cluster of ideas, sentiments, and public behavior patterns that characterize this syndrome cannot be subsumed under the title "ideology" as this term is commonly understood. If it did indeed include any systematic philosophy with direct implications for social and political action, this remained only a part of a larger whole.[25] Moreover, a *Weltanschauung* can properly define this phenomenon only when it is understood in the broadest possible sense. Perhaps a better term, one that is more easily associated with basic human action and needs while not excluding philosophy, science, and the arts, is culture, "the total interconnected set of ways of thinking, feeling, and acting." Ideology and *Weltanschauung* are easily subsumed under this concept, which is considered "a great symbolic unit" that is shared and learned by individuals in the process of their socialization and eventually serves to unite them in "a particular and distinct collectivity."[26] Furthermore, "culture" also

---

[23] As an example see John J. Ray, "Is Antisemitism a Cognitive Simplification? Some Observations on Australian Neo-Nazis," *The Jewish Journal of Sociology* 14(2), 1972, 207–13.

[24] Adorno, *The Authoritarian Personality*, 151–288; Sanford, "The Roots of Prejudice"; Richard Christie and Marie Jahoda (eds.), *Studies in the Scope and Method of "the Authoritarian Personality,"* Glencoe, IL, Free Press, 1954.

[25] For the meaning of the term "ideology," see Clifford Geertz, "Ideology as a Cultural System," in David E. Apter (ed.), *Ideology and Discontent*, London, Free Press of Glencoe, 1964, pp. 47–76, especially 47–60. Compare with Carl J. Friedrich and Zbigniew K. Brzezinski, *Totalitarian Dictatorship and Autocracy*, Cambridge, MA, Harvard University Press, 1956, pp. 73–5.

[26] The term "Weltanschauung" is often used rather loosely in historical writing, indeed often too loosely to be of much value. It was given a critical but limiting philosophical interpretation by Wilhelm Dilthey, "Die Typen der Weltanschauung und ihre Ausbildung in den metaphysischen Systemen," in *Gesammelte Schriften*, Berlin, B.G. Teubner, 1931,

includes traditions that consciously and subconsciously affect such a collectivity, habits of mind, a variety of automatic reactions, and a plethora of accepted norms.

We often assume that a national society, in the framework of a particular nation-state, has such a single culture, although recently there are increasing doubts concerning the validity of such cultural cohesion, and the existence of various types of dividing lines, even in societies that appear cohesive, receives growing attention. In Imperial Germany too, several subcultures co-existed, albeit not always in harmony. Sociologist Rainer Maria Lepsius used the term "milieu" to define four such "cultural contexts" in Wilhelmine Germany: the Conservative, the Liberal, the Socialist, and the Catholic.[27] Relying on the class and ideological contours that guided Lepsius's view, one could further argue that in the Germany of the last quarter of the nineteenth century, yet another milieu had surfaced, one that encompassed those who did not feel comfortable in any of the above subcultures. It was the milieu of those who felt most acutely threatened by modernity: the discontented, those hoping for a change in the existing order, those not planning to achieve it in any of the ways acceptable to the rest of society; it was a milieu marked primarily by its members' more or less explicit antisemitism.

While accepting Lepsius's categories, other divisions of German society at the time may also be relevant. After all, no one scheme can do justice to the complexity of a society of its kind. Still, there are some dividing lines that are particularly illuminating and better serve our purposes than others. They may not be useful for all issues at hand, but they are useful for some. Thus, I would suggest, that it is helpful, at least in our context, to split the social, political, and, above all, cultural world of Imperial Germany into two major camps. Accordingly, two subcultures co-existed at the bosom of this society and antisemitism served to draw the dividing line between them. One such subculute was undoubtedly the one that found its spiritual expression in the "German ideology." Marked by a radical

vol. 8. Karl Mannheim provided the best available theoretical treatment in his "On the Interpretation of Weltanschauung," in *Essays on the Sociology of Knowledge*, London, Routledge & Kegan Paul, 1952, pp. 33–88, as well as the best case study: "Conservative Thought," in *Essays on Sociology and Social Psychology*, London, Routledge & Kegan Paul, 1953, pp. 74–164. Admittedly, the word "culture" is equally ambiguous. Here and in what follows I use Geertz's approach in "Ideology as a Cultural System."

[27] Rainer M. Lepsius, "Parteiensystem und Sozialstruktur: Zum Problem der Demokratisierung der deutschen Gesellschaft," in Wilhelm Abel (ed.), *Wirtschaft, Geschichte und Wirtschaftsgeschichte*, Stuttgart, G. Fischer, 1966, pp. 371–93.

anti-modern mentality, it rejected liberalism and capitalism on the one hand, and revolutionary or even moderate socialism on the other. United by a staunch opposition to democracy and a desire to finally establish, or rather re-establish, a single, cohesive national community based on harmony and justice, the members of this subculture were extreme Nationalists who shared a sweeping imperial dream, an enthusiasm for an imminent war, and loyalty to a pre-industrial moral code. The variations on this general pattern were many. Significant were, for instance, the diverging views on Christianity and on the role and position of the *Junker* aristocracy in the *Kaiserreich*.[28] A comparison of the attitudes of men in the Pan-German League, the *Bund der Landwirte*, and the *Deutschnationaler Handlungsgehilfenverband* (National-German Commercial Assistants' Association), for instance, with an in-depth study of the internal divisions within each one of these organizations is bound to bring forth many important differentiations and ongoing shifts of accent.[29] This diversity, however, should not be allowed to obstruct a view of the whole. Despite these differences, there was much in common in the beliefs, ideas, style of life and thought of the members of these associations. They shared a common ethos, a basic pattern of ideals, an unmistakable culture. Finally, that culture was invariably associated with antisemitism.

In 1912, in a book carrying the title *Had I Been the Kaiser*, Heinrich Class, the leader of the Pan-German League, published a complete political program based on the "Germanic" worldview.[30] Class was famous for his antisemitism, but he held firm views on many other matters as well. His book caused something of a sensation and was apparently very widely read. By the beginning of World War I, some 25,000 copies were sold, a handsome figure for this time by all accounts. In the book, Class

---

[28] For the distinction between Christian and anti-Christian antisemitism, see Uriel Tal, *Christians and Jews in Germany: Religion, Politics and Ideology in the Second Reich, 1870–1914*, Ithaca, NY, Cornell University Press, 1975, especially pp. 223–89. On Junker antisemitism, see Pulzer, *The Rise of Political Anti-Semitism*, 108–17, in contrast to Puhle, *Agrarische Interessenpolitik*, 125–40.

[29] Puhle, *Agrarische Interessenpolitik*, 72–140; Iris Hamel, *Völkischer Verband und Nationale Gewerkschaft: Der Deutschnationale Handlungsgehilfen-Verband 1893–1933*, Frankfurt a. M., Europäische Verlagsanstalt, 1967; Mildred S. Wertheimer, *The Pan-German League 1890–1914*, New York, Columbia University Press, 1924; Roger Chickering, *'We Men who feel most German': A Cultural Study of the Pan-German League, 1886–1914*, Boston, G. Allen & Unwin, 1984.

[30] See *"Wenn ich der Kaiser wär" – Politische Wahrheiten und Notwendigkeiten*, Leipzig, Dieterich, 1912. The book was published under the pseudonym Daniel Frymann.

developed a critique of the German government's foreign policy, rejecting the concept of a "saturated Germany" and the values of a "just peace" by which it should resign itself to a supposedly inferior position in the international arena. He demanded expansion to the East and the acquisition of overseas colonies, protesting against the manner in which the superpowers had treated Germany in the various international crises up to this point. He then openly called for a war of national rejuvenation and campaigned for a new type of social and economic legislation designed to stop and reverse the various trends of modernization. Above all, he was concerned with putting an end to "racial intermingling," which posed a grave danger to the true "German soul." Class pleaded for agrarian reforms, constitutional changes, and a new educational program – all to save what could still be saved, in his view. No major issue of the day was left untouched in his text, and the various proposals were strongly tied together not by their irrefutable logic or the force of his didactic fervor, but by the underlying cultural values discernible behind them: blind worship of power equated with manliness and virility; search for uniformity conceived as harmony; authority conceived as leadership; and anti-egalitarianism expressed in racism, misogyny, and hostility to democracy. Hatred of Jews fit only too neatly into this mix. Nevertheless, Class's book may be accurately described as antisemitic only if one chooses to denote that entire mixture of ideas and beliefs expressed by him, that entire cultural complex represented in his book, as "antisemitic." Indeed, both at that time and later, many would apply this label as a "shortcut"; an indication for a much larger phenomenon.

The *Alldeutscher Verband*, headed by Class since 1907, was not originally an openly antisemitic body. The "Germanic syndrome" was all there, but by the early 1890s, antisemitism did not as yet seem unavoidable within it. Significantly, it was always the Berlin chapter of the Pan-Germans that pressed for a more outspoken stand on the "Jewish question."[31] At the heart of the Empire, the association between antisemitism and Pan-Germanism, its militarism and authoritarianism, had apparently become meaningful before it was realized elsewhere in the country. Gradually, however, the *alldeutscher Verband* as a whole adopted an anti-semitic stand, combining its distaste and resentment of Jews with militant anti-Slavism and repeated diatribes against the Poles. In fact, all groups and associations that propagated militant nationalism, imperial expansion, racism, anti-Socialism, militarism, and support for an authoritarian

---

[31] Pulzer, *The Rise of Political Anti-Semitism*, 226–8.

government professed antisemitism, too.[32] The 1892 convention of the *Deutschkonservative Partei*, known as the "Tivoli Convention," marked the course. There was clearly an element of opportunism in the party's conversion to open antisemitism at this stage, adopting a blunt "antisemitic clause" in its new platform. Antisemitism was useful in appealing to elements of the lower middle classes who were still skeptical in their attitude toward the aristocratic conservative party. But by then it was also an integral part of their overall doctrine, increasingly inseparable from their sweeping anti-modernism and their social and economic reform programs. With or without the "antisemitic clause," the Conservatives belonged in that emerging "culture" that combined the old and the new Right. Their initial lack of enthusiasm was soon compensated for by radical antisemitism, which was propagated by their own men in the more openly militant *Bund der Landwirte* and by a variety of other conservative agitators. These seemed to show more initiative than the old leadership and appeared to have a better understanding of the social environment within which they were operating.[33]

The range of this subculture is well reflected in the breadth and quality of the literature produced by its advocates. In 1914, the G. Hedeler publishing house in Leipzig published a small guide to the literature of the "*Deutschbewegung*," as the vociferous and distinctly nationalist stream in Germany was often called.[34] It listed some 800 titles and more than 80 periodicals, encompassing religion and philosophy, biology and the natural sciences, anthropology, history, genealogy, language, art and literature, economics, politics, and law. The greater part of this literature is entirely unknown today, but its scope and intellectual aspirations are truly impressive. Significantly, no special section in the list was concerned exclusively with Jews or with the "Jewish Question," but a look at the list of titles and authors confirms the impression that many of the "highly recommended" items dealt extensively, if indeed rarely in isolation, with that issue. Antisemitism was a permanent aspect of the multifaceted subculture represented here, a naturally fitting element. In an unusually

---

[32] Chickering, "*We Men who feel most German*" and Richard S. Levy, *The Downfall of the Anti-Semitic Political Parties in Imperial Germany*, New Haven, CT, and London, Yale University Press, 1975, choose to underestimate the antisemitic tone in these organizations, as opposed to Pulzer, *The Rise of Political Anti-Semitism*, 228–9, and Jochmann, *Gesellschaftskrise und Judenfeindschaft*, 71–3, 87–94.

[33] Pulzer, *The Rise of Political Anti-Semitism*, 118–26; Puhle, *Agrarische Interessenpolitik*, 111–40.

[34] Rudolph Rüsten (ed.), *Was tut not? Ein Führer durch die gesamte Literatur der Deutschbewegung*, Leipzig, G. Hedeler, 1914.

perceptive passage, Friedrich Lange, a rabid antisemite writing in 1893, asserted that antisemitism had to be "but one element, and not the most important one in an overall broader and higher national worldview and policy."[35] Lange's "broader and higher" ideal was "pure Germanism," upon which he endlessly elaborated in his journal and pamphlets. It included high-pitched nationalism, an elevation of war and conflict to the level of an independent cultural good, an insistence on the need for German territorial expansion, a program for economic reforms to achieve autarchy, and social reforms to preserve the traditional *Mittelstand*. It offered treatments for all of Germany's social ills.[36]

Thus, antisemitism gradually became the hallmark of the right, perhaps even the center-right, in Germany, too, a permanent feature of its worldview and cultural style. In the situation of social and ideological polarization in Germany at the turn of the century, it became a cultural code.[37] Expressing antisemitic sentiments and attitudes – even by some Jews – was proof of belonging to this patently "German" subculture, a sign of rejecting anything perceived as valuable and meaningful by the "other side." On that other side, indeed, opposition to antisemitism has likewise come to mark belonging, belonging to what might be called the "camp of emancipation," supporting democracy, parliamentarism, and an array of economic and cultural goods associated with modernization. Antisemitism was not merely a singular aspect of a worldview typical of a certain cultural camp in Germany; rather, it was an unequivocal indicator of that culture. By the late nineteenth century, it had a unique role in demarcating the borderline between two major positions in the German public sphere. It thus acquired a new role, one that it never had before.

As we have seen, the arsenal of the anti-emancipatory, nationalist culture of Bismarckian Germany had already been forged by the late 1870s. This peculiar combination had been given expression in the works of Marr, Glagau, and Treitschke and was later cemented in the writings of Paul de Lagarde, Eugen Dühring, and a host of lesser publicists. It was by the mid-1890s, that the cluster of ideas, values, and norms that these men represented had been absorbed by part of the social fabric of Germany to become an infrastructure for a distinct subculture. The heated sermons

---

[35] Friedrich Lange, *Reines Deutschtum: Grundzüge einer nationalen Weltanschauung*, Berlin, Duncker, 1905 [1893], 109. The title article quoted here was first published on April 11, 1893.
[36] Ibid., 135–87.
[37] Though here too I rely on Clifford Geertz, he finds the term "code" inappropriate. See Clifford Geertz, "Thick Description: Toward an Interpretive Theory of Culture," in his *The Interpetation of Culture. Selected Essays*, 1993 [1973], pp. 3–30, especially 9.

of the 1870s were replaced with the businesslike tone of the 1890s. The large-scale antisemitism that was earlier considered a novelty, carrying an exciting new gospel, became later a routine part of the familiar public discourse. It is interesting to compare Lagarde's antisemitic pathos with Julius Langbehn's equanimity only twelve years later.[38] Lagarde's antisemitism was intense and fanatical while Langbehn's, though it was equally fundamental, was proclaimed with composure and even some indifference. The worst social and economic crisis of the 1870s and the period of political disorientation during the first decade of the new *Kaiserreich* were over by then. The possible therapeutic function of antisemitism was losing significance. Antisemitism became part and parcel of a familiar combination of cultural elements, a permanent fixture in the aggressively nationalistic and anti-modern discourse of the Second Reich.

The link was made so self-evident that even people of Jewish origin sometimes succumbed to its logic. Maximilian Harden, an energetic and gifted journalist and one of Wilhelmine Germany's sharpest social and political critics, is an interesting case in point. Although Harden occasionally criticized the antisemitic movement, direct and indirect anti-Jewish comments were common in the pages of the *Zukunft* (The Future), a weekly he was editing single-handedly.[39] During the Dreyfus affair, Harden distinguished himself by viciously attacking the Dreyfusards – those who defended the French-Jewish officer accused of spying for Germany and believed in his innocence. Harden's attitude gave rise to two conflicting interpretations. In his book on Jewish self-hatred, Theodor Lessing used Harden as an example to prove his point and saw in him a convincing case of this peculiar Jewish pathology. Others tried to defend Harden against the charge of antisemitism by trying to underline his consistent fight for justice and individual freedoms, clearly incongruent with it.[40] Commentators agree, however, that Harden's position on the Jewish question was primarily an outgrowth of the way in which he conceived the struggle between the forces of light and darkness in his days. The Dreyfus affair was for him, as well as for many others, a symbol of this fight, a historic battle between "traders" and "warriors." He took sides

---

[38] See Paul de Lagarde, *Deutsche Schriften*, Munich, Lehmann, 1937 [1885], pp. 30, 41, 421–22; Julius Langbehn, *Rembrandt als Erzieher*, Leipzig, Hirschfeld, 1922 [1893], pp. 36–7, 242–4. See also Fritz Stern, *The Politics of Cultural Despair*, 61–4, 139–45.

[39] Harry F. Young, *Maximilian Harden, Censor Germaniae: The Critic in Opposition from Bismarck to the Rise of Nazism*, The Hague, M. Nijhoff, 1959, pp. 10–15; Theodor Lessing, *Der jüdische Selbsthass*, Berlin, Jüdischer Verlag, 1930, pp. 167–94.

[40] Lessing, *Der jüdische Selbsthass*, 189, 194–7.

against Dreyfus because, like many, he sensed that what lay in the balance was not the fate of the defendant, but France's future, and that in France, too, the "Jewish Question" had become a symbol of the struggle not only between two political camps, but also and perhaps primarily between two styles of thought, between two cultures.[41] The analogy to the German conditions was all too obvious. The Dreyfusards were the republicans, the democrats, and the modernists. Harden was none of these. He could not support a Jewish officer charged with treason. After all, there was nothing more sacred for him than the country he so lovingly regarded as his own – Germany. It came as no surprise when, during the war years later on, Harden passionately joined the loudest annexationists and established himself, at least for a time, as a zealous Pan-German. His attitude toward Jews was a corollary of his other views. Despite his personal history and its embarrassing and eventually tragic consequences, Harden felt compelled to express hostility toward them. It was in fact the best way he could prove his absolute loyalty and his belonging to the "proper" camp.

Harden well sensed his own dilemma. In an early 1890s interview with Hermann Bahr, he complained of being labeled an antisemite only "because I set myself against the spirit of brokers and middlemen, against the rabble of the stock exchange, against the egotism and laziness of the bourgeoisie." And then, referring to the names of prominent Jewish journalists and to Hermann Ahlwardt, one of the antisemites in the Reichstag, he added:[42]

What should I do, if I am immediately labeled an antisemite [because of this]? What should I do, if Judaism declares it solidarity with the Wolffs, the Leipzigers and the Sommerfelds? What should I do if one cannot set out against the spirit of commerce without being immediately labeled as one of the Ahlwardts?

Indeed, such a separation of issues was no longer possible. By then the lines of cultural conflict in Germany were clearly drawn, and at some juncture one had to accept either the totality of emancipation or the totality of antisemitism. The attitude toward Jews – for or against them, but especially for or against their integration – now came to symbolize the two opposing cultural syndromes of the time. This role was an integral part of contemporary discourse and was taken for granted by most Germans. For many rightwing, nationalist, and patriotic Jews, as well as for a minority of prejudiced individuals in the "emancipatory camp,"

[41] See Chapter 7.
[42] Hermann Bahr, *Der Antisemitismus: Ein internationales Interview*, Berlin: S. Fischer, 1893, pp. 50–1.

this posed a bitter dilemma. It was by then impossible to separate one's attitude toward Jews and Judaism from the rest of one's ideological and cultural "package deal." Not all contemporaries were consciously aware of the signifying function of their attitudes toward Jews, but some saw it clearly. In the same interview series by Hermann Bahr, Theodor Barth, the progressive politician, asserted that Jews were taken as "a symbol of the time," and the aged Theodor Mommsen, still optimistic in his hopes for the inevitable disappearance of antisemitism, interpreted it as hatred not of Jews alone but of *"Bildung,* freedom and humanity."[43] Eduard Bernstein, the revisionist leader of Germany's Social Democracy, warned against the position taken by his colleague Franz Mehring, who, in compliance with his party line, continued to oppose both antisemitism and the so-called philosemitism with the same passion. Bernstein claimed that such a position was no longer relevant, because the battle had long become one of slogans and symbols. Under these circumstances, he argued, it was urgent to take special precautions to avoid any possible identification of Social Democracy with antisemitism.[44] Just as an antisemitic stand in Wilhelmine Germany meant in effect an anti-emancipatory position and a resistance to the various manifestations of "the modern social and political struggle for freedom," so did an opposition to antisemitism signify a commitment to emancipation, not of Jews alone but of civil society at large.[45] Nationalist, state-supporting patriots could hardly avoid signifying their resolute stance through professed antisemitism while their opponents were inevitably caught in the same snag. It was no longer possible to remain neutral on the Jewish Question.

[43] Ibid., 13, 28–9.
[44] *Die Neue Zeit* XI(2), 1893–1894.
[45] On the concept of emancipation see Jacob Katz, "The Term 'Jewish Emancipation': Its Origins and Historical Impact," in *Emancipation and Assimilation: Studies in Modern Jewish History,* Farnborough, MA, Gregg International, 1964, pp. 1–16, and Reinhard Koselleck, "Emanzipation," in Otto Brunner, Werner Conze, and Reinhart Koselleck (eds.), *Geschichtliche Grundbegriffe: Historisches Lexikon zur politisch-sozialen Sprache in Deutschland,* Stuttgart, E. Klett, 1972–1997, vol. 2, pp. 153–97, especially 153–70.

6

Norms and Codes

Two Case Studies

a. The Case of Social Democracy

The meaning and implications of antisemitism as a cultural code in Imperial Germany may be illustrated in various ways. Here I have chosen to address two issues: The first is the case of the Social Democrats, who in the past never hesitated to voice their anti-Jewish sentiments and who by the late nineteenth century became increasingly more cautious in this respect. The second is the case of anti-feminism that was another widely shared attitude in Wilhelmine Germany, but one that was rather a general norm and could therefore never fulfil the complex role of a cultural code.

In the older literature on antisemitism, the position of European Socialism regarding the so-called Jewish Question was commonly examined by collecting the relevant quotes from the writings of various Socialist theorists or from the sayings of the Labor movement's prominent leaders. This method easily produced a series of debasing statements, both about Judaism as a religion and about Jews as individuals or as a group. Yet, such a collection of statements produce only a partial view of the matter. Clearly, Socialism was seriously infected with Jew-hatred from the outset. The harshest indictment was and remained Karl Marx's early essay, *Zur Judenfrage* (On the Jewish Question), written in 1843 and later often exposed as "the source of the antisemitic tradition in modern Socialism."[1] The essay reeks of spite to Judaism and the Jews. Nevertheless, it too must be read with the conceptual and political contexts of the time in mind, and

---

[1] See, for instance, Edmund Silberner, *Sozialisten zur Judenfrage*, Berlin, Colloquium Verlag, 1962, pp. 142, 119–27.

its relative influence, or, in this case, especially the lack of it, should not be forgotten. Marx's *Zur Judenfrage* was written in response to another similarly titled essay that was written by the left-Hegelian publicist Bruno Bauer.[2] In fact, Marx's predominant concern was to analyze the relationship between the state and civil society under the conditions of capitalism. In this context, "Judaism" represented for him the single most articulate manifestation of the profit-seeking spirit, the flagship of a new bourgeois society, and the symbol of its moral degeneration. At the same time, the degree to which the Jews (as individual members of a given society and not as a group, of course) enjoyed political and civil rights was considered by him the most telling indicator of a country's level of modernity. He unequivocally demanded the abolition of all discrimination against them, seeing in their full civil and political emancipation a major, logical consequence of the very premises of bourgeois society. For Marx, however, a full and final emancipation of Jews and Christians alike could in any case only be achieved by the complete overthrow of the present social order.

Nevertheless, for noncontemporary readers, and barring a careful examination of the author's assumptions, Marx's vitriolic language in this essay could have certainly been used to justify or strengthen anti-Jewish sentiments and in any case, together with various other manifestations of antisemitism in the ranks of the German labor movement, this essay also throws doubt on the argument that regards socialism as an a priori enemy of antisemitism and the labor movement as inherently immune to its poison. Peter Pulzer, in one of the first comprehensive studies of modern antisemitism in Germany and Austria, stressed that German Social Democracy was "clearly related to nineteenth century Liberalism" and therefore inspired by "a revulsion against tyranny and poverty, by optimism and a belief in progress, by the assumption that if a formula could be found to explain how society worked, spread by education and applied, the world's evils could be abolished." Social Democracy was diametrically opposed to antisemitism, which was concerned "not with more emancipation but with less," and which "set forth the primacy of the national and the integral over the universal."[3] Sociological research also has often

[2] Karl Marx and Friedrich Engels, *Marx, Engels: Werke*, Berlin, Dietz Verlag, 1959, vol. 2, pp. 91–5, 99–104, 112–25. From among the many commentaries, see especially Shlomo Avineri, "Marx and Jewish Emancipation," *Journal of the History of Ideas* 25, 1965, 445–50.
[3] Peter G. J. Pulzer, *The Rise of Political Anti-Semitism in Germany and Austria*, New York, Wiley, 1964, p. 259.

asserted the thesis of the proletariat's inborn immunity to prejudice. But most well known in this context are surely the comments by Jean Paul Sartre. In his *Anti-Semite and Jew*, he writes:

We find hardly any antisemites among the workers . . . Shaped by the daily influence of the materials he works with, the workman sees society as the product of real forces acting in accordance with rigorous laws. His dialectical "materialism" signifies that he envisages the social world in the same way as the material world.[4]

Even if we accept this argument in principle, it does not explain the countless instances of antisemitism making inroads into the worker movement's rank and file and leaving its mark on its leadership.

In fact, German Social Democracy in particular, like socialism in general, all too often fell victim to this affliction. The slips of tongue and pen by many prominent Socialists have frequently been recalled, and in addition, a careful examination of the entire corpus of the party's publications – not only its daily papers but also its popular magazines and the relevant literature it inspired – reveals many of the negative stereotypes generally attached to Jews in Imperial Germany. In caricatures, sketches, stories, and popular songs, all printed under party sponsorship, the Jew's ridiculous and threatening image is ubiquitous.[5] The everyday antisemitism that was so characteristic of German society at the time, did not skip the workers' ranks, and even the resolute Social Democratic leadership could not, or was not willing to, completely uproot it. And yet, from the early 1890s, the party adopted an unambiguous public *anti*-antisemitic stance.

This was an important transition period in the history of Social Democracy. The year 1890 brought about the end of the legal oppression of the Socialist movement under the Bismarckian anti-Socialist legislation. Concurrently, the early nineties saw the completion and intensification of important changes in both the ideology of the German labor movement and in the fixing of its sociological makeup. With the acceptance of the Erfurt Program in 1891, Marxism was officially endorsed as a party

---

[4] Jean-Paul Sartre, *Anti-Semite and Jew*, New York, Schocken Books, 1973, pp. 35–6 (originally in French, 1946).

[5] For a detailed discussion see Rosemarie Leuschen-Seppel, *Sozialdemokratie und Antisemitismus im Kaiserreich*, Bonn, Verlag Neue Gesellschaft, 1978. It is interesting that, in the large historiography dealing with socialism and the working class in Imperial Germany, relations to Jews or antisemitism are treated at best in passing. See, for example, the voluminous synthesis (part of the series *Geschichte der Arbeiter und der Arbeiterbewegung in Deutschland seit dem Ende des 18. Jahrhunderts*), Gerhard A. Ritter and Klaus Tenfelde, *Arbeiter im Deutschen Kaiserreich, 1871 bis 1914*, Bonn, Dietz Verlag, 1992.

doctrine, and while this by no means brought an end to the ideological controversies within the party, it did signify a transformation in their content and rhetorical nature. Simultaneously, Social Democracy increasingly became a fully organized proletarian movement. German industry kept growing rapidly even during the years of the so-called Great Depression (1873–1896), and its growth rate took off afresh under the improved economic conditions afterwards. The Socialist Trade Unions, which were at last free from police supervision and government repression, were now growing by leaps and bounds. The characteristic feature of this growth was the recruitment of unskilled laborers, who found employment in heavy industry and the newly built giant plants. Their joining the workers' organized struggle was now likewise reflected in the social composition of the Social Democratic Party membership and its voting public. By the mid-1890s, the SPD became a party of industrial workers, drawing its strength from the overwhelmingly Protestant industrial regions and big towns. It was essentially a class party, a Marxist proletarian movement.

Concurrently with the changes in the nature and composition of German Social Democracy, the 1890s also signify an important turning point in the development of political antisemitism. It was a kind of scissor effect that resulted in a widening gap between the two movements. Up until about 1880, socialism and antisemitism had much in common. Above all, they shared an anti-liberal worldview and were both eager to demonstrate their rejection of the capitalist system. In addition, both had then recruited considerable support from a similar social element, the lower *Mittelstand*. This was particularly true for the Lassallean branch of German socialism. Ferdinand Lassalle had distanced himself early in life from Judaism, and although he must have occasionally experienced the awkwardness of his position as a Jew in a predominantly gentile society, he did not shy away from injecting a fair amount of anti-Jewish verbiage into his own agitation.[6] From the very beginning of his political and organizational activities, Lassalle had conceived of the Liberals as his main enemies and had made it quite clear that he preferred an alliance with the leading forces of the authoritarian Prussian state to any dealings with the Liberals of his day. Anti-Liberalism had been the backbone of both Lassalle's socialist theory and practice, and antisemitic rhetoric seemed to serve well his purpose in degrading and abusing his liberal opponents. Jews, and not only Judaism in the abstract, were for him a symbol of liberal

---

[6] On Lassalle in this context, see Shlomo Na'aman, *Ferdinand Lassalle: Deutscher und Jude*, Hannover, Buchdruckwerkstätten, 1968.

hypocrisy and their greedy capitalist schemes of exploitation. Lassalle had readily identified the bourgeoisie in general with the Jewish bourgeoisie, and anything "rotten" in the modern world – with Judaism.

But in the early 1860s, at the peak of Lassalle's activity, he was clearly not alone in making use of this convenient equation. The equation of Judaism and Liberalism was by that time prevalent in public discourse. Above all, it was an indispensable element in the writings of a growing number of Conservatives, who had developed by then a social theory that was often referred to as "state-Socialism." These politically reactionary thinkers had belatedly begun to take notice of the *Soziale Frage* in Germany and soon concluded that it was urgent for the affluent in Germany to concern themselves with the problems of the so-called Fourth Estate, that is, the day laborers, the poor, and the needy. It was necessary to take concrete steps for the improvement of their lot.[7] All of these thinkers had been making use of antisemitism in a more or less overt and articulated form. Although Lassalle's political leaning was quite different from theirs, he had close personal contacts with most of them. His meetings with Bismarck, who also toyed with social-conservative plans, as a counterweight to his political alliance with the Liberals at the time, are common knowledge. Less known are his correspondence with Social Conservative intellectuals, such as Karl Rodbertus, or his public exchange of views with the socially active Catholic Bishop Emanuel von Ketteler or the conservative proponent of the new Cooperative Movement, Victor Aimé Huber. Lassalle shared with all of them a virulent anti-liberalism tinged with antisemitism, and some of his followers took over this ideological mix from him. It was, in any case, quite apparent in the agitation, as well as in the literary work, of Johann Baptist von Schweitzer and in the journalism of Wilhelm Hasselmann in the early part of the 1870s, both of whom were Lassalle's direct followers.[8]

This combination of "state-Socialism," anti-liberalism, and an anti-Jewish stance had been Lassalle's legacy to the German Social Democratic Party. The stock-exchange collapse of 1873 and the ensuing economic crisis helped to strengthen those in favor of state intervention in the economy, and as the writings of Rodbertus, Wagener, and other Social-Conservatives became increasingly popular, a considerable group of Social

---

[7] See Shulamit Volkov, *The Rise of Popular Antimodernism in Germany: The Urban Master Artisans, 1873–1896*, Princeton, NJ, Princeton University Press, 1978, pp. 203–11.

[8] See Paul W. Massing, *Rehearsal for Destruction: A Study of Political anti-Semitism in Imperial Germany*, New York, Harper, 1949, pp. 198–9.

Democratic leaders attempted to ride the same wave. Suffering from the
lack of a unified and coherent economic theory, the Lassalleans tended
to borrow from the arsenal of state-socialism, while the "Eisenachers" –
labor leaders originally based in the Saxonian town of Eisenach and traditionally seen as the movement's mainstream – were looking everywhere
for solutions to the new difficulties. Possessing only a very rudimentary
knowledge of Marx and Engels's work, they too were temporarily drawn
toward the myriad of reformist conservative programs that were accessi-
ble at the time. For instance, Eduard Bernstein, who later became the
champion of the revisionist faction of the German Labor Movement,
was originally deeply influenced by the writing of Eugen Dürhing, the
energetic and relentless antisemite.[9] The generally balanced prose of the
official Social Democratic organ, the *Sozialdemokrat*, of which Bernstein
was the editor-in-exile during the 1880s, was frequently tainted with anti-
Jewish statements.[10] Even the *Freiheit*, the periodical of the anarchistic
branch of Social Democracy, got carried away in this rhetoric, under the
influence of both the Lassalleans and the anarchists' antisemitic tradition
since Proudhon.

The sources of antisemitism in the ranks of the Socialist movement were
thus diverse. Furthermore, Social Democratic voters at the time were easily swayed in this direction. The party's appeal was by then not only, not
even primarily, directed at working-class voters. Since a true industrial
proletariat hardly existed in the Germany of the 1860s, Social Democracy tended to turn to laboring men in small industry and in the traditional handicraft trades. The dividing line between self-employed and
hired hands, or even between small employers and skilled employees, was
still very fluid, and mutual influences among them were inevitable. Thus
the socialists, like the conservative antisemitic agitators who were already
active at that time, appealed to workers and employers alike, and the original nucleus of both their supporters came from a mixed stratum, including
self-employed and independent artisans and tradesmen. The combination
of anti-liberalism and vocal antisemitism was highly popular in this target
audience. It was, for instance, to these men that Adolf Stöcker, the conservative court-priest in Berlin of the late 1870s, was addressing his passionate orations. Stöcker's *Christlich-Soziale Arbeiterpartei* (Christian-Social
Workers' Party) attempted to compete with the Socialists on the innocent

---

[9] Vernon L. Lidtke, *The Outlawed Party: Social Democracy in Germany 1878–1890*,
   Princeton, NJ, Princeton University Press, 1966, chap. 6.
[10] See, e.g., *Der Sozialdemokrat*, February 16 and October 26, 1882.

souls of the workers, bringing them back to Crown and Church. His success was in fact limited at first, but in the 1881 election, alarming signs could easily be observed. In the 2nd Berlin voting district, where Stöcker was himself campaigning for a Reichstag seat, the Social Democratic vote dropped from 26.3 percent in 1878 to 9.5 percent in 1881. This was not a typical working-class district, so it may not have been indicative of a desertion of Social Democracy by the Proletariat. It did, however, indicate that its former supporters were now able to express their discontent and anxieties by taking their vote elsewhere. The Socialist vote in more typical working-class areas of Berlin also dropped in the 1881 election. In the 4th district, where August Bebel, perhaps the most outstanding Social Democratic leader at the time, was the candidate for a Reichstag seat, the Socialist vote dropped from almost 50 to 32 percent, and in the 6th district, a typical working-class area, it dropped from 41 to 27 percent.[11] This was clearly a result of a number of factors. Nevertheless, in a letter to Engels in November 1881, activist Louis Viereck wrote that he was convinced that the majority of the 47,000 antisemitic votes that Stöcker had won in Berlin had been recruited from among previous supporters of Social Democracy.[12] From Vienna, too, Karl Kautsky, a senior Social-Democrat, likewise reported to Engels on the serious danger that the Viennese oppositional antisemitic movement had posed for the budding workers' movement there. He was clearly aware that the antisemites had managed to gain support not only of potential Socialists, but also of some actual former Socialists.[13] They were clearly posing a threat to the movement. In Berlin, Bernstein was later forced to admit that there had been many who, "without really wanting to do the Jews any harm, regarded the antisemitic slogans as an inevitable addition to the struggle, since in their eyes the Jews were after all the representatives of capitalism, an outgrowth of the trade system."[14]

The Socialists' later resolute anti-antisemitic stance is thus far from self-evident. Still, even as early as 1881, the SPD refused to cooperate with antisemitic candidates in run-off elections, and in the 1884 Berlin election campaign, when the left-liberal candidate Rudolf Virchow, a highly respected Berliner, ran against Stöcker, all Social Democratic leaders in town made it their business to support him against the antisemitic pastor.

---

[11] The numbers are provided by Lidtke, *The Outlawed Party*, 163.
[12] Ibid., 163–4.
[13] See Pulzer, *The Rise of Political Anti-Semitism*, 265.
[14] Eduard Bernstein, *Die Geschichte der Berliner Arbeiterbewegung*, Berlin, Vorwärts, 1907, vol. 2, pp. 76–7.

With one or two exceptions, this remained the official policy that was followed by Social Democrats from the mid-1880s to the end of the Wilhelmine era.[15] By that time, Marxism had become increasingly influential among prominent Socialists in Germany, providing them with a powerful alternative to state socialism and increasingly making antisemitism redundant and irrelevant for them. Simultaneously, with the expansion of the urban proletariat in Germany, the party no longer had to rely so heavily on *Mittelstand* voters and could afford to distance itself from antisemitism without sustaining a significant loss at the polls. It was this combination of ideological and social factors that dictated the explicitly anti-antisemitic stance of the socialist movement from the 1890s onward.

In addition, socialists too were now required to formulate their position on antisemitism more explicitly, as the issue became increasingly more prominent in Germany's public sphere. Scorn and disregard were no longer sufficient. In May 1890, Friedrich Engels set the tone in an open letter to the Viennese *Arbeiterzeitung*. Writing from London, Engels was not inhibited by any practical, party-political considerations that must have burdened the Social Democratic leadership in Germany.[16] Indeed, Bernstein, Kautsky, and Bebel were never able to match Engels's outspoken and decisive stand on the Jewish Question. They did, however, participate, each in his own way, in the workers movement's intellectual and propaganda project of formulating a proper response to the antisemitic challenge, corresponding to their inner conviction and serving their practical needs.

In their analysis, the Socialists first wished to show that the special function of Jews in capitalism, a function that made them a prototype of the exploitative factor of that system, was merely the result of an age-old discrimination and not a proof of their corrupt nature. Second, their analysis sought to expose the social basis of antisemitism in Germany, warning against its unique appeal not only among the "decaying *Mittelstand*" but also among the peasantry, parts of the Junker aristocracy, and the unsuccessful elements of the educated elite. The antisemitism of these groups was understandable, they claimed, but mistaken, a clear case of false class-consciousness. They believed that, in due course, at least some of these social groups would see the light, abandon antisemitism, and transfer their allegiance to Social Democracy.

---

[15] Ibid., 56–76; Massing, *Rehearsal for Destruction*, 173–4; Richard S. Levy, *The Downfall of the Anti-Semitic Political Parties in Imperial Germany*, New Haven, CT, and London, Yale University Press, 1975, p. 174.

[16] Marx and Engels, *Werke*, Vol. 22, 49–51.

Still, the practical implications of this analysis remained curiously ambiguous. While the party leadership was indeed forced to distance itself from antisemitism, it could continue to underestimate its real power and regard it as a transient phenomenon. Thus it did not seem too unreasonable or too dangerous to continue to attack the Jews, despite the opposition to organized antisemitism. This was, for instance, the position taken by Franz Mehring, a belated Marxist and a long-time anti-Liberal campaigner. In a series of articles on the subject in *Die Zeit*, the central periodical of German Socialist theory, he insisted on the importance of maintaining the proper balance between attacking antisemitism on the one hand and rejecting philosemitism, on the other. The latter, in his view, was nothing but a manifestation of progressive liberalism. He thus kept condemning the hypocrisy of the left-liberals, who saw themselves as the protectors of the Jews, while in fact, Mehring argued, all they ever wanted to defend was capitalism.[17] In a comprehensive study of the history of German Social Democracy, published in the mid-1890s, Mehring still asserted that "compared to the likes of Eugen Richer," a leading Liberal parliamentarian, "Stöcker may be considered a model of truth-loving."[18] And other leading Social Democrats apparently shared his views. By 1893, when the antisemitic parties grew stronger and their danger became more apparent, Eduard Bernstein had joined the controversy, and although he had never tried to conceal or deny his Jewish origin, he too was careful to refrain from defending "Jewish Capitalism," and the "repulsive qualities" usually associated with the Jews.[19]

In the early 1890s, then, the socialist leadership could still afford a measure of ambiguity in its pronouncements on the Jewish Question. In fact, even the resolution brought forth by Bebel and accepted by the 1893 party congress in Cologne reads as a strangely watered-down and vague document.[20] At Bebel's initiative, the congress agreed that, given the social basis of antisemitism, the fight against it was at this point simply irrelevant. It is but a mere by-product of bourgeois society, which is doomed anyway, the resolution read. It then ended with an expression of hope that the

---

[17] *Neue Zeit*, IX, 2, 1890–91; X, 2, 1891–1892.
[18] Franz Mehring, *Geschichte der deutschen Sozialdemokratie*, Berlin, Dietz Verlag, 1960 (first complete edition 1903/4), p. 490.
[19] *Neue Zeit* XI, 2, 1893–1894.
[20] *Protokoll über die Verhandlungen des Parteitages der Sozialdemokratischen Partei Deutschlands abgehalten zu Köln am Rhein*, Berlin, Sozialdemokratische Partei Deutschlands, 1893, pp. 223–4. The protocol contains the full version of Bebel's speech, which was later distributed as a separate pamphlet in a slightly amended version under the title "Sozialdemokratie und Antisemitismus," Berlin, 1906.

antisemites would eventually join the socialist struggle against capitalism and for the establishment of a new socialist society. It contained no
attempt to defend the Jews and said nothing about the need to stop equat-
ing them with the hated capitalist system. This caution surely expressed
the socialist movement's difficulty to detach itself from its former supporters. Despite the rapid changes in Germany's economic structure and
its development into a successful industrial country, the SPD of the early
1890s was still making efforts to gain electoral support from peasants
in Germany's rural regions, especially in the south, and to recruit craftsmen in urban small industry.[21] As late as 1906, a note of admiration and
envy could still be detected in Philip Scheidemann's description of the
antisemites' success in accessing the Hessian countryside during the early
1890s, where he had then lived, working as an organizer on behalf of the
SPD.[22] The antisemitic propagandists, he recalled, knew how to make
politics appealing even to the smallest peasant in the remotest area, to
men who previously could not be bothered about political issues of any
kind. Scheidemann applauded the democratic impulse manifested in the
activity of Otto Böckel, the leading antisemite agitator in Hesse, his stand
against military and naval budgets proposed by the government, and his
independent positions vis-à-vis the reactionary conservatives vying for the
same voting public.

Thus it was only when the SPD had given up on its efforts to win *Mittelstand* support that it could finally formulate its distinctly anti-antisemitic
stance. But from then on, Social Democracy has been clearly free of any
deviations in this respect, especially in the public sphere. Any affinity with
the champions of that "Socialism of the fools," as antisemitism came to
be known among the socialists, was now considered by party leaders to
be a betrayal not only of their values but also, and primarily, of their
class. Sporadic expressions tinged with antisemitism could still be found
in the socialist leadership's private correspondence, but these were usually
confidential, sometimes written in a brutal language that was clearly no
longer legitimate in the open.

Culturally, too, Social Democracy found it difficult to overcome the
antisemitism of many of its followers. The party press, for instance, was
not absolutely free of stereotypical caricatures and could not shake off
the identification of the Jew with the ruthless, exploiting capitalist that

---

[21] Hans-Georg Lehmann, *Die Agrarfrage in der Theorie und Praxis der deutschen und
internationalen Sozialdemokratie*, Tübingen, J.C.B. Mohr, 1970, pp. 62ff.
[22] *Neue Zeit* XXIV, 2, 1905–1906.

was so prevalent in the conceptual world of the movement's early days. The socialists' total negation of any attempt to define a national identity for the Jews, mainly within the borders of the Austro-Hungarian Empire, was also tainted with antisemitism.[23] Antipathy toward Jews was so deeply ingrained in German society, including its working class, that overcoming it was nearly impossible, even through a deliberate effort. Yet in a society contaminated by antisemitism across the board, even a tentative, occasionally faltering anti-antisemitic stance could become a signifying cultural code, the hallmark of distinctly oppositional groups and individuals: socialists, radical and staunch liberals, as well as a motley assortment of ideological "outsiders." It was now neither politically nor culturally correct to express antisemitism in the leftwing camp. Such sentiments no longer belonged in its legitimate arsenal of beliefs. They were too clearly associated now with the other, opposing subculture, the constant target of Socialist critique.

b. Antisemitism and Anti-Feminism

The singular status of antisemitism in Wilhelmine culture may be better understood when compared to the status of anti-feminism at about the same time. In 1781, the first and most seminal book on the position of Jews within the Prussian monarchy, written by Christian Wilhelm Dohm, a "secret" archivist – as his title read – and a foreign affairs adviser in the Prussian state department, was published in Berlin.[24] It was entitled *On the Civil Improvement of the Jews* and immediately became the focus of a lively public debate. A dozen years later, in 1793, another "secret" public servant, later revealed to be Theodor Gottlieb von Hippel, a "war advisor," regional police commissioner, and mayor of the city of Königsberg in East Prussia, published a book under a similar title, *On the Civil Improvement of the Women*. In contrast to the commotion raised by Dohm's book, von Hippel's arguments made almost no mark at the time, and the book's influence was limited to the author's close circle of friends.[25] Even

[23] For a full analzsis of this issue see Shlomo Na'aman, *Marxismus und Zionismus*, Gerlingen, Bleicher Verlag, 1997, pp. 99–154.

[24] The complete edition, including responses to various critiques, entitled *Über die bürgerliche Verbesserung des Juden*, was published in Berlin/Stetin 1783. For a modern biography of Dohm, see Ilsegret Dambacher, *Christian Wilhelm von Dohm*, Frankfurt a. M., Lang, 1974.

[25] On von Hippel's life and work, see *Biographie des königlichen Preuß. Geheimkriegsraths zu Königsberg: Theodor Gottlieb von Hippel, zum Teil von ihm selbst verfasst,*

100 years later, when an active and militant women's movement was already operating in Germany, the book remained pratically unknown. Yet, despite the radical differences in the reception of the two books, they offer an interesting perspective into a pivotal connection between what was later termed "the emancipation of the Jews" and the processes of "the emancipation of women."

This connection was by no means limited to late-eighteenth-century Prussia. Von Hippel's book, written in the faraway eastern part of the continent, was published almost simultaneously with Mary Wollstonecraft's book, *Vindication of the Rights of Women*, which appeared in London in 1792. A further reminder of the apparently inadvertent application of the identical terms in the discussion of the status of Jews on one hand and the rights of women on the other, along with the international contexts of the debate, may be found in Moses Mendelssohn's almost contemporary translation of a 1656 book by Menasseh Ben Israel, entitled *Vindication of the Jews*. The link and its political significance were visible in the early 1790s in France, too. The National Assembly had initially been swarmed with petitions and pamphlets urging, if not the full equality of women, at least their right to education and improvement of their legal status. In 1790 an essay by Condorcet concerning the possibility of granting women full civil rights, aroused considerable public attention.[26] At the time, the Assembly was in the midst of deliberating the status of the Jews in France, and in the fall of 1791, indeed, they were granted full citizenship by the revolutionary republic. In contrast, achievements on the women's front were rather meager. No substantial progress in this respect was made anywhere in Europe during the revolutionary era.[27] Practical achievements were not reached until some hundred years later. Nevertheless, the affinity with the Jewish case, the theoretical analogy,

Gottha, 1801 (new printing, Hildesheim, Gerstenberg, 1977). See Juliane Jacobi, "Der Polizeidirektor als feministischer Jakobiner T. G. von Hippel und seine Schrift 'Über die bürgerliche Verbesserung der Weiber', in Viktoria Schmidt-Linsenhoff (ed.), *Sklavin oder Bürgerin? Französiche Revolution und Neue Weiblichkeit 1760–1830*, Frankfurt a. M., Historisches Museum Frankfurt, 1989, pp. 357–72, and her Introduction to the new edition of von Hippel's book, *Über die bürgerliche Verbesserung der Weiber*, Vaduz/Lichtenstein, Topos-Verlag, 1981, pp. ix–xli.

[26] "Essai sur l'admission des femmes au droits de cité," 23 Juillet 1790. Originally published in *Journal de la Société de 1789*, No. 5.

[27] There is a considerable body of literature on the subject. See Jane Abray, "Feminism and the French Revolution," *American Historical Review* 80(1), 1975, 43–62; Joan B. Landes, *Women and the Public Sphere in the Age of the French Revolution*, Ithaca, NY, Cornell University Press, 1988. For a useful summary see Gisela Bock, *Women in European History*, Oxford, Blackwell Publishers, 2002, chap. 2, pp. 82–126.

and the principal similarities were and remained striking. The situation of social groups demanding equality, women and Jews, indeed, but also the peasantry and the poor, were often discussed in similar terms and raised similar questions.

Yet this similarity has often escaped the scrutiny of modern historiography. Although von Hippel's and Dohm's works were closely related in many respects, they were seldom treated together by historians.[28] Now, von Hippel was undoubtedly familiar with Dohm's treatise as he set out to compose his own. But, more importantly, it is obvious that both were nourished by the same intellectual milieu that was typical of the Prussian top bureaucrats and both addressed the basic ideas of the European Enlightenment regarding human equality. Interestingly, both also accepted as given the inferiority and inadequacy of the group in question, attributed this inferiority to its history, and believed in the ability of its members to adapt to the needs of the modernizing state with the help of a balanced and progressive education. The principal arguments in these parallel discourses are strikingly similar. Their weaknesses too are typical of the world in which they were conceived.

Just as Dohm's text clearly reveals his ingrained anti-Jewish prejudice, so does von Hippel's book disclose the author's biased attitude toward women.[29] In an earlier work, *On Marriage*, published in 1775, in which he sharply criticized the status of women in contemporary society, Hippel's fundamental ambivalence was equally apparent. Von Hippel not only set exceedingly strict moral standards for women but also repeatedly stressed their inability to uphold them. He argued that women were incapable of acquiring education in "abstract fields" or of creating any work of substance on their own. He may have changed his mind later, perhaps under the influence of the French Revolution, but even then he

---

[28] Some exceptions are Julius Carlebach, "The Forgotten Connection: Women and Jews in the Conflict between Enlightenment and Romanticism," *Leo Baeck Institue Yearbook* XXIV, 1979, 107–38; Robert Liberles, "The Historical Context of Dohm's Treatise on the Jews," in *Das deutsche Judentum und der Liberalismus – German Jewry and Liberalism*, Königswinter, Comodock-Verlagsabteilung Sankt Augustin, 1986, 44–69; Ute Frevert, "Die Innenwelt der Außenwelt: Modernitätserfahrungen von Frauen zwischen Gleichheit und Differenz," in Shulamit Volkov (ed.), *Deutsche Juden und die Moderne*, Munich, R. Oldenbourg, 1994, pp. 75–94. Compare also Ute Planert, "Reaktionäre Modernisten? Zum Verhältnis von Antisemitismus und Antifeminismus in der völkischen Bewegung," in *Jahrbuch für Antisemitismusforschung 2000*, pp. 31–51.

[29] See the Introduction to the 1981 printing of von Hippel's book, *Über die bürgerliche Verbesserung der Weiber*, pp. xlii–xliii.

remained cautious and avoided any topic that proved to be too embarrassing or radical. Unlike the dry and businesslike Dohm, von Hippel proved to be quite an able, slightly chatty, satirist. This, in addition to the issue at hand, could explain why Dohm's more serious and more practically oriented work opened almost 100 years of intensive discussion on the position of Jews in Germany, while Hippel's finally remained no more than a a literary episode.

It was only in the late 1820s, following the first wave of post-revolutionary reaction across Europe, that public debate on the legal and political status of groups still deprived of what was considered their "natural rights" was revived. A new term, *emancipation*, was then coined and quickly applied to diverse causes: the status of Catholics in England, the slavery issue, and gradually and ever more frequently to the Jewish Question, too.[30] In fact, within a few years, public attention in Germany was turned to the question of the emancipation of the bourgeois society at large, focusing on its main constituents rather than on its marginal groups. The original sense of the term "emancipation" in the Roman codex denoted a process of gradual "maturing" along with the symbolic legal act, indicating a separation from paternal authority. This sense was now transferred to a broader, more complex context. The Enlightenment as a whole, let us not forget, had already been defined as the process by which man was "leaving his self-caused immaturity" (Kant), and somewhat later the main objective of the time, wrote Heinrich Heine in 1828, was emancipation, "not only of the Irish, the Greeks, the Jews of Frankfurt, the blacks of the West Indies, etc., but the emancipation of the whole world, and of Europe in particular," that Europe that was finally setting itself free of its age-old iron shackles.[31]

Europe – perhaps, but certainly not the women of Europe. While the debate about the status of the oppressed – Catholics, slaves or serfs, peasants, workers, and even Jews – intensely and almost incessantly engaged public opinion in Europe in general and in Germany in particular during

---

[30] In the context of women's status, this term was in use earlier, but not as the preferred term. Compare Reinhart Koselleck, "Emanzipation," in Otto Brunner, Werner Conze, and Reinhart Koselleck (eds.), *Geschichtliche Grundbegriffe: Historisches Lexikon zur politisch-sozialen Sprache in Deutschland*, Stuttgart, E. Klett, 1972–1997, vol. 2, pp. 153–97, especially 185–6.

[31] Kant's phrase is taken from the first sentence of his "What is Enlightenment?" (1784), in Carl J. Friedrich (ed.), *The Philosophy of Kant. Immanuel Kant's Moral and Political Writings*, New York, Modern Library, 1949, p. 132 (editor's translation). The quote from Heinrich Heine is from his "Reisebilder," in *Sämtliche Werke*, Leipzig and Vienna, Bibliographisches Institut, 1887–1890, vol. 3, p. 275 (my translation).

much of the first two-thirds of the nineteenth century, the discussion of women's status was hardly on the agenda, certainly not until 1848.[32] The spark ignited during the French Revolution was quenched for the time being. During these early years, the debate about women's rights took place only in literary circles, if at all. Romantics of all shades were often eager to sketch the contours of women's uniqueness while others wished to use their "findings" to delineate a woman's separate sphere, uniquely feminine, and ultimately justify her exclusion from public life. Even during the revolutionary months of 1848, the struggle for women's rights never translated into a substantial social or political force. During the "Spring of Nations," bourgeois society, born under the belated sign of the Enlightenment, had to confront its own counter-universalistic, excluding tendencies. It tended to define itself at this point more aggressively, mainly in ethnic terms, searching for ways to form a robust and integrative national society, overriding its fundamental class hierarchy. The Jewish Question seemed symptomatic in this context, but the Women's Question was usually marginalized. Indeed, it was only after the debate about the legal emancipation of the Jews in Germany had been settled, following the passage of the bill governing their status within the liberal framework of the North-German Confederation and later within the Bismarckian Reich and its various states, that the women's movement finally emerged. After modest beginnings, its cause won real momentum toward the end of the nineteenth century. But by then Jews were already fighting another battle. Their legal emancipation had long been completed. To a large extent, at least the men among them now felt that it had fulfilled its promise and enabled them to be successfully integrated in the non-Jewish world. As far as they were concerned, there was only one battle left to fight – the battle against antisemitism, that "new," post-emancipatory kind of Jew-hating and its diverse manifestations.

Even in this shifting context, despite the years in which the ways of Jews and women so markedly parted in their respective struggles, certain links between them could still be noticed. One hundred years of deliberations, which were at times tumultuous in every respect, fundamentally changed the precise nature of these links, but by no means did they void them.

---

[32] For a brief description of the status of women in the early decades of bourgeois society, see George L. Mosse, *Nationalism and sexuality: Respectability and Abnormal Sexuality in Modern Europe*, New York, H. Fertig, 1985, chap. 5, and now more fully, in Bock, *Women in European History*, chaps. 3 and 4, pp. 82–173. Compare also, Ute Frevert, *Women in German History: From Bourgeois Emancipation to Sexual Liberation*, Oxford, Berg, 1989 (originally in German, 1986), chap. 2.

At the turn of the nineteenth century, as at the turn of the eighteenth century before, there was a renewed interaction between the struggle over women's place in society and the struggle over the Jews' place in it. Locating the "other"' in *fin de siècle* Germany was still no less problematic than in the past. A great many obstacles were still laid on the path to integration of anyone other than an adult, relatively educated, and well-to-do male in contemporary bourgeois society.

During these years, between the late nineteenth century and World War I, and despite its apparent cohesion and respectability, Germany was, in fact, fragmented and conflicted on many levels.[33] Two rival camps were gradually formed at its margin: the radical left and the extreme right. They were a distinctly modern bloc on the one hand and an outspoken anti-modern bloc on the other. Antisemitism, as I have argued above, was of only secondary importance at the time, but it has gradually evolved into the hallmark of one of the camps, an identifying element of the "rightwing subculture." To be sure, it was never identical to the general nationalistic Volk culture that, at the time, was receiving its final contours on the German right, old and new. Nor was it merely one of its aspects. As I have shown in the previous chapter, antisemitism had by then attained a symbolic value. Identification with sworn antisemites and radical antisemitism in Germany of that time became a tool of self-definition. It marked an affiliation with a certain ideational and political camp. Within the prevailing conceptual environment, antisemitism helped those who embraced it to diagnose the presumed symptoms of their malaise, to foresee imminent danger, and to explain what often appeared as an unexplicable world. Antisemitism helped to point out everything that was loathed and feared by the prophets of Germany's anti-modern culture.

This picture assumes a society in which blatant antisemitism, however widespread, was not a norm. In fact, violent attacks against Jews, such as those attached to the spreading of blood libels against them, were considered unacceptable even by the conservative authorities of the day.[34] Reinforced military and police units were dispatched to affected regions to restore order, and the courts were strict in punishing those responsible for the agitation. In the Reichstag, antisemites were often the butt of jokes. Responding to an openly antisemitic memorandum that was submitted

---

[33] Compare Chapter 5.
[34] For an interesting reconstruction of one of these cases, see Helmut Walser Smith, *The Butcher's Tale: Murder and Antisemitism in a German Town*, New York, Norton, 2002.

to him, Bethmann-Hollweg, who was the chancellor at the time, commented that ideas such as those were best ignored, while the Kaiser noted on his own copy that the whole thing was "childish" and stressed that the anti-Jewish policy that was proposed by the author would "only make Germany regress a hundred years back" and "cut it off from the company of civilized nations."[35] Even that German leadership that was toying with the idea of a coup to rid itself once and for all of the restrictions placed on it by the constitution, a leadership that finally wreaked havoc on Germany by leading it into a war of previously unknown proportions; even that leadership which was never overly sympathetic to the Jews regarded such a radical, action-craving brand of antisemitism as pathetic fantasy.

I have characterized antisemitism in Wilhelmine Germany as a cultural code, signifying the radical right. Concurrently, one may regard explicit *anti*-antisemitism as characteristic of the oppositional camp on the left, combining all supporters of emancipation, including those who worked to fortify Liberalism and even some who were daring to back a moderate and reformist Social Democracy from the very heart of the bourgeois establishment.

A case in point is the German peace movement.[36] Many of the pacifist leaders expressed themselves openly and aggressively on the issue of antisemitism, too. It is fascinating to trace the ideological course of such diverse figures as historian Ludwig Quidde or the Viennese Baron von Suttner and his wife Bertha, all of whom were peace activists before World War I. Known as one of the movement's prominent leaders, Quidde first earned a reputation when he participated in the public debate on antisemitism back in 1881.[37] In an acerbic polemical essay entitled "Antisemitic Propaganda and German Students," he attacked the "new" antisemitism, explaining

---

[35] See Hartmut Pogge von Strandmann, "Staatsstreichpläne, Alldeutsche und Bethmann-Hollweg," in his and Imanuel Geiss, *Die Erforderlichkeit des Unmöglichen. Deutschland am Vorabend des Ersten Weltkrieges*, Frankfurt a. M., Europäische Verlagsanstalt, 1965, pp. 22, 25–6.

[36] See Karl Holl, *Pazifismus in Deutschland*, Frankfurt a. M., Suhrkamp, 1988; and for a specific emphasis on the Kaiserreich, see Roger Chickering, *Imperial Germany and a World without War: The Peace Movement and German Society, 1892–1914*, Princeton, NJ, Princeton University Press, 1975.

[37] See *L. Quidde, Caligula. Schriften über Militarismus und Pazifismus*, Hans-Ulrich Wehler (ed.), Frankfurt a. M., Syndikat, 1977; On Bertha von Suttner, see Gisela Brinker-Gabler (ed.), *Kämpferin für den Frieden – Bertha von Suttner, Lebenserinnerungen, Reden und Schriften*, Frankfurt a. M., Fischer Taschenbuch Verlag, 1982, and Beatrix Kempf, *Suffragette for Peace: The Life of Bertha von Suttner*, London, Wolff, 1972 (originally in German, 1962).

it away as yet another manifestation of a raging social crisis that was typical of life under the Imperial system. Ten years later, in early 1891, Baron von Suttner established in Vienna the Austrian Association for the War on Antisemitism, in parallel with the similarly named but considerably larger body operating in Germany at that time.[38] This was shortly before he joined his wife Bertha, a tireless peace activist, in establishing the local chapter of the peace movement. Other pacifists were also known to be active in the fight against antisemitism, though the link between pacifism and anti-antisemitism has not always proven unbreakable. When World War I broke out, almost the entire German Association for the War on Antisemitism (known as the *Abwehrverein*) was swept up in patriotic zeal. Still, some of its leaders continued to be active in the peace movement. Theodore Barth, for instance, a president of the *Abwehrverein* for many years, was and remained a strong supporter of the peace movement. His successor, Georg Gothein, was an unswerving pacifist and member of the Association for International Understanding even before the war. He later openly opposed the German government's annexationist policy, and as a Reichstag delegate repeatedly protested the authorities' abuse of the peace activists.

Thus, by the beginning of the twentieth century, one could discern not only an ideological syndrome typical of the German right but also a clear ideological syndrome that was characteristic of the left. That syndrome encompassed the liberal-democratic position, which was sometimes pacifist in one form or another and distinctly *anti*-antisemitic. In this milieu, *anti*-antisemitism and unrelenting support for the idea of full equality for the Jews were incontestable tenets. As in the mirror image examined previously, here, too, in leftwing culture, these were not necessarily the central issues at hand, but they had powerful symbolic value and an unambiguous identifying role. Antisemitism, on the one hand, and *anti*-antisemitism, on the other, were both used in marking membership in these two competing camps. For this reason, both acquired a long-standing special status in Imperial Germany. It should be noted that this was made possible because neither antisemitism nor anti-antisemitism were ever the norm in Wilhelmine society. In the atmosphere of prosperity in early

---

[38] See especially, Barbara Suchy, "The Verein zur Abwehr des Antisemitismus (I) – From its Beginnings to the First World War," *Leo Baeck Institute Yearbook* XXVIII, 1983, 205–39; "The Verein zur Abwehr des Antisemitismus (II) – From the First World War to its Dissolution in 1933," *Leo Baeck Institute Yearbook* XXX, 1985, 67–103.

twentieth-century Germany, both unbridled antisemitism and an outspoken advocacy of the Jews were the exceptions. They could therefore both serve as indicators of belonging, each marking one of the opposing camps, fighting, so to speak, over the soul of German culture.

But the clearest affinity between these four components – antisemitism and *anti*-antisemitism, feminism and *anti*-feminism – even more distinct than the one between *anti*-antisemitism and feminism – was forged between antisemitism and *anti*-feminism.[39] The proximity of these two components was born during the nineteenth century, parallel to the emergence of nationalism. In a series of pioneering studies, George Mosse argued that German nationalism emerged as "a cult of masculinity."[40] While both men and women could be expected to show genuine patriotism, it was clear to all that they could not be treated as equals in terms of the nation's needs and its political life. After all, women – apparently like Jews – were not endowed with the "moral earnestness" that marked the German man. They could not be regarded as equal partners in the national community. Furthermore, the old argument about a woman's true "essence" that had become familiar since at least the Enlightenment remained relevant well into the twentieth century.[41] It was in the beginning of that century, indeed, when the repercussions of the feminist struggle in England first reached the Continent, and with the debate about women's rights raging in Germany, too, that pure masculine exclusivity within the national community was in danger of being jeopardized for the first time. At this junction it seemed to need urgent protection.

Among the clearest theoretical statements on this issue was Otto Weininger's. This young Viennese Jew managed to raise a real, though short-lived, storm with the publication of his book, *Geschlecht und*

---

[39] See, for example, Friedrich Lange, *Reines Deutschtum: Grundzüge einer nationalen Weltanschauung*, Berlin, Duncker, 1905 [1893], p. 166. On antisemitism in the context of the struggle for women's rights, see Richard J. Evans, *The Feminist Movement in Germany, 1894–1933*, London, Sage Publications, 1976, pp. 175–82, and Pulzer, *The Rise of Political Anti-Semitism*, 221–2. Marion Kaplan discusses the issue from a different point of view in her "Sisterhood under Siege: Feminism and Antisemitism in Germany, 1904–1938," in Jehuda Reinharz and Walter Schatzberg (eds.), *The Jewish Response to German Culture: From the Enlightenment to the Second World War*, Hanover and London, University Press of New England, 1985, pp. 242–65.

[40] Mosse, *Nationalism and Sexuality*, 78–9.

[41] See Carole Pateman, *The Sexual Contract*, Cambridge, Polity Press, 1994; Sylvana Tomaselli, "The Enlightenment Debate on Women," *History Workshop* 20, 1985, 101–24.

Charakter (Sex and Character), in May 1903.[42] As mentioned before, Weininger focused primarily on the fundamental dualism between the sexes and on feminine inferiority, but he also labored to compare "femininity" with "Jewishness," reiterating older analogies, and suggesting new links between them. The struggle against Judaism and femininity was one and the same, Weininger argued, and his message evoked a range of cultural associations, striking dormant and familiar notes in the minds of his contemporaries. In retrospect, the popularity that his rather tiresome book had enjoyed in Vienna, a city brimming with levelheaded and incisive minds is striking, indeed. It was no doubt aided by the fact that the young author committed a very dramatic, or rather melodramatic, suicide shortly after its publication. But the book's unique attraction was not mere coincidence. It was rooted in a much broader context, that of the attitude toward all "others" in Europe in general and in the German-speaking countries in particular. For our purpose, of paramount importance is the associative link between Jew and woman that had been forged more than 100 years earlier and was finally being expressed in a most extreme and somewhat perverse manner by Weininger. The German public was in fact busy defining the essence of "otherness" for a long time. The concepts formulated in the process became a cornerstone in the struggle to preserve ethnic as well as masculine exclusivity within the boundaries of the national community. Eventually, the biological-racial explanation was appended to buttress this ideological structure, augmenting the rather intuitive explanations of the Enlightenment with a presumably bona fide scientific theory. The new mix was clearly much harder to resist.

The preoccupation with difference was a stabilizing factor in bourgeois society at the turn of the century. It was in the center of the intellectual as well as the social and political response to the challenge of the modern age. The Enlightenment propagated the creation of a new, open society that was free of any preference or discrimination. Throughout the

[42] Compare Chapter 2, and see Otto Weininger, *Sex and Character*, London, W. Heinemann, 1906 (originally in German, 1903). By 1904 there were already four editions, by 1914 there were fourteen, and by 1925 it had reached twenty-six editions. Ute Frevert, *'Mann und Weib, und Weib und Mann': Geschlechter-Differenzen in der Moderne*, Munich, C.H. Beck, 1995, p. 120. Luckhardt devotes the last section of her study to the discussion of this book, see Ute Luckhardt, "Die Frau als Fremde: Frauenbilder um die Jahrhundertwende," *Tel Aviver Jahrbuch für Deutsche Geschichte* XXI, 1992, 99–126, here 120–6. Compare also with Jacques Le Rider, *Der Fall Otto Weininger: Wurzeln des Antifeminismus und Antisemitismus*, Munich and Vienna, Löcker, 1985 (originally in French, 1982). My discussion is based on a new edition of Weininger's book, Munich, Matthes & Seitz, 1980, pp. 403–41.

nineteenth century, various attempts were made to formulate the principles that would permit the use of exclusionary tactics despite this egalitar-
ianism. These were first and foremost conceived in terms of social class,
but also in terms of ethnicity, biology, and gender. The colonial-imperialist
discourses, as well as the domestic social and local ones, were all affected
by such considerations. From the 1860s onward, talk of race had been
linked to the *Judenfrage* and, above all, to the attempts to exclude Jews
from the mushrooming public sphere of the new bourgeois society. As the
struggle for women's rights intensified, the use of biological arguments
along with racial theories became central to that struggle, too. It was a
weapon designed to neutralize feminine influence and preserve the traditional role of women at the margin of public life.[43]

By the late nineteenth century, even those wishing to defend the Jews
or support the women's struggle found themselves forced to address the
analogy between these two groups. Some even attempted to consider
this combination a positive sign, though they were few and far between.
Theodor Lessing, for instance, a rather controversial philosopher at the
time, mentioned previously as the author of *Jewish Self-Hatred*, published in 1910, an essay that had been written years before under the
title "Weib, Frau, Dame" (Woman, Wife, Lady).[44] Upon its publication,
it was inevitably regarded as a response to Weininger's book, and the
debate over *Sex and Character* may have indeed brought Lessing to pub-
licize his own views. In any case, it was a resolute statement in defense of
the link between women and Jews. The moral and intellectual supremacy
of these two, ran Lessing's argument, was the result of their ongoing efforts
to overcome age-old oppression, suffering and dependence. It was under
these dire circumstances that their negative traits also were developed,
and, as a way of overcoming them, Lessing offered two radical remedies:
feminism and Zionism.

An equally unusual combination of feminism with philosemitism can
be found in the writings of Leopold von Sacher-Masoch, who gave his

---

[43] Compare George L. Mosse, *Toward the Final Solution: A History of European Racism*,
London, J.M. Dent, 1978, and his *The Crisis of German Ideology: Intellectual Origins
of the Third Reich*, New York, Grosset & Dunlap, 1964, pp. 145–66. In addition to Ute
Frevert's book, *Mann und Weib, und Weib und Mann*, see Ute Planert, *Antifeminismus
im Kaiserreich: Diskurs, soziale Formation und Mentalität*, Göttingen, Vandenhoeck &
Ruprecht, 1998, pp. 83–93.

[44] Theodor Lessing, *Weib, Frau, Dame: Ein Essay*, Munich, Gmelin, 1910. Compare also
Chapter 2 and Lawrence Baron, "Theodor Lessing: Between Jewish Self-Hatred and
Zionism," *Leo Baeck Institute Yearbook* XXVI, 1981, 323–40; pp. 330–2 are specifically
on this work.

name to masochism and was notorious at the time for his scandalous essays on the presumably true nature of the relationships between the sexes. Less known is the fact that Sacher-Masoch had always been fascinated with scenes from the Jewish milieu, mainly in Galicia, and with what he considered Jewish life in general. He was particularly captivated by the situation in which an allegedly passive man was permanently preoccupied by study while his wife assumed the active role of a breadwinner, managing the entire household, including the worldly affairs of her own husband.[45]

Comments on the primitive, authentic nature of sexuality that was typical of both Jews and women are to be found in the writings of Otto Rank, one of Freud's more original and independent disciples. Rank considered the individuals who made up these groups as leading the struggle against the repression of what he saw as "natural" sexuality. He saw them as having a liberating and therefore essentially positive mission.[46] Less positive analogies appeared in the writings of Hans Gross, a pioneering criminologist, and Georg Groddeck, who was later known in Freud's circle as the "wild analyst" – each from his own singular perspective.[47] In *fin de ciècle* European culture, it was possible to find a great variety of attitudes toward the supposed link between women and Jews. Some foresaw and advocated the feminization of society while regarding

---

[45] On Sacher-Masoch, see Hans Otto Horch, "Der Aussenseiter als 'Judenraphael': zu den Judengeschichten Leopolds von Sacher-Masoch," in Hans Otto Horch and Horst Denkler (eds.), *Conditio Judaica: Judentum, Antisemitismus und deutschsprachige Literatur vom 18. Jahrhundert bis zum Ersten Weltkrieg*, Tübingen, M. Niemeyer, 1989, Part II, pp. 258–86; David Biale, "Masochism and Philosemitism: The Strange Case of Leopold von Sacher-Masoch," *Journal of Contemporary History* XVII, 1982, 305–23. I also relied here on an unpublished lecture given by Ms. Alison Rose at the Comparative European History Seminar held during the academic year 1991/2 at Tel Aviv University, entitled "Exotic Temptress or Ideal Housewife? The Representation of Jewish Women in Vienna in the Late Nineteenth Century."

[46] Otto Rank, "Das Wesen des Judentums" [1905], translated in Dennis B. Klein, *Jewish Origins of the Psychoanalytic Movement*, New York, Praeger, 1981, Appendix C. On Rank, see E. James Lieberman, *Acts of Will: The Life and Work of Otto Rank*, New York, Free Press, 1985, and Esther Menaker, *Otto Rank: A Rediscovered Legacy*, New York, Columbia University Press, 1982.

[47] Both, along with others, are discussed in Jacques Le Rider, *Modernity and Crises of Identity*, New York, Continuum, 1993, pp. 101–46. Hans Gross, who, together with psychiatrist Paul Näcke, established the first periodical in criminology (1898), was from 1905 a professor for "Kriminalstatistik" in Graz. See Franziska Lamott, "Prof. Dr. Hans Gross gegen seinen Sohn. Zum Verhältniß von Wissenschaft und Subjektivität," in Jean Clair, Cathrin Pichler, and Wolfgang Pircher (eds.), *Wunderblock. Eine Geschichte der modernen Seele*, Vienna, Löcker, 1989, pp. 611–19. On Groddeck, see Carl M. and Sylva Grossman, *The Wild Analyst. The Life and Work of Georg Groddeck*, New York, G. Braziller, 1965.

the Jews as an obstacle in the process. Others, witnessing the budding women's movement, anxiously observed what they saw as a "feminine takeover" and rose to the defense of "masculine" rationality in the face of the inherently feminine irrationality principle. In this "last battle," most of them regarded the Jews as dangerous enemies. In the prevailing atmosphere, only a few were able to formulate a positive connection between women and Jews or to cultivate a line of action supporting both feminism and the Jewish equality. At the center of attention were those who overtly expressed their contempt for both women and Jews and viewed them as inferior, the enemies of culture and a threat to the existing social order.

Still, despite the persistent discourse on the affinity between women and Jews, the position of antisemitism in Wilhelmine Germany was not identical to that of anti-feminism. Identification with antisemitism was indeed common enough in various social milieus of the right, but blatantly antisemitic expressions were typical of its margins only. It was there, and there alone, that antisemitism had been sweeping and unequivocal. The opposition to women and their demand for equality, in contrast, was more culturally widespread and more generally acceptable. Except for a few radical democrats, everyone seemed to regard them as intruders into public life, in higher education, and in politics. Such views were common among conservatives and liberals, modernists and anti-modernists, anti-socialists and even some socialists – men and women alike.[48] Clearly unambiguous was the conservative stance in all its shades; the position of moderate liberals, who now found themselves drifting away from their movement's progressive views, was more complex. But most intriguing was the attitude of the staunch modernists, who were active in Germany's progressive cultural scene and who had devised a way to combine creativity and innovations with an unyielding antagonism to women's emancipation. In late-nineteenth-century Vienna, some of the well-known modernists, such figures as composer Arnold Schoenberg and architect Adolf Loos, held only contempt for anything they saw as "feminine." Perhaps fearful of revealing the feminine aspect of their own personalities, they insisted on keeping their distance from anything they regarded as feminine: the "femininity" of the contemporary decadent style, the materialism and overt simplicity that were considered to be distinctly feminine traits.

---

[48] For examples see Evans, *The Feminist Movement in Germany*, 146–75; Jean H. Quataert, *Reluctant Feminists in German Social Democracy 1885–1917*, Princeton, NJ, Princeton University Press, 1979, and especially Planert, *Antifeminismus im Kaiserreich*.

From this perspective, George Mosse's thesis in his *Nationalism and Sexuality,* stressing the uniform attitude of Germany's nationalist society to all "others" within it, seems all too encompassing.[49] Mosse's presentation of the conformist facet of the nationalist movement underlines its emphasis on a specific kind of masculinity along with its characteristic repulsion of any kind of "deviation." He argues that, throughout the nineteenth century, the champions of nationalism – many liberals among them – feared feminization and devoted themselves to establishing "bourgeois decency," complete with a puritanical sexual ethos. Not all "others" in this society, however, were treated equally. Homosexuals, indeed, were disqualified from equal membership in the national community by the large majority of those who regarded themselves as its legitimate members at the turn of the century. The opposition to women's equality, while sometimes less vehement, was consistent and shared by the majority. In contrast, the Jews, who in the days prior to 1848 were commonly rejected by the various ideological camps – liberals included – were by now regarded as complete outsiders only by a relatively small antisemitic minority. In support of his position, Mosse refers to the antisemitic activities of that time: the book by the Frenchman Eduard Drumont, the politics of Herman Ahlwardt', and the publications of Carl Wilmanns and Otto Weininger, of course. However, in comparison with the short-lived popularity of the antisemitic agitators, authors, and politicians, we should consider the large-scale and long-term effects of those who were then preoccupied with matters of sexual identity: Ivan Bloch, the most prominent sexologist in the early twentieth century; Sigmund Freud himself; and almost all contemporary psychologists, psychiatrists, physicians, and criminologists.[50] From today's perspective, most of the members of this group seem troubled and cautious defenders of bourgeois values, but at the time they were the heralds of a generally progressive and enlightened sanity. Prior to World War I, blatant antisemitism was shared by a minority on the far right, a marginal minority albeit one that was often loud and, contrary to expectations, eventually very influential. Anti-feminism, in contrast, was

[49] Mosse, *Nationalism and Sexuality,* especially the conclusion, pp. 181–91.
[50] Mosse (Ibid.) discusses contemporary sexologists in his chap. 2, with an emphasis on the issue of homosexuality. On Freud see mainly the fifth volume of his collected writings, *Sexualleben,* Frankfurt a. M., 1972. A vast body of literature exists on this aspect of his theory. See, for instance, Frank J. Sulloway, *Freud: Biologist of the Mind: Beyond the Psychoanalytic Legend,* Cambridge, MA, Harvard University Press, 1992, especially chap. 8. See also Peter Gay, *Freud: A Life for Our Time,* New York, Norton, 1988, pp. 501–22 and the bibliographical references on pp. 773–4.

an element of mainstream culture, represented equally on both the left and the right, and carried a message that reflected a well-established norm that was shared by the entire spectrum of Wilhelmine society, indeed by much of European society as a whole.

Feminism, finally, was upheld by a small group of men, and a somewhat larger group of women – a tiny and rather inconsequential minority. In addition, its location on the German political scene was much less definable. Only Liberals and Socialists of a very distinct shade supported equal rights for women, while at the same time, a milder and more conservative version of feminism, one that rejected egalitarian and stressed the unique "essence of femininity," had also emerged. This kind of feminism put special emphasis on motherhood as the ultimate feminine role, motherhood that could serve as a basis for launching an attack on the presumably cold and inhuman nature of modern society. Ideologically and socially, then, feminism, and not only in Germany, lacked a clear and consistent backbone.[51] Moreover, it often found itself in rather strange company. While nationalism was indeed designed especially for men, women too could apparently find their place within it. On the eve of World War I, most women's organizations embraced the national verbiage of the time, often with open enthusiasm, and during the war some of them even propagated their own sort of chauvinism. This was by no means a phenomenon limited to Germany. Some of Europe's most prominent feminists climbed on the bandwagon of nationalism at that time.[52] This was particularly conspicuous in the case of Emmeline and Christabel Pankhurst, the militant leaders of Britain's Women's Social and Political Union (WSPU). Even before the war, the two were freely borrowing from the nationalist vocabulary, and in 1916 they publicly urged a special feminine contribution to the war effort based on the "natural patriotism" of Britain's women, their highly developed sense of duty, and their proven courage. In that conceptual framework, Germany was conceived of as a particularly despicable masculine nation, and the call for victory over its army was thus made

---

[51] See Gisela Bock and Pat Thane (eds.), *Maternity and Gender Policies: Women and the Rise of the European Welfare State, 1880s–1950s*, London, Routledge, 1991, and Ann T. Allen, *Feminism and Motherhood in Germany, 1800–1914*, New Brunswick, NJ, Rutgers University Press 1991.

[52] For a comparative look, see Margaret R. Higonnet et al. (eds.), *Behind the Lines: Gender and the Two World Wars*, New Haven, CT, Yale University Press, 1987, and Billie Melman (ed.), *Borderlines: Gender and Identities in War and Peace, 1870–1930*, New York, Routledge, 1998, pp. 65–84, 421. See also Susan Kingsley Kent, "The Politics of Sexual Difference: World War I and the Demise of British Feminism," *Journal of British Studies* XXVII(3), 1988, 232–53.

self-evident from a feminist point of view, too, an extension of the fight for women's rights. The inclusion of nationalism within the overall feminist syndrome in early twentieth-century Europe occurred just as swiftly and as smoothly as the parallel inclusion of nationalism as a legitimate aspect of socialism. Thus, at no stage was feminism ever the hallmark of one specific political camp or social group. It was much too weak to serve as a signifier of a particular cultural milieu, and it was much too rare to be regarded as a social norm in any contemporary context. Thus it was the belief in emancipation on the one hand and antisemitism on the other that served as the signposts of the two extreme political cultures co-existing in Wilhelmine Germany. Feminism and anti-feminism were important battle cries but neither of them, each for a different set of reasons, could assume the role of cultural code.

7

Comparing Germany with the French Republic

A comparison with the position and role of antisemitism in France may further explain the special place of antisemitism in Germany of the late nineteenth and the early twentieth centuries; the apparent similarities between the two countries may also shed some light on the fundamental differences between them.

The history of French antisemitism has received far less attention than its German equivalent.[1] General books on the history of the Third Republic mention, of course, Edouard Drumont and the astounding success of his *La France Juive*, published in 1886, not only among the general reading

---

[1] A pioneering work was Robert F. Byrnes, *Antisemitism in Modern France: The Prologue to the Dreyfus Affair*, New Brunswick, NJ, Rutgers University Press, 1950. See also Stephen Wilson, *Ideology and Experience: Antisemitism at the Time of the Dreyfus Affair*, Rutherford, NJ, Fairleigh Dickinson University Press, 1982, and two of his earlier articles: "The Antisemitic riots of 1898 in France," *The Historical Journal* 16(4), 1973, 789–806, and "Le Monument Henry: La structure de l'antisémitisme en France 1898–1899," *Annales* 32(2), 1977, 265–91. Also see Philip Nord, *The Republican Moment: Struggles for Democracy in Nineteenth-century France*, Cambridge, MA, Harvard University Press, 1995, and Pierre Birnbaum, *The Anti-Semitic Moment. A tour of France in 1898*, New York, Hill and Wang, 2003 (originally in French, 1998). From the older literature, I found the following useful: Pierre Sorlin, *La Croix et les Juifs (1880–1899)*, Paris, B. Grasset, 1967; Jeannine Verdes-Leroux, *Scandale financier et antisémitisme Catholique*, Paris, Éditions de Centurion, 1969; and Pierre Pierrad, *Juifs et Catholiques Françaises*, Paris, Fayard, 1970. For the overall intellectual and political atmosphere, see Zeev Sternhell, *La Droite Révolutionnaire 1885–1914*, Paris, Editions du Seuil, 1978, and René Rémond, *The Right Wing in France from 1815 to de Gaulle*, Philadelphia, University of Pennsylvania Press, 1966 (originally in French, 1963). The essay on which I base the following chapter was written earlier than some of the above-mentioned works. I believe, however, that its argument still stands, despite the additional research in this field.

public but also among some of France's most prominent intellectuals. The Dreyfus affair is also discussed extensively. But one cannot help but wonder how slanted the picture of the past has become through hindsight and in view of later events in Germany. For our purposes it is not necessary to go into the details of France's tradition of antisemitism. Suffice it to recall that, since the early part of the nineteenth century, manifestations of anti-Jewish sentiments could be found in France, as in Germany, on both the left and the right, nourished no doubt by mainstream Catholic hostility toward the Jews, and that during the later part of the century, French antisemitism, despite its apparent uniqueness, could easily have been defined in terms quite similar to the ones used in the German case.[2] Here, too, it was characterized by the introduction of new ideological elements, sporadic organizational experiments, and, above all, the particular cultural function it had fulfilled in the public life of the Third French Republic prior to World War I.

On the ideological front, a measure of novelty – this time on a European scale – came indeed from the pen of Edouard Drumont. His *La France Juive* won more popularity and gained more serious treatment in well-placed circles than anything produced by the German antisemites at the time.[3] In its cultural prestige it could only be compared with Houston Stewart Chamberlain's best-selling *Grundlagen des neunzehnten Jahrhunderts* (1899) and perhaps also with Langbehn's *Rembrandt als Erzieher* (1890). None of these, however, won the popularity of Drumont's treatise; nor did they receive good press or so lenient a historiography. While the German educated elite spurned most of the antisemitic literature, Drumont was discussed and seriously evaluated in the best Parisian papers.[4] Yet Drumont's book suffers from all the shortcomings that were typical of the works of his German contemporaries; *La France Juive* is a

---

[2] For an overall comparison see Christian Wiese, "Modern Antisemitism and Jewish Responses in Germany and France," and Vicki Caron's comment in: Michael Brenner, Vicki Caron, and Uri Kaufmann (eds.), *Jewish Emancipation Reconsidered*, Tübingen and London, Mohr Siebeck, 2003, pp. 127–53.

[3] On Drumont see, in addition to Byrnes, *The Prologue to the Dreyfus Affair*, Michel Winock, *Nationalism, Anti-Semitism and Fascism in France*, Stanford, CA, Stanford University Press, 1998 (originally in French, 1982), pp. 85–102, 111–30.

[4] See Byrnes, *The Prologue to the Dreyfus Affair*, 150–4. On Drumont's intellectual impact, see also, Zeev Sternhell, "National-Socialism and Antisemitism: The Case of Maurice Barrès," *Journal of Contemporary History* 8, 1973, 47–66, and Michael Curtis, *Three Against the Third Republic: Sorel, Barrès and Maurras*, Princeton, NJ, Princeton University Press, 1959, pp. 203–20. The following discussion is based on these sources as well.

confused, eclectic, and tedious book. From today's standpoint its popularity is astonishing. Expressing a wide range of fears and resentments, the book apparently reflected the general malaise that was prevalent in those transitional years of the Third Republic, when the French democracy was facing rapid change and accelerated modernization.

The success of Drumont's book also resulted in the reprinting in France of some of the French and German antisemitic "classics," such as Toussenel's *Juifs, Rois de l'époque* (1845) and August Rohling's *Der Talmudjude* (1873). New antisemitic writers also appeared on the scene, all of them eager to make their mark and exploit the sympathetic reading public. But the French antisemitic literature of those years somehow managed to preserve a reputation for not being racist. While the racial elements in the works of Drumont, Barrès, and Maurras are indisputable, the consensus seems to be that the moral and social-cultural aspects of antisemitism in their texts are still more important. The preference for cultural arguments, however, was apparent in the position taken by the leading German antisemites, too, while a distinctly racist literature was by no means a strictly German phenomenon. Gobineau's book, as has been recently reasserted, was far better known in France than had been previously assumed; Taine provided an original French version of social racism; and in the late nineteenth century, France, rather than Germany, was the European center of racial anthropology.

Antisemitic political parties of the kind known from the German experience may not have existed in the Third Republic. But the *Ligue antisemitique française*, which may not have been a "proper" political party, nevertheless gained considerable popularity in France of the late 1890s. It aggressively promoted its candidates in municipal and national elections, and the group of self-declared antisemitic delegates eventually sent to the Chamber was loud enough, though not very effective. By 1898, an antisemitic bill managed to win close to 200 votes in an early reading, exploiting the hostile atmosphere that immediately followed the publication of Zola's *J'accuse*. The *Ligue*'s showing in urban constituencies was particularly impressive, and in January and February of 1898 it managed to organize or encourage some sixty anti-Jewish riots throughout France. These developed into real pogroms only in Algeria, but in France much damage was done to Jewish property, and the Jewish population was thoroughly intimidated. The political potential of a populist antisemitic movement in France was further demonstrated by the Marquis de Morés, operating in the early 1890s especially in the Ist Paris *arondissment*, and later by Jules Guarine in the popular XIXth. By the peak year of 1898, the *Ligue* and its satellites had managed to carry on loud street agitations and organize street marches and parades, trying its hand in all kinds of anti-Jewish propaganda across France.

In the long run, these were probably meager successes, but at the time they were not entirely unimpressive, even in comparison with Germany. In fact, the German parties and associations never managed to secure as much public support as did the French anti-Dreyfusards at the turn of the century. Neither was the distribution of antisemitic attitudes along the French social spectrum so very different from the German. Indeed, Stephen Wilson's analysis of the list of contributors to the "Monument Henry," a foundation to support the widow of Colonel Hubert Henry, who was responsible for Dreyfus's conviction in his first trial, supports such an assertion. The composition of the list, which was published periodically by *La Libre Parole* from December 1898 to January 1899, suggests that the support for the antisemites in late nineteenth-century France came from social elements similar to the ones attracted by antisemitism in Germany. It was apparently more common among the working class and, understandably, among the Catholic priesthood. But otherwise, in France, too, one can identify army officers, small employers, students, and members of the free professions as the most highly over-represented groups on the list.[5] All in all, the antisemitic preoccupation in France may have been less intense than in Germany but not less widespread, although pre-Nazi German antisemites neither experienced the high point that French antisemitism had reached by 1898, nor did they suffer such a demise as their French counterparts did in the aftermath of the Dreyfus affair.

Regardless of these differences the role of antisemitism and its function, which were observed in Wilhelmine Germany, recurred in France, too. At least from the early 1880s, antisemitism had been an integral component of the newly constructed right wing nationalism in France. The Jew as the foreigner, the perennial outsider, provided the negative archetype of all that was presumably purely French – authentic, unique, and diffused with the special signs of national greatness and promise. Antisemitism appeared whenever the need arose to obliterate class differences for the sake of a united and glorious France. This, for instance, happened during the election campaign of the Boulangist movement in the early 1880s, when an effort was made to enlist the workers and the lower middle classes to support the ambitious general. In Drumont's and Barrès' writings, too, antisemitism was systematically considered a unifying element,

5 Wilson, "Le Monument Henry."

and it became an indispensable part of Maurras' Integral Nationalism. France did not have to face the severe identity crisis that was imposed on Germany by the Bismarckian unification process. Nevertheless, during the latter years of the century it was engaged in fundamental internal controversies over the "real" meaning of modern nationalism. Similarly, French industrialization was never as intensive or as rapid as that same process in Germany. But in France, too, society was seeking ways to deal with the implications of a new, emerging national market and the unmistakable and often painful symptoms of industrial capitalism. Thus, antisemitism, in France as in Germany, played a role in the channeling of socio-economic disaffection and dissatisfaction that was engendered by the economic transformations and the social restructuring of those years. This is too well known to repeat at length. Suffice it to mention the surge of antisemitic sentiments following the collapse of the *Union Générale* in 1882 and the increasingly antisemitic tone of the catholic newspaper *La Croix*, which gradually became the mouthpiece for this type of anti-industrial, anti-capitalist and anti-modern reaction in France. Among the antisemitic literary stars, the social theme had been prominent throughout. It was Drumont, once again, who gave an early French version to the familiar antisemitic theme that was so effective in the streets of Berlin and in the rural areas of Hesse and Westphalia. "Antisemitism," he proclaimed, "had never been a religious question. It had always been an economic and social question."[6]

Furthermore, the political function of antisemitism in France during the profound transformation of the late nineteenth century was parallel to its function in Germany. Along with the new nationalism, it engendered "a whole combination of ideas, sentiments and values henceforth considered the birthright of Radicalism" and transformed them from the revolutionary left to the political right in France.[7] Between 1879 and 1899, explains René Rémond, the historian of the French right, the left-center in French politics moved slowly and by degrees to the right, making for an important change in the political map of the country. While the newly created right mostly used the arsenal of political ideas and ideals borrowed from the tradition of the two empires, only one new major element was added – antisemitism. It was antisemitism that also helped to reshape both the ideological and the social compositions of the main political camps in Republican France.

---

[6] Quoted in Strenhell, *La Droite Révolutionnaire*, 117.
[7] Rémond, *The Right Wing in France*, 224.

Finally, French antisemitism seems to have become a cultural code, too, serving as a sign of belonging. Even if the controversy during the Dreyfus affair was not primarily a matter of justice versus patriotism, or generally a fight over principles, the struggle itself helped to crystallize the two main blocks in French politics, their overall style and subculture. On the one hand, the anti-Republican right was regrouping its forces and testing its muscle. On the other, the Republicans were gradually joining hands, despite deep internal divisions, including that over the issue of Dreyfus's innocence. The case of the Socialists was, moreover, in France as in Germany, particularly instructive. In the late 1880s, antisemitism was still widely diffused across the social and political spectrum of France. As late as 1887–1889, even *La Revue Socialiste*, the semi-official organ of the Socialist movement, had published a series of antisemitic articles dealing with the Jewish Question, although it did open its columns to opposing views, too. The Blanquist and Proudhonist traditions of the French Socialist left were in any case saturated with antisemitic elements. But as an explicit anti-Jewish position increasingly became the identity card of the new anti-Republican right, the Socialists felt obliged to distance themselves from it. By 1892, the Socialist Party line became more *anti*-antisemitic than ever, although its position on the Dreyfus affair remained ambivalent. It was only in 1898, after the public appearance of Zola on the Dreyfusards' side, and as the specter of the *Ligue* in the streets of Paris was becoming ever more alarming, that the Socialists had to reformulate their position. From that point onward, they seemed to have grasped the political, and indeed cultural, meaning of antisemitism. Like the Social-Democrats in Germany, they too could not entirely divest themselves of all traces of antisemitism. But on the public level and in their overt political pronouncement, from then on there was no longer any doubt about their position.[8] The Dreyfus affair made the cultural function of antisemitism in France quite clear, indeed in a more overt manner than any other parallel event has ever been able to do in Germany.

Two points of diversity are usually mentioned when the French and German versions of antisemitism are compared. Historians usually note the fact that the French Jewish population was considerably smaller than the German one and that, at the time, France had been, unlike Germany,

---

[8] On the Socialists' position, see Byrnes, *The Prologue to the Dreyfus Affair*, 156–78; Stren-hell, *La Droite Révolutionnaire*, 184–96, 237–41, and the interesting interpretation in Jean-Pierre Peter, "Dimensions de l'affaire Dreyfus," *Annale* 16(6), 1961, 1141–67. Compare this also with Hannah Arendt, *The Origins of Totalitarianism*, New York, Harcourt, Brace, 1951, pp. 98–120.

a relatively stable republic armed by a strong egalitarian tradition that naturally conveyed a clear *anti*-antisemitic message and was structurally well equipped to guard against antisemitism. In fact, by 1900, the French Jewish community comprised only 80,000 members whereas their number in Germany, in proportion to the general population, was five times larger.[9] In addition, with the endorsement of the Republican regime, the Dreyfus affair did finally end with a victory for the emancipatory camp that amounted to a reassertion of its faith in liberty, equality, and fraternity. Although that victory may have indeed been achieved despite, and not because of, the pressure exerted by public opinion or the press, the very fact of victory was enough to imbue nationalists and antisemites with bitterness and a sense of impotence that seemed never to be erased – even after the upheavals of two world wars. On the contrary, it gave the Republican Dreyfusard forces a solid awareness of their power and responsibility, as well as the necessary self-confidence to continue the battle. Equally important was the sense of security that this victory gave to the French Jewish community, along with a lasting faith in the benevolence of French civilization.

The German nation and society never experienced such a test case, and we shall never know how they would have withstood it. But it is instructive to remember that many in Germany at the time saw in the affair proof of the inferiority of the French system, and most German Jews reacted with concern fit for the better-situated brother. Although they were accustomed to various manifestations of hostility, they seemed confident that antisemitism in such extreme and overt form as in France would not be tolerated in Wilhelmine Germany. I indicated in the previous chapter that in the few known riots against Jews at the time of the *Kaiserreich*, in Neustettin (1881), Xanten (1891), and Konitz (1900), the authorities proved completely reliable. In the Reichstag, the German antisemites never managed to get their various bills beyond even the initial parliamentary stage. The German leadership in the Wilhelmine era

---

[9] On the French Jewish community, see Michael R. Marrus, *The Politics of Assimilation: A Study of the French Jewish Community at the Time of the Dreyfus Affair*, Oxford, Clarendon Press, 1971; Paula Heyman, *From Dreyfus to Vichy: The Remaking of French Jewry 1906–1939*, New York, Columbia University Press, 1979, and her *The Jews of Modern France*, Berkeley, CA, University of California Press, 1998. Also relevant is Jean-Denis Bredin, *The Affair: The Case of Alfred Dreyfus*, New York, G. Braziller, 1986 (originally in French, 1983), and Pierre Birnbaum, *The Jews of the Republic. A Political History of State Jews in France from Gambetta to Vichy*, Stanford, CA, Stanford University Press, 1996 (originally in French, 1992).

undoubtedly feared the revolutionary implications of a radical popular movement, even if its main purpose was the harrassment of the Jews. It was well aware of the incommensurability of the antisemitic propagandists' concrete demands for action with the most minimal standards of contemporary civilization.[10] And, despite the Dreyfus affair and the events that surrounded it, the picture in France was basically similar. In both countries, antipathy towards Jews was socially widespread; antisemitic literature in various forms was popular, and a certain amount of social discrimination was routinely practiced. However, in both countries, integration proceeded along and there was no real intent to execute any kind of official or semi-official antisemitic policy. Beyond the socially prevalent antipathy, the main legacy of pre-war antisemitism, in Germany as well as in France, was a written, "literary" one.

With the possible exception of Adolf Stöcker, whose tenacity we have already witnessed, the antisemitic politicians of late nineteenth- and early twentieth-century Germany quickly moved from the streets and mass public rallies into the comfort of the Reichstag's parliamentary halls, where they were drawn into the impotence of the Reichstag's endless speechmaking. They dissipated their energy in internal strife and showed no talent for carrying out any of their grandiose schemes. While Stöcker and Treitschke assured their respective audiences that they had no intention of going back on emancipation as such, Marr and Glagau did occasionally toy with the idea of new restrictive measures to rein in Jewish influence on the German economy and public life.[11] But neither they nor their younger and more practical heirs in the organized antisemitic movement had any concept of the kind of desirable or feasible action that was needed to bring such measures about. Among the early ideologues, only Eugen Dühring really expanded on any "practical" proposals for the solution of the Jewish Question. He may have been convinced, indeed, of the inevitability of physically exterminating the Jews to realize his goals, but this seemed preposterous even to him. Essentially, Dühring was far too pessimistic to

---

[10] Compare the more in-depth discussion in Chapter 6.

[11] Compare, in addition to the literature cited in Chapters 4 and 5, Shaul Esh, "Designs for Anti-Jewish Policy in Germany up to the Nazi Rule," *Yad Vashem Studies* VI, 1967, 83–120 (originally in Hebrew, 1966). Daniel J. Goldhagen, *Hitler's Willing Executioners. Ordinary Germans and the Holocaust*, New York, A.A. Knopf, 1996, sends a rather mixed message in his chap. 2, which deals with nineteenth-century antisemitism in Germany. On p. 69 he is "astonished" that "a large percentage of the antisemites proposed no action at all...," while on p. 71, he argues that "fully two thirds of these prominent antisemites....uttered, indeed called for a genocidal response." Clearly, however, the gist of his argument on this issue runs against mine. On Goldhagen, compare Chapter 4.

bother with drawing detailed blueprints. No European government, he argued, was in a position to employ the measures he would have liked to offer, so that, in any case, more specific plans could not materialize under the existing circumstances. One was left to wage only a personal struggle, he concluded, a war of "enlightenment and self-defense."[12] The eccentric blind scholar was primarily busy re-editing his old antisemitic opus or attempting new versions of it. Together with most of the other antisemites, he dealt with written words, attempting to convert his readers to his views, but not to recruit them for actual battle.

The antisemites in Wilhemine Germany were part of its written culture. A rich and diversified one, it included the whole linguistic gamut between the bureaucratic Potsdam style and the romantic, Wagnerian grandeur. Despite the authoritarianism of the regime in which it developed and the direct and indirect censorship it exercised, this culture also gave rise to Fontane's moderate tone and to Thomas Mann's reflective elegance. It was also the culture that served, to use George Steiner's phrase, as "the real homeland of the Jews."[13] Marr, Dühring, and Lagarde always remained bitter and frustrated at its margin. Witness their continuous attacks on Jewish intellectuals and men of letters. The verbal aggression of the antisemites often gives the impression of a public ritual. They were endlessly preoccupied with the same themes, returning to the same historical examples and personal experiences, always hammering away at the same grievances. In his analysis of the written comments added by the contributors to justify the erection of the Monument Henry, Stephen Wilson found them to have had the object and the function of a liturgy. Theirs, he added, was "a reaction typical of magic," serving an end in its very expression and not meant to lead to further action.[14] Much of the antisemitic verbiage in Germany of that time fulfilled the same function.

Hitler had no use for this verbiage. From the very beginning, he sensed the basic irrelevance of this "written" antisemitism and consciously set out to change its premises and objectives. In *Mein Kampf* he kept emphasizing the superiority of the spoken word over the "written matter."

---

[12] See Eugen K. Dühring, *Die Judenfrage als Rassn-, Sitten- und Kulturfrage*, Kralsruhe, Reuther, 1880, especially pp. 113–35.

[13] For this entire description, see George Steiner, "The Hollow Miracle," in *Language and Silence: Essays 1958–1966*, London, Faber and Faber, 1967, pp. 117–32; "The Language Animal," in *Extraterritorial Papers on Literature and the Language of Revolution*, London, Faber and Faber, 1972, especially part 4, pp. 71–88. See also Shaul Friedländer, *Nazi Germany and the Jews: The Years of Persecution, 1933–1939*, New York, Harper Collins, 1997, chap. 3, pp. 73–112.

[14] Wilson, "Monument Henry," 286–7.

All world-shaking events, he argued, were brought about not by *"Geschriebenes"* but by *"das gesprochene Wort."* His two examples were the French Revolution and Marxism. In both cases, he claimed, it was oratory and not ideology, propaganda and not ideas, that won the day. In passing, as was often Hitler's habit, he poured scorn at the German *"tintenritter"* (knights of ink) and the highly educated but entirely purposeless *"Schreibseele"* (scribblers' souls). Hitler despised and ridiculed the written matter, which, he said, always smacked of barren intellectualism. He himself wrote extensively only once, when political activism and the speaker's platform were forcibly denied him in a prolonged house arrest; *Mein Kampf*, the book he wrote during that period, remained, to borrow his own terms, a book *"das geredet ist"* (that is being spoken).[15]

Striving for power, it was Goebbels, the prime speechmaker, who quickly became second only to Hitler himself within the hierarchy of the Nazi party. Men like Alfred Rosenberg were considered rather useless. Hitler probably never really read his *Mythos des 20. Jahrhunderts,* although he claimed to have been well versed in the earlier antisemitic literature. His admiration was clearly reserved for the great rabble-rouser of his youth in *fin-de-siécle* Vienna, Mayor Karl Lueger, and his own antisemitism was apparently picked up in conversations, in beer cellars, on street corners, and in mass rallies. He remembered his own conversion to antisemitism by the spoken word and was certain that he could best transmit its message through the same medium; and, in his case, the medium was, indeed, the message.

Nazism was a spoken culture. Its language was speech devoid of literary dimensions, intimacy, and individuality. It was the language of demagogy, declamations, and shouts, with flags flying in the wind and red-and-black swastikas as far as the eye could see.[16] It was a culture in which verbal aggression was not a substitute for action, but a preparation for it. In contrast to the language of Wilhelmine Germany, Nazi language was a medium that was in all seriousness meant to lead to deeds. In his so-called *"grundlegende Rede über den Antisemitismus,"* Hitler sounded his faith in a final victory saying: "finally the day will come, when our words are silenced and the doing begins."[17] Hitler spurned the written

---

[15] Adolf Hitler, *Mein Kampf*, Munich Franz Eher, 1939 [1925]. All quotes are from chap. 9.

[16] Compare Victor Klemperer, *LTI, Die unbewältigte Sprache: Aus dem Notizbuch eines Philologen*, Leipzig, Reclam, 1946. I used the 1991 edition, pp. 17–49.

[17] See Reginald H. Phelps, "Hitler's grundlegende Rede über den Antisemitismus," *Vierteljahreshefte für Zeitgeschichte* 16, 1968, 395–99.

word; and the spoken word was for him but a preparation for action. His rhetoric thus forced a transformation of antisemitism. He initially may not have had a clear plan for "handling" the Jews once he seized power in Germany, but his antisemitism was, from the very beginning, entirely and consciously a matter of action. In his hands, the old written stuff turned into explosive, dangerous material that led finally to catastrophe. To his audiences, though, the change of meaning was often imperceptible. His contemporaries were easily fooled by his language; historians still struggle to comprehend it.

The old, tenacious tradition of European antipathy toward the Jews no doubt contributed to making them the target for Nazi persecution, ostracism, and eventually extermination. This tradition prepared the crowds of on-lookers throughout Europe for their silent consent to the Holocaust in their midst. More than anything else, the antisemitism of the pre–World War I years helped to preserve this tradition and adapt it to modernity and its social and political contexts. As such, it was significant in shaping the particular human environment at the time and turning the old Jew-hatred into a key element in the spiritual world of modern Europeans. But the murderous acts of the Nazis were of a different category. The crime of extermination must be understood by the singular terms specific to the time and circumstances, not in terms of early and gradual preparation in the faraway past. This crime must be discussed through the elucidation of its own dynamism and not by reliance on its "beginnings." Here is how Marc Bloch concluded his chapter on the "idol of origins."[18]

In a word, a historical phenomenon can never be understood apart from its moment in time. This is true of every evolutionary stage, our own and all others. As the old Arab proverb has it: "Men resemble their times more than their fathers." Disregard of this oriental wisdom has sometimes brought discredit to the study of the past.

[18] Quoted from Marc Bloch, *The Historian's Craft*, New York, A.A. Knopf, 1953 (originally in French, 1949), 35.

PART III

THE GERMAN-JEWISH PROJECT OF MODERNITY

8

Excursus on Minorities in the Nation-State

It is not by chance that this book, which is dedicated to the history of Jews in modern Germany, reaches its main topic only in the third part. After all, the special interest that many of us have in this topic is usually related to the bitter end of these Jews, and from this point of departure antisemitism almost naturally gains primacy. I, too, have started by dealing with it. Stressing antisemitism when thinking about Jewish history, however, may be misleading in the end. Salo Baron, one of the outstanding Jewish historians of the last half-century, argued, in fact, that the undue stress on Jew-hatred and the Jewish suffering throughout the ages have tended to turn their history into a "lachrymose" tale.[1] The events comprising it were all too often made to fit a mere chain of calamities. In particular, when writing German-Jewish history, even historians who are not primarily preoccupied with antisemitism place great emphasis on analyzing the relationships between Jews and non-Jews and study what may be termed "the seam lines" between the majority and minority while often neglecting the so-called internal aspects of the narrative. In the introduction to one of Jacob Toury's works on German Jewry that covers the third quarter of the nineteenth century, Toury makes explicit his intention to avoid any discussion of Jewish internal history, focusing instead on the areas of contact between them and the Germans, or on what he termed the process of their "Germanization."[2] Jacob Katz, in contrast,

---

[1] Salo Baron, "Newer Emphases in Jewish History," *Jewish Social Studies* XXV(4), 1963, 240
[2] Jacob Toury, *Soziale und politische Geschichte der Juden in Deutschland 1847–1871*, Düsseldorf, Droste Verlag, 1977, p. 7.

alternately turned his attention either to strictly internal matters or to the important areas of mutual contact between Jews and non-Jews, the reciprocal influences between them, the issue of equality versus particularity, and emancipation on the one hand and assimilation on the other. Indeed, historians who do not regard antisemitism as their main concern often choose to concentrate on these two latter issues. In the following chapters, I too will pay close attention to the meaning and consequences of emancipation and assimilation. But in addition to these, I will scrutinize yet another aspect of the narrative. By stressing the manifestations of the process of modernization in the context of Jewish history, I hope to achieve a combination of internal and external perspectives, at the center of which stands what I like to call the Jewish project of modernity.

Since the end of the eighteenth century, when the "ghetto walls" finally fell, as historian Jacob Katz metaphorically described the decreasing isolation of the Jews, they too were gradually made partners in the transformation affecting Europe. During that time, and up until the Nazi rise to power, Jews were active participants in the modernization of the European economy; the transformation of its social structure, the demographic fluctuations; the reshaping of politics; the processes of secularization; and the many-sided artistic, scientific, and intellectual changes that accompanied all of them. Jews were not merely passive victims of European history but acting agents within it. Furthermore, their life did not necessarily center on the attitudes of others toward them, and their collective endeavor was not merely about achieving equality or about successfully being integrated into the non-Jewish world. For many, it was far more important to climb up the ladder of economic and social success, to live a more satisfying and richer life, to provide their children with an education that would equip them for what they saw as a proper existence in the modern world, and to watch them thrive and prosper in its various spheres.

The emerging modern world required adaptation and adjustment by everyone, including the Jews. In many ways, their story was not very different from that of many others. But not in all ways. Unexpectedly, it was the process of emancipation as part of the creation of the modern civil society that turned the Jews into a "problem." The "Jewish Question" was a by-product of the deep transformation that marked the emergence of that society. Unlike the old order of estates and the feudal state in all its variations, the modern state needed a high level of cohesion and at least the appearance of social uniformity. One should bear in mind that such uniformity never existed in the old Europe. Equality, except among the peers of the realm, was of little value, both in theory and in practice.

Traditional society was fundamentally nonegalitarian. Every distinct element within it was explicitly defined; its rights and duties were separately and often legally determined and applied differentially according to local custom. Professional groups, guilds, and corporations of all kinds had a prescribed place within this social system, and in this sense the Jews too were part of the whole, yet another kind of corporate body within a corporate society. In addition to their religious distinction and as a result of various long-term economic processes, they were concentrated in certain vocations and not in others and lived under restrictions of various kinds. It was the modern concept of a central and unified nation-state that turned them into a "minority" in the full sense of the term, and it was only the uncompromising demand for ethnic or cultural homogeneity, in contrast to the reality of class and status diversification, that turned their very existence into a "problem."

It is true that the Jews were an exceptional community even within the social fabric of the old regime. They were the paradigmatic infidels in Christian society, the ultimate "other" in a world where religion was the determining factor of everyone's identity. They further remained unique even while the Reformation destroyed the religious unity of Western Europe and created a multitude of new minorities that were no longer mere heretical factions of limited and short-term influence. Discrimination and persecution of minorities now often resulted in population shifts and conflicts on the one hand, efforts at adaptation and assimilation, on the other. A complete absoption was only rarely achieved. The Mennonites, for example, migrated from their original homeland in the Dutch plains to the Weichsel Delta, where they were admitted by the Prussian government, like the Jews, for various economic reasons. They preserved their language and customs and remained a distinct minority for generations. In other areas of Europe, too, such cultural and ethnic enclaves were in the process of formation. Migrating Saxons, for instance, settled in Transylvania, where they preserved a kind of embryonic national consciousness for hundreds of years. During the eighteenth century, Protestants from the vicinity of Salzburg, as well as many French Huguenots, migrated into the eastern provinces of the Prussian kingdom and were welcome there as fellow Protestants. At the time, the so-called enlightened monarchs across Europe were busy establishing centralized states in which all subjects were equally subordinated to their rulers and were all expected to be honest and legally registered taxpayers. Under the new circumstances, new definitions of minorities were needed. In fact, minorities – in the full sense of this term – emerged only then, gaining clearer contours with the growing prominence of the nation-state.

Signs of the efforts to redefine the status of Jews in Germany in national rather than religious terms were evident as early as the beginning of the so-called era of emancipation. In response to Dohm's book on the civil "betterment" of the Jews in the early 1780s,[3] the renowned orientalist Johann David Michaelis sought to explain how ancient monotheism had shaped the national character of the Jews in antiquity, and why their age-old distinction could never be obliterated.[4] Similar attempts were made throughout the nineteenth century, all of them characteristic of the persistent link between nationalism and antisemitism that marked the movement for German unification even in its early liberal phase. With the newly established Bismarckian Reich and the apparent difficulties of political and social integration within it, Jewish uniqueness – that stubborn distinctness – seemed to have become increasingly annoying. It was Heinrich von Treitschke, the doyen of the Prussian historical school to whom I have alluded previously, who best expressed this vexation: "The question of how we can blend this foreign *Volkstum* with our own, becomes daily more serious," he lamented in 1879. What German Jews ought to be doing in this respect was clear to him: "They should become Germans," he stated, "feel themselves simply and completely Germans." Alternatively, they should all "make up their mind to become Germans," because nothing could be more dangerous to the new state, which is currently in the midst of constructing its own lifestyle, than a *Mischcultur*.[5] If Treitschke may be considered a hostile witness, let us recall the attitude of his decidedly more liberal colleague at the respectable University of Berlin, Theodor Mommsen, the illustrious historian of Ancient Rome. In replying to Treitschke's anti-Jewish tirades, Mommsen, marshalling the forces of his liberal conviction, summarized his argument in the following manner:

The entry into a great nation must have its price; the Hanoverians and the inhabitants of Hesse as well as we, the men of Schleswig-Holstein, are ready to pay it. We feel content in knowing that we too have given a bit of ourselves. After all, we

[3] See part II, chap. 6, fn. 24.
[4] Michaelis' major work is *Mosaisches Recht*, in six volumes, first published in Frankfurt a. M., Johann Gottlieb Garbe, 1770–1775. See Anna-Ruth Löwenbruck, *Judenfeindschaft im Zeitalter der Aufklärung: Eine Studie zur Vorgeschichte des modernen Antisemitismus am Beispiel des Göttinger Theologen und Orientalisten Johann David Michaelis*, Frankfurt a. M., P. Lang, 1995.
[5] Reprinted in Walter Boehlich (ed.), *Der Berliner Antisemitissmusstreit*, Frankfurt a. M., Insel-Verlag, 1965, pp. 7–14, especially 9, 10 and 14.

give it for the common fatherland. Now, no Moses seems to lead the Jews back into the promised land; so be it as *Hosenverkäufer* or as book-writers, it is their duty, as much as they can – without acting against their conscience – to detach themselves, on their own part, of their uniqueness, and break down completely the barriers between themselves and the rest of the German citizenry.[6]

I have quoted Mommsen at length so that his tone and his sympathetic leaning are not lost. Still, while the disparity with Treitschke ought to be kept in mind, the similarity is undeniable. In his own way, Mommsen too seeks to underline assimilation as the price of entry. In this he was following a liberal tradition that began no later than the time of Wilhelm von Humboldt and was repeatedly expressed throughout the nineteenth century. By the time of the establishment of the Bismarckian nation-state, this was a common position. In its new state clothes, the nation now reaffirmed its demand for concessions of all sorts. Above all, to overcome internal divisions, it constantly had to be on guard against any centrifugal forces. Most crucial for achieving the required homogeneity was the breakup of the old corporations, and since, as Jacob Katz has argued, Jews had often been seen as "a state within a state," they were now made a major target of the nationalist effort.[7] In the past, this kind of accusation was also leveled at artisans' and merchants' guilds, the Jesuits, and even the Freemasons, who were suspected, each for different reasons, of exacerbating the schisms in the national body. Once the legislative process granting Jews full citizenship and equal rights had been complete, this accusation was flung at them whenever they seemed to neglect their side of the unwritten contract, namely their assimilation. The demand for the negation of any sign of uniqueness was not in itself antisemitic; it was a reflection of one of the basic tenets of modernity.

In his book *Modernity and Ambivalence*, Zygmunt Bauman underlined the immanently individual character of the process of Jewish assimilation and the campaign against Jewish collectivity that had always been, according to him, its concomitant.[8] It is indeed worth repeating that the initial principle of emancipation that was formulated during the French Revolution was "Everything – to the Jew as individual; nothing – to Jews as a group," and there was nothing accidental about this formulation. It was intrinsic to the new order, which the revolutionaries sought to

---

[6] Mommsen's reply, "Auch ein Wort über unser Judentum," is likewise reprinted in Boehlich, *Der Berliner Antisemitismusstreit*, 212–27. The quote is from p. 227.

[7] Jacob Katz, "A State within a State: The History of an Anti-Semitic Slogan," *The Israel Academy of Sciences and Humanities Proceedings IV*, 1969/70, 29–58.

[8] Zygmunt Bauman, *Modernity and Ambivalence*, Cambridge, Polity Press, 1991. Here I used the 1995 paperback edition.

establish, and, according to Bauman, it likewise manifested a basic principle of modernity as such. The non-Jewish society, runs the argument,
made an offer to individual Jews to join in, although, of course, the offer
always had some preconditions attached. First and foremost, Jews were
forced to dismantle their community structure. And when they failed to
achieve such total dismemberment, one must add, the state categorically
refused to recognize their separate institutions and grant them legal status.
In fact, the modern state, despite its efforts, never managed to destroy all
the corporate, intermediary bodies under its jurisdiction, Jewish or otherwise. Many of these bodies proved exceedingly resilient, not only to public
criticism but also to repeated legislation that was intent on their abolish-
ment. In more than one German state, the guilds, for instance, fought for
their independent existence for almost 100 years after they were first dissolved.[9] In Prussia, even the nobility retained many of its privileges well
into the second half of the nineteenth century. The Jews, however, were
required to keep their part in the unwritten agreement of their emancipation instantaneously and in full. It is thus hardly surprising that many
representatives of organized Judaism were fearful of emancipation. In
fact, its enthusiastic embrace by so many of them, notwithstanding such
fears, could have only been possible at that time, which was a particularly low point in Jewish community life, as the traditional rabbinate was
losing much of its power and a new leadership was as yet unavailable.

In this context, it is interesting to review the debate between
Moses Mendelssohn and Christian Wilhelm Dohm. As a characteristic
spokesman for the Prussian enlightenment, Dohm was primarily interested in the benefits of emancipation for the monarchy he served. Despite
his trust in the principles of universalism, he was willing to leave at
least some measure of particular authority in the hands of the Jewish
communities, to prevent their rapid disintegration and facilitate state
control. Mendelssohn was strongly opposed to these "concessions" and
spoke publicly against what he saw as the unnecessary preservation of
the Jews' organized distinctness. This may have echoed his earlier struggles with some of the established rabbinical authorities in Germany, but
Mendelssohn surely saw this as a matter of principle, too. As Horst Möller,
one of the experts on the German enlightenment, explained, Mendelssohn
immediately realized the significance of Dohm's supposedly generous offer
for the safeguarding of communal autonomy. Such an offer, runs the

---

[9] See Shulamit Volkov, *The Rise of Popular Antimodernism in Germany: The Urban Master
Artisans. 1873–1896*, Princeton, NJ, Princeton University Press, 1978, pp. 173–8.

argument, "though it may seem so tolerant and well-meaning, could only strengthen the special status [of Jews]," and its consequences could finally only be "regressive."[10] But the debate could also be interpreted from a different angle. Bauman, for instance, is strongly critical of the uncompromising demand by spokesmen of the enlightenment to eradicate Jewish community life. For him, the destruction of communal life was surely no sign of progress; it was merely a manifestation of the pressure exerted by the nation-state over society at large, including the Jews, to attain total uniformity. Emancipation according to him, was not about equality but about homogeneity. It was neither progressive nor regressive but rather unmistakably oppressive.

Hannah Arendt, in contrast to Bauman and despite her ambivalent position with regard to modernity as such, could be listed among the many defenders of emancipation. In her classic *Origins of Totalitarianism*, she described favorably the dismantling of the relics of feudalism by the modern state and the consequences of this process for the abolition of discrimination against the Jews. She, too, acknowledged that emancipation was a package deal. On the one hand, the way was now open for the Jews to enter bourgeois society. On the other hand, their corporative privileges were to be entirely revoked. "Jewish restrictions and privileges had to be abolished together with all other special rights and liberties," she wrote.[11] But unfortunately, according to Arendt, this general principle, although crucial for the constitution of the modern state, was not fully applied. Vital as it was for the construction of the new state, that same state had, in addition to its lofty ideals, some other urgent interests. Above all, it was permanently in need of cash. And because Jews had already been for some time its main cash suppliers, the state found it impractical to abolish their special financial and trading privileges right then and there. Arendt argues that the modern state – apparently until quite late in the nineteenth century – had an interest "in preserving the Jews as a special group and preventing their assimilation into class society." That state's interest, she added, suited only too well the Jews' anachronistic ambition to preserve their collective self.[12] Throughout the period, according to Arendt, Jews

---

[10] Hosrt Möller, "Aufklärung, Judenemanzipation und Staat: Ursprung und Wirkung von Dohms Schrift 'über die bürgerliche Verbesserung der Juden'," in *Deutsche Aufkälrung und Judenemanzipation*, Beiheft 3, *Jahrbuch des Instituts für Deutsche Geschichte*, Tel Aviv University, 1980, pp. 119–53. The quote is a translation from pp. 146–7.

[11] Hannah Arendt, *The Origins of Totalitarianism*, New York, Harcourt, Brace, 1951. Here I used the 1964 paperback printing. The quote is from p. 11.

[12] Ibid., 13.

sought to evade the inevitable consequences of the new universal principles of the modern state. By so doing, they enraged their fellow citizens.
Assimilation was imperative under the new circumstances, yet the Jews
refused to comply.

Thus, while Bauman complains of the Jews' eagerness to assimilate at
any cost, Arendt finds fault with their resistance to it. While he wishes
to explain their destruction by stressing their readiness to forsake their
group identity, she stresses the catastrophic results of their insistence on
its preservation. Neither of them has a shortage of evidence for these contradictory positions, because one makes all Jews in the image of a small
elite of the well educated and the highly cultured while the other focuses
on a small, elite group of the rich and the powerful. Superficially, these
two sociologist-philosophers may be taken to represent the two main
schools of German-Jewish historiography: the Zionist and the Liberal, the
one asserting the hopelessness of emancipation and the shame of assimilation, while the other supports emancipation as a strategy of equality
and justice and laments its failure. But, in fact, neither Arendt nor Bauman take part in this old historiographic controversy. What sets them
apart is not their conception of Jewish history but their conception of the
essence of modernity. The discourse in which they participate is not the
one about the fate of the Jews but the one dealing with the pros and cons of
modernity.

Inasmuch as modernity embodies the principles of universalism and
equal citizenship, Arendt heartily approves of it. For her, the creation of a
nation-state based pon these two was and still remains a worthy goal. In
addition, while she is aware of the dangers of too radical a nationalism, it is
not here that she puts the blame. At the very outset, Arendt makes sure that
we identify neither the Nazis, nor the totalitarian rulers of Soviet Russia, as
"simple nationalists." Theirs was a "supranational approach to politics,"
she claims.[13] One should not forget, she repeatedly notes, that the sources
of evil were antisemitism and imperialism – not nationalism, and still less
the modern nation-state itself. The problem with the Jews, she seems to
suggest, was their insufficient commitment to the principles of modernity.
They failed to embrace wholeheartedly and consistently the project that
sought to end their isolation once and for all. They hesitated when offered
the combination of equality with assimilation that constituted the essence
of emancipation, and they therefore carry at least some blame for its
ultimate failure.

[13] Ibid., 3.

The Zionists, too, after all, favored the "project of modernity."[14] Despite her explicit preference for universalism over particularism, Arendt is closer to them than Bauman. Alt-Neuland, the new state that Theodor Herzl sought to establish, was to fit perfectly the basic tenets of modernity as she defined them. Bauman's approach, which at first seems to be more consistent with Zionism on account of his attack on assimilation, is eventually revealed to be farther away from it. According to him, the establishment of a modern Jewish state is doomed to fail, because it is a project that merely replicates the mistakes of European society. A Jewish state, he argues, could not hope to avoid the fate of other nation-states. It too would ultimately be based on a uniform structure that claims to be egalitarian but is actually striving for a one-dimensional and oppressive centralism, for the abolition of internal differences, and the eradication of all aspects of multiculturalism. In opposition to both Arendt and the Zionist viewpoint, Bauman is highly critical of modernity. He regards the entire effort to create a homogenous national society buttressed by the institutions of the nation-state as misguided. Bauman does admit that this route has had certain beneficial consequences that represent a certain improvement over the *ancient régime*. But his claim is that these new solutions only led to another kind of tyranny that was necessarily destructive of the chances for true human freedom and oppressive with respect to human creativity. For Bauman, modernity is not the quest for rationality, justice, or equality; it is primarily concerned with "the production of order," as he puts it, from the top down, geared to the "struggle against ambivalence." The catastrophic outcome of modern history was not a tragic mistake but a bitter, predictable end. Furthermore, it was the immanent "horror of mixing" that made the Jews' entry into European bourgeois life so threatening.[15] All in all, he insists, modernity was an attempt to replace the natural, somewhat chaotic and mixed state of things by an imposed and controlled order. This order's tolerance of individuals, as Bauman sees it, was nothing but the lit side of "intolerance aimed at collectives, their ways of life, their values, and, above all, their value-legitimizing powers."[16] From this point of view, toleration was nothing but another form of manipulation and immorality. Emancipation

[14] This phrase was coined by Jürgen Habermas in "Die Moderene – ein unvollendetes Projekt?" – a speech reprinted in his *Kleine politische Schriften I–IV*, Frankfurt a. M., Suhrkamp, 1981, pp. 444–64.
[15] Both quotes are from Bauman, *Modernity and Ambivalence*, 14–5.
[16] Ibid, 105, 107. See also Zygmunt Bauman, *Intimations of Postmodernism*, London, Routledge, 1992, p. xiv.

and assimilation, too, were thus but vehicles for establishing the modern order. Their sole purpose was to blur the distinctness of "others" and enhance social homogeneity. Seen from this perspective, Zionism, too, was nothing but yet another effort at reproducing modernity. If Jewish emancipation turned out to be a fraud, if they could not be truly assimilated, then they should be uprooted, displaced, and relocated in a separate state that displayed the same yearning for uniformity, the same dread of ambivalence, and the same timid rejection of contingency. The only saving grace of emancipation, in Bauman's terms, was its inevitable failure. Jews never managed to be truly like others and never ceased to cultivate their "creative ambivalence." The best of them were finally able to "call the bluff of imagined totalities" to see the true contents of modernity through its glamorous envelope, exposing its weaknesses and subverting its authority.[17]

I find Bauman's narrative, replete with admiration for the small Jewish cultural elite and its outstanding contribution to European culture, just as questionable as the demonization of the rich Jewish bankers and moneylenders by Arendt. Yet we can derive some insights from the controversy that has never taken place between them. It is not necessary to accept Bauman's ideational package as a whole – surely not his one-dimensional view of modernity. Modernity was, in fact, more than the drive for a unified order and the horror of ambivalence. But acknowledging such drives and such horrors as constitutive of its overall message is essential for the study of minorities. To be sure, a pluralist liberal vision that accepts a measure of social *difference* is not entirely a new vision. As early as the 1830s, Alexis de Tocqueville had already realized that the power of American democracy lay in its inherent pluralism and not in its uniformity. And a half-century later this truth was repeated by Lord Acton, who saw in the ethnic variety of European societies the source of their vitality and dynamism. Even in the midst of modernity, within the enlightened tradition itself, the controversy over pluralism never stopped raging. And in practice, intermediary institutions and various kinds of corporations were never entirely abolished from modern European societies. Nor was assimilation undertaken on the individual path alone.

From the point of view of modernity, despite Bauman's critique, minorities were entitled to nothing more, but also nothing less, than tolerance with a measure of equality. The modern German nation-state, albeit one that was often awash in self-righteous verbiage, had been obliged to

---

[17] Bauman, *Modernity and Ambivalence*, 185–6.

abolish many of the discriminations against them. In pratice, this state
was far from meeting the ideal of uniformity described by Bauman. Some
40 percent of the inhabitants of the Bismarckian Reich were Catholics,
for whom the primarily Protestant and Prussian vision of German nationalism meant only little. The Poles in the east and later the French in the
west; the Danes in their northern corner as well as the enclaves of local
patriotism in southern Germany – none of these ever adapted to this
vision. Jewish efforts at assimilation must therefore be examined within
this complex context, not against a constructed, ideal-type nationalism.
The image of a homogeneous national block that was only slightly and
occasionally irritated by foreigners knocking at its doors is thus partial
and misleading. It represses the frailty of nationalism, the deep schisms in
German society during the era of modernization, and the actual participation of minorities in all the tribulations of ambivalence brought about
by that era – not as outsiders but as part of the ever-problematic whole.
The story of Jewish life at this time is indeed exemplary. It is not only
a chapter in the history of a marginal minority but one that represents
the general tension embedded in modernity in general. It is a particularly
complex and difficult chapter, forever to be seen through the fact that it
ended in calamity.

9

Climbing Up the Social Ladder

a. Becoming Bourgeois

From the perspective of the Weimar Republic, before the crises of the late 1920s and prior to the Nazis' rise to power, Jews were clearly full citizens of the new republic, enjoying equal rights and fulfilling all their civil duties. They were overwhelmingly urban dwellers who were occupied mostly in commerce with a small but prominent minority in the free professions, and it is often mentioned that they were over-represented in the scholarly, scientific, and artistic communities of Germany at the time. As a rule, Jews belonged to the more-or-less educated and affluent middle class – the somewhat feeble backbone of the new democracy. From this perspective, German Jews may be regarded as true *Bürger* according to both meanings of the term: They were now full citizens (*Staatsbürger*), secure as members of the *Bürgertum*.

Looking back in time to the *Kaiserreich*, prior to World War I, the picture appears similar, if by no means identical. Apart from some de facto restrictions, which obstructed Jewish entry into the top echelons of the state bureaucracy and the upper ranks of academia; apart from being precluded from any post in Prussia's military establishment, Jews were full citizens of the *Kaiserreich*, too. By the time of its foundation, many of them had already achieved a measure of both *Bildung* and *Besitz* (property), which were regarded as the minimum requirements for belonging to the bourgeoisie. It is only when we move further back in time, to the years prior to the establishment of the *Kaiserreich*, that the scene becomes dramatically more complicated and less promising.

First, the juridical status of Jews in the pre-1871 period varied significantly from one German state to another. The legal standardization of their status, which was finally achieved on July 3, 1869 through a law of the North German Federation, was indeed a radical novelty. Prior to it, they were dependent on local legislation, always containing discriminating clauses and restrictions of various types.[1] As we look further back into the early nineteenth century, the mosaic grows in complexity, and a closer examination of the Jews' living conditions in this pre-emancipatory era reveals a bleak social picture. At the point of origin of our discussion, toward the end of the eighteenth century, the overwhelming majority of German Jews were paupers. They barely eked out an existence from peddling and a few other permitted occupations. Although they often lived in towns, they could hardly be considered a part of the city bourgeoisie, even in its modest forms at the time. Jacob Toury estimated that some 80 percent of the Jewish population in late eighteenth century Germany was "living from hand to mouth," and, according to his calculations, for at least two-thirds of them, the idea of ever being able to bridge the gap between themselves and the German middle class around them was practically inconceivable.[2]

Toward the end of the *ancient régime*, in the later decades of the eighteenth century, the Holy Roman Empire of the German Nation was considered an anachronism even by contemporaries. It was a hierarchical body that was essentially based on old feudal power relations and headed by the Habsburg emperor, the undisputed ruler of some 360 independent political units. The strongest among them were kingdoms in their own right, such as Prussia and Hanover; the weakest were tiny princedoms, such as those located along the Rhine, or free hometowns, mainly in southern and central Germany. The relative independence of these political units relied on the power of the emperor, who guaranteed their safety against the aggression of the ever-ambitious kingdoms and medium-sized principalities. Yet, despite the *Reich*'s crucial role in preserving this fragile political arrangement, it was quickly losing influence. During the eighteenth century, the *Kaiser* was entangled in wars, not only against neighboring European powers but also – and repeatedly – against Prussia,

---

[1] For full details, see Jacob Toury, *Soziale und politische Geschichte der Juden in Deutschland 1847–1871*, Düsseldorf, Droste, 1977, pp. 334–61, 384–9.

[2] Jacob Toury, "Der Eintritt der Juden ins deutsche Bürgertum," in Hans Liebeschütz and Arnold Paucker (eds.), *Das Judentum in der deutschen Umwelt*, Tübingen, J.C.B. Mohr, 1977, pp. 149–50.

that other German power in the north. The other ruling dynasties, too, were continually undermining the Habsburgs' traditional predominance and thus weakening the authority of the *Reich*. Its borders were perpetually modified, and, in practice, that Germany under its often only virtual rule was deeply divided and in an advanced stage of disintegration.

Division and heterogeneity marked the Jewish community in these areas as well. Changes that had a great impact on the Jews in Berlin, the capital of Prussia, did not usually concern those living in other parts of Germany, or even in other Prussian towns. The transformations in rural regions were different in pace and in character from those affecting the cities. North and south, east and west – everywhere there were various laws that regulated Jewish life, their rights of residence, their special privileges, and, more often still, their special duties. Jacob Katz has estimated that in the middle of the eighteenth century some 21,000 Jewish households, or about 70,000 people, were living in the territories of the old *Kaiserreich*.[3] By the early nineteenth century, as a result of rapid demographic growth and fundamental border changes in the aftermath of the Napoleonic wars, this number almost doubled. Concurrently, a large Jewish population resided in the Austrian regions of the Habsburg Empire, and during most of the nineteenth century they too were part of that amorphous community of German-speaking Jewry. Around 1750, some 70,000 Jews lived in the Habsburg lands, most of them in the provinces of Bohemia and Moravia, while some 200,000 additional Jews lived in the part of Galicia annexed to Austria when Poland was divided among its neighboring powers during the last third of the eighteenth century. Thus, in early modern times, about half a million Jews inhabited German-speaking central Europe, constituting approximately 1 percent of the total population. About half of them were Prussian residents, and one-fifth resided in the Bavarian Kingdom. Only in the small Hessian States was the percentage of Jews slightly higher, reaching 3 percent of the total population, and only in Saxony, as a result of a consistent policy prohibiting Jewish settlement, their share in the population was as low as 0.05 percent. While data for Austria are even less accurate than for other German states, it can be estimated that Jews comprised slightly less than 2.5 percent of the population there, even when one adds the territory of Galicia, where they accounted for almost 7 percent of all inhabitants.

---

[3] These data are based on Jacob Katz, *Out of the Ghetto: The Social Background of Jewish Emancipation, 1770–1870*, Cambridge, MA, Harvard University Press, 1973, pp. 9–10.

Relative to western European countries, these were high numbers, while in comparison to Poland, for instance, or the Russian "pale of settlement," the German Jewish community was rather small.

The living conditions of Jews in the various German states varied greatly, too. In Prussia, for instance, most of the Jews were only allowed to live in towns. Occasionally, as in the case of Berlin, they were encouraged by the authorities to enter the city in the hope that they would contribute to its financial and commercial fortunes. In contrast, Bavarian Jews were generally banned from cities and usually lived in small rural communities, mainly in Franconia. These rules, however, were never without exceptions. For example, Jews were forced to literally beg for the right to reside, even temporarily, in the Prussian city of Magdeburg, while in Fulda, in the heart of Bavaria, there was a large and thriving Jewish community. In other regions, such as the Grand-Duchy of Baden, in the Palatinate, and in Westphalia, Jews settled in villages and small towns and provided diverse commercial services to the local population. In the Habsburg Empire, too, Jews inhabited mostly villages, while Vienna, despite a plethora of prohibitions, included a fast-growing Jewish community at that time. In fact, around 1780, Jewish communities of over 1,000 people existed only in eight cities: Vienna, Frankfurt, Berlin, Hamburg-Altona; Mannheim, and Fürth in Bavaria; Glogau in lower Silesia; and Zülz in Upper Silesia.

Up until the end of the eighteenth century, and in many cases well into the nineteenth, the majority of Jews were still living mostly among their kind and their contacts with non-Jews, though perhaps more intense than one usually assumed, remained within clearly defined boundaries. They spoke a western Yiddish that was close to a German medieval dialect, and their conspicuously different dress marked them as strangers everywhere. Their religious laws and ways of life unmistakably set them apart from the non-Jews in their vicinity. While they were not officially enclosed in real ghettos, they did usually live on certain streets (*Judengassen*) and in separate houses (*Judenhäuser*), most likely near the synagogue and the rest of the community's public services. Their social and often their economic status, too, was greatly affected by local customs, in addition to the official local rules and regulations. Nevertheless, they had a place within the social order of the old regime. After all, the concept of individual freedom of movement was generally unfamiliar in this society, so that restrictions on Jews in that respect were not conceived as unusual, and in a society based on professional corporations, the vocational restrictions imposed on the Jews almost everywhere in the Christian world did not really stand out. Finally, in a world of serfdom and feudal restrictions, it was not surprising that Jews were occasionally forbidden to marry and that the authorities routinely interfered in their private affairs. Only the notorious *Leibzoll* (body tax), a duty that was levied specifically on individual Jews at the many German border crossings, and the exorbitant community tax that Jews were often forced to pay, were considered exceptional, particularly humiliating forms of government harassment. Although Jews were still considered foreigners, mainly because of their religion, they were not perceived as posing a unique problem. They enjoyed a certain internal autonomy that enabled them to live according to the Halachic law, and rabbinical courts had jurisdiction over many unsettled issues among them. The *Judenfrage* in its modern sense did not exist in this context.

Current historiography tends to emphasize the depth and breadth of the relationships between Jews and non-Jews even in strictly traditional societies, but, during the second half of the eighteenth century, these relationships grew rapidly closer and became ever more common and intense.[4] At that time, central European cities began to grow at an unprecedented pace, and within these growing cities a dynamic public sphere gradually emerged that was characterized by lively educated discourse and the many-sided activities of civil associations of all kinds. Wealthy Jews as well as certain professionals – medical men, perhaps, above all – could now meet members of the general population more easily. The partitions that had separated them seemed to be set aside more frequently. Yet this sporadic openness could not yet challenge the old order or replace it with a new one. Because German Jewry was still primarily characterized by its wretched poverty, it simply could not afford to participate in the new public life. Jews were left out of the emerging bourgeoisie, just like the rest of the poor. The historiography is indeed replete with allusions to outstanding Jewish intellectuals and the legendary "Court Jews," but while they were conspicuous for their reputaion and splendor, they were

---

[4] On direct and indirect contacts and even mutual influences between Jews and Christians as early as the Middel Ages, see, for example, Israel J. Yuval, *'Two Nations in your Womb.' Perceptions of Jews and Christians* [Hebrew], Tel Aviv, Alma, 2000; David B. Ruderman, *Jewish Thought and Science in Early Modern Europe*, New Haven, CT, Yale University Press, 1995; and Shmuel Feiner, *The Jewish Enlightenment in the Eighteenth Century* [Hebrew], Jerusalem, Merkaz Shazar, 2002. All three relate especially to intellectual ties, but new work on Jewish daily life also tends to support this revision. See Marion Kaplan, Robert Lieberles, Stevem M. Lowenstein, and Trude Mauerer (eds.), *Geschichte des jüdischen Alltags in Deutschland. Vom 17. Jahrhundert bis 1945*, Munich, C.H. Beck, 2003, especially the first part, pp. 19–122.

but a tiny minority.[5] Other Jews could not even see them as potential role models. For the ordinary German Jew, the life experience of this elite was just as irrelevant as the leisurely salons in Berlin or the grand court life of the German principalities was for the majority of other German subjects.

One hundred years later, the situation was radically different. Over 600,000 Jews lived within the boundaries of the German Empire, two-thirds of them in Prussia and only less than one-tenth in Bavaria. This shift meant a desertion of rural residential areas and a process of urban concentration. As a result, a great majority of all German settlements had no Jewish inhabitants in them at all, and more than one-half of the Jews were now members of communities comprising more than 1,000 members.[6] While the vast majority continued to be engaged in various trades and in commercial occupations, their economic situation had changed radically. The following details are repeatedly cited in every history book dealing with German Jews: In the early twentieth century, Jews in Frankfurt am Main were paying four times more taxes than Protestants and eight times more than Catholics in town. In Berlin, the taxes paid by Jews constituted some 30 percent of the municipal revenues even though they themselves constituted only 15 percent of the taxpaying population and a little over 4 percent of the inhabitants in the German capital.[7]

Still, some qualifications are due even here. The emphasis we usually put on a small group of the very rich and the very famous among the Jews results in a slanted view. Such emphasis was indeed characteristic of the antisemitic polemics at the time and of Jews who insisted on stressing, even glorifying, Jewish achievements. A more balanced picture, however, is also more interesting. The process through which Jews became bourgeois in Germany was no doubt rapid and comprehensive, but its pace was not uniform and it did not really include all strata of the Jewish population. That process, while fast and dramatic until the late nineteenth century, was much slower afterward. By the end of the century, the income of many Jews – about one-quarter in some of the major cities – was still lower than the minimum required for paying taxes. Across Germany,

[5] For a good summary see Mordechai Breuer's chapter on the Court Jews in Michael A. Meyer (ed.), *German-Jewish History in Modern Times. Vol. I: Tradition and Enlightenment: 1600–1789*, New York, Columbia University Press, 1996, pp. 104–26.
[6] See Jakob Thon, *Die Jüdischen Gemeinden und Vereine in Deutschland*, Berlin, Verlag des Bureaus für Statistik der Juden, 1906, pp. 68–85; see also the *Zeitschrift für Demographie und Statistik der Juden* (ZDSJ), 1911, 44–7; 1907/8, 47.
[7] ZDSJ, 1905, 12; 1908, 78.

Jewish income was usually quite modest, under 3,000 Marks annually. Their occupational structure likewise fails to corroborate the assumptions about their economic prominence or the discourse about their happy integration in the elite of the day. In 1895, more than one-half of the Jews in Germany were still engaged in commerce, mostly on a local and small scale. As many as 20 percent of them were registered as workers in various industries. Despite the ideological verbiage employed by the Jewish leadership to stress the "normality" of Jewish life in Germany and the broad "productivization" they had undergone during the century of the emancipation, their social composition was still highly untypical and distinctly different from that of the general population.

Nevertheless, by 1870 at the latest, in parallel with the establishment of the Bismarckian *Reich*, the Jews, it was generally agreed, had "made" it. After a prolonged debate and repeated delays, they acquired full citizenship rights, and within two or three generations a great majority among them could be considered part of the German bourgeoisie. How did that happen? What do we know about the process by which they became bourgeois?

Of course, Jews were not the only ones who became bourgeois during the nineteenth century. The emergence of a dominant middle class in Germany had been a general process that involved a considerable number of lower class men and women. In a society that was just opening up to talent and learning to reward its members for initiative, ambition, hard work, and tenacity, many were eager to try their luck. The Jews represent but one of the segments of society to join the race. We do, however, possess relatively much material about their experience. Jews seem to have had a particularly intense need to describe it, usually for the benefit of the younger generations. In numerous memoirs, they analyzed the process and its various phases, the forces driving it, and, of course, above all, the agonies associated with it. Considering their point of departure, Jews were perhaps particularly aware of the importance of the process they were undergoing and made sure to monitor it consistently and carefully, not without a dose of self-congratulation. Rising to the levels of *Bildung* and *Besitz* that were required for entering bourgeois society, being integrated into it, assimilating its lifestyle – these were major goals in life for many Jews during much of the nineteenth century, though certainly not for all of them. They provided an important yardstick for success or failure and criteria for self-esteem. Furthermore, aside from observations concerning individual routes to success, there was also a kind of "collective reflection" through which this entire social upgrading project was evaluated as a collective issue. Within it individual success had an impact on the status of the group, and vice versa. The new Jewish *Öffentlichkeit*, which had been developing in parallel to the general one since the late eighteenth century, was incessantly preoccupied with tracing this group process, commenting on its course, interpreting every relevant move, and arguing the advantages and disadvantages of its various tactics. The Jewish press provided constant encouragement, reporting, and preaching, taking pride in the individual members of the community who had accomplished their goals successfully and castigating those who found themselves, willingly or unwillingly, left by the wayside.

The terminology used at the time in this context was often vague and confusing. There was talk of "emancipation" but also of *Annäherung* (getting closer), *Anpassung* (adaptation), *Eingliederung* (incorporation), and *Identifizierung* (identification). The terms *Verschmelzung* (merging), *Aufgehen* (being absorbed), and *Auflösung* (dissolving) were used interchangeably. Occasionally there was talk of *Anbürgerung* (becoming bourgeois), too.[8] While this terminological confusion was in itself indicative of the mixed intentions of those taking part in the process, it should not blind us to its main characteristic. What was at stake here was clearly, above all, entry into the German *Bürgertum*. Despite the conceptual vagueness, the process of Jewish *Verbürgerlichung* remained a particularly clear-cut example of a process through which an ambitious population group that was persistently climbing up the social ladder managed to change its status from that of poor outcasts to one comparable to the prosperous and established middle class. The Jews' determination and self-awareness every step of the way made their own "bourgeoisification" a model of the process for many others. In fact, the procedure by which an aspect of German Jewish history turns out to serve as a paradigm for the study of German society as a whole is no novelty in the historiography. The German attitudes and policies toward minorities have often been studied with reference to the Jews, and the wealth of Jewish sources on becoming bourgeois may likewise be seen as a paradigm.

The middle class, which in England is considered to have been on the rise since the sixteenth century, began to make its mark on the culture, economy, and even the politics in Germany during the later half of the eighteenth century. Jürgen Habermas described the formation of a public sphere at that time, giving voice to this emergent class both in Europe in

---

[8] See Jacob Toury, "Emancipation and Assimilation. Concepts and Conditions" [Hebrew], in: *Yalkut Moreschet* 2, 1964, 167–82.

general and in Germany in particular.[9] Naturally, the process was manifested in different ways in the different countries. In England, for example, it was the economic contribution of the middle class that was particularly important at that time, above all their contribution to the so-called first industrial revolution. In France, it was the unwritten contract between the *noblesse de robe* and the top bourgeois bureaucrats under the rule of a centralizing absolutism, which fueled the Great Revolution. And in Germany, while commercial and financial barons as well as the bureaucracy of the absolutist states played an important role in facilitating change, it was the growing middle class of educated and semi-educated men that took the lead. A civil society that was initially local and timid was becoming a force to be reckoned with in Germany, too. Dozens of periodicals were published in these days, most of them staying afloat only a few months, covering every possible topic from literature, philosophy, economics, and statistics, to science, technology, and the new "science of man." They grappled with new subjects, had a clear stand on any given issue, and gradually created a new vocabulary to suit their purposes and facilitate communication. The image of a static and backward German society as seen from the perspective of either the French or the Industrial Revolution, is misleading. Despite the relative political calm in the various German states in the late eighteenth and early nineteenth centuries and the sluggish rate of economic growth, Germany too was undergoing a fundamental transformation. The mountaintops rising over the seemingly tranquil surface of this obedient and provincial society were the great idealist philosophers along with the authors and poets who produced what were soon to become the classics of German culture. Enlightenment in Berlin took its own special course. Weimar was a magnet for theatergoers and lovers of literature; Jenna was the hometown of witty conversation and a meeting place for readers and writers of the new romantic poetry. Vienna in the late eighteenth century hosted a group of musicians whose work feeds our culture to this very day. And all these were milestones in the emergence of a fairly large stratum of educated citizenry, indicating the approach of great changes and pushing them along.

The Jews came from a different background and their story had other features, yet they too were active participants in this process since its inception. Their entry into bourgeois society took place concurrently with its emergence; it was not merely a matter of adaptation or their absorption of

[9] Jürgen Habermas, *The Structural Transformation of the Public Sphere*, Cambridge, MA, MIT Press, 1989.

German norms and values. Assimilation, which is so prominent in any discussion of German Jewish history, did not begin as a process of imitation, nor was it ever solely dependent on the good will of non-Jews. Above all, it was based on upward mobility and the active participation of Jews in the construction of a new social class previously a nonexistent creature: the modern German bourgeoisie. The conditions for entry that were applied to Jews and non-Jews alike were highly fluid. "Belonging" was based on an invisible and subtle symbolic network. Moreover, those who were responsible for defining and controlling entry continuously changed the rules and the prerequisites. Indeed, perhaps only Kafka's fable of the castle properly describes this process in all its complexity and finally also in all its hopelessness.

The German *Bürgertum* was never a legally defined estate within the *ancient régime*, nor was it an economic "class," as it was argued later on. Above all, it was the social vehicle of a certain culture that was characterized by its shared moral values and social norms and was defined by a lifestyle whose strict rules applied to anyone wishing to "enter."[10] But even so, no single category, such as property, income, or professional prestige, was ever sufficient to characterize the new bourgeoisie. While it is impossible to define it in strictly economic terms, it is apparent that its members could never be indifferent to economic achievement. To maintain a bourgeois lifestyle, one needed a considerable permanent income. The culture of the bourgeoisie was just as dependent on economic prosperity as the previously dominant culture of the aristocracy. Even if economic success was not the heart of the matter, it was indispensable for social climbing. It was indispensable but often not enough. Because the standards were always changing, it was never quite clear how much *Besitz* or *Bildung* was necessary,. And Jews repeatedly experienced rebuff even when they seemed to possess both in abundance.

Rahel Levin, better known as Rahel Varnhagen, or just Rahel, was the daughter of a Jewish Berlin merchant. Aided by the income she shared with her mother after her father's death, Rahel financed one of Berlin's most prominent social salons in the 1790s. This was undoubtedly a very costly enterprise. In addition, she traveled extensively and in lavish style to other

[10] These points are discussed in great detail in the relevant literature in German. For an example, see the translated essays in Jürgen Kocka and Allen Mitschell (eds.), *Bourgeois Society in Nineteenth-Century Europe*, Oxford and Providence, RI, Berg, 1993. A full bibliography, concentrating on the Jewish case, is now available in Andreas Gotzmann, Rainer Liedtke, and Till van Rahden (eds.), *Juden, Bürger, Deutsche. Zur Geschichte von Vielfalt und Differenz 1800–1933*, Tübingen, Mohr Siebeck, 2001, pp. 419–32.

cities and various resorts, associating there with the "best circles" – the local aristocrats, artists, writers, and theater enthusiasts. Rahel constantly lived beyond her means until finally, with her mother's death in 1809, her fortune sank so low that the woman who always delighted in her multiple contacts was soon forced back onto her limited and exclusively Jewish acquaintances. Even her circle of correspondents, with whom she maintained frequent and intensive contacts for many years, as was customary at the time, was suddenly "reduced" to Jews only.[11] For Rahel, who was an independent and ambitious woman, this was a harsh blow. After her glorious days, she was now experiencing both disappointment and humiliation. But these were inevitable under the circumstances. The half-open bourgeois society, or "semi-neutral" as it was termed by Jacob Katz, was by then ready to accept Jews, indeed even Jewesses, only on the condition that they had everything: money, education, talent, and social brilliance. And it was certainly not willing to offer them any special concessions. Impoverished aristocrats may have been allowed to keep their social status, at least for a while, but impoverished Jews, let alone impoverished and not particularly pretty Jewesses, such as Rahel, were promptly excluded.[12]

We can look at the fate of another successful Jew a half-century later, the banker Gerson Bleichröder, in order to view from another perspective the role of wealth in the process of entry. After being present as a guest of honor in Versailles at the creation of the new *Kaiserreich* in January 18, 1871, Bleichröder returned triumphantly to Berlin decorated with the Iron Cross of the second order. "He was Berlin's most renowned private banker and one of its wealthiest citizens; he was Bismarck's adviser and the counselor of much of the elite."[13] But, as his biographer, Fritz Stern, comments, even at that time "it was easier for a poor man to become rich than for a rich man to become honorable." Indeed, like Rahel, Bleichröder aspired to enter not merely into the *Bürgertum* but into the highest social circles in the land: a mixed elite where not only Jewish but also many Christian *Bürger* were considered parvenus. His life, successes, and disappointments could indeed serve as an example for what a Jew could achieve but also for what he could not; it was a

[11] On Rahel see Hannah Arendt, *Rahel Varnhagen. The Life of a Jewess*, London, East and West Library, 1957. Compare also Hannah Arendt, *The Origins of Totalitarianism*, New York, Harcourt, Brace, 1951, the 1964 paperback edition, pp. 56–67.

[12] See chap. 4 in Katz. *Out of the Ghetto*, as well as Deborah Herz, *Jewish Society in Old Regime Berlin*, New Haven and London, Yale University Press, 1988.

[13] Fritz R. Stern, *Gold and Iron: Bismarck, Bleichröder, and the Building of the German Empire*, New York, A.A. Knopf, 1977, p. 164.

cautionary tale about the limited efficacy of wealth, of the things that all the money in the world could not buy.

Wealth was indispensable, but it was definitely not enough. There were many doors it could not open. Daniel Itzig, a Berlin minter and banker who received extensive privileges in the city in the 1760s and was formally naturalized a full Prussian citizen in 1791, was made an object of admiration and pride for many Jews, but he had never managed to enter the heart of Berlin's high society. It was Moses Mendelssohn, an observant Jew from Dessau who had come to Berlin in 1743 with most modest means, who eventually became a veritable "star" in the world of German *Bildung*. But his entry, too, could only proceed up to a certain point. The laws governing this process were never clear. They were constantly changing. There was always more than one way to achieve the goal, but it was never possible to know exactly how things would run their course. The main difficulty was in anticipating where new obstacles would crop up.

b. Language and Proper Behavior

To appreciate the scope of the Jews' efforts to "enter," let us expose the ambivalent demands placed on them on their "way to the top" beyond those related to wealth and property and even beyond the formal requirements of *Bildung*. Interestingly, it was usually the state bureaucracy that in Prussia as well as in the Habsburg territories and in southwestern Germany decided on these demands, albeit rarely in explicit terms. In the atmosphere of the old, so-called Enlightened Absolutism, high-level bureaucrats saw themselves not only as guardians of the state who were responsible for its functioning and prosperity but also as the avant-garde of Enlightenment. They too were an element of the new *Bildungsbürgertum* while serving as its representatives vis-à-vis the state. According to them, it was precisely the new *Bildungsbürger* alone among the underprivileged that the state had to accommodate, and the sooner the better. They were to turn from submissive and powerless subjects into free and active citizens who had a say in decisions concerning their future as well as the future of their new, reforming state. Some bureaucrats were willing to grant rights to other groups, too, even to the Jews, but they always made sure to stipulate at least one clear precondition: All those wishing to enter had to undergo a comprehensive process of *Verbesserung* (improvement). They had to adapt to the intellectual and ethical ideals of the reformers and accept the code of behavior that was typical of their bourgeois environment.

I already alluded to Christian Wilhelm Dohm's book, *Über die bürgerliche Verbesserung der Juden*, which was published in 1781; it was no doubt a classic of its kind.[14] It was a work infused with the educational optimism of the Enlightenment and an unwavering belief in the beneficial effects of an enlightened environment. Other bureaucratic blueprints for "improvement" were equally infused with this spirit. They all shared the assumption that becoming bourgeois was the basic prerequisite for Jewish emancipation and agreed on the four key elements that were to be set before the Jews as preconditions for their *Verbürgerlichung*: a reform of the community's occupational structure, full acquisition and usage of the German language, adoption – indeed, absorption – of the ideals of learning (*Bildung*), and compliance with the formative bourgeois ethos and its pattern of moral behavior (*Sittlichkeit*).

Much has been made of the demand for "productivization," namely, the challenge set before the Jews to take up so-called "productive" occupations and relinquish their traditional roles as small traders and moneylenders. This issue was customarily stipulated as a precondition for emancipation. However, it was rather secondary for most reformers, and despite some measures attempting to encourage its implementation, it was never actually pursued by the various German governments as a realistic policy. The Jews, for their part, were likewise content with the lip service they paid almost ritually to this matter ever since it had been raised. In the mostly rural environment of pre-industrial Central Europe, there was no substitute for either the door-to-door peddling services provided by Jews or for their ability to offer financial help for needy individuals and hard-pressed governments. In an era of market expansion, accelerated urbanization, and massive economic restructuring, it would have been odd for the Jews to relinquish these occupations just as they were becoming more crucial and in ever-growing demand. Thus, the calls for productivization remained a sanctimonious hope. The Jews had never seriously considered taking to agriculture at a time when an increasing number of those employed in this sector were deserting it. They had no intentions of becoming artisans when even traditional craftsmen were often looking for other, more lucrative occupations. In these early phases of industrialization there was no point in pushing the Jews into traditional occupations. Authorities everywhere were opting for more feasible reforms, indeed, and concentrated on areas in which

---

[14] See Part II, Chapter 6, fn. 24.

government's interests were more generally consistent with the interests of the Jews.[15]

As early as 1739, Jews in the principality of Hessen-Kassel had been ordered to use only German in their business transactions. Both Yiddish, the normal colloquial language among them, and Hebrew, the language of their more formal communication, were forbidden.[16] Yiddish in particular was apparently held suspect, even in this small German state and long before the issue of emancipation ever came up. Indeed, Yiddish was often seen as a language of secret business transactions at best, and the language of gangsters and thieves at worst. Joseph II's first *Toleranzpatent*, aimed at the Jews in his Bohemian territories and promulgated in 1782, stipulated that Jews were to achieve full mastery of German and use it exclusively in all public occasions within two and a half years. Similar articles were later introduced into all other *Toleranzpatente*, and in the one drafted for Galicia, Jews were also forbidden to use Polish. In fact, any language other than German was considered suspect by the bureaucracy. The main goal was surely to strengthen central government control, but at the same time, the bureaucracy was also seeking to create a common cultural ground across the Empire to promote its enlightened educational ideals. In many of the German states in those days we find this typical combination: bureaucratic blueprints for strengthening the state in the guise of enlightened, mostly educational reforms. In Baden, the success of the constitutional edict of 1809 with regard to the Jews was primarily, though not exclusively, measured by the degree to which Jews in that Grand Duchy were taking on German family names and using German colloquially and in writing. Language was also a central theme in the Prussian edict of 1812, which later came to be known as the Edict of Emancipation, and the stipulations in this regard reappeared virtually unchanged in the 1833 legislation concerning the status of Jews in the province of Posen. There it was also made a precondition for naturalization and for receiving the crucial right of emigration.[17]

---

[15] For the years 1848–1871, see Toury, *Soziale und politische Geschichte*, 69–99, and his appendices A and J. For the years 1840–1860, compare the statistical data in Henry Wassermann, "Jews, Bürgertum and Bürgerliche Gesellschaft in a Liberal Era in Germany (1840–1880)" [Hebrew], Diss. Hebrew University of Jerusalem 1978, chap. 3.

[16] Toury, "Der Eintritt der Juden," 177.

[17] See Reinhard Rürup, "Die Emanzipation der Juden in Baden," in *Emanzipation und Antisemitismus: Studien zur 'Judenfrage' der bürgerlichen Gesellschaft*, Göttingen, Vandenhoeck & Ruprecht, 1975, pp. 37–73, especially 49; on Prussia, see Ismar Freund, *Die Emanzipation der Juden in Preußen unter besonderer Berücksichtigung des Gesetzes vom 11. März 1812*, 2 vols., Berlin, M. Poppelauer, 1912; and the Introduction

The language question was seriously discussed in Jewish enlightened circles, too. Yiddish was no more popular among Jewish *Maskilim* (enlightened scholars) than among German bureaucrats. The circle around Moses Mendelssohn in Berlin was unwavering in its opposition to the hated, "indecent," and "corrupt jargon," lashing out at Jews for disdaining both proper Hebrew and proper German. Initially, many of the early *Maskilim* aimed at the revival of Hebrew usage among Jews so as to provide them with a "pure" language that was equal in status to the languages used by other peoples of culture and sophistication. The Hebrew monthly, *Ha'Meassef* (The Collector), was first published in 1784 in Königsberg, then in Berlin, and finally, between 1794 and its closure in 1797, in Dessau.[18] Even Mendelssohn's translation of the Pentateuch, presenting the original Hebrew text alongside his new German translation, printed in Hebrew letters, was probably no less intent on bringing about an improvement in the Jewish community's use of Hebrew than on the introduction of German.[19] It was only toward the beginning of the nineteenth century that this duality was finally dissolved. High German, and in its most perfect, hypercorrect form, was to be the language of the Jewish *Bildungsbürgertum*, and German proficiency became an unequivocal demand directed at anyone wishing to join it.

But the use of Yiddish among German Jews never ceased. Continuous waves of Jewish immigration from Posen, Silesia, Galicia, and Russia persistently revived it, despite the fact that, for the local Jewish bourgeoisie, this was a constant source of embarrassment. It seems that in early twentieth-century Vienna, Jakob Wassermann was no less irritated by the Yiddish of many of his co-religionists than was Moses Mendelssohn a century and a half earlier in Berlin. However, even those who resented the use of Yiddish, regarding it as a mark of "otherness" and an assertion

in Monika Richarz (ed.), *Jüdisches Leben in Deutschland. Selbstzeugnisse zur Sozialgeschichte 1780–1871*, Stuttgart, Deutsche Verlags-Anstalt, 1976, pp. 19–26.

[18] On *Ha'Meassef* see Michael A. Meyer, *The Origins of the Modern Jew: Jewish Identity and European Culture 1749–1824*, Detroit, MI, Wayne State University Press, 1967, pp. 115–9; Walter Röll, "The Kassel 'Ha'Meassef' of 1799: An Unknown Contribution to the Haskalah," in Jehuda Reinharz and Walter Schatzberg (eds.), *The Jewish Response to German Culture: From the Enlightenment to the Second World War*, Hanover and London, University Press of New England, 1985, pp. 32–50. For the intellectual background of this periodical, compare Selma Stern-Taeubler, "The First Generation of Emancipated Jews," *Leo Baeck Institute Yearbook* XV, 1970, 3–40.

[19] See Julius Carlebach, "Deutsche Juden und der Säkularisierungsprozess in der Erziehung," in Liebeschütz and Paucker, *Das Judentum in der deutschen Umwelt*, 55–94, especially 73–6.

of "nonbelonging," were often unable to set themselves completely free of its linguistic hold. Processes of linguistic shift are notoriously long and complex. After all, the normative language eventually accepted as the standard German had reached this status through continuous competition with a multitude of dialects and local vernaculars, and it was no earlier than the second quarter of the eighteenth century that it finally became the norm in Germany. Only gradually did *Hochdeutsch* become the spoken language among the educated. Its use eventually came to mark, outwardly as well as inwardly, the individual's sense of belonging. In the context of political, religious, and social diversity that was characteristic of the Holy Roman Empire, German was a unifying element that was crucial for the identity of the *Bildungsbürgertum*. Local dialects, in turn, were the sign of lower social status and lacking a sense of national belonging. In North Germany, for example, it was particularly difficult to overcome the local jargon, and as late as the 1830s, nationalists were attacking the use of the local *Plattdeutch* in terms very similar to those applied by the Jews to discredit Yiddish.[20]

Yet there must have been something particularly irritating about "the language of the Jews." In an article in one of those bourgeois periodicals flooding the market at the time, published in 1804 in the Hamburg-based *Journal zur Geschichte der Zeit, der Sitten und des Geschmaks* (Journal of Contemporary History, Manners and Good Taste), the author laments that[21]

Viewed from every possible angle, I find it entirely incomprehensible why our Jews in their large majority should persist so obstinately on speaking the language of the country in which they have their homes, the language that has become their mother tongue, in a mutilated form that is most offensive to the ear. Even when they speak the correct language without any alien admixture, they do it in an accent that is no less unpleasant than the mutilation of language itself. . . .

The most striking and influentail text in this context is Richard Wagner's *Das Judentum in der Musik* (The Jews in Music), which was first published – anonymously – in 1850. Having expressed his repugnance toward the Jews, complaining of their external appearance, about which there is something "insurmountably and unpleasantly foreign," Wagner

---

[20] Peter Freimark, "Language Behaviour and Assimilation: The Situation of the Jews in Northern Germany in the First Half of the 19th Century," *Leo Baeck Institute Yearbook* XXIV, 1979, 157–77.

[21] Ibid., 164.

turns to what he considers an even more important matter, namely, the question of language. Here is what he had to say about it:[22]

The Jew speaks the language of the nation in whose midst he dwells from generation to generation, but he speaks it always as an alien... [He] talks the modern European languages merely as learnt, and not as mother tongues... A language, with its expression and its evolution, is not the work of scattered units, but of an historical community: only he who has unconsciously grown up within the bond of this community, takes also a share in its creations. But the Jew has stood outside the pale of any such community, stood solitarily with his Jehova in a splintered, soilless stock, to which all self-sprung evolution must stay denied, just as even the peculiar (Hebraic) language of that stock has been preserved for him merely as a thing defunct.

For those who refused to take such an outspokenly hostile and pessimistic stand on this matter, the acquisition of High German came to be the entry ticket into the German *Kulturnation*. Participation in the discourse about science, art, and public affairs carried on in this common language was the key measurement of the will and ability to belong. To be sure, the Jews, as well as many other lower and often rural social elements in Germany, had often remained outside the limits of this discourse not because of any concrete language barrier, but because they did not share that whole world of reference and communication associated with it. Although we do have some reports of Jews visiting the theater and getting involved in setting up public libraries or literary societies during the eighteenth century, this could have only been the concern of very few at that time.[23] Even by the end of that century, a major effort was needed to introduce Jews to the language of educated society and interest them in the consumption of German literary products. The enthusiasm that later became a passion for generations of German Jews began as a marginal phenomenon. There were indeed those who hired private language tutors for their sons and even their daughters. As early as 1781,

---

[22] Richard Wagner, *Judaism in Music*, Reedy, WV, Liberty Bell Publications, 1978, p. 6 (originally under pseudonym in *Neue Zeitschrift für Musik*, September 1850). See also Wagner's "Über das Dirigieren," in *Sämtliche Schriften und Dichtungen*, Leipzig, Breitkopf & Härtel, 1871–1911, vol. 7. The text contains several antisemitic comments by Wagner (e.g., on pp. 266–7), but these, unlike the attack in *Das Judentum in der Musik*, have gone practically unnoticed.

[23] On the early Enlightenment among German Jews, see Asriel Shochat, *Der Ursprung der jüdischen Aufklärung in Deutschland*, Frankfurt, Campus Verlag, 2000 (originally in Hebrew, 1960), and Jacob Katz, *Tradition and Crisis: Jewish Society at the End of the Middle Ages*, New York, Schocken Books, 1971 (originally in Hebrew, 1958), pp. 245–59. For a comprehensive view see Shmuel Feiner, *The Jewish Enlightenment*.

David Friedländer, one of Mendelssohn's closest students and associates, founded the Free School in Berlin, intent on providing secular education (mostly German and arithmetic), in addition to religious instruction, for its needy pupils. And similar schools were then established in Frankfurt, Breslau, Dessau, and Hamburg, although, unlike the Berlin school, these were usually no charitable institutions. On the contrary, they constituted a new type of school for the children of the rising Jewish *Bürgertum*, training a new generation of eager Jews who were to be proficient in religious studies but also willing and ready to take on the challenge of attending the regular German *Gymnasium* or even the university.[24] The *Toleranzpatente* in the Habsburg Empire, like many stipulations made in other contemporary legal documents, ordered the Jews either to open new schools for themselves or to send their children to the general public schools established at the time. Thus the process was simultaneously carried out voluntarily from "below" and by order from "above." The teaching of German became central to Jewish education, and by 1822, even the traditional Talmud Torah in Hamburg, a conservative institution established in 1805, introduced German-language evening classes for its students. Mastery of the German language had become a *sine qua non*. Anyone wishing to enter the bourgeoisie, Jews and non-Jews alike, was obliged to comply.

Enlightened Jews and non-Jews found a common platform on other minimum requirements for belonging to the *Bürgertum*. In addition to the language issue, they were convinced of the necessity to refine and improve their social manners. Here was another key aspect of the acculturation process, and it was, like language, equally adopted from below and commanded from above. Like the use of Yiddish, this too remained a relevant issue well into the twentieth century, kept alive by the continuous Jewish immigration from the East and the waves of migration from villages to towns. Efforts at acculturation, of assimilating the cultural aspects of the non-Jewish world, found clear expression in the first German-language Jewish newspaper, *Sulamith*, which began to appear in 1806. Its editors never tired of exhorting Jews to adopt German *Bildung* and *Sittlichkeit*.

---

[24] On Friedländer, see Meyer, *The Origins of the Modern Jew*, 57–84. On the new Jewish schools and Jewish education, see Mordechai Eliav, *Jewish Education in Germany during Enlightenment and Emancipation* [Hebrew], Jerusalem, Ha'Sochnut Ha'Yehudit, 1961, pp. 71–141. A shorter German version is available in the *Bulletin des Leo Baeck Instituts* 3, 1960, 207–15. On the Jews' place in the general educational system, there are mainly works dealing with specific towns or areas. See the detailed bibliography in Gotzmann et al. *Juden, Bürger, Deutsche*, 263–98.

Its professed goals were the development of Jewish capacity for *Bildung* and the encouragement of their "proper conduct." In 1807, the paper examined the conditions of the Frankfurt Jews, judging their "degree of enlightenment" by the standards of their cleanliness, the propriety of their manners, and their sexual mores and attitudes.[25] Moreover, *Sittlichkeit*, like the use of language, was not merely a personal matter. In the process of becoming bourgeois, the community as a whole had to learn to conform to the standards of the bourgeoisie. Appeals for more respectable praying habits, especially for putting a stop to swaying and outward expressions of passion during service, were made part of the general communal exertion to "adjust." Often, as in Sachsen-Weimar-Eisenach, a government edict forbade "improper" behavior in synagogues while both the community and its leadership exerted considerable pressure on anyone reluctant to relinquish old, "faulty" habits. Leopold Zunz, who was involved in such activities as a young man, found it necessary to urge Jewish worshippers to put an end to "wailing" during prayer. Here, again, the convergence of the ideals of the enlightened bureaucracy and of Jewish reformers of all kinds could be clearly observed. It was a convergence based on an emerging bourgeois culture, to whose norms the Jews both contributed and were required to conform. As "foreigners," they were probably even more committed to these norms than ordinary German citizens.

Like the standard German language, the new bourgeois code of behavior began to take final shape only in the latter half of the eighteenth century, and its acceptance necessitated a concerted educational effort, not only among the Jews. Except for those manners that the middle class adopted from the aristocracy and which were therefore generally familiar to the higher classes of Germans, the details of the new code of behavior remained fluid for a long time. To make things even more difficult, this code included not only rules pertaining to outward behavior but also those that defined an inner ethos. It was an ethos promoting the values of frugality, the strict fulfillment of duty, and constant restraint of passion. Anyone attempting to become part of the new bourgeois culture had to learn to abide by these rules, and this for many meant a radical departure from previous patterns of behavior. In addition, the newly prescribed conventions were never completely unequivocal. They often

---

[25] See George L. Mosse, "Jewish Emancipation between Bildung and Respectablity," in Reinharz and Schatzberg (eds.), *Jewish Response*, 1–16; see also Mosse's *Nationalism and Sexuality: Respectability and Abnormal Sexuality in Modern Europe*, New York, H. Fertig, 1985, pp. 1–22.

remained ambivalent, being shaped and reshaped and continuously re-articulated. Under these circumstances, the legitimacy of particular rules could occasionally be contested, but most particularly it was always possible to criticize the extent of compliance to it by individuals or groups.

Thus, although Jewish mastery of German was more often than not beyond reproach, there was incessant pressure on Jews to adjust not only their language proficiency but also their presumably foreign intonation. Although Jewish behavior was usually impeccable, or at least equal to that of most other members of the educated middle class, there were repeated complaints about their impropriety. Though possibly no other group in Germany had so fully internalized the requirements of the dominant bourgeois code or tried so hard to conform, they were repeatedly branded as outsiders. Faced with these attitudes, it was difficult for the Jews to accurately evaluate their own success. Some of them were therefore never free from an embarrassing sense of insecurity and self-criticism. Even a writer of Franz Kafka's caliber often alluded to his doubts about the legitimacy of his own use of the German language.[26] Here, too, lay the ground for the constant unease of local Jews at the plainly nonbourgeois behavior of Jewish immigrants from the east, often their direct relatives. Some of Arthur Schnitzler's and Georg Hermann's characters in works from the late 1890s poignantly express the depth of their pain at the realization that their behavior was seen by others as "a Jewish matter," a daunting proof of their failure to assimilate.

Two other issues illustrate the problems associated with Jewish acculturation: the relatively simple, though immanently paradigmatic problem of dress and fashion, and the more fundamental matter of theological and religious reforms. Anthropologist Hermann Bausinger has pertinently discussed the history of the hat in German bourgeois culture.[27] Adjusting to the prevalent custom was a particularly vexing problem for the Jews. Because head covering was and still is such a long-standing Jewish religious habit, Jews had great difficulties participating in the *Bürgers'* sophisticated hat-on/hat-off rituals. Eventually, the need to adapt in all matters of outward appearance within the public sphere in Germany was so critical that even orthodox Jews felt obliged to conform. Early in the nineteenth century, they began to give up head covering in government offices or city cafés, while on the streets, where their

[26] Compare Part I, Chapter 2.
[27] Hermann Bausinger, "Bürgerlichkeit und Kultur," in Kocka (ed.), *Bürger und Bürgerlichkeit*, 121–42, especially 124–30.

custom luckily coincided with common practice, they could keep their tradition intact. By the second half of the century, the uncovering of the head under all roofed spaces, in accordance with bourgeois style, was the rule everywhere, even among nonreforming Jews. Some rabbis even allowed bareheaded oath taking in courts, if the judge categorically demanded it.[28] This seemingly marginal aspect sheds unexpected light on the entire process of acculturation and on the uniqueness of the Jewish experience of it. The problem of accommodating new and unfamiliar customs of dress and head covering was surely not unique to the Jews. Non-Jews from various regions, and mostly those migrating from rural areas, were often entangled in the web of changing rules of etiquette. But even in this respect, it was more complicated for Jews. Due to the religious nature of many routines in Jewish life, they were repeatedly faced with having to make principled decisions whenever they attempted to adapt. On every trivial matter, an explicit discussion and a prescribed solution, often a compromise, were called for, both on the individual and the collective levels.

Similar problems arose in another sphere, one that was indeed much more fundamental and touched on deeper levels of Jewish life. Acculturation in the sphere of religion often required the application of two basic strategies. On the social level, emphasis had to be shifted from the religious practices in public to those performed at home, and on the theological level, a parallel shift was to be carried out from the collectivity to the individual. Reformers who emphasized Judaism's concept of duty and morality over its legal, ritualistic, and Halachic dimensions undertook both these shifts. The early *Haskalah* (Jewish Enlightenment) firmly believed in the need to reform Jewish life through absorbing bourgeois notions but without deserting the sense of shared Jewish fate and culture. By the beginning of the nineteenth century, it was already clear that emancipation would jeopardize the values of Jewish communality. Judaism then underwent a transformation very similar to the one experienced by both Catholicism and Protestantism in Germany, a process in which individual faith and ethics came to take precedence over joint, communal presentations of religiosity.[29]

---

[28] Mordechai Breuer, *Modernity within Tradition: The Social History of Orthodox Jewry in Imperial Germany*, New York, Columbia University Press, 1992 (originally in German, 1986), pp. 8–9, 255–8.

[29] For a full and concise summary of these changes, see Thomas Nipperdey, *Germany from Napoleon to Bismarck, 1800–1866*, Princeton, NJ, Princeton University Press, 1996 (originally in German, 1983), chap. IV, 1.

The need to bridge the widening gap between religion and the emerging national culture was for a long time a major problem for non-Jews in Germany, too. The Catholic Church held an ongoing internal debate concerning the introduction of *Bildung* into the Church. The absorption of certain enlightened concepts seemed to have accentuated the need to develop Catholicism away from dogma, institutions, and authority and in the direction of humanism and a more "inward," personal religiosity. For Protestants, in turn, the search for an acceptable synthesis of religion and liberal values became a major theme during the early nineteenth century. Tendencies to stress the importance of the pious heart, the inner feeling, and the experience of sin and repentance were made ever more predominant now. Schleiermacher's reformulation of Protestantism had a deep influence indeed on all theological considerations at that time. His romantic solution to the dilemma of religion in the "Age of Reason" had left its mark on a century of Protestant theology. But while romantic concepts of religiosity were still debated among Christian reformers, they were slowly incorporated into the Jewish world, and not by radical thinkers only. Such prudent and moderate reformers as Leopold Zunz and even Samson Raphael Hirsch, the future founder of Neo-Orthodoxy, were deeply concerned about these matters.[30] The stress on the individual's inner faith on the one hand and the insistence on the ethical character of the community on the other were considered novel in the context of Judaism. But in view of parallel developments in Christianity and particularly as a response to the demands of entry into the bourgeoisie, the adoption of a new religious style seemed almost inevitable. Reforming Jewish preachers often attended Schleiermacher's sermons, as he may well have occasionally listened to theirs, and their concept of Judaism was fundamentally transformed in the process. It was gradually made more palatable to a whole generation of educated Jews who were seeking to become an integral part of the *Bidungsbürgertum*. The new religiosity was consistent with their changing cultural tastes and the relentless demands of their new lifestyle.

While changes in Jewish community lifestyle and even in the spirit of Judaism paralleled those taking place in the wider society, they do,

---

[30] On Zunz, see Meyer, *The Origins of the Modern Jew*, 44–182; Ismar Schorsch, "History as Consolation," in his *From Text to Context: The Turn to History in Modern Judaism*, Hanover and London, University Press of New England, 1994, pp. 334–44. On Hirsch, see David Sorkin, *The Transformation of German Jewry 1780–1840*, New York, Oxford University Press, 1987, pp. 156–71; Breuer, *Modernity within Tradition*, passim and especially 55–89

once again, present us with a particularly extreme case of the general phenomenon. By the beginning of the nineteenth century, Judaism was often considered a strictly legalistic religion. More than the two other monotheistic religions, ran the argument, it relied heavily on Talmudic law, namely on a rigorous corpus of rules and regulations. Thus, in the Jewish case, a religious reform in the spirit of *Bildung* and romanticism seemed a more radical break with the past than in other cases. It was a deviation from tradition that was much deeper than in both the Catholic and the Protestant contexts. Indeed, for some of the early reformers and their followers, the dilemmas presented by the need to conform may have eventually, despite all contrary arguments, led to conversion.[31] For those who remained within the fold, it meant a life-long inner struggle accompanying the efforts at adaptation. Overall, however, German Jews who were in the process of becoming bourgeois managed to generate their own modern religious identity. They created their own mix of *Bildung* and *Sittlichkeit* and formulated a new version of Judaism, one that was more domestic than communal and more ethical than legal – making room for their new existence as "German citizens of the Jewish Faith."

c. Advantages and Disadvantages

The process through which German Jews in the late eighteenth century and the early nineteenth century became bourgeois was similar to that experienced by others. All social climbers and all those moving from the periphery into the center were obliged to accept some changes in their worldview, lifestyle, and value system. Despite the similarities, however, the Jewish experience was unique not merely in degree or scope. The Jews had some initial advantages as well as disadvantages in this context. While they often faced insurmountable obstacles, they could occasionally benefit from unexpectedly advantageous starting points. To begin with, emancipation carried for them an unprecedented message. After all, Jews had been the ultimate "other" of European Christian society for generations, and those among them who wished to overcome their isolation and join the surrounding world were almost invariably forced to use the ultimate tool, namely, to convert. By contrast, emancipation suddenly provided them with an entry permit into non-Jewish society without having to relinquish Judaism, stipulating an altogether different set of demands. It raised the need for a new kind of synthesis that had to include both Jewish

---

[31] Compare Chapter 13.

and non-Jewish elements, mixing advantageous traits from both cultural arsenals. They had to forge new tools that would enable them to press forward the process of becoming bourgeois. This was an extremely difficult and complex project. At the same time, however, it was a challenge holding great promise and prospects.

Everywhere in Germany, Jews enjoyed some key advantages on the road to success. Their accumulated experience in the world of trade and finance was surely one such valuable asset. But gradually other advantages outside the economic sphere were made apparent, too. It is probably unnecessary to take as extreme a position as that taken by Julius Carlebach, who in a 1978 article argued that the corpus of Jewish religious tradition included "all the basic norms and values which eventually became the universally accepted ideology of West-European *Bürgerlichkeit.*"[32] However, this corpus certainly included a number of such norms and values that were long a part of Jewish everyday life. Many of the demands now facing anyone wishing to become bourgeois seemed fully consistent with elements of age-old Jewish traditions. Thus, some Jewish customs were smoothly integrated in the new bourgeois ethos. It is difficult to ascertain the importance of moderation, frugality, cleanliness, or industry in the old Jewish lifestyle of the pre-bourgeois era. It can, however, be argued that, because such values were religiously prescribed for Jews, the demands of the new bourgeois world were more tolerable for them. They seem to have had little or no difficulty in accommodating and internalizing the principal requirements that had become the hallmarks of bourgeois culture.

In some areas, the effectiveness of old Jewish habits can be demonstrated statistically. Even in pre-modern times, for example, the child mortality rate among Jews was considerably lower than that of the general population. The exact reasons for this have not been determined. More responsible childcare and closer parental supervision may have been involved. In any case, the new bourgeois attitude toward children, no longer regarding them as a cheap and available labor force, as had been common in traditionally rural areas, but as heirs and bearers of bourgeois culture, was clearly in line with pre-existent Jewish practice. The traditional emphasis on children's education was similarly useful in the process of becoming bourgeois. From this point of view, even the "Cheder," that

---

[32] See Julius Carlebach, "The Forgotten Connection: Women and Jews in the Conflict between Enlightenment and Romanticism," *Leo Baeck Institute Yearbook* XXIV, 1979, 107–38, especially 115–8; the quote is on 116.

religious elementary school that was so vehemently attacked by enlightened reformers, had played a positive role. The Jewish literacy rate was remarkably high long before emancipation, an achievement that must be attributed at least in part to the tyrannical teaching methods of that Cheder, where generations of lower class Jews acquired learning habits and a basic respect for, or perhaps only awe of, the learned. Everyday customs within the traditional Jewish family also may have helped ease Jewish entry into the *Bildungsbürgertum*. In fact, during much of the nineteenth century, Jewish family life was considered exemplary and was celebrated even by non-Jewish spokesmen of the *Bürgertum*. The traditional customs of private and intimate collectivity that was so characteristic of Jewish homes fit perfectly into the image of the family cultivated by the German bourgeoisie at the time. In their move toward life as part of non-Jewish society, Jews were sometimes, no doubt, forced to change some elements of their lifestyle, but they usually did not have to revolutionize them altogether.[33]

Along with these obvious advantages, Jews also faced some grave disadvantages. The most formidable among them was surely their mark as "others," the memory of their long existence as a separate people that made their loyalty and patriotism forever untrustworthy. While the German Enlightenment had been primarily cosmopolitan in tone and attitude, even as early as the mid-eighteenth century, when the modern debate on emancipation had just began, love of the fatherland was placed high in the order of virtues that the new bourgeois was obliged to exhibit.[34] George Mosse has argued that patriotism in its new, national variety was indispensable for the development of a bourgeois ethos from its inception. In his opinion, it was because only it was capable of channeling the emotional and sexual energies of contemporary young men into the safe haven of a nationalist pathos and collective enthusiasm, thereby restraining any manifestation of *unsittlichkeit* (impropriety).[35] In any case, first patriotism and then nationalism undoubtedly played a major role in forming the self-awareness of the German *Bürger* in general and of the *Bildungsbürger* in particular. Here the Jews were faced with an intractable obstacle. Despite the great respect he enjoyed from his non-Jewish surroundings, even Moses Mendelssohn's patriotism was apparently not very

[33] See Wassermann, "Jews, Bürgertum and Bürgerliche Gesellschaft," 124–36.
[34] The classic work on the shift from cosmopolitan bourgeoisie to nationalism is by Friedrich Meinecke, *Weltbürgertum und Nationalstaat*, Munich, 1907 (English translation, *Cosmopolitanism and the National State*, Princeton, NJ, Princeton University Press, 1970).
[35] Compare Mosse, *Nationalism and Sexuality*, especially chap. 4.

convincing. His circle of Jewish *Maskilim* was primarily dedicated to the belief in the brotherhood of mankind and the universality of reason that they all shared. In the wake of the Napoleonic wars, just as the Jews were ready to display their loyalty, the newly developing concept of the nation was becoming ever more exclusive.

Enlightened Germans had always regarded themselves as champions of a single German nation whose collective culture transcended the borders of particular German states and served as the infrastructure of genuine national unity. Now they were gradually becoming responsible for safeguarding that nation's homogeneity by fighting off any manifestation of pluralism. Upward social mobility and entry into the bourgeoisie were eventually to be regarded as acts of assimilation into the nation. Any sign of particularism among the Jews, trivial as it may be, was construed as their failure to assimilate and proof of their defective national consciousness. Throughout the nineteenth century, they made incessant attempts to overcome this hurdle. The so-called Jewish census of 1916, which was presumably designed to examine the extent of Jewish participation in the war effort, was but the final blow dealt them just before the final collapse of the *Kaiserreich*. Jews felt that the census was aimed to show, once again, even at this crucial hour, their disloyalty and cowardice. To count them separately was seen as a deep humiliation, an attempt to exclude them from the national body just as they were spilling their blood in its defense. "It was the most shameful disgrace of our community since the emancipation, an uncondonnable shame," a Jewish journal wrote in retrospect.[36] Apparently, no act of heroism or sacrifice could ever eradicate their basic otherness.

Much earlier, however, the *Bildungsbürgertum*, which claimed to be principally open to all, revealed its ambivalence. In fact, it never opened its gates more than half-heartedly. And that did not change with time. Even as other popular subcultures in Germany were being accepted as legitimate under the influence of Romanticism and the social upheavals of rapid urbanization during the first half of the nineteenth century, Jews continued to be regarded as outsiders. Nor did the realization that nation building could be achieved only through a slow evolutionary process rather than a violent revolutionary act help in their case. Yiddish, for example, continued to be mercilessly derided as a contemptible, repulsive jargon, while

---

[36] Quoted from Eva G. Reichmann, "Der Bewußtseinswandel der deutschen Juden," in Werner E. Mosse and Arnold Paucker (eds.), *Deutsches Judentum in Krieg und Revolution 1916–1923*, Tübingen, J.C.B. Mohr, 1971, p. 516.

local village dialects were upgraded in the spirit of romantic nationalism. The legalistic nature of the Jewish religion and the apparent oddity of everyday life under Halachic law continued to be viewed as reprehensible, even among those who accepted the principles of emancipation. And efforts by Jewish intellectuals to improve the reputation of Judaism, its unique traditions, customs, and manners, through the development of a *Wissenschaft des Judentum* (Science of Judaism), had failed to render the characteristics of Jewish "ethnic" culture as a whole legitimate or respectable. There was a constant clash between the Jews' long-standing sense of group solidarity and shared past and the relentless demands of German nationalism. While initially the tension did not seem very grave or hopeless, it did eventually exacerbate, and by the end of the century, the lines of its contour were clear and strictly defined.

For the Jews, becoming bourgeois never meant only a process of adjustment to the style and ethos of the non-Jewish society. For them it meant living *with* non-Jews as much as living *like* them. Assimilation had been a vehicle for achieving full membership in the surrounding society, not for total self-denial. The educated bourgeoisie, which seems to have set the terms for "entry" at least until the mid-nineteenth century, dictated, as an absolute minimum, that those wishing to join it had to become sufficiently and properly educated. It also established a whole new institutional structure into which new candidates must fit – a complex set of organizations, associations, clubs, and public and semi-public gatherings.[37] Previously banned from joining guilds or corporations, the Jews now made every effort to participate in the new organizational structure. Sources on this matter are scarce, but they leave no doubt as to the severity of the obstacles placed before the Jews in this area. The best initial research was surely Jacob Katz's study on the position of Jews in the European Masonic lodges.[38] Here, too, where the tenets of universalism, human equality, and

---

[37] The key article here is Thomas Nipperdey, "Verein als soziale Struktur in Deutchland im späten 18. und frühen 19. Jahrhunderts," which now appears in his *Gesellschaft, Kultur, Theorie. Gesammelte Aufsätze zur neueren Geschichte*, Göttingen, Vandenhoeck & Ruprecht, 1976, pp. 174–205. See also Nipperdey's *Germany from Napoleon to Bismarck*, chap. 2. Following Nipperdey, there has been much research on this topic. For a summary with a rich bibliography, but an emphasis on rural, mainly Catholic south German cases, see Oded Heilbronner, "The German Bourgeois Club as a political and social Structure in late Nineteenth and early Twentieth Centuries," *Continuity and Change* 13, 1998, 443–73.

[38] Jacob Katz, *Jews and Freemasons in Europe 1723–1939*, Cambridge, MA, Harvard University Press, 1970 (originally in Hebrew, 1968). See also, with clear divisions into periods of more or less openness, Stefan-Ludwig Hoffmann, *Die Politik der Geselligkeit. Freimauererlogen in deutschen Bürgergesellschaft, 1840–1918*, Göttingen,

religious tolerance were supposedly unshakable, Jews were never automatically accepted, surely not always and not without debate. At the
turn of the eighteenth century, Jews occasionally managed to join various bourgeois associations, mainly the literary societies sprouting across
Germany in the course of building a single national learned society. It
was at that time that Jews – and Jewesses – began to feature prominently
in the intellectual salons of Berlin, too. But, while historians found this
phenomenon fascinating and exotic, it was quite marginal at the time.
It involved a tiny group of Jewish or formerly Jewish men and women
who, for a brief period, took part in the life of the city's cultural elite as it
was attempting to break free of the conventions of class, gender, and all
other forms of prejudices. There was a ray of hope there, perhaps a sign
of things to come, but no model for contemporaries to imitate. Nowhere
else were the gates likewise opened to welcome the Jews. A crack in the
alienation wall could at times be traced and possibly even widened a bit
through persistent efforts, but nothing more.

This too was not a unique Jewish phenomenon. Based mainly on the
infrastructure of a common culture and perhaps a shared national ideology, the bourgeois associations were almost always restrictive, despite
their universalistic verbiage. Confessional barriers remained crucial, and
class distinctions were strictly kept. The majority of literary societies during the second half of the eighteenth century and into the nineteenth
normally excluded lower class elements, although they seldom openly
declared such policies. An exception was the statute of the local literary society in Aschaffenburg, which stipulated that "individuals of lower
rank" were not allowed.[39] Women were also systematically excluded from
all participation in the various bourgeois associations at the time. As in
the case of the Jews, exceptions were occasionally made, but they only
proved the rule.[40] Fluctuations in the degree of openness of these associations may be observed and analyzed across time. The position of rifle
clubs, sports and singing associations, and the like had no consistent
policy with regard to accepting Jews. On the whole, entry was made
more difficult during the patriotic wave at the time of the Napoleonic

Vandenhoeck & Ruprecht, 2000. In English, see his "Brothers or Strangers: Jews and
Freemasons in nineteenth-century Germany," *German History* 18, 2000, 143–61.
[39] Quoted in Marlies Stützel-Prüsener, "Die deutschen Lesegesellschaften im Zeitalter der
Aufklärung," in Otto Dann (ed.), *Lesegesellschaften und bürgerliche Emanzipation: Ein
europäischer Vergleich*, Munich, C.H. Beck, 1981, p. 77.
[40] Ute Fervert, *Women in German History: From Bourgeois Emancipation to Sexual
Liberation*, Oxford, Berg, 1989 (originally in German, 1986), pp. 4–5. See also the relevant bibliography there.

wars than during the heyday of the Enlightenment that preceded them. Later, in the 1840s and 1860s, which were relatively liberal periods, doors seemed to open with greater ease, while in the nationalistic 1880s the rules grew stricter once again.[41] At this point, however, the alternatives appeared much clearer and hints of the various possible strategies abound.

As early as 1800, there were three types of literary societies in Frankfurt am Main: mixed, for Christians only, and for Jews only. During the nineteenth century, Jews established separate associations of every kind, primarily in large cities but also in smaller towns and villages. They gradually learned to accept the closeness of bourgeois society, and since full entry for their likes seemed impossible, they had no choice but to establish their own societies. This was a tactic of "negative integration"[42] that was based on emulating the customs of the surrounding world while remaining within the confines of one's own collectivity.

Once again, such tactics were not reserved for Jews alone. Both women and workers reacted similarly to the barriers erected by the bourgeoisie. They, too, established parallel sets of associations through which they gave expression to their own bourgeois values. Members of such groups became bourgeois without becoming part of the bourgeoisie. Indeed, bourgeois society had managed to instill its values and principles among broad strata of the public, not just in Germany, without losing its selective, increasingly elitist, and, in many respects, strictly homogeneous character.[43] Although the rationale for not allowing Jews in was different from

---

[41] For this and the following discussion, see Wassermann, "Jews, Bürgertum and Bürgerliche Gesellschaft," 71–96. There is now research literature suggesting a considerable openness to Jews, as, for example, in the gymnastics clubs up until World War I. See Hartmut Becker, *Antisemitismus in der deutschen Turnerschaft*, Köln, Sankt Augustin, 1980. For good examples of the workings of local associations, see, i.e., Till van Raden, *Juden und andere Breslauer: Die Beziehungen zwishcen Juden, Protestanten und Katholiken in einer deutschen Grossstadt von 1869 bis 1925*, Göttingen, Vandenhoeck & Ruprecht, 2000; Stephanie Schüler-Springorum, *Die jüdische Minderheit in Königsberg/Preussen, 1871–1945*, Göttingen, Vandenhoeck & Ruprecht, 1996; and as an example for a rural area: Ulrich Baumann, *Zerstörte Nachbarschaften. Christen und Juden in badischen Landgemeinden, 1862–1940*, Hamburg, Dölling und Galitz Verlag, 2000.

[42] This term is borrowed from Dieter Groh, *Negative Integration und revolutionärer Attentismus: Die deutsche Sozialdemokratie am Vorabend des Ersten Weltkrieges*, Frankfurt a. M., Propylaen, 1973. A similar view was proposed earlier by Günther Roth, *The Social Democrats in Imperial Germany: A Study in Working Class Isolation and National Integration*, Totowa, NJ, Bedminster Press, 1963.

[43] The only full analysis of such a process I am familiar with is in the English context. See Harold J. Perkin, *The Origins of Modern English Society 1780–1880*, London, Routledge & Kegan Paul, 1969, pp. 271–340.

that used against the entry of women or workers, the problems it eventually posed and the solutions that had to be devised were common to all these groups. They reflected an important aspect of bourgeois society in general.

The strategy of "negative integration" was applied throughout the nineteenth century, even as the defining borders of the bourgeoisie were changing, its entry requirements transformed, and its "leading sector" re-composed. As late as the mid-nineteenth century, the financial entry requirements of the *Bildungsbürgertum* were still rather low, and even the formal educational requirements were relatively modest; upwardly mobile families could hope to enter without undue effort. But after 1848, when the links between the *Bildungsbürgertum* and the *Wirtschaftsbürgertum*, between the educated and the well off, were strengthened, both the property and the educational prerequisites for prospective newcomers were raised considerably. The so-called bourgeois society became increasingly more differentiated. Groups and subgroups were vying for leadership, and the borderlines between and among them were constantly shifting. Jews were one such group that managed to master the art of effectively and quickly adjusting to changes so as not to lose what had previously been gained. They learned to preserve the standing they had so painstakingly managed to secure for themselves and continued to promote themselves into and within bourgeois society.

Up until the middle of the nineteenth century, perhaps even later, Jewish fathers, who were eager no doubt to provide proper education for their sons, were at the same time directing them toward employment in the family businesses. They were all too often fearful of taking uncalled-for chances. In the second half of the century, however, the number of Jewish youth who recieved a higher education and then chose not to return to their father's business grew sharply. In 1895, about 7 percent of the Jewish workforce could be found in the category of "Liberal Professions and Officials," compared to 6.4 percent in the general population. Their movement into these occupations was particularly conspicuous in the larger cities, and above all in the *Reich*'s capital, Berlin.[44] Since Jews only rarely sought careers in the state bureaucracy because promotion in the public sector was practically impossible for them, their share among the free professions was in fact far higher than the data indicate. Toward the years

---

[44] See Usiel O. Schmelz, "Die demographische Entwicklung der Juden in Deutschland von der Mitte des 19. Jahrhunderts bis 1933," *Zeitschrift für Bevölkerungswissenschaft* 8(1), 1982, 31–72, especially 64.

of the Weimar Republic, about one-half of the private solicitors in Berlin were Jews, and their share among the capital's physicians was equally large. Already during the *Kaiserreich*, Jews were clearly over-represented in institutions of higher learning. Studies have shown that even when taking into account the Jews' relative economic well-being, their percentage of the student population was remarkably high.[45] It was not only well-to-do Jews who provided university educations for their children; less affluent Jews also saw it as a way to assist their offspring in their social climbing. Nor was this strategy merely a Jewish phenomenon. By the late nineteenth century, the children of many lower class non-Jews practically flooded German institutions of higher learning.[46] Gradually, even bourgeois girls were no longer content with displaying perfect manners, fluency in foreign languages, and piano playing. Women were beginning to strive for greater, formal education and the chance to take the *Abitur* (matriculation exams) and attend universities as regular students. Like Jews, they too wished to compete as equals in the job market of the liberal professions. And for them, too, this was part of their aspiration for fuller personal freedom and a more meaningful participation in bourgeois society.

This mounting pressure from outer groups knocking at the doors explains, in part at least, the changing nature of the bourgeoisie itself. Concurrently, however, something happened to those wishing to enter, too. For Jews, the most intriguing aspect of it all was the change in their final goal. From about mid-century, Jews began to reformulate their individual and collective ambitions, and the process continued most emphatically during the years of the *Kaiserreich*. On its establishment, they did finally acquire equal legal status, indeed, but disappointment was quick to follow. Despite the formal implementation of emancipation and the prominent achievements of some Jews in some spheres, it often seemed as if their integration into bourgeois society was becoming only more problematic. Antisemitism raised its head and set up all kinds of hurdles on their route. The project of assimilation grew more complicated precisely

---

[45] Norbert Kampe, "Jews and Antisemitism at Universities in Imperial Germany (I): Jewish Students: Social History and Social Conflict," *Leo Baeck Institue Yearbook* XXX, 1985, 357–94.

[46] Konrad H. Jarausch, *Students, Society and Politics in Imperial Germany*, Princeton, NJ, Princeton University Press, 1982, pp. 114–34, and Fritz K. Ringer, "Bildung, Wissenschaft und Gesellschaft in Deutschland 1800–1960," *Geschichte und Gesellschaft* 6, 1980, 5–35.

as the Jews shed most of their marks of distinction. At the same time, it turned out that social ascent, rapid modernization, and, above all, the ever-growing individual and collective success of Jews in the economic and cultural spheres were no longer perceived as mere vehicles for the coveted integration within German society. By now, they had become independent objectives, legitimate goals in themselves.

10

Paradoxes of Becoming Alike

a. Who Came to Resemble Whom?

Assimilation, then, is more complex and dialectical than one usually assumes. An attempt to make informed use of the term quickly proves problematic. To begin with, it is shaded by thick ideological dust. With the onset of the era of emancipation, assimilation still had a clearly positive meaning, and this meaning was still occasionally in use even at the end of the nineteenth century.[1] By then, however, especially in the context of the struggle between Zionists and their opponents, the word gradually assumed a negative, even derogatory connotation. As part of the Zionist discourse, assimilation conjured up a picture of people who were ready and willing to eradicate their own self, foolishly and blindly thereafter facing a hostile world. From this point of view, assimilation was considered a dishonorable process that was to be resisted by all means. To examine the history of German Jews in a more balanced manner, even if complete objectivity continues to evade us, it is helpful to bear in mind that, in other contexts, assimilation is often enough seen as a positive affair. Within the "melting pot" ideology in the United States, for instance, it was for a long time a fundamental principle that contributed to the system's viability. Immediately after the establishment of the State of Israel, the integration of newcomers into a similar "melting pot" was likewise a primary objective, though it was, significantly, named absorption rather than assimilation. It is only recently, under the influence of the post-modern rethinking of

---

[1] Jacob Toury, "Emancipation and Assimilation. Concepts and Conditions" [Hebrew], in *Yalkut Moreschet* 2, 1964, 167–82.

these processes and the revaluation of multi-culturalism, that the positive sign previously attached to this term has lost its credibility.

Be that as it may, assimilation is a confusing term not only from a normative point of view. It is also analytically vague. It alludes to social, cultural, and psychological processes without distinction and tends to blur the element of reciprocity that is so vital to all of them. In addition, the term marks a protracted development and its final outcome at one and the same time. Now, such misleading terms are rather common in the historical jargon, and they are known to be very persistent. Because we cannot bypass them, we ought to at least clarify the manner in which we use them. In my case, the emphasis is on the process of assimilation rather than the supposedly final state to which it may lead. I focus on the manner in which both Jews and other outsiders were being transformed while they were becoming more integrated in, and presumably more similar to, the core elements of German bourgeois society.

The story of German Jewry is part of the collective memory of Jews of our times. It is interlaced in the ideological wars among them and is a vital component of their different worldviews. Many would argue that, on the eve of World War I, Jews were completely integrated into German society. They were both avid consumers and outstanding contributors to its culture. Others insist that such integration had never occurred and that a real Jewish-German dialogue never took place. Finally, opinions also differ regarding the impact of these processes on the self-identity of German Jews. As I have argued previously, accusations of self-denial and even self-hatred often appear along with a clear sense of pride in the astonishing achievements of this Jewry. Bafflement at these Jews' presumed blindness in the end is merged with awe at their success.[2]

Part of the dispute stems from the multiple facets of the phenomenon itself. Toward the end of the nineteenth century, its internal dialectics could no longer be doubted. While it seemed then that Jewish integration was no less than exemplary, antisemitism was gradually becoming a permanent aspect of Germany's social and cultural life. Despite their success, or maybe because of it, Jews were now cornered into a defensive position. At the same time, Zionism had begun to penetrate various layers of Jewish society and was jeopardizing the moderate Jewish-German concord from the other extreme. The *Centralverein Deutscher Staatsbürger jüdischen Glaubens* (knows as the CV) was established as a pressure group for the protection of Jewish interests, but even among its members religious

---

[2] See Part I, Chapters 2 and 3, and Part II, Chapters 4 and 5.

identity was often replaced by an ethnic one that stressed culture, origins, and roots. Here, as an example, is an excerpt from Eugen Fuchs, one of the prominent leaders of the CV, in a public meeting held in May 1913:

> By my nationality I am a German; but according to my religion and tradition – I am a Jew. Just as my affiliation with Prussia, with my motherland Silesia, with my family business and with my profession, affects my character, so do the nature of my Jewish home and the Jewish environment in which I have grown up and still live, deeply inscribe my personality.[3]

There was an abundance of such statements in those years, even if the confident and optimistic tone of Fuchs's speech was not as common. In the styles of Theodor Lessing and Walther Rathenau, these same arguments sounded more like lamentations or cries of agony. But for many others, these were simply expressions of daily reality with whose many facets they had to keep grappling. What, then, was the meaning of that "Jewishness" or "Judaism" that had gained recognition and reaffirmation from people who had already strayed from religion and occasionally even relinquished their links to the organized Jewish community? These were, after all, German citizens, faithful patriots, and often bona fide nationalists. Was their continuing dependence on their Jewish identity nothing more than the so-called *Trotzjudentum* (Jewishness for spite), a reaction to anti-semitism, a decision to stand by the weak and the humiliated? It certainly was, in part. Is there a link here to the racial thinking of the time that was used by antisemites, to be sure, but also by many others, often as a matter of course? This, too, is surely part of the answer. But was this holding on to Jewishness only a reaction to the conduct and pressures of the external world? Could the change in self-perception that was so common among German Jews toward the end of the nineteenth century be explained by ideological and psychological shifts alone, or can we also relate it to some tangible changes in their social and cultural environments? What actually happened within this environment that could help to explain the shift in self-identity and the renewed stress on Jewish uniqueness?

Let us first return to some of the basic data. I have already pointed out the high level of urbanization among German Jews by the early 1900s and their tendency to concentrate in the larger cities. Germany as a whole underwent an overall process of urbanization during the nineteenth century, at a relatively moderate rate in the first half and then very rapidly later on. Jews, indeed, often preceded the urbanization of the rest of the

---

[3] Quoted in Jehuda Reinharz, "Deutschtum und Judentum in the ideology of the Centralverein deutscher Staatsbürger Jüdischen Glaubens 1893–1914," *Jewish Social Studies* XXXVI(1), 1974, 37–8.

population. By the early twentieth century, more than one-quarter of all Jews in Germany resided in cities of more than 100,000 people, while the corresponding rate for the entire German population was less than one-eighth. In Saxony, 85 percent of the Jews lived in cities, and even in Bavaria, which was known for its rural Jewry, about 70 percent of the Jewish population in 1900 was already living in cities. In the non-Prussian north, 65 percent of the Jews lived in the great port city of Hamburg. In southwestern Germany, about one-quarter of the Jews lived in Mannheim and Stuttgart.[4] Some of them intentionally wished to be near their co-religionists, but for the majority, it was a mere by-product of parallel courses of action that were decided on out of similar motivations and in attempting to achieve similar goals. Jews had always been more urban than the rest of the central European population, and toward the end of the nineteenth century, at the peak of the flow from country to city, their urbanization was clearly more complete than it was for non-Jews. For various reasons – old and new – they were ahead of the rest of the population in their readiness to adjust to new conditions in the modern metropolis.

In the years between the establishment of the Bismarckian *Reich* and the beginning of World War I, the gap that opened between the two populations, the great majority of Germans on the one hand and the small minority of Jews on the other hand, had, in fact, widened in other respects, too. The Jewish occupational structure, for example, which was both the cause and the effect of the urbanization processes, remained unique. All the data, as we have seen, confirm the fact that, even by the end of the nineteenth century, trade was the main source of livelihood for the Jewish population. In 1895 more than one-half of the Jewish workforce in the *Kaiserreich* was employed in the trade sector, compared to merely 10 percent of the general population. In the cities the gap was obviously smaller, but the data for Berlin in the early 1900s still indicate that 42 percent of the Jews were engaged in trade, compared to 25 percent of the rest of the working population; and in Hamburg, 55 percent of the Jews were engaged in trade, compared to 32 percent of the rest of the population.[5]

---

[4] The data are taken from the *Zeitschrift für Demographie und Statistik der Juden* (*ZDSJ*). For Prussia see 1911, 153–7; for Saxony: 1908, 108–9; for Bavaria: 1912, 12; for Baden and Wurtemberg: 1907, 47; for Pomerania: 1911, 146–9.

[5] For these data see Jakob Segall, *Die beruflichen und sozialen Verhältnisse der Juden in Deutschland*, Berlin, M. Schildberger, 1912, pp. 28–30. For Berlin, see *ZDSJ* 1911, 28. For Hamburg, see Helga Krohn, *Die Juden in Hamburg, Die politische, soziale und kulturelle Entiwcklung einer jüdischen Großstadtgemeinde nach der Emanziaption 1848–1918*, Hamburg, H. Christians, 1974, pp. 71–2.

Toward the early 1900s, the general vocational distribution in Germany showed the typical symptoms of a rapidly industrializing economy: The percentage of those employed in trade decreased while the percentage of the number of employees in various industrial sectors increased. In those years, a slight decrease in the percentage of Jews in trade was also discernible. But, except for the Jews' growing tendency to the professions, their overall occupational structure remained stable.[6] A study of the Jewish community of Altona, a medium-sized community in northern Germany that was not particularly affluent, can demonstrate the typical social developments during this time.[7] Precisely because of the relatively modest standing of this community, it is possible to infer from its data some general conclusions regarding German Jewry.

My starting point here were two enumerators' copybooks of censuses taken in the community of Altona first in 1867 and then in 1890. The first census counted 2,359 Jews, and the second listed 2,070 men and women.[8] An earlier community census from the year 1840 counted 2,100 Jews, comprising 7.7 percent of the population in town, which was then under the rule of the Danish Crown. In nearby Hamburg there were some 8,000 Jews at about the same time, amounting to 4.4 percent of the town's population. At that time, only in one other city in Germany was the percentage of Jews higher, and that was Frankfurt am Main, where the Jewish population amounted to 10 percent of the population. It is noteworthy that, as early as 1867, the number of Jews in Altona sank to the level of 3.3 percent of the population, and in 1890 it was only 1.5 percent, only slightly higher than the percentage of Jews in the general population of the German *Reich*. These data reflect a general phenomenon. Despite the Jews' rapid urbanization and the natural growth of their community, the parallel processes in the general German population were taking place at an even faster pace. As a result, the share of Jews decreased in many

---

[6] See the discussion on the minority character of the Jewish occupational structure in Avraham Barkai, "The German Jews at the Start of Industrialisation – Structural Change and Mobility 1835–1860," in Werner E. Mosse, Arnold Paucker, Reinhard Rürup (eds.), *Revolution and Evolution: 1848 in German-Jewish History*, Tübingen, J.C.B. Mohr, 1981, pp. 123–49.

[7] All the data on Altona rely on Shulamit Volkov, "Die jüdische Gemeinde in Altona, 1867–1890. Ein demographisches Profil," in *Das jüdische Projekt der Moderne. Zehn Essays*, Munich, C.H. Beck, 2001, pp. 97–117. This article was first published in a *Festschrift* for Gerhard A. Ritter in 1994.

[8] See the General Archive of the Jewish People in Jerusalem, files 157–160 for Altona. The numbers given by the official Altona census were slightly higher. Compare the *Bericht über die Gemeindeverwaltung der Stadt Altona 1863–1900* (two parts), Altona 1905–1906, Part 2, 26, which lists 2,109 Jews for 1890 (1,008 men and 1,101 women).

TABLE 10.1. *Social Division of Jewish Heads-of-Family in Altona (percentage)*

	Lower Class	Middle Class	Upper Class
1867	26.1	69.8	4.1
1890	25.6	67.2	7.2

large German cities, including Frankfurt, Hamburg, Breslau, and eventually even Berlin.[9] Between 1867 and 1890, the population in Altona increased by 30 percent while the number of Jews in the city shrank by 12 percent. This process continued, and in 1910, Jews made up only 1 percent of all city residents. It was finally in 1925, as a result of the great wave of immigration following World War I, that the number of Jews in the city reached an all-time high of 2,400 – a last-minute success and an ephemeral achievement, indeed.

A look at the occupation structure of the Altona Jewish community reveals the familiar pattern: Forty-one percent of the working Jewish population in 1867 was employed in trade.[10] At the same time, about 13 percent of the Jews were employed in various crafts, a somewhat higher percentage than was common elsewhere in German towns; 7 percent were laborers working in home industries and a variety of industrial shops; and the remaining 39 percent were divided among the various other urban occupations. The picture for 1890 is strikingly similar. A social division of the Jewish community into three large classes based on the occupational structure of heads of families reveals a picture similar to the one shown in Table 10.1.

Avraham Barkai's estimates, which were theoretically based on Simon Kuznetz's model for the economic behavior of minorities, seem to be corroborated by these data.[11] Both argue that the socio-economic structures of minority groups show signs of social "abnormality" that remain

---

[9] For further data on large cities during 1871–1910, see Bruno Blau, *Die Entwicklung der jüdischen Bevölkerung in Deutschland*, Berlin, 1950 (manuscript, a copy of which is held at the Leo Baeck Institute's Library in Jerusalem). See also Heinrich Silbergleit, *Die Bevölkerungs- und Berufsverhältnisse der Juden im Deutschen Reich*, Vol. 1, Berlin, Akademie-Verlag, 1930; and Jakob Lestschinsky, *Das wirtschaftliche Schicksal des deutschen Judentums*, Berlin, Zentralwohlfahrtsstelle der Deutschen Juden, 1932.

[10] From this point onward and unless otherwise indicated, all figures for Jews in Altona follow the collated or calculated data based on the 1867 and 1890 censuses in Volkov, "Die jüdische Gemeinde in Altona, 1867–1890."

[11] Barkai, "The German Jews at the Start of Industrialisation," 44–7, relies mainly on Simon Kuznets, "Economic Structure and Life of the Jews," in Louis Finkelstein (ed.), *The Jews, Their History, Culture and Religion*, New York, Harper & Row, 1960, 1597–1666.

TABLE 10.2. *Occupation Division of Jewish Heads-of-Families (percentage)*

	Independents in better or lesser trades		Employed in trade	Employed in crafts	Peddlers
1867	18.7	23.3	4.9	7.5	4.3
1890	27.9	11.1	7.0	3.5	2.5

Note: In all other occupations in 1867: 41.4%; in 1890: 48.0%.

unchanged even in generally dynamic situations. However, a closer look at the data of the Jews in the two major workforce groups, that is, trade and industries/crafts – even if the data only apply to one particular town at this point – does reveal some important changes (see Table 10.2).

Under closer examination, a change in the social position of the Jews in Altona can easily be seen, and it is clearly for the better. Improvement is evident in the massive transition of Jewish heads-of-family toward the more lucrative and respectable occupations, and a certain decrease is discernible in the share of handicrafts employees and peddlers, the most debased form of trade. Thus, while usually staying in the same sectors, Jews were now moving up within them.

Marked improvement can also be seen from a careful analysis of the residence patterns of the Jewish population within the various city districts (*Bezirke*). For example, in 1867, 9 percent of the Jewish population in Altona resided in the 7th district, the poorest one, whereas by 1897 their share in that area went down to 5 percent. In 1867, some 3 percent of the Jews in town resided in the 13th, most affluent, district, while in 1890 that number rose to about 7 percent. The majority of the Jews continued to reside in the 18th, 15th, and 9th districts, creating a Jewish "territorial continuity" in the inner city. With it they were apparently moving into nicer and more affluent areas, albeit at a rather moderate pace. Finally, a clear trend of improvement was manifest in both intragenerational and intergenerational analyses of the situation. Even in this modest community, whose most successful members probably opted to move to nearby Hamburg, economic improvement in the circumstances of the Jews was noticeable by the late 1890s. Their social distinctiveness, however, was not blurred. On the contrary, additional distinctive features had been added in the meantime.

The social structure of other Jewish communities in Germany stood out remarkably, too. Helga Krohn's study of the Jewish community of Hamburg indicates that the city's Jews were divided into a broad well-to-do group that boasted several extremely wealthy families and a narrower stratum of Jews of limited resources who were often genuine paupers.[12] This division also found expression in the municipal tax reports for the relevant years. As was already noted, at the beginning of the twentieth century, tax reports indicated the economic robustness of German Jewry and its distinctiveness as a well-to-do group in most German cities.[13] Indeed, friends and foes alike noticed the extraordinary concentration of Jews in the larger cities, their peculiar occupational structure, and their favorable economic status. All of these were construed as further signs of their otherness, even as their older, familiar identity marks were becoming increasingly blurred. If indeed the social process of Jewish integration was designed to bring about progressive assimilation of the minority within the majority, and while certain Jewish individuals had actually experienced the fruits of such an assimilation, no doubt, this was not their general, collective experience.[14] Their otherness in the pre-modern world had gradually worn off, but now they were clearly different in other respects once again. Whereas they previously seemed to lag behind the dynamic and ever-changing non-Jewish society, now they had become the leading edge of modernization. In many ways, it was the non-Jews who were now trying to catch up with the Jews. The old concept of assimilation now had to be radically redefined.

b. Demography and Intimate Culture

Beyond this general overview, which mainly describes the Jews' efforts at assimilation as a group, assimilation was still trickier for individuals. Acculturation on the individual level was usually observed from the perspective of those outstanding Jews who became prominent contributors to Germany's high culture. But culture is never solely manifested in the creative arts or in the world of philosophy and science. Accordingly, signs of acculturation also can be traced in other spheres of life. In addition to the outward manifestations of clothing, shared customs, and behavior patterns in public, more intimate areas of human experience also shed light on the process. Thus it may be interesting to divert our attention from the

---

[12] See Krohn, *Die Juden in Hamburg*, 65–8.
[13] See, in addition to Krohn, the statistical data in Marsha L. Rozenblit, *The Jews of Vienna, 1867–1914*, Vienna, Böhlau, 1988, chap. 3.
[14] A far greater stress on successful assimilation at the upper social echelons is the main thesis in Dolores Augustine, *Patricians and Parvenus. Wealth and High Society in Wilhelmine Germany*, Oxford and Providence, RI, Berg, 1994.

open and explicit cultural modes to the intimate world of German Jews and examine their acculturation process from this perspective.

A key slogan of the Jewish Enlightenment that was coined by Yehuda Leib Gordon, a Jewish poet and activist in Tsarist Russia, was, "Be a man outside and a Jew at home." While German Jews adopted the customs of their surrounding world and mastered the German language, they indeed continued to preserve their uniquely Jewish domestic lifestyle for a long time. In the third quarter of the nineteenth century, the spokesmen of the bourgeois-liberal society in Germany were still wildly praising the safe and warm Jewish home. Its ethos was highly consistent with the values of that society; its preservation did not imply detachment or withdrawal but rather accommodation and integration. The traditional pattern of the Jewish home, along with its values and culture, was therefore sustained much longer than that of Jewish public life. Gradually, however, toward the end of the century, it had lost many of its traditional elements. Failure to observe the Sabbath became rather commonplace, except, of course, among the Orthodox. Family celebrations associated with the High Holidays gradually lost their unique charm, too. This is evident from many memoirs, autobiographies, and oral accounts.[15] Yet while the Jewish family and its home life lost their particularity, cultural assimilation into the general society did not automatically follow. Although the Jews increasingly shed their traditional distinctiveness, they did not grow more "German" in the process. They forged a new Jewish family life that was modern but still uniquely their own.

The following discussion addresses two aspects of this intimate culture: the emergence of a new approach to family planning and family size, and the reformulation of attitudes toward children's upbringing and education. These two themes are, of course, central to the history of the family in general, since they clearly reflect the changing cultural values and social norms. Jews reacted to modernization in theses spheres with great alacrity and efficiency. By doing so, they were not attempting to emulate the common habits of their non-Jewish environment but instead were trying to form their own modern modes of behavior, thus eventually leading the way for others.

---

[15] In addition to Gershom Scholem, *From Berlin to Jerusalem: Memories of my Youth*, New York, Schocken Books, 1980 (originally in German, 1977), see Richard Lichtheim, *Rückkehr: Lebenserinnerungen aus der Frühzeit des deutschen Zionismus*, Stuttgart, Deutsche Verlags-Anstalt, 1970, pp. 17–26. As a useful summary, see Steven M. Lowenstein's chpaters in: Michael Meyer (ed.), *German-Jewish History in Modern Times*, New York, Columbia University Press, 1997, vol. 3, especially pp. 103–8.

Complete or accurate data regarding marital fertility are not available. One is left with a mélange of partial statistics that are open to various interpretations. Still, some good figures on birth rates among the population in general and among Jews in particular can be obtained from Prussia going back to the early nineteenth century. Birth rates for the Jewish population were originally slightly lower than the rates for the general population, with a difference of only five to six births per thousand from the early 1820s to the late 1860s. During this period, both populations exhibited a gradual, parallel, and sustained decrease in birth rates. But by the 1860s, the gap began to widen as the rate of change among Jews accelerated. From the years 1875–1879, and for the next twenty years, the birth rate among Prussian Jews dropped by over 10 percent every five years, clearly marking the onslaught of a deep demographic change. While the birth rate among them was 32.2 per thousand in 1887, plummeting to 20.1 per thousand by 1895, the birth rate in the non-Jewish population only decreased from 41.4 to 38.7 per thousand within that same time span. The drastic drop in the birth rate of the general population in Germany, the one that resulted in the demographic reversal that was familiar for every modernizing society, occurred only after 1900, with perhaps only Berlin showing signs of an earlier trend, possibly as early as the mid-1880s. In any case, by the beginning of the twentieth century, the birth rate among Jews was less than one-half the rate for the general population.[16]

Similar figures can be drawn from birth statistics in some of the larger German cities, and because the Jewish population was mostly urban, these data are especially important to us. By the first decade of the twentieth century, while the birth rate among Protestants in Hamburg and Frankfurt was 28.7 per thousand, it was only 16 among the Jews in these two cities. In Berlin, the rates for the general population were 32.2 births per thousand and 13.3 for the Jews. Even in small, homogeneous Charlottenburg, a suburb of the Prussian capital at the time, a gap of 10 births per thousand was maintained between Jewish and non-Jewish birth rates.[17] Based on these data, both populations seem to have undergone a similar decline in birth rates, but among the Jews, this trend, too, like that of urbanization mentioned previously, began earlier and proceeded faster. In

[16] Compare Silbergleit, *Die Bevölkerungs- und Berufsverhältnisse*, vol. 1, 14–15. For a more detailed presentation of the analysis here, see Shulamit Volkov, "Erfolgreiche Assimilation oder Erfolg und Assimilation: die deutsch-jüdische Familie im Kaiserriech," *Wissenschaftskolleg zu Berlin, Jahrbuch* 1982/83, 373–87.

[17] For Frankfurt, see *ZDSJ*, 1907, 61–2; for Hamburg, see Krohn, *Die Juden in Hamburg*, 68; for Breslau, *ZDSJ*, 1907, 111; for Berlin, 1908, 172; for Charlottenburg, 1907, 78.

1910, the gap between Jewish and non-Jewish birth rates in Prussia was double its value in the first decade of the *Reich*.

Turning to changes in marital fertility, which is a better indicator of shifts in cultural and social values than changes in birth rate, the picture seems to be somewhat more complicated. Several factors determine the difference between Jews and other Germans. First, the rate of extramarital births was considerably lower among Jews than among non-Jews in Germany. Second, the marriage rates according to age groups among Jews were quite different from the rates for the general population, and as a whole they were much lower. Third, the number of miscarriages among Jewish women was significantly lower than among women in general. Finally, and perhaps most importantly, infant and child mortality rates among Jews were consistently lower. By the first decade of the twentieth century, general child mortality rates in Prussia were double the rates reported for the Jewish population of that country.[18]

Declining infant mortality rates are generally considered a clear indicator of demographic modernization. In fact, even in the early nineteenth century, such rates were already lower among Jews than they were for others in Germany, whether in the eastern, western, or southwestern provinces. The gap can still be observed in the early twentieth century, and even outside of Germany: in Russia, the Austro-Hungarian Empire, England, and the United States. Figures for large urban centers, such as St. Petersburg, Budapest, Amsterdam, London, New York, and Baltimore, confirm this pattern.[19] Now, differences in child mortality are usually strongly correlated with economic status. In the case of the Jews, however, the data indicate a low and steadily declining infant mortality almost regardless of the local population's economic standing. Relatively low rates were found both in cities where the majority of the Jews were members of the established middle classes, such as Berlin, Hamburg, and Munich, and in towns where the Jews were particularly poor, such as Krakow, Budapest, and London. In most of these cities, a wider gap in infant mortality rate was discernible between Jews and the urban laboring poor than between Jews and the middle classes, but the gap was always there, maintained across the entire social spectrum.

Using child mortality data based on professional and economic groups in Germany to get a more accurate picture of the Jews' specific edge in this respect, I performed the following demographic exercise: I tried to

---

[18] For data on Prussia see *ZDSJ*, 1907, 42–54; 1924, 26–7.
[19] See Usiel O. Schmelz, *Infant and Early Child Mortality among the Jews of the Diaspora*, Jerusalem, Hebrew University, Institute of Contemporary Jewry, 1971.

calculate the infant mortality rate for a hypothetical, nonexistent social group comprised of non-Jewish Germans whose occupational and social-class makeup is identical to that of the Jews. Data for the social structure of the Jewish population in 1907 are available in Jacob Segall's studies, which I have slightly adjusted to fit other sources, and general information on infant mortality in Germany calculated by profession and class division for the years 1906–1907 were obtained from a study by Reinhardt Spree that was published in his 1981 book, entitled *Social Inequality in Sickness and Death*.[20] The result is a mortality rate of 13.9 per thousand births, while all available data for Jews are considerably and consistently lower. The relevant number for Jews in Frankfurt at that time was 6.5, in Munich it was 8.1, and even in Krakow the figure for 1905–1909 was only 11.4.

All of these figures are meaningful in trying to understand the intimate life of German Jewry. They indicate marital patterns that were different from those prevalent among the rest of the population and were probably dependent on a higher level of personal hygiene and perhaps also on a different attitude toward childcare. While what we have seen in the area of birth rates is typical for the process of demographic modernization in general, Jewish data concerning child mortality point to the relative advantage of the Jews throughout the process. Lower rates here seem to be a result of old traditions, not of the impact of modernization. At least initially, the Jews had a favorable starting point, one that was independent of the general social changes that took place in contemporary society. In addition, these two factors – birth rate and infant mortality rate – are important for examining a third, equally important element, that of marital fertility. There are various methods for calculating this rate. Prussian statisticians normally calculated the ratio between the annual number of marriages and the annual number of births. While this is not the common modern method of calculation, it does take into account the variance in marriage rates and in extramarital births, so that it holds some advantages over the basic birth rate data we saw previously. Indeed, it reveals a number of telling facts. The typical Jewish family in Germany prior to 1860 was considerably larger than that of non-Jews. The Halachic command of procreation was apparently observed everywhere among the Jews in the diaspora and influenced a number of demographic factors. While the marriage age in pre-modern Europe was not especially low, contrary to what was often assumed, Jews customarily married off their sons – and

[20] See Segall, *Die beruflichen und sozialen Verhältnisse*; Reinhard Spree, *Health and Social Class in Imperial Germany: A Social History of Mortality, Morbidity, and Inequality*, Oxford, Berg, 1988 (originally in German, 1981).

most importantly, their daughters – at a very early age, and longer years of women's fertility within the scope of marriage together with lower infant mortality rates, as we saw previously, combined to create Jewish families that were very large by any standard. In Prussia, too, the birth-to-marriage ratio among Jews was more than 5.2 even in the 1820s, compared to 4.3 for the rest of the population. In the 1870s, this ratio among Protestants in the former Polish province of Posen was 4.13, while it was still as high as 4.87 among Jews. Only in 1880 was the ratio 4.3 for Jews and 4.6 for non-Jews in Berlin, indicating the beginning of a convergence that would eventually change the picture altogether. As one type of gap was being bridged, a new one immediately widened. Traditional Jewish customs that manifested in high marital fertility rates were now disappearing, perhaps in an attempt to resemble the rest of the population and possibly in response to other stimuli associated with modernization. But the process continued so vigorously that, by the late nineteenth century, the balance was fully redressed. By then the size of the Jewish family was 2.8, while the family size in the general population stood at 4.4. The convergence process was short-lived and immediately followed by an opposite process of divergence.

Another indicator of family fertility that is commonly used in historical demography and includes infant and child mortality rate considerations is the ratio of children under the age of five to all married fertile women. I have been able to calculate the relevant values for this indicator for two German cities in the early twentieth century, Hamburg and Munich. Focusing on large urban centers has enabled me to examine Jewish demographic characteristics in comparison to the non-Jewish population living under principally similar conditions. Here we could expect to find smaller gaps than those observed for Germany or for Prussia as a whole. In fact, the differences revealed in this context are no less impressive. For the two cities, the family fertility of Jews was found to be lower than that of non-Jews by 28 percent (although for technical reasons the data for the two cities cannot be compared).[21] Similar results were obtained by demographer-historian John Knodel. It is noteworthy that his data, indicate family fertility rates among Jews in 1875 Munich that were 20 percent lower than the ratio for Catholic families but only 3 percent

---

[21] The data for Munich (1900) are from the *ZDSJ*, 1907, 57–9; for Hamburg (1905), *ZDSJ*, 1910, 31. The data for Munich provide the ratio of children aged 1–5 years to married women aged 16–50. The data for Hamburg refer to children under age 5 and women in age groups between 15 and 50. Thus a comparison may be made between the ratio among Jews and non-Jews in each of these cities but not between the two cities.

lower than the ratio for Protestant families. In the early 1890s, however, the gap was apparently rapidly growing. It amounted to 43 percent for Catholics and 22 percent for Protestants. In Berlin, according to Knodel, Jewish family fertility was measured at a level that was 18 percent lower than the fertility he calculated for the rest of the population in the 1890s, but there, and only there, the gap gradually shrank with time.[22]

Of course the differences in fertility rates between Jews and non-Jews could be merely the result of the Jews' social standing. While the high level of urbanization among them loses its significance when we compare data for the large urban centers only, the differences in social stratification within the cities could still provide the easiest explanation for Jewish uniqueness. In order to clarify this point, I have first compared Jewish family fertility data in the *Reich* in general with that calculated for several large cities by John Knodel, broken down according to industries and occupational groups. The results consistently suggest that Jewish marital fertility rates were at least one-third lower than those reported for employers in trade, for example, or for business owners and white-collar workers in industry.[23] It seems that a new and special kind of "Jewishness" was responsible for these strikingly low rates among Jews, both in comparison to the general population and to more or less comparable social groups within that population. This is further corroborated by Calvin Goldscheider's demographic studies of ethnically mixed populations in Rhode Island.[24] Goldscheider's figures, using contemporary data, are much more reliable than ours. He showed marital fertility rates among Jews in the United States to be particularly low, especially during the last half-century, suggesting that this cannot be explained away by differences in the level of urbanization or in social stratification, or by differences in education calculated separately for men and women. His findings seem to indirectly validate the likeliness of ours, concerning the Jews of Germany.

[22] John E. Knodel, *The Decline of Fertility in Germany 1871–1939*, Princeton, NJ, Princeton University Press, 1974, p. 136.

[23] The data were processed based on Silbergleit's tables in his *Die Bevölkerungs- und Berufsverhältnisse*, Vol. 1, *14, *47, *69.

[24] For a general discussion, see Frances E. Korbin and Calvin Goldscheider, *The Ethnic Factor in Family Structure and Mobility*, Cambridge, MA, Ballinger, 1978. For birth rates in particular, see Calvin Goldscheider and Peter R. Uhlenberg, "Minority Group Status and Fertility," *American Journal of Sociology* 74(4), 1969, 361–72. See also Tamara K. Hareven, Maris A. Vinovskis, "Marital Fertility, Ethnicity and Occupation in Urban Families: An Analysis of South Boston and the South End in 1880," *Journal of Social History* 8(3), 1975, 69–93. Other studies addressing birth rate differences between various groups tend to put less emphasis on ethnicity.

TABLE 10.3. *Age Structure: Jewish (and General) Population (percentage)*

Age (years)	1867 Jews	1890 Jews	1890 Others
0–1	2.3	2.1	3.1
1–5	8.3	6.9	9.4
5–10	10.7	8.1	10.3
10–20	20.3	17.8	18.5
20–30	16.2	17.7	19.8
30–40	11.7	15.1	15.4
40–50	10.1	11.8	10.6
50–60	8.6	8.5	6.8
60–70	7.6	6.5	4.0
70–80	3.3	4.0	1.7
More than 80	0.9	1.5	0.5

There, too, the smaller family norm apparently evolved about one generation prior to its acceptance by the general population. It was a telling indicator of the difference between Jews and non-Jews concerning their family life, expressing their choices, values, aspirations, and hopes.

The particular character of the demographic modernization of Jews in Germany mainly during the last third of the nineteenth century is suggested by my study of the Altona community, too. Illuminating information may be gleaned from examining the age structure of the community in 1867 and 1890 as well as from a comparison between the age structure of Jews and that characteristic of the rest of the population (see Table 10.3).

Dividing these age groups into three categories (young, adult, and elderly) promptly reveals what I have argued previously, namely, that the so-called demographic revolution that so clearly marked the shift from a traditional to a modern society began for the Jews in Altona, conservative as they may have been, a generation before it did for the rest of the population. The share of the elderly among the Jews, which was just over 20 percent in 1867, remained the same in 1890. The decrease in mortality rates that is generally viewed as a preceding step of the "demographic revolution" seemed to have occurred even before that earlier date. By 1890, the share of the elderly in the general population (Jews included) was only 13 percent. Massive shifts are also discernible at the other end of the Jewish age spectrum during the years between 1867 and 1890. The young, amounting to 41.6 percent of the overall Jewish population in Altona in 1867, were only 34.9 percent in 1890. The decrease in its birth rate was already at its peak. In fact, the share of the young in the general town population in 1890 was marginally higher than their share among the Jews even twenty-five years earlier. Clearly, the Jews were ahead of the rest of the population in the key factors determining modernization. For some reason, their demographic revolution took place a whole generation before the rest of the population. More on the background for this phenomenon may be gleaned from Tables 10.4–10.7.

I have chosen to present in these tables four series of data, all referring to "completed families," in which women were older than forty-five years of age on the day of the census. The data on women's age at the birth of their first child, given in Table 10.4, are usually regarded as a good substitute for data on marriage age in the community, which were otherwise unavailable in this case. It seems that by the late nineteenth century, a lower marriage age for women was already established, or perhaps indeed reestablished, among the Jews in Altona. The share of women who had already given birth before age twenty-five in 1890 was almost double the figure for 1867. By 1890, about one-half of the Jewish married women in town had their first child when they were under the age of thirty.[25] In a society that adopts a family model in which there are only two to four children, the ability to marry earlier, thus prolonging women's fertility period within marriage, must be closely linked to the ability to plan family size and use contraception. The decline in the age of women at the birth of their last child (Table 10.5) suggests the same trend. These are distinct signs of modern behavior. Concurrently, typical of this phase of modernization is the tendency for men to marry at an older age, so as to be able to provide their wives and children with the resources needed to lead proper bourgeois life. Thus, Table 10.6 suggests an increasing gap between the ages of women and men in marriage among Altona Jews. Finally, the data regarding family size (Table 10.7) complete the picture: Even in the traditional Jewish community of Altona, the number of couples with five or more children had declined significantly from 1867 to 1890, while a growing number of Jewish couples were now content with less children and were apparently capable of effectively planning their family size. This eased their way into the bourgeoisie and secured for their children the means for keeping up their social position. The average Jewish family in Altona in the year 1867 had 3 children; in 1890, it had less than 2.5. For both years, this number was considerably lower than

---

[25] The figures in this table must be treated with some caution, because they are based on a census that lists only children living at their parents' home. There were of course children (mostly older) who were living away from home, and deceased children as well.

TABLE 10.4. *Age of Women at Birth of First Child*

% of women at age	1867 (*n* = 108)	1890 (*n* = 87)
Under 25	11	20
25–30	27	27
30–35	35	34
35–40	21	15
Over 40	6	4

TABLE 10.5. *Age of Women at Birth of Last Child*

% of women at age	1867 (*n* = 87)	1890 (*n* = 83)
Under 30	5	9
30–35	14	25
35–40	30	29
40–45	27	20
Over 45	9	10
Unknown	15	7

TABLE 10.6. *Age Difference Between Married Men and Women*

% of	1867 (*n* = 141)	1890 (*n* = 121)
Women older than men	27	19
Women same age as men	8	7
Women younger – up to 5 years	22	24
Women younger – up to 10 years	21	17
Women younger – more than 10 years	17	27
Age unknown	5	6

TABLE 10.7. *Size of Family*

% of families	1867 (*n* = 141)	1890 (*n* = 121)
With no children	23	26
With 1 child	13	17
With 2 children	15	13
With 3 children	12	16
With 4 children	12	12
With 5 children or more	25	16

those available for the general population (4.67), even specifically for the commercial middle class in town (4.3). The average family size of less than 3 children, such as had been reported for Jews of Altona as early as 1867, was first reported for independent traders in Germany only after the turn of the century, in the years immediately preceding World War I. Clearly, the Jews in that town adopted new marriage patterns no later than 1890, despite the fact that so many of them were religiously orthodox and belonged to the lower middle class. It seems that by any demographic measure, the Jews of Germany were already more modern than the rest of the population by that time. They were even more modern in relation to their immediate reference group in the general population – the group of small traders in large towns.

How did contemporary Jews manage to achieve this feat? And why did they consider this effort so worthwhile? Now, much has been written about the reasons for the decline in marital fertility following industrialization. The recurrent argument, mentioned previously, is that middle-class families tend to have fewer children, to be able to provide for them and eventually help them to establish respectable bourgeois homes.[26] This is particularly true in times of economic hardship. From the 1870s onward, the German bourgeoisie has indeed undergone a period of instability, at least in comparison to the prosperity and growth years during the third quarter of the century. Following the stock exchange crisis of 1873, the fluctuations in the national economy and the protracted deflation had all taken their toll, especially on the middle classes. For Jews, who were then also faced with a renewed wave of antisemitism, the burden may have been particularly heavy. Studies regarding their contribution to German industrialization suggest, in fact, that, contrary to their behavior in previous times, Jews were slower to respond to the needs of the industrialized economy at that time. By the late nineteenth century they were primarily concerned with fortifying their position and intensifying their social-cultural integration. To be sure, other groups in similar circumstances exhibited similar trends. In every case, the conspicuous result of such circumstances is a decline in marital fertility. Social minority groups in particular, eager to assimilate in the general population, would prefer to decrease family size and opt for "quality" over "quantity."

[26] See, in addition, Joseph A. Banks, *Prosperity and Parenthood: A Study of Family Planning among the Victorian Middle Class*, London, Routledge & Kegan Paul, 1954, and Charles Tilly (ed.), *Historical Studies of Changing Fertility*, Princeton, NJ, Princeton University Press, 1978.

This attitude explains the link between marital fertility and another characteristic feature in the intimate culture of German Jews: the nearly obsessive emphasis on children's education. In a society where education beyond the elementary level was very expensive, Jewish parents labored to provide not only their sons but also their daughters with as broad an education as possible. While Jewish sons had traditionally enjoyed a better education than their German counterparts,[27] the gap between the two groups grew dramatically toward the end of the nineteenth century. While Jewish children went to schools of various types, they almost invariably received better and more comprehensive education than non-Jewish children. In Prussia, the share of Jewish children with a higher-than-elementary education was eight times larger than that of other children in the same age group. In some cities, the differences were smaller, indeed, but they did remain significant there, too. In Frankfurt, Jewish boys amounted to 14 percent of the number of high-school pupils in town, although the Jews made up only 7 percent of the city population. In Berlin, one-quarter of the *gymnasium* students and almost one-third of the students in the more modern *Realgymnasia* were Jews, and this ratio remained virtually unchanged from the early 1900s to the eve of the First World War, despite the shrinking relative share of Jews in the relevant age groups. During these years the Jews made up 4.26 percent of the city's population, 7.5 percent of the trading sector, and 4.6 percent of those occupied in the free professions.[28]

The emphasis on children's education was undoubtedly a prominent characteristic of the Jews in the *Kaiserreich*. Moritz Goldstein, who later became a successful journalist, had to repeat classes twice in the Berlin gymnasium he attended, and was a failing and bored student throughout. His parents, however, never considered transferring their son to a different learning institution or sending him out to the general labor market.[29] Philosopher Theodor Lessing graduated from the gymnasium in Hanover when he was more than twenty years old, under terrible pressure, which

---

[27] For Hamburg, see Krohn, *Die Juden in Hamburg*, 84–8, and *ZDSJ*, 1905, 11. Another useful source is Jakob Thon, *Der Anteil der Juden am Unterrichtswesen in Preußen*, Brelin, Verlag des Bureaus für Statistik der Juden, 1905. For Frankfurt, see *ZDSJ*, 1908, 142; for Berlin, see a highly detailed account in an article by Jakob Segall, in *ZDSJ*, 1909, 113–21.

[28] Arthur Prinz, *Juden im deutschen Wirtschaftsleben: Soziale und wirtschaftliche Struktur im Wandel, 1850–1914*, Tübingen,, J.C.B. Mohr, 1984, p. 167. The data are valid for 1907.

[29] Moritz Goldstein, *Berliner Jahre: Errinerungen, 1880–1933*, Munich, Verlag Dokumentation, 1977, p. 18.

included a host of daily private tutors and a veritable hell to endure from his father at home.[30] But the insistence on Jewish girls' education is even more outstanding. While the education of boys had always been of crucial importance among Jews and retained its primacy as they were trying to improve their social standing, the education of girls had no traditional roots. Nevertheless, Jewish girls' enrollment in the various Prussian high schools was ten, twelve, and even fifteen times higher than other girls in the various provinces, and in Frankfurt, where Jewish boys were, as we have seen, 14 percent of the high school population, the Jewish girls comprised 24 percent of the girls' population in parallel institutions. In Berlin, one-third of all high school girls were Jewish.[31] This was a distinctly modern phenomenon. It did not rely on any previous Jewish tradition and had no apparent significance within the context of Jewish aspirations at the time. Certain comments in Ruth Bondy's autobiographical account of her life in Prague on the eve of World War II indicate how careful we must be in generalizing from the stories of a handful of educated women at the time. In Bondy's home, as she recounts, everyone had reservations about her literary passion. "Don't you have anything better to do?" her mother used to ask whenever she caught her immersed in a book at midday.[32] It is likely that in the Jewish environment of the German-speaking world of the nineteenth century, girls were not necessarily encouraged to venture beyond the minimum educational requirements. Stephen Zweig describes in his *World of Yesterday* how the daughters of wealthy Jewish families were constantly encouraged to "improve" themselves, to prevent them from entertaining improper thoughts on other issues, mainly on sex.[33] Indeed, examples from the literature point to a complex and interesting pattern in this respect. Katya Mann recalls how she was educated, together with her twin brother, first at home, then by private tutors, and later, when her brother was sent to school, by a succession of gymnasium teachers who frequented the Pringsheim's mansion year in year out in a concerted effort to prepare the talented and charming daughter for taking her matriculation and entering the university. Lawyer Ettinger from Karlsruhe made sure every one of his six daughters got at least a full

[30] See Theodor Lessing, *Einmal und nie wieder*, Gütersloh, Bertelsmann Sachbuchverlag, 1969 [1935], pp. 104, 246.

[31] Thon, *Der Anteil der Juden am Unterrichtswesen*, 33–4.

[32] Ruth Bondy, *Mehr Glück als Verstand: eine Autobiographie*, Gerlingen, Bleicher Verlag, 1999, pp. 106 (originally in Hebrew, 1997).

[33] Stefan Zweig, *The World of Yesterday: An Autobiography*, Lincoln, NE, University of Nebraska Press, 1964, pp. 67–83 (originally in German, 1944).

high school education, and Rachel Strauss, who came from an orthodox home of limited means, attended the first girls' gymnasium in Karlsruhe and later became the first woman to study medicine at the University of Heidelberg.[34]

The Jewish family was thus unique not only in its urbanity, stable bourgeois position, and low fertility rate. In some ways the woman in that Jewish milieu was also different from her non-Jewish counterpart. The likelihood of her being employed outside the home was lower than among non-Jewish women.[35] But even though her education was not considered vital, she was often better educated and more urbane than a non-Jewish woman in similar circumstances. A unique kind of Jewish woman emerged in this period – both as an expression of the norms and aspirations of the Jews in German society and as a tool for effectively inscribing such norms and such aspirations in future generations.[36]

From the mid-nineteenth century onward, the assimilation process of the Jews in Germany suggests new directions that were gradually clarified and accentuated toward the end of the century. In the *Kaiserreich*, the Jews retained their unique geographical distribution, and it grew ever more conspicuous. Their social stratification was fundamentally different from the typical stratification of a rapidly industrializing society such as Germany at the time. In many ways, they grew less similar to the rest of the population. The differences, however, were no longer based on tradition; they were modern differences of a new kind. Above all, they relied on a particular intimate culture that evolved among the Jews during those years. Within the Jewish home tradition no doubt lost much of its importance, but a new Jewish code of behavior, a new world of concepts and values, a common way of looking at and reacting to the surrounding world emerged instead. In the process, a new Jewish family

[34] Katia Mann, *Meine Ungeschriebenen Memoiren*, Frankfurt a. M., S. Fischer, 1974, pp. 9–11 (also available in English: *Unwritten Memories*, New York, A.A. Knopf, 1975); Monika Richarz, *Jüdisches Leben in Deutschland: Selbstzeugnisse zur Sozialgeschichte im Kaiserreich*, Stuttgart, Deutsche Verlags-Anstalt, 1972, pp. 347–54; Rahel Strauss, *Wir Lebten in Deutschland; Errinerungen einer deutschen Jüdin*, Stuttgart, Deutsche Verlags-Anstalt, 1961, p. 66. Compare also Claudia Huerkamp, "Jüdische Akademikerinnen in Deutschland, 1900–1938," *Geschichte und Gesellschaft* 19, 1997, 311–31, and especially Harriet Pass Freidenreich, *Female, Jewish, and Educated. The Lives of Central European University Women*, Bloomington, IN, University of Indiana Press, 2002.
[35] Segall, *Die beruflichen und sozialen Verhältnisse*, 75–86.
[36] Compare the full-length treatment of this and related subjsects in Marion Kaplan, *The Making of the Jewish Middle Class: Women, Family, and Identity in Imperial Germany*, Oxford, Oxford University Press, 1991.

evolved, one that embraced modern values with astonishing alacrity. In many respects, Jewish society pioneered change in the general German society. If the meaning of assimilation is indeed a process in which one group eventually resembles another, then it would seem that the order was occasionally reversed in this case. Germans of course did gradually progress into the various spheres of modern life but the Jews preceded them by almost an entire generation. Eventually this could have led to a certain convergence. Following the First World War, German society reached a new level of modernity. The gaps between Jews and non-Jews that widened unpredictably during the *Kaiserreich* were now shrinking. But this process was nipped in the bud. We shall never know how it might have ended.

In any case, during the years between 1870 and 1914, Jewish assimilation was progressing unevenly on various fronts. Jews participated in the intellectual life of the new Germany with enthusiasm and striking success; they were avid consumers of its cultural and material products. At the same time, however, unintentionally, they had developed their own "private" culture. It is not surprising, therefore, that their senses of self, identity, and belonging were so often vague and conflictual. The process of their integration was indeed fraught with paradoxes. Jews did manage to penetrate society at large; they mastered its language and adopted its customs and standards of living. They were integrated into new professions and residential areas and relinquished much of their unique heritage, ancient customs, and separate social institutions. But while many of them personally experienced this integration as a great achievement, as a group they still remained unique in many ways. This was not because their efforts were insufficient nor because their talents failed them, and not, or at least not only, because of the new surge of antisemitism. It was because the entire process was always brimming with inherent contradictions and conflicts. As it progressed relentlessly in certain areas, assimilation was dealt severe blows in others. In addition, integration was not the Jews' sole objective, and at times it was not even their main objective. Jews never accepted the equation between emancipation and a partial or total eradication of their Jewishness.[37] All too often success was as important to them as assimilation. In fact, their economic, social, and cultural mobility mattered to them as much, if not even more.

---

[37] Jacob Katz, "The German-Jewish Utopia of Social Emancipation," in *Emancipation and Assimilation: Studies in Modern Jewish History*, Farnborough, MA, Gregg International, 1964, pp. 91–110.

The Case of Jews in Science

a. The Social Origins of Success

Jewish success in certain spheres was indeed so quick and sweeping that contemporaries and later historians too tended to describe it in superlative terms and even historical categories. This grew especially significant after the appearance of political antisemitism in the late 1870s. To defend themselves against the campaign of defamation, Jews had to develop a variety of strategies. Central among them was their effort to stress their contribution to German culture, in the visual arts, music, literature, and especially in the various fields of science. Significantly, even at the outset of the process of emancipation, defending oneself by arguing for the equality of all human beings was inadequate for the task. Instead, the "practical" argument became increasingly more common; namely, given legal and social equality, Jews were eminently capable of contributing to the welfare of state and society in one way or another, and they should be granted emancipation for this if for no other reason. Aspirations for full equality and claims pertaining to their unique accomplishments became inextricably linked throughout German Jewish history. At the time of late absolutism, the potential *economic* contribution of Jews was the central issue at stake. Later, and especially after the foundation of Bismarck's *Kaiserreich*, the debate focused on their *cultural* contribution. Once again, this was an implicit justification for their acceptance as full citizens and an integral part of non-Jewish society. Their contribution was construed as a kind of returned favor, measure for measure.

To be sure, this argument never made an impression on the antisemites. On the contrary, Jewish distinction only fed their resentment. At the same time, however, Jews held to it ever more tenaciously. The claim concerning their achievements became a constitutive element not only in their fight for equal rights but also in the making of their self-understanding. For while integration and assimilation were only partially realized, Jewish economic and cultural successes seemed positively overwhelming. They could serve as compensation for incomplete assimilation, making life in a world that was often hostile and unreceptive more bearable.

With the National Socialist seizure of power, Jewish accomplishments could no longer even be mentioned in public. The new rulers were determined to "cleanse" Germany's spiritual sphere of all traces of Jewish talent and creativity long before they seriously embarked on the physical extermination of the Jews. Yet, at this stage, too, Jews held on to the "service argument." They found it unimaginable that they would be so brutally rejected, as individuals and as a collectivity, given their achievements in and for Germany. It was as late as 1934 that Sigmund Kaznelson, the director of the *Jüdischer Verlag* in Berlin, and a group of distinguished co-authors hastily compiled a voluminous manuscript entitled *Juden im deutschen Kulturbereich* (Jews in the German Cultural Sphere). In accordance with the new regulations, it was submitted to the censorship board and its publication was promptly prohibited. The manuscript contained compilations of Jewish accomplishments in approximately forty areas of culture and scholarship as well as in politics and society. Despite Kaznelson's claim to have written an "unpolemical reference work," it uniquely mirrored the feeling of pride mingled with disappointed love that was so characteristic of the German-Jewish attitude at the time.[1]

Of the 1,000 pages in Kaznelson's book, finally published in 1959, only 150 were devoted to the exact and natural sciences. This, however, does not reflect the prominence of Jews in these spheres. The fact that almost one-third of all German Nobel laureates during the first four decades of the twentieth century were Jews is oft repeated.[2] The renown of those who

---

[1] The book was not published until 1959. I have used Siegmund Kaznelson (ed.), *Juden im deutschen Kulturbereich*, 3rd edition, Berlin, Jüdischer Verlag, 1962.

[2] Lewis S. Feuer, "The Scientific Revolution and the Jews," in *The Scientific Intellectual: The Psychological and Social Origins of Modern Science*, New York, 1963, p. 302; Colin Berry, "The Nobel Scientists and the Origins of Scientific Achievement," *British Journal of Sociology* 32(3), 1981, 381–91, especially 383. Berry calculated the number of Nobel Laureates (through 1977) per million persons in 1900. For Germany, the index for Protestants is 0.7 and for Jews it is 20.0. On this, see also Charles Singer, "Science and Judaism," in Louis Finkelstein (ed.), *The Jews, Their History, Culture and Religion*, New York, Harper & Row, 1960, pp. 376–429.

were forced out of German universities and research institutions when the
National Socialists came to power may also serve as a measure of their
prominence. A great majority among them, though by no means all of
them, were Jews. Approximately 30 percent of the academic staff in the
natural sciences, more than 40 percent in the medical faculties, and almost
50 percent of the mathematicians in German universities were dismissed at
this time.[3] The story of their achievements in their new places of residence
and their later academic influence everywhere in the Western world need
not be retold here.[4] They undoubtedly constituted a formidable group.

Their story, however, is often fraught with unfounded and inaccurate
polemics. A notable example is Benjamin Disraeli, who made one of the
characters in his first novel, *Conningsby*, published in 1844, declare that
Jews already had "almost a monopoly" over university chairs in Germany.
Accuracy was thus set aside and the facts turned into legends. In addition, various explanations for the leading role of Jews in universities,
particularly in the natural sciences, are at hand. Chaim Weizmann, the
first president of Israel and a prominent chemist, formulated the most
prevalent among these in his autobiography:

Our great men have always been a product of the symbiosis between the ancient,
traditional Talmudic learning, in which our ancestors were steeped in the Polish
or Galician ghettos or even in Spain, and the modern Western universities with
which their children came in contact. There is as often as not a long list of Talmudic scholars and Rabbis in the pedigree of our modern scientists. In many
cases they themselves have come from Talmudic schools, breaking away in their
twenties and struggling through Paris or Zurich or Princeton. It is this extraordinary phenomenon, a great tradition of learning fructified by modern methods,
which has given us both first-class scientists and competent men in every branch
of academic activity, out of all proportion to our numbers.[5]

A generation later, Lewis Feuer, the American historian and sociologist of knowledge, chose to describe the development of the interest in

[3] See David L. Preston, "Science, Society and the German Jews, 1878–1933," Diss. University of Illinois 1971, pp. 118–24.
[4] Paul K. Hoch, "The Reception of Central European Refugee Physicists of the 1930s: USSR,
UK, USA," *Annals of Science* 40, 1983, 217–46; Jarrell C. Jackman and Carla M. Borden
(eds.), *The Muses Flee Hitler: Cultural Transfer and Adaptation, 1930–1945*, Washington,
DC, Smithsonian Institution Press, 1983; Donald Fleming and Bernard Bailyn (eds.), *The
Intellectual Migration: Europe and America, 1930–1960*, Cambridge, MA, Belknap Press
of Harvard University Press, 1969. See also Herbert A. Stern (ed.), *Jewish Immigrants of
the Nazi Period in the USA*, 3 vols., New York, K.G. Saur, 1978–1982, especially vol. 2,
parts I, II; David Nachmansohn, *German-Jewish Pioneers in Science 1900–1933*, New
York, Springer, 1979, especially pp. 343–72.
[5] Chaim Weizmann, *Trial and Error: The Autobiography of Chaim Weizmann*, London,
H. Hamilton, 1949, p. 440.

science among Jews since the end of the eighteenth century as a "scientific revolution" and designated it as "the greatest [revolution] that has ever seized and transformed a people."[6] He, too, emphasized the significance of the generations of intellectual training of Jews through their religious studies as a possible explanation for this phenomenon, but at the same time, unlike Weizmann, he showed greater sensitivity to the enormous difficulties involved in moving from traditionalism to the world of secular science. This was anything but a friction-free process. Apart from the spiritual strain, open conflicts with one's family or a flight from home were often an inevitable part of it. The route was fraught with risks and only the particularly gifted, and above all the particularly motivated and the particularly persistent, could overcome the obstacles. The similarities between the story of Salomon Maimon during the late eighteenth century and that of Leopold Infeld, a renowned physicist and later a collaborator of Albert Einstein in Princeton, some 150 years later, are indeed remarkable.[7] They highlight the fact that the difficulties of moving from a yeshiva to a university did not become any easier with time. The test of nerve involved in such a move was indeed extremely demanding. Furthermore, was it really the respect for religious studies that was so deeply anchored in Jewish tradition that spurred Jews to the highest achievements in the world of worldly, modern science? Was not the respect for science among them yet another indication of their secularization, their abandonment of previous values, and their fundamental modernization? Even if this was a matter of some compensatory mechanism, in which respect for religious scholarship was transposed bit for bit onto modern secular science, this could not have been a direct, straightforward "progress" but a complex, many-sided development that could not be taken for granted. After all, only a handful of Jewish scientists in the last two centuries moved straight from religious Jewish tradition to modern science. Most of them were the sons of already radically secularized families who often lacked any religious roots. They may have brought with them a basic respect for scholarship as such, but not much more than that.

Another attempt to explain Jewish success in science that crops up repeatedly both in scholarly literature and in ordinary discourse has been succinctly stated in a little-known article by the American sociologist and economist Thorstein Veblen. The article appeared in the 1919

---

[6] Feuer, *The Scientific Intellectual*, 311.

[7] Cf. Salomon Maimon, *Lebensgeschichte*, Munich, G. Müller, 1911 [1792], especially chaps. 6, 13, 14, 20–24, and Leopold Infeld, *Quest: An Autobiography*, New York, Chelsea Pub. Co., 1980 [1941], pp. 232–6.

volume of the *Political Science Quarterly* and bore the title "Intellectual Pre-eminence of Jews in Modern Europe."[8] Veblen was apparently greatly impressed by Albert Einstein's scientific fame. Trying to explain this extraordinary achievement, he saw fit to underline the role of the Jews as such on the margin of European society and pointed to their typical "creative skepticism" as an indirect consequence of their unique position. Because they were never fully accepted by society at large, Veblen argued, Jews had turned into skeptics "by force of circumstances" and were therefore particularly suited to intellectual pursuits. A few years later, Veblen's thesis received unexpected support from a comment made by Freud in one of his private letters: "Because I was a Jew," Freud wrote, "I found myself free of many prejudices, which restrict others in the use of their intellect. As a Jew I was prepared to be in opposition and to give up agreement with the 'compact majority.' "[9]

That is no doubt an interesting insight. But while it may be useful in explaining individual achievements, it is not unproblematic if applied to Jews as a group. First, the description of Jews in the natural sciences in Germany as marginal and outsiders is far too one-sided.[10] In fact, most of them felt that they were an inseparable part of the German scientific community, and, despite occasional antisemitic incidents, they were usually well integrated into it, proud of its achievements, and partners in its many successes. Their reaction of scandalized disbelief vis-à-vis the National Socialist policies of Jewish exclusion after 1933 reflects their previously self-confident state of mind.[11] If they did feel excluded because of their Jewishness, they tended to react with exaggerated conformism rather than with "typical skepticism," as I shall later try to show.

---

[8] Veblen's article is also available in Max Lerner (ed.), *The Portable Veblen*, New York, 1950, pp. 467–79.

[9] Ernst L. Freud (ed.), *Letters of Sigmund Freud*, New York, Basic Books, 1960, p. 367. The expression "compact majority" is a quote from Ibsen's play, *An Enemy of the People*.

[10] See Ulrich Sieg, "Der Preis des Bildungstrebens: Jüdische Geisteswissenschaftler im Kaiserreich," in: Andreas Gotzmann, Rainer Lidtke, and Till van-Rahden (eds.), *Juden, Bürger, Deutsche. Zur Geschichte von Vielfalt und Differenz 1800–1933*, Tübingen, Mohr Siebeck, 2001, pp. 67–96. Sieg stresses the marginality of Jews in the humanities, and it is, indeed, possible that they were more clearly marked as outsiders in these fields.

[11] See also Weizmann's reports in *Trial and Error*, chap. 32. Of particular interest are his comments about the chemist Richard Willstätter, who reacted strongly to antisemitism: "For a long time Willstätter refused [...] to understand what was taking place in Germany. [...]; but, though deeply disturbed, he would not believe that the German people and government would go any further in their anti-Jewishness" (433).

Second, if Veblen's hypothesis is to be generally applicable to the natural sciences, it requires the additional assumption that success in this area indeed presupposes the rejection of convention and a certain intellectual rebelliousness. Yet even historians of science who emphasize the revolutionary character of scientific progress point to the importance of scientific conformity and the convergent character of research in these fields. In an essay written in 1959, Thomas S. Kuhn stated that "almost none of the research undertaken by even the greatest scientists is designed to be revolutionary, and very little of it has any such effect." "Only investigations firmly rooted in the contemporary scientific tradition" he adds, "are likely to break that tradition and give rise to a new one."[12] Ludwik Fleck had argued the same point, perhaps even more radically, as early as 1935, and Lewis Feuer demonstrated this point in one of his books, *Einstein and the Conflict of Generations in Science.*[13] In it he convincingly showed that even the most inventive and productive scientist in modern times had a basically nonrevolutionary attitude.

To avoid generalized and abstract assumptions and get closer to the life experience of Jewish scientists in Germany, I have chosen for study a select group of the most successful among them in Germany at that time, attempting to draw their group portrait and infer their motivations, worldviews, and particular courses of action. The group selected for this study consists of all those Jewish scientists named by Kaznelson under the rubrics of chemistry, physics, and medical research and who also appear in the 1980 edition of the most exhaustive encyclopedia of scientific biographies, the *Dictionary of Scientific Biography (DSB)*. The group is made up of forty scientists: nine physicists, eighteen chemists, and thirteen medical researchers; thirty-nine men and one woman. They do not make up a random sample; the group includes all the truly exceptional Jewish scientists in the selected fields. They were "Jewish" according to Kaznelson's criteria, providing that they were at least born Jews and were not baptized at birth. They were "exceptional" according to the *DSB*, whose fifteen volumes contain the concise biographies of leading scientists, beginning in ancient Greece and encompassing the entire world.

[12] Thomas Kuhn, "The Essential Tension: Tradition and Innovation in Scientific Research," in *The Essential Tension: Selected Studies in Scientific Tradition and Change,* Chicago and London, University of Chicago Press, 1977, pp. 225–39; the quote is from 227.
[13] Ludwig Fleck, *Genesis and Development of a Scientific Fact,* Chicago, University of Chicago Press, 1979 (originally in German, 1935); Lewis S. Feuer, *Einstein and the Generation of Science,* New York, Basic Books, 1974, especially part 3.

Some members of the group were world-famous. Ten of them were Nobel laureates: Paul Ehrlich (1908), Otto Meyerhof (1908), and Karl Landsteiner (1930) in medicine; Otto Wallach (1910), Richard Willstätter (1915), and Fritz Haber (1919) in chemistry; and Albert Einstein (1921), James Franck (1926), Otto Stern (1943), and Max Born (1954) in physics. All the others were leading experts in their respective fields, too. The only woman in the group, physicist Lise Meitner, did convert at some point, but she was born a Jewess in Vienna; was later famous for her research at the Kaiser Wilhelm Institute in Berlin; and finally emigrated, briefly to Copenhagen and then to Stockholm, in 1938. Although all of the scientists in this group were active during the years of the *Kaiserreich*, some of them were born as early as the 1820s, while others – not until the 1880s. To do justice to the dynamic changes within this span of time, they were first divided into three generations. The first generation comprises those born in the first half of the nineteenth century who were already active scientists by the third quarter of the century. The second generation encompasses those born between 1850 and the mid-1870s who studied and worked during the *Kaiserreich*. Finally, the third generation includes those born in the last quarter of the nineteenth century and, while having begun their academic careers before World War I, had achieved status and fame only during the period between the two world wars.

For thirty-five out of the forty scientists in the selected group, we have more or less exact, though often minimal, social data regarding their family origins and the schematic course of their life. As we scan this material, the affluence and respectable family backgrounds of the majority of our scientists are immediately apparent. More than one-half of them came from wealthy families of the upper middle class; if we add up the self-employed and the academic *Bildungsbürgertum*, 85 percent of the fathers of our scientists seem to have belonged to that widely defined category. This, indeed, could have been expected, considering the length of time necessary for university education, its cost, and the protracted period of economic uncertainty that was typical of the early stages of an academic career in Germany.[14] Still, the figure is extremely high. It is all the more outstanding in comparison with our admittedly fragmentary knowledge

---

[14] This phase of life is comprehensively discussed by Franz Eulenburg, *Der "akademische Nachwuchs": Eine Untersuchung über die Lage und die Aufgaben der Extraordinarien und Privatdozenten*, Leipzig and Berlin, B.G. Teubner, 1908, especially pp. 111–43. See also Alexander Busch, *Die Geschichte des Privatdozenten: Eine soziologische Studie zur grossbetrieblichen Entwicklung der deutschen Universitäten*, Stuttgart, Enke, 1959, pp. 148–62 (which also contains an appendix on Jewish staff members in German universities).

of the social origins of all faculty members in Germany and specifically with those in the relevant scientific disciplines. The social background, or more precisely the fathers' occupation of university teachers and professors, was examined for the years 1864–1954 by Christian von Ferber of Göttingen University in a detailed study that was published in 1956.[15] Ferber established that, up to the end of the *Kaiserreich*, approximately 25 percent of all the fathers of university lecturers in Germany belonged to the "economically self-employed" bourgeoisie, including, of course, some very rich ones; some 60 perecent of them belonged to the *Bildungsbürgertum*, that is, to the academic, teaching, artistic, and journalistic professions. Superficially, the similarities with the Jewish group are striking, but the numbers are misleading. Jews had no access to many of the bureaucratic and civil-service professions included in the category of the "educated" (the higher civil servants, church functionaries, of course, the army officers or the noble landowners). Furthermore, comparing the more relevant figures, one finds that sons of merchants and industrialists, representing over 50 percent of *our* group, composed only some 20 percent of the fathers of *all* faculty members in German universities during the *Kaiserreich*. The self-employed, academics, and teachers formed one-third of the fathers of Jewish scientists, but only 18 percent of the fathers of university teachers in general. A more detailed breakdown shows even more extreme contrasts: As many as 20 percent of the Jewish fathers of the scientists in our group were lawyers, whereas lawyers constituted only 1.6 percent of the fathers of all university teachers, Jews and non-Jews alike. While the percentage of the "economically self-employed" in trade among the fathers of university lecturers in medicine was particularly low, this was not the case for the Jews in medicine. Seven of the twelve fathers of those Jewish physician-scientists known to us were not merely "self-employed" but businessmen, bankers, and factory owners.

Clear indications of social mobility are only discernible among Jews in the first generation and mostly among the physicians. The medical profession had long provided a unique possibility for upward mobility everywhere in Europe and not specifically for Jews.[16] As long as medical practice and medical research formed a self-evident, single profession,

---

[15] Christian von Ferber, *Die Entwicklung des Lehrkörpers der deutschen Universitäten and Hochschulen 1864–1954*, Göttingen, Vandenhoeck & Ruprecht, 1956, pp. 163–86.

[16] Monika Richarz, *Der Eintritt der Juden in die akademischen Berufe: Jüdische Studenten und Akademiker in Deutschland, 1678–1848*, Tübingen, J.C.B. Mohr, 1974. See also Jacob Toury, "Der Eintritt der Juden ins deutsche Bürgertum," in Hans Liebeschütz and Arnold Paucker, (eds.), *Das Judentum in der deutschen Umwelt*, Tübingen, J.C.B. Mohr, 1977, pp. 139–242, here 179–84.

some upwardly mobile physicians occasionally found themselves in fields that could have led them to take up a scientific career. In social terms, this was less rewarding than the normal medical route, but it was an attractive possibility for the scientifically talented and committed. From the mid-1850s onwards, the practical and scientific aspects of medicine increasingly diverged, and the latter gradually lost its attraction for upwardly mobile men. Among the Jewish physician-scientists of our second and third generations, members of the affluent upper middle class were already in a clear majority; for them, social position was already of secondary importance. Their parents had secured it.

Likewise, there are almost no representatives of the lower classes among the Jewish chemists in our group, in contrast to non-Jews in this field of science. By the middle of the nineteenth century, chemistry had finally "emancipated" itself from medicine and joined the other natural science disciplines within the philosophical faculty. It thus became attractive to upwardly mobile individuals, as many new career opportunities now presented themselves in industry.[17] Around 1900, approximately two-thirds of all chemists who earned a doctorate in Germany came from a modest social background; only about 50 percent of them received the typically bourgeois education in a humanistic gymnasium, while the other half graduated from *Realschulen*, the more modern and more scientifically oriented high schools. Among the Jewish chemists in our group, however, thirteen of the fathers known to us were well situated: Nine were wealthy industrialists or businessmen, mostly from the textile trade; two were lawyers; and two were university professors. Only one, Richard Willstätter's father, was a somewhat less successful entrepreneur who eventually emigrated to American to try his luck there, leaving his wife and children behind. Richard, like many non-Jews in his position, decided on chemistry because medical studies, which was his first choice, were longer and more expensive.[18]

Finally, the eight fathers known to us of the nine physicists in our group were even better situated: Two were bankers, two were wealthy

---

[17] On the growing number of positions for chemists in some important chemical firms, see Hans H. Müller (ed.), *Produktivkräfte in Deutschland 1870 bis 1917/18*, Berlin (east), Akademie-Verlag, 1985, p. 345, and table 92. See also Carl Duisberg, "The Education of Chemists," *Journal of the Society of the Chemical Industry* 15, 1896, 427–32. He reports that, in 1896, in 83 of the largest chemical concerns in Germany, 68% of the chemists had received doctorates at universities and polytechnics.

[18] Richard Willstätter, *Aus meinem Leben*, Weinheim, Verlag Chemie, 1958 [1949], pp. 38, 55–6.

entrepreneurs, one was a successful lawyer, and one was a practicing scientist. Only two among them could be subsumed under the category of small- or middle-scale traders. In fact, upward social mobility was rarely a motivational force for Jews in the natural sciences. In physics it may have been no longer relevant for non-Jews either.[19]

Nevertheless, entering the world of science still held special promise for the Jews. While the majority of German Jews at that time were prepared to regard their economic success as an acceptable substitute for full social integration and often felt more secure within the confines of their own Jewish subculture, Jewish scientists could still hope for a fuller acceptance in the supposedly open, competitive, and egalitarian world of science. Robert K. Merton has defined universalism as one of the typical and most vital norms of the scientific community.[20] In practice, no doubt, scientific procedures may often deviate from the normative ethos of science, as critics of Merton's thesis have noted.[21] But science did remain attractive, especially for those Jews whose fathers had already attained the highest levels of economic or cultural success. The emphasis on merit within the social and institutional frameworks of science held the promise of a community without limits, where recognition could be attained through personal talent and exertion, regardless of distinctions of race or religion, and free of any prejudice or discrimination.

Our comparison between the social origins of Jewish and non-Jewish scientists is, however, highly problematic. It casts a select group of the best and brightest Jews against the entire academic staff of Germany, which naturally included some exceptional scientists, no doubt, together with a majority of mediocre ones. In a later study, I tried to overcome this hurdle by defining two groups, Jews and non-Jews, each consisting of twelve scientists, all of them remarkably successful. This time the non-Jews were highly accomplished scientists, too. Some of them were Nobel laureates, and some were directors of leading research institutions. All of them are renowned to this day. This second comparison, then,

[19] Lewis Pyenson and Douglas Skopp, "Educating Physicists in Germany, circa 1900," *Social Studies of Science* 7, 1977, 329–66. For the scientists' affluent background, see also Leo Moulin, "The Nobel Prizes for the Sciences, 1900–1950," *British Journal of Sociology* 6(3), 1955, 246–63, especially 260–1.

[20] Robert K. Merton, "The Normative Structure of Science" (1942), in: *The Sociology of Science: Theoretical and Empirical Investigations*, Chicago, University of Chicago Press, 1973, pp. 267–78, especially 270–3.

[21] For a summary of the discussion, see Nico Stehr, "The Ethos of Science Revisited: Social and Cognitive Norms," in Jerry Gaston (ed.), *Sociology of Science*, San Francisco, Jossey-Bass, 1978, pp. 172–96.

234 The German-Jewish Project of Modernity

while further corroborating the above conclusions, highlighted another aspect of the Jewish uniqueness. The remarkably successful non-Jewish scientists mainly came from families of academic men, while Jews who reached key positions in the scientific sphere came straight from homes of *Besitzbürger* (property-owning bourgeois). In our group of outstanding non-Jewish natural scientists, seven of the twelve fathers were academicians themselves: Two held university chairs, one in the faculty of medicine and the other in theology. The picture is different in the Jewish case. Here, too, the successful scientists came from affluent homes. But out of the twelve Jewish fathers known to us in this group, only two were academicians: the father of physicist Max Born, who was a professor of anatomy, and the father of chemist Friedrich Paneth, who was a renowned physiologist. Eight fathers were well-to-do merchants; among them were two extremely wealthy bankers, the fathers of Emil Warburg and James Franck, and a prosperous grain merchant from Breslau, Otto Stern's father. Wallach's father was a clerk. While some of the Jewish parents who were engaged in commerce had certain cultural aspirations, most were regular merchants and businessmen. They had already achieved economic success and social standing, but science could provide their sons entry into the German cultural community, too.

An academic career for a German Jew during the nineteenth century was seldom a simple or self-evident matter. In the winter semester of 1909–1910, 2.5 percent of all full professors in Germany were Jews, while the entire Jewish community made up only a little more than 1 percent of the total population.[22] But of course professors are not chosen from the "total population." They constitute the upper echelon of a particular academic generation and are selected through a prolonged process from the overall student body. At the beginning of the twentieth century, Jews constituted as many as 9.4 percent of all Prussian students.[23] They were over-represented by a factor of about seven during the first two decades of the *Kaiserreich*. On the eve of World War I, after some fluctuations, they were still over-represented by a factor of about 5.5.[24] Even as early

---

[22] Bernhard Breslauer, *Die Zurücksetzung der Juden an den Universitäten Deutschlands (Denkschrift im Auftrag des Verbands der deutschen Juden)*, Berlin, 1911, p. 12, table 1a.

[23] See on this especially Norbert Kampe, "Jews and Antisemitism at Universities in Imperial Germany (I)": Jewish Students: Social History and Social Conflict," *Leo Baeck Institute Yearbook* XXX, 1985, 357–94, especially 389–90, table 3.

[24] A survey of the literature of the time can be found in Kampe, ibid., 361–4, and in the bibliographical information provided there. See also Jakob Thon, *Der Anteil der Juden am Unterrichtswesen in Preußen*, Brelin, Verlag des Bureaus für Statistik der Juden, 1905, pp. 1–47, and Jakob Segall, *Die beruflichen und sozialen Verhältnisse der Juden*

as the 1890s, statisticians and social observers sought to explain this pre-dominance by the relatively intensive urbanization of the Jews and their unique social stratification. We now know that Jewish students did not come exclusively from wealthy families, and many of them had to rely on financial support from various official bodies and private foundations. In any case, considering their over-representation among the well-to-do urban middle classes, their prominence as university students was impressive but hardly surprising.

Higher up in the academic hierarchy, however, the picture is increasingly unfavorable. As early as 1874–1875, Jewish occupants of university chairs constitued only 14.5 percent of all Jewish faculty members at the universities, whereas the figure was almost 58 percent for the non-Jews. Later, this gap seemed to shrink, as in 1889–1890, there was a higher percentage of full professors among the Jewish personnel. But, by the academic year 1909–1910, the equalization process seems to have been reversed once more and the figures indicate a return to the conditions of the 1870s.[25] Innumerable personal testimonies suggest that there was massive institutional discrimination against Jews at the top of the university hierarchy. The higher they climbed up the university ladder, the more official and non-official difficulties they could expect. Richard Willstätter remembered that as a successful, upwardly striving young chemist at the university of Munich, he had been openly advised by his teacher and mentor Adolf von Baeyer, who was also of Jewish descent, to be baptized to ease his path to the top.[26] Willstätter rejected the offer; but others did attempt to take this route. Fritz Haber, for example, who later became one of Willstätter's closest friends, was already baptized as a young man. He then accepted a minor position at the Technical University in Karlsruhe, where he had to remain for twelve years with hardly any advancement before he was appointed to a chair in this institution.[27]

in Deutschland, Berlin, M. Schildberger, 1912, pp. 67–75. Based on the Prussian *Bene-fizienstatistik* ("beneficiary statistics"), Kampe has shown that Jewish students received scholarships more often than, for example, Protestant students. Kampe's data also indicate that they did not necessarily come from the heavily urbanized parts of Germany.

[25] Breslauer, *Die Zurücksetzung der Juden*, 13.

[26] Willstätter, *Aus meinem Leben*, 78–80.

[27] Morris Goran, *The Story of Fritz Haber*, Norman, OK, University of Oklahoma Press, 1967, pp. 38–41, and the summary in Charles C. Gillispie (ed.), *Dictionary of Scientific Biography (DBS)*, 16 vols., New York, Scribner, 1980, vol. 6, pp. 620–3. Unless otherwise noted, all biographical data of the scientists mentioned below are from the *DSB*. On Haber, see also Fritz R. Stern, "Fritz Haber: The Scientist in Power and in Exile," in *Dreams and Delusions: The Drama of German History*, New York, A.A. Knopf, 1987, pp. 51–76.

Others were sometimes luckier. But while absolute numbers show that more Jews were pursuing a university career and more were managing to reach the very top, the ratio between those who were baptized and those who remained Jews was practically constant. In 1875, twenty baptized Jewish professors and ten Jews were employed in German universities. In 1909, forty-four converts and twenty-five nonconverts were occupants of university chairs.[28]

For many, no doubt, to bid farewell to Judaism, which they often experienced as nothing but a burden anyway, was not too high a price to pay for professional advancement. Apathy toward their Jewish identity, if not outright rejection of it, is reflected in the high rate of interfaith marriage among them. The available data are neither complete nor very accurate. It seems, however, that between 35 percent and 50 percent of them chose to marry outside the Jewish community. This is a far higher percentage than in even some of the larger and more modern cities in Germany at the time.[29] Furthermore, only one member of the forty selected scientists in our group was active in some manner in the life of the Jewish community. Albert Einstein was continually concerned with Jewish matters. He was an exception in this, as in many other respects.[30] The Jewish identity of the scientists in our group was clearly diminishing, while a life in science provided the promise of social recognition and full integration in Germany. Later on, none of the members of this group settled in Palestine after the Nazis seized power, although other high-ranking German-Jewish specialists in various fields did find their way to the budding academic institutions there.[31]

In addition, the push for extraordinary achievement seems to have been particularly strong in an environment that emphasized assimilation. Jews had learned over many generations to trust the tactic of outstanding achievement as a means of attaining social recognition. Toward the end of the nineteenth century, it was a mere truism among Jews that a decent fulfillment of their tasks was never sufficient for their professional advancement; brilliance and excellence were required. In his biography,

---

[28] Breslauer, *Die Zurücksetzung der Juden*, 12, and his remarks on 9.

[29] For the discussion on mixed marriages, see Chapter 13, a.

[30] Another exception is the chemist Ernst Lassar-Cohn from Königsberg. See *Encyclopedia Judaica*, Jerusalem, Keter Pub. House, 1970, vol. 5, p. 381. On Einstein's position on Judaism, see primarily Albert Einstein, *The World as I see It*, London, J. Lane, 1935 (originally in German, 1934), pp. 90–112.

[31] On the disappointment of the Zionist leadership, see Weizmann, *Trial and Error*, chap. 32.

Willstätter remembers the elation he experienced when he finally managed to bring home a B, that is, "Good," in Latin. His mother cast a cursory glance at his report card and uttered, "Good is bad."[32] As a rule, in fact, "Good" was never "good enough." In the words of Freud, one expected of Jews exceptional conscientiousness, continual enthusiasm, and extraordinary talent.[33] Still, ambition alone was not always sufficient, not even for the most gifted. So what else could explain their remarkable success?

b. Succeeding within the System

Let us first briefly consider the career patterns of the scientists in our group. Of the twelve Jewish scientists selected for comparison with non-Jews, eleven graduated from a humanistic Gymnasium. Only one, Richard Willstätter, attended a *Realschule*. Among the twelve non-Jews, four attended a *Realschule*, the more modern school, two of whom were offspring of typical families of the *Bildungsbürgertum,* for which the Gymnasium represented the epitome of *Bildung*. Indeed, Jews had long been known for the emphasis they placed on the "proper" education of their children. Paul Ehrlich's father was so eager to provide his son with the right kind of schooling that he sent him away from home, to lodge with strangers in Breslau, so that he could attend the humanistic Gymnasium there. Otto Wallach's father was gratified to be transferred by his employers from East Prussia to the capital, because he then could send his gifted son to the highly rated humanistic Gymnasium in Potsdam. In his studies of internal immigration patterns of Jews in Germany, Avraham Barkai suggested that a major reason for their intensive urbanization had been the wish to avail themselves of better educational facilities. At home, too, economic well-being was often used by Jews to create a lifestyle centered on *Bildung* to enhance full acculturation, at least for the benefit of future generations.

This educational strategy allowed Jews to enter the academic race well prepared, and the advantages they initially enjoyed may have compensated for the negative effect of more or less open discrimination against them. Thus, at this stage, having completed their doctoral dissertations and obtained the coveted *Venia legendi,* the right to teach in the university, there seem to be no noticeable differences between the career paths of Jews and of other Germans. The average number of years during

[32] Willstätter, *Aus meinem Leben*, 27–8.
[33] Freud, *Letters of Sigmund Freud*, 68–9.

which Jews were stranded as *Privatdozenten* (untenured university lecturers) was about the same as the average for the overall academic staff in Germany as well as for my select group of outstanding non-Jewish scientists. The more brilliant ones, both Jews and non-Jews alike, seemed to spend more time in this position – and not less, as might be expected – than other candidates for promotion. Paradoxically, this might have contributed to their later success. It all depended on the common division of labor between full professors and their subordinates at the German universities of that time. Clearly, the status difference along this hierarchy was of immense importance. Those in subordinate positions, however, enjoyed some advantages, too. While full professors were obliged to offer a broad survey of their subject in series of open lectures, taking other sciences into consideration and exhibiting comprehensive knowledge, the *Extraodrinarius* and the *Privatdozent* were able to combine teaching and research in more restricted and well-defined topics. A lower ranking position in a German university allowed its holder to specialize and even treat some controversial issues.[34] At a time when specialization in science was becoming indispensable, indeed a precondition for progress, this had far-reaching consequences. This may have been a disadvantage for a normal academic career, but it was a useful tactic for the particularly talented. The fate of the specialists depended on the particular situation, of course. In some cases they were able to establish their narrower research fields as proper scientific disciplines, so that separate chairs and new academic positions were created for them. In others, while no new chairs were created, special research institutions were set up, occasionally even outside the established universities. In these special settings distinguished scientists could enjoy excellent terms of employment and a respectable standing.

In medicine, it was physiology that emerged as a new scientific discipline in the mid-nineteenth century.[35] Between 1855 and 1875, new chairs in physiology were established in twenty-four medical faculties

[34] Breslauer, *Die Zurücksetzung der Juden*, 49–55. See also Joseph Ben-David, "Scientific Productivity and Academic Organization in 19th Century Medicine," *American Sociological Review* 25(6), 1960, 828–43, here 836–8; Avraham Zloczower, *Career Opportunities and the Growth of Scientific Discovery in 19th Century Germany (with Special Reference to Physiology)*, Occasional Papers in Sociology, the Hebrew University of Jerusalem (no date), 18–28 (published as a book under the same title by Arno Press, New York, 1981).

[35] The discussion is based on Zloczower, *Career Opportunities*, 49–74, and on Peter Lundgreen, "Differentiation in German Higher education," in Konrad H. Jarausch (ed.), *The Transformation of Higher Learning, 1860–1930*, Stuttgart, Klett-Cotta, 1983, pp. 149–79, especially 153–9.

in Germany. Five of the six medical researchers in the first generation of our group of Jews in science were physiologists. The sixth was presumably a pathologist, but he too worked on themes that were considered marginal in his discipline. In the last quarter of the century, the situation changed. Physiology became established and scientific progress in this area began to slow down. Only one of the academic physicians of the second generation (Rudolf Magnus) was a physiologist who specialized in the then relatively less advanced field of neurophysiology. Two others, Richard Semon and Martin Heidenhaim, managed to enter one of the more reputable branches of medicine and became anatomists. The others were specialists in new subdisciplines like immunology, chemotherapy, and genetics (August Wassermann, Karl Landsteiner, Paul Ehrlich, and Richard Goldschmidt). Only three of these seven finally became *Ordinarii* (full professors), one of them outside Germany, in Utrecht, and that too only after many lengthy delays. In the third generation, new chairs were created almost exclusively for clinical disciplines, and although here, too, specialization played a central role, no analysis of the Jews in these disciplines has been attempted yet. Indeed, there are no academic physicians in the third generation of our group. The most famous example outside this group was Sigmund Freud, who wished to continue his work in the highly regarded physiological laboratory at the University of Vienna, but as a Jew he was practically forced to leave. To achieve success and have the financial security he so eagerly sought, Freud gave up his original research plans and moved, against his inclination, to less central clinical areas, first to neurology and then to psychiatry.[36] The non-Jews in my comparison group also left their marks on new areas of specialization. The German academic system offered the best of them research opportunities that may have been considered marginal at the time, but in which scientific and research opportunites were particularly promising.

This can also be observed in chemistry.[37] Nine of the thirteen chemists in both the first and second generations of our group, that is, all those who were born before the last quarter of the nineteenth century, worked in

[36] For a discussion of Freud's decision to abandon research and become a clinician, see Ernest Jones, *The Life and Work of Sigmund Freud*, edited and abridged by Lionel Trilling and Steven Marcus, London, Hogarth Press, 1965, pp. 22–46. See also Peter Gay, *Freud: A Life for Our Time*, New York, Norton, 1988, pp. 22–37.

[37] On developments in chemistry and on the history of this academic discipline, see the tables in Lundgreen, "Differentiation in German Higher Education," 175, and the detailed discussion in Aaron J. Ihde, *The Development of Modern Chemistry*, New York, 1964, pp. 257–471.

organic chemistry, which was undoubtedly the most important branch of
chemistry at the time. Six of them, all members of the second generation,
worked in "physiological chemistry," better known today as "biochem-
istry," and another worked in physical chemistry. At that time, physiological chemistry was a decidedly unattractive and low-prestige discipline.
For chemists, who were proud of their new independence from medicine,
this field smacked of its supposedly practical origins and was held in low
esteem. Physical chemistry also suffered from a lack of prestige, although
for exactly the opposite reasons. Despite the brief flicker of interest evinced
in the circle of Friedrich Wilhelm Ostwald and his pupils in Leipzig, very
few new chairs were created in this field. It was held to be an unimportant,
controversial, and marginal subdiscipline.[38] As one could now guess, of
the five chemists in the last generation of our group, three worked precisely in these fields: Otto Meyerhof in physiological chemistry and Herbert Freundlich and Otto Stern in physical chemistry.[39] Unlike physiology,
however, physiological chemistry and physical chemistry took a long time
to move into the center of scientific interest and continued to be regarded
as problematic in terms of professional advancement. Both disciplines,
however, eventually proved to be of exceptional scientific interest. They
were both typical "creative niches" in which the basis for future developments was laid. Jews who were forced into these niches (though naturally
not only Jews) found promising ground for research there. Their academic
advancement may have been reduced to a slower pace, but their scientific
achievements proved exceptional. Naturally, not all marginal areas turned
out to be so promising. Some were merely dead ends. Equally, not every
subordinate academic position offered possibilities for independent creative work. In many of the cases examined here, however, Jews who were
forced into such positions, often as victims of discrimination and against
their will, found themselves at the scientific frontier, in true "creative
niches," of which they then took full advantage.

　　This mechanism, in which the periphery induced achievement, was further supported by the unique geographical and institutional structure of
the German scientific establishment. Indeed, specialization in subdisciplines with little recognition or controversial repute often went hand in
hand with positions in universities in the provinces and in second and
third class scientific institutions. New and unorthodox disciplines often

---

[38] Compare R. G. A. Dolby, "The Case of Physical Chemistry," in Gerard Lemaine et al.
    (eds.), *Perspectives on the Emergence of Scientific Disciplines*, The Hague, Mouton, 1976,
    pp. 63–73. See also Ihde, *Modern Chemistry*, 391–417.

[39] It is interesting to note that both of the Nobel laureates in this group received their prizes
    not for chemistry but for medicine (Meyerhof) and physics (Stern).

developed more easily in such places.[40] Specialists who were invited to teach there could often insist on being appointed to full professors in their own special discipline or at least on obtaining the requisite personnel, equipment and finance for developing it. While this was often impossible in more illustrious centers of learning, it could occasionally be realized in the periphery. Thus, the renowned physiologist Emil Du Bois-Reymond remained an *Extraodinarius* for years because the medical faculty of the University of Berlin, despite the warm recommendations of the occupant of the chair, was not prepared to split it between its two traditional components, anatomy and physiology. His friend and colleague, Carl Ludwig, who was appointed to a parallel position in Zurich in 1849, succeeded in doing just that: splitting the chair, not officially to be sure, but in practice. Du Bois-Reymond was then invited to join him, concentrating on physiology and eventually turning it into an independent discipline.[41] Smaller universities in the periphery of German science could more easily afford such experiments, in the hope of increasing their reputation by encouraging achievements in new areas that would eventually, albeit in the long term, compensate them for their courage and originality.

In fact, Jews were often appointed to universities on the periphery and, after the establishment of the new polytechnics, to academic positions in these, rather less prestigious institutions. The forty scientists in my group clearly demonstrate this fact: Of the tenty-four Jewish *Ordinarii* in that group, five were appointed to positions actually outside Germany (in Leiden, Utrecht, Milan, Florence, and Oslo). Albert Einstein, as is well known, held his first position in Prague. Six other Jews in the group, all chemists, began their academic careers as professors at polytechnic institutes: one in Karlsruhe (Haber), one in Berlin (Liebermann), one in Stuttgart (Meyer), and three at the renowned Eidgenossische Technische Hochschule (ETH), the Federal polytechnic in Zurich (Lunge, Bamberg, and Willstätter). Some later moved to more central positions in Germany, but as a rule not before they had become directors of independent research institutes elsewhere.[42]

---

[40] See Ben-David, "Scientific Productivity and Academic Organization," 839–40. Universities on the periphery were often relatively new universities that were located in cities that did not have a reputation as traditional centers of learning in Germany. For this, I am drawing on Zloczower, *Career Opportunities*, who proposed a hierarchy of German universities according to their prestige, 29–40.

[41] Ben-David, "Scientific Productivity and Academic Organization," 832.

[42] Thus Willstätter, who had been the director of the Kaiser Wilhelm Institute for Chemistry since 1912, was called back to Munich in 1916. See Willstätter, *Aus meinem Leben*, 233–6, and details in *DSB*, Vol. 13.

The various branches of the Kaiser Wilhelm Institut (KWI) in Berlin played a central role in the process. In fact, the Prussian bureaucracy often used it to bypass the senates of the various German universities, especially in matters of appointments.[43] Richard Goldschmidt arrived there in 1905 as head of the genetics department until he emigrated to the United States in the summer of 1935. Herbert Freundlich, who never managed to become an *Ordinarius* in the Braunschweig Technische Hochschule, joined Fritz Haber's staff at the KWI during World War I, and Haber himself, who had been an *Ordinarius* at the Technische Hochschule in Karlsruhe, moved to Berlin in 1912 to head the KWI's department of physical and electrochemistry, where he stayed until he was forced out by the Nazis. Willstätter, his close friend, left a full professorship in Zurich to work at the KWI. He probably had reason to regret his later decision to prefer the University of Munich, since as early as 1924 he became so deeply alienated by the open antisemitism of his colleagues there that he eventually felt forced to resign.

Furthermore, some twenty Jews in our group received their doctoral degrees in the universities of Berlin, Heidelberg, Göttingen, Vienna, and Munich, and ten were eventually appointed to professorial positions at these universities. But the pattern of their careers shows that they often stayed in one, relatively peripheral, place for a long time and moved only very slowly, if at all, into the center. Moreover, a comparison of the careers of twelve Jewish scientists with twelve non-Jews reinforces the assumption that the Jews' path was indeed often blocked by antisemitism. Of the twelve non-Jewish scientists in my added group, as many as four ended up full professors at the most prestigious university in Germany, that of Berlin. Three became *Ordinarii* in Munich; two in Göttingen; and one each in Freiburg, Tübingen, and Leipzig. Only one, Eduard Buchner, who was known for his unruly behavior, ended up as a professor at the less prestigious College of Agriculture in Berlin. Among the twelve Jews, however, only two finally landed in Berlin: Emil Warburg, relatively early, in 1895, and Albert Einstein in 1914. Three held chairs in Göttingen: Wallach, Born, and Franck, the latter two only during the Weimar Republic. In 1923, Otto Stern was appointed to the chair of physics at the new University of Hamburg. Finally, Paul Ehrlich was sixty years old, a man with an unusually distinguished scientific career behind him, when he was finally appointed *Ordinarius* following the establishment of a university

[43] See also Jeffrey A. Johnson, *The Kaiser's Chemists: Science and Modernization in Imperial Germany*, Chapel Hill, NC, University of North Carolina Press, 1990.

in Frankfurt in 1914.[44] In fact, only the career of Emil Warburg seems as unhindered and brilliant as that of all the non-Jews in my control group. Even this, however, is misleading. Warburg, who was born in Altona in 1846, completed his doctorate at the University of Berlin in 1867 and his *Habilitation*, the second dissertation, in 1870. When his long-standing and closest colleague, August Kundt, was appointed *Ordinarius* in Strasburg, he insisted that Warburg get an appointment, too, if only as an adjunct professor, a position created especially for him. Six years later, Warburg was appointed as the first professor of physics at the University of Freiburg, and he remained the only physicist there for almost twenty years. By then, Kundt, a skillful experimentalist but by no means a physicist of Warburg's stature, moved on to Berlin, and once again it was he who insisted that Warburg be promoted as well. Warburg finally did get his appointment and stayed in Berlin until his retirement in 1922.

Due to the deep, latent antisemitism within the German academic system, Jews could only rarely assume central positions. It did not hinder them from attending the best universities and then continuing their research endeavors, but it ususally forced them into less prestigious positions in less prestigious locations. However, it was precisely there that these brilliant individuals seemd to thrive. They were part of the lively academic establishment of the time, engaged in their fields of special interest, and hoping to eventually break through all the restrictions by their extraordinary achievements. In certain instances, they did, indeed; in many others, their scientific fame failed to be reflected in their academic positions. The success they gained was, of course, primarily a result of their special talents, but the system had an inadvertent effect as well. This exact dosage of acceptance and rejection, which was so typical of Germans toward German-Jews, played a major role in their becoming scientific "stars." That dosage enabled them to optimally groom themselves for lives in research, drove them to excel at every step of the way, and, by pushing them to the sidelines, encouraged them to specialize in areas that were considered less prestigious yet often proved to hold unforeseen research potentials that were ripe for major scientific breakthroughs.

Now, tracing the careers of our group of excelling scientists reveals another fact, for which analogies are also to be found in other spheres of cultural life in Germany: Wherever Jews found themselves, be it in

[44] See Fritz R. Stern, "Paul Ehrlich: Der Forscher in seiner Zeit," in *Verspielte Größe*, Munich, C.H. Beck, 1996, pp. 151–75.

professional centers or in the periphery, in prestigious or in parochial universities, they never ceased to aspire to the top. This was reflected not only in their formal achievements but also in their style.

It is important to remember that, well into the nineteenth century, the natural sciences were not considered areas of particular prestige. In a cultural environment that focused on the principles of *Bildung*, *Wissenschaft* still had a pejorative meaning and tended to indicate a measure of narrowness and limited horizons. In 1877, a leading German scientist still complained that only those who occasionally made grammatical errors or happened to forget an important date were likely to be considered uneducated and *ungebildet* ("uncultured"), but not those who "did not know what brings about the change of seasons or the physiological meaning of breathing."[45] Paradoxically, while the status of scientists was already improving, the old values still prevailed, even among the scientists themselves. Max Planck liked to relate how low his family regarded physics, as well as the other natural sciences. His great-grandfather was a professor of theology, his father a professor of jurisprudence, and his uncle a leading historian. As the sixth son in his family, Planck had modest ambitions that paradoxically made him "content" with a career in science.[46] Indeed, Jews, whose status was low by definition, were first tolerated in the medical faculties, even as early as the eighteenth century, and were only gradually less frowned on in other disciplines. As difficult as it is for us to believe today, even in Wilhelmine Germany achievement in science did not in itself confer social prestige, even among the educated; scientists acquired social standing especially through their roles as full university professors or heads of institutes. In any case, to be considered an equal member of the *Bildungsbürgertum*, one had to demonstrate a proficiency in one of the humanistic subjects or the arts, in short, in a legitimate aspect of German *Bildung*. Alternatively, scientists could attain recognition if they could parade an extensive and highly comprehensive knowledge of their fields. Throughout the nineteenth century, mere "specialists" were ranked at the bottom of the academic prestige ladder.

It was historian Fritz Ringer who coined the fitting term "mandarins" to characterize the German academic elite.[47] While Ringer's research focused on the humanities and the social sciences, this term is equally

[45] Emil Du Bois-Reymond, *Reden*, Leipzig 1912, 606.
[46] John L. Heilbron, *The Dilemmas of an Upright Man: Max Planck as Spokesman for German Science*, Berkeley and London, University of California Press, 1986.
[47] Fritz K. Ringer, *The Decline of the German Mandarins: The German Academic Community 1890–1933*, Cambridge, MA, Harvard University Press, 1969.

applicable to the natural sciences. By the later part of the nineteenth century, there were, of course, those scientists who adhered to the older style of a comprehensive and so-called balanced education, while others, who were seen as "modernists," were more open toward the cultural implications of the new scientific and technological era. These were more pragmatic men who were less reverent in their attitude to *Bildung* and less likely to live by its strict standards and often anachronistic demands.[48] The more "orthodox" scientists were usually educated in humanistic Gymnasia and maintained a "general" approach to science while entertaining an active personal interest in philosophical, literary, or artistic subjects in their leisure time. The more modern scientists often attended the *Realschule*; were usually proficient in at least one other modern European language, albeit weaker in Latin and Greek; and opted for specializing in defined and limited areas that promised more focused and effective research. They did not share the admiration of high culture that was so prevalent in the social world of the *Bildungsbürgertum*, and instead put a higher premium on modern science and technology. Often they were also more politically open and even more democratic in their views.

Jews, Ringer observed, tended to be "modernists." Because of their unique position, they were often counted among the "radical critics" of the establishment in general and the academic establishment in particular.[49] This may be true for the humanistic and social sciences but cannot be proven for the Jewish natural scientists. Despite the fact that many of them came from a commercial middle-class background without far-reaching cultural pretensions, and despite the fact that they were often employed in technical institutes of higher education and not in the traditional and prestigious universities, Jewish scientists seemed to aspire to the "mandarin" image just as their non-Jewish counterparts did, if not more. Among the twelve scientists in my Jewish group, whom I chose for comparataive purposes against the twelve non-Jews, only Einstein attended a technological university, the ETH in Zurich, and graduated from it. Most of the others did not succumb to the demands of specialization and pragmatic research, regarding themselves instead as men of comprehensive scientific knowledge who were "cultured" in the good old sense. In fact, almost all the scientists in both my groups adopted this traditional

---

[48] Jonathan Harwood, *Styles of Scientific Thought: The German Genetics Community 1900–1933*, Chicago, University of Chicago Press, 1993. See also his essay, "Mandarins and Outsiders in the German Professoriate 1890–1933: A Study of the Genetics Community," *European History Quarterly* 23, 1993, 485–511.

[49] See Ringer, *Decline of the German Mandarins.*

scientific style. Among the physicists, even Einstein was publicly renown for his musical abilities. Proficient in classical languages and a gifted pianist, Emil Warburg taught and published scientific papers in every conceivable branch of physics. Born, Franck, and Stern were versatile scientists renowned for both their "comprehensive" approach and their interest in cultural matters. At least four of the five Jewish chemists in my group also fit this model. They had an active interest in the historical and philosophical aspects of science, in art, literature, and music. And among his contemporaries, none incorporated the characteristics of the old-style, "mandarin" scientist more than the biologist Richard Goldschmidt. In his youth, Goldschmidt attended the humanistic Gymnasium of Frankfurt am Main and went on to study at the universities of Heidelberg and Munich. While his later career was greatly hindered by his Jewish origin, he was nevertheless universally admired as a comprehensive scholar who was highly knowledgeable in the history of science and the writer of many popular books on science. It was in congratulating Goldschmidt on his seventieth birthday that Alfred Kuhn, a distinguished colleague, praised him as "a whole biologist, who always keeps the diversity of the natural world in view."[50]

The scientists in my small group of non-Jews, despite their initial stronger link to the *Bildungsbürgertum*, show a more varied profile. Among the physicists, to be sure, all four were typical "mandarins." Max Planck was a prime exemple. He had a lasting concern for poetry, literature, and the theater and was a pianist of such caliber that Joseph Joachim, who was probably the most renowned violinist of the day, occasionally joined him for private concerts at his Grunewald villa in Berlin. Among the biologists, Kuhn and Spemann were also "comprehensives"; they were graduates of famed humanistic Gymnasia and avid students of Renaissance art and the canonic literature of their time. But the most illustrious figure in this group, chemist Friedrich Wilhelm Ostwald, was, unexpectedly perhaps, an avid "modernist." In his autobiography, Ostwald recalls his first trip to Rome, where he was invited to participate in a scientific conference. "I have already mentioned," Ostwald writes, "that I completely lack that capacity for respecting things and places of 'historical meaning' and that I can only appreciate things that are of value in the present." Rome, in fact, left him with a feeling of "exalted boredom."

[50] Harwood, "Mandarins and Outsiders," 491. On Goldschmidt see also his autobiography: Richard B. Goldschmidt, *In and Out of the Ivory Tower*, Seattle, WA, University of Washington, 1960.

On a visit to the Sistine Chapel he concluded that the "artistic needs of today's man" cannot be satisfied by the work of Michelangelo, just as his own "scientific needs" cannot be fulfilled by Euclid or Aristotle.[51] In contrast, it is hard not to think of Freud's enthusiastic rhapsody during and after his first visit to Rome and the impression some of Michelangelo's works had made on him.[52] In any case, Jews could hardly afford to display such heretical attitudes toward the practically sacred values of *Bildung*. None of the Jews in my group had ever engaged, like non-Jewish chemist Eduard Buchner, for example, in hunting or mountain climbing. None of them shared the hobbies of Walther Nernst, who enjoyed riding, swimming, and car racing. None of them behaved like outsiders.

With the exception of Einstein, none of the Jews in my group was a "radical critic." In fact, they were usually not critics at all. Instead, they tended to belong to the typical mandarins, though in comparison with non-Jews, they might have felt less threatened by the "modernists." Their attitude toward science was rarely "pragmatic," and their cultural preferences were usually those of their traditional colleagues, all respectable members of the *Bildungsbürgertum*. Although they were often pushed by antisemitism to the margins of the academic milieu, their ambition – both scientific and social – was to transcend all remnants of their status as outsiders and join the mainstream. Indeed, they usually managed to overcome discrimination by taking great care not to rock the boat of convention. Even as they often found themselves in marginal institutions or in marginal scientific disciplines, they held on to the cultural lifestyle of the respectable German environment, of which they strove to become an integral and indistinguishable part.

[51] Wilhelm Ostwald, *Lebenslinien: Eine Selbstbiographie*, 3 vols., Berlin, 1927, vol. 3, pp. 337–8.
[52] See Siegmund Freud, *Briefe an Wilhelm Fliess, 1887–1904*, Frankfurt a. M., S. Fischer, 1986, p. 493, in a letter of September 19, 1901, and the description in Gay, *Freud*, 135–36, 314–17.

12

The Ambivalence of *Bildung*

George Mosse regarded the Jews as the ultimate representatives and last defenders of the German humanistic culture at its best.[1] By the late eighteenth century, he claimed, Jews had collectively embraced *Bildung*, a compound cultural ideal that represented the essence of European Enlightenment. Defined by luminaries such as Lessing, Goethe, Schiller, and Humboldt, together with other, less illustrious figures, who all worked out its precise content, the *Bildung* ideal was then formulated and given individual as well as communal meanings. It emphasized rationality and a vision of humanity acting under its guidance. *Bildung* meant above all the process of individual self-development, gradually manifesting man's – indeed usually not woman's – spiritual potential and his capacity to become a free, creative, and autonomous person living in harmony with like-minded men in a spirit of tolerance, solidarity, and friendship. As in the special case of science discussed in the previous chapter, this general ideal held the promise of total openness and, in its radical version, even the promise of full civil equality among all who were ready to commit themselves to its principles, regardless of race or class.

---

[1] See George L. Mosse, *German Jews beyond Judaism*, Bloomington, IN, University of Indiana Press, 1985. Of Mosse's numerous essays, those especially relevant to the following discussion are "Jewish Emancipation between *Bildung* and Respectability," in Jehuda Reinharz and Walter Schatzberg (eds.), *The Jewish Response to German Culture. From the Enlightenment to the Second World War*, Hanover and London, University Press of New England, 1985, pp. 1–16, and "Das deutsch-jüdische Bildungsbürgertum," in Reinhart Koselleck (ed.), *Bildungsbürgertum im 19. Jahrhundert, Teil II: Bildungsbürger und Bildungswissen*, Stuttgart, Klett-Cotta, 1990, pp. 168–80.

While this was the point of departure, Mosse continued, things began to go wrong soon afterward. While at first it seemed that the promise embodied in *Bildung* was being fulfilled, hopes were soon shattered. Jews could join the new community of *Bildung*, manifesting their deep dedication and extraordinary talent, but a fundamental conflict within the educated camp gradually complicated matters. Toward the end of the nineteenth century, it became evident that while Jews were hanging on to the old ideal, educated Germans allowed it to be recast, transformed, and rephrased in different and occasionally even contradictory terms. With time, German *Bildung* was contaminated by two major nineteenth-century counterforces: Romanticism, or rather the recurrent waves of neo-Romanticism, and nationalism. The ideal of *Bildung* was radically limited by these forces, and the messages of rationality and universalism were blurred in the process. Jews, however, refused to acknowledge the change, according to Mosse. Having lost contact with their ancient religion and their ethnic traditions, they had no way back. Thus they found themselves in the last defense line of this original *Bildung*-specific mixture of cultural values and moral tenets, posed against all its would-be destroyers.

Mosse's is a powerful thesis. It spans almost two centuries and offers an overall vision of German cultural history as well as an analysis of the peculiarities of German Jewry. Above all, it suggests an explanation of the Jews' immense trust in German culture and their insistence on holding on to it even as the earth was shaking under their feet. It is also consistent, for instance, with a widespread belief in the special role of Jews to uphold the best of this culture, and with the assumption concerning the nonconformity and basic radicalism of Jews within it. Mosse himself, to be sure, pointed out certain areas in which German *Bildung*, from its inception, had not been as pure and simple as it was purported to be. The concept of *Sittlichkeit*, that familiar bourgeois sense of respectability, for instance, was meant to ensure conformity and retain a moral code that was typified by strictly controlled emotions and conventional sexuality. Against the enlightened demands for individual autonomy and the notion of masculine community of friendship that had been propagated by *Bildung*, Mosse explained, the bourgeoisie felt obliged to defend the supremacy of family values as well as other, dominant social hierarchies. But beyond this initial ambivalence, admitted and analyzed by Mosse, the ideal of *Bildung* proved contentious in other respects, too.

By the late Enlightenment, some of these were already evident. Most obvious was the dual nature of the Enlightenment à la Dohm, combining a call for equal rights with the needs of the authoritarian Prussian state.[2] This was one of the inherent paradoxes of the Enlightenment, especially but not only in Germany: allowing the co-existence of a radical call for individual freedom with subordination to the far-from-liberal existing regimes. Also typical for these critical years was the tension created between the continuing emphasis on the predominance of rationality and the growing realization of the role of sensuality and passion. A great deal of *Innerlichkeit*, an intuitive and passionate emotional world, was by then considered indispensable for creativity in all fields. It was later to become a major focus of Romanticism but had been present, indeed influential, at least since the days of *Sturm und Drang*. In fact, the individual who was developing according to the principles of *Bildung* was already by the later part of the eighteenth century expected to achieve not just a higher sort of rationality but rather the right mixture of reason and passion, a true harmony between conflicting forces.[3]

In addition, from its inception, the concept of *Bildung* contained the tension between universalism and nationalism. Patriotism, as we have already seen, was by then a prerequisite for being a true German *Aufklärer*.[4] The proper education for free citizens in this framework had always been a general "Nationalerzierhung" (national education) that presumably was intended for all but in actuality was limited to care for the specific interests of the absolutist state. In any case, while Goethe and Humboldt continued to underline the process of perfecting the individual even under Napoleon's rule, Schleiermacher and Fichte were already far more concerned with the contribution of the individual to the nation and with the cultivation of a selfless patriotism, ready for any sacrifice, under conditions of occupation and foreign rule. Thus, even at this early moment, the threats to the emancipatory ideal of *Bildung* posed by Romanticism and nationalism was in evidence. Fraught with inner contradictions from its very inception, this ideal was never fully egalitarian

---

[2] For bibliographical details and relevant literature, see Part II, Chapter 6, fn. 24, 26.

[3] See Peter Gay, *The Enlightenment. An Interpretation*, Vol. 2: *The Science of Freedom*, New York, Norton, 1977, pp. 187–207, and especially for Germany, Rolf Grimminger, "Aufklärung, Absolutismus und bürgerlichen Individuen," in Rolf Grimminger (ed.), *Deutsche Aufklärung bis zur französischen Revolution 1680–1789*, Vol. 3/1 of *Sozialgeschichte der deutshcen Literatur*, Munich, Deutscher Taschenbuch Verlag, 1980, pp. 15–103.

[4] See Chapter 9, c. On eighteenth century German bourgeois patriotism, see especially Rudolf Vierhaus, "Patriotismusbegriff und Realität einer moralisch-politischen Haltung," *Wolfenbüttler Forschungen* 8, 1980, 9–29, and his article "Bildung" in Otto Brunner, Werner Conze, and Reinhart Koselleck (eds.), *Geschichtliche Grundbegriffe: Historisches Lexikon zur politisch-sozialen Sprache in Deutschland*, Stuttgart, E. Klett, 1972, vol. 1, pp. 509–51.

or universal. The seeds of danger were ingrained and did not go unnoticed by contemporaries. Yet the Jews, like so many other Germans, were not deterred and lated on developed strong affinity to Romanticism as well. They too were carried away by its emphasis on heroic individualism, comprehension through passion, and a community based on cultural partnership.

Heinrich Heine's legacy reflects well this ambivalence of attraction and aversion that many Jews felt toward the romantic version of *Bildung*. On the one hand, he was a true son of the Enlightenment and a most outspoken critic of Romanticism; on the other, his poetry, at least in certain parts and always in his own peculiar way, constitutes one of the most subtle and refined expressions of the spirit of that same Romanticism. His political rhetoric was saturated with the spirit of the Enlightenment, while at the same time he was concerned and often in pain about his beloved Germany. Heine was an ardent German patriot, no doubt.[5]

Toward the end of the nineteenth century, another typical German-Jewish writer, albeit one far from Heine's stature, presented this mixture of attitudes again. The Jewish characters in Georg Hermann's novels, especially in his popular *Jettchen Gebert*, first published in 1906, are all finished products of the Enlightenment. The reader's sympathy, however, is clearly kept for Jettchen, the romantic heroine of this novel. Carried away by her pressing emotional needs, Jettchen probably made Hermann the most widely read writer among German Jews before World War I. They were engrossed by romantic literature just like other educated Germans, and there is no reason to think that they reacted to it any differently than their non-Jewish counterparts. Romantic music was also a part of their aesthetic and cultural diet. The attraction of so many Jews to the music of Richard Wagner represents perhaps the peak of their romantic enthusiasm.[6] Jews, likewise, never rejected late Romanticism or "Neo-Romanticism," as it was sometimes named. One can easily recall

---

[5] On Heine as a Romantic poet, see Gillian Rodger, "The Lyric," in Siegbert S. Prawer (ed.), *The Romantic Period in Germany*, London, Weidenfeld and Nicolson, 1970, pp. 147–72, and Jeffrey L. Sammons, *Heinrich Heine: The Elusive Poet*, New Haven, CT, Yale University Press, 1969, especially with regard to the young Heine, pp. 26–87. For Heine's (ironic) attack on Romanticism, see his "Die Romantische Schule," written in Paris in the fall of 1835, in *Sämmtliche Schriften in sechs Bände*, Vol. 3, Munich, Carl Hanser Verlag, 1978.

[6] On the "crowd of Jewish abject followers" of Wagner, see Peter Gay, "Hermann Levi: A Study in the Service and Self-Hatred," in *Freud, Jews and Other Germans. Masters and Victims in Modernist Culture*, Oxford, Oxford University Press, 1978, pp. 189–230. Also compare Ruth Katz, "Why Music? Jews and the Commitment to Modernity," in Shulamit Volkov (ed.), *Deutsche Juden und die Moderne*, Munich, R. Oldenbourg, 1994, pp. 31–8.

Jewish talent flocking to the *Kreis* around Stefan George, undeterred by
its nationalist and even racist ambience, or Gustav Mahler and the young
Arnold Schoenberg in fin de siècle Vienna.[7]

Clearly, this is a rather haphazard gallery; it fails to represent the cultural preferences of the Jewish community as a whole. But then, neither
does the list composed of Ludwig Börne, Berthold Auerbach, Stephan
Zweig, and Emil Ludwig cited by George Mosse to corroborate his position. It is true, of course, that Lessing's humanistic vision and Friedrich
Schiller's poetry of freedom were particularly admired by the majority of
Jewish readers. But Jews were also fascinated by Fichte, Schopenhauer,
and, of course, Nietzsche.[8] Neither Romanticism nor the various forms of
nationalism ever deterred them from joining the mainstream of German
culture that they adored.

Nationalism was, of course, more difficult for Jews to identify with
than most other aspects of the Romantic worldview. During the early
years of the nineteenth century, because it was normally joined to liberalism, German national patriotism was adopted with relative ease by
assimilating German Jews. While Germans often refused to acknowledge the possibility of a genuine patriotic passion among Jews, the latter never tired of demonstrating its depth and extent among them. During the Revolution of 1848 many Jews already played a considerable
role in the liberal, nationally oriented movement in Germany, and by
the 1850s they were openly active and well represented in the *Nation-
alverein* (National Union), the most prominent political association in
Germany at the time and the main organ of the reviving national-liberal
movement. The Jews were devoted volunteers to the Prussian army from
the *Befreiungskrieg* against Napoleon in 1813 to the battlefields of World
War I. Their self-identification as Germans was not shaken by Treitschke's
antisemitic diatribe during the autumn of 1879 or by the repeated waves
of anti-Jewish sentiment during the following years. Indeed, nationalism
could not have failed to be absorbed and internalized in the intellectual
environment where members of the Jewish *Bildungsbürgertum* felt so
much at home. A study of the content of instruction in several disciplines

<hr>

[7] See Frederic V. Grunfeld, *Prophets Without Honor: A Background to Freud, Kafka,
Einstein and their World*, New York, Holt, Rinehart and Winston, 1979, pp. 67–95,
on Karl Wolfskehl, Theodor Lessing, and Carl Sternheim.

[8] On Jewish attraction to Nietzsche, see Steven Aschheim, "Nietzsche and the Nietzschean
Moment in Jewish Life (1890–1939)," *Leo Baeck Institute Yearbook* XXXVII, 1992, 189–
212, and Chapter 3 of his *The Nietzschean Legacy in Germany, 1890–1990*, Berkeley, CA,
Berkeley University Press, 1992, pp. 93–112, and the full bibliography cited there.

regularly taught within the walls of the German Gymnasium, where so
many Jews earned their education during the *Kaiserreich*, demonstrated
the strength of an open, nationalistic indoctrination that was typical of
this institution.[9] During the last six years of school, much of the instruction time was devoted to German history – mainly that of the Prussian
monarchy – and to training for discipline and loyalty in the best Prussian military tradition. Topics for free composition, especially as part of
the *Abitur*, were of an emphatically nationalist tone, as were all festive
occasions, ceremonies, and the general atmosphere in and out of these
schools. The Jews rarely opposed this nationalist Imperial message. And
while the list of Jewish humanists, pacifists, socialists and revolutionaries
at that time, all *Gymnasium* students in their youth, of course, is eminently
impressive, these were still the exceptions that proved the rule.

A recurrent example in arguments regarding the unique cultural role
of German Jews is their admiration for Goethe. Mosse claimed that the
basis for this admiration was the famed poet's unwavering commitment
to humanism and universalism. But Goethe's position as a national cultural hero and poet laureate could have fueled his appeal just as well.
Jews were prominent among Goethe scholars in both academic and
popular circles. Often criticized as "foreigners," they felt compelled to
show a particular enthusiasm for Germany's most influential genius, thus
parading their truly felt admiration as well as their unequivocal national
attachment.[10]

Beyond the tension between reason and passion or between universalism and nationalism, the *Bildung* ideal contained another inherent contradiction – between openness and exclusion. We have repeatedly seen the
ways this tension affected the Jews. Despite its claim to be principally open
to all, *Bildung* was an extremely manipulative tool. In *Wilhelm Meister*,
Goethe's programmatic *Bildungsroman*, the author made it abundantly
clear that for *Bildung* to be real, one must have not only sound mind and
sharp reason, but also the proper physical form, appearance, and manner
of speech. It was a matter of taste and not only of manners, of the right
kind of attitude, and not only of self-discipline. Pierre Bourdieu made
this issue a central theme of his theory of education and his sociology

[9] Ulrich Hermann, "Über 'Bildung' im Gymnasium des Wilhelminischen Kaiserreich," in
Reinhart Koselleck (ed.), *Bildungsbürgertum im 19. Jahrhundert*, Stuttgart, Klett-Cotta,
1990, pp. 46–68.
[10] Wilfried Barner, *Von Rahel Varnhagen bis Friedrich Gundolf: Juden als deutsche Goethe-
Verehrer*, Göttingen, Wallstein, 1992, pp. 29–35.

of the arts.[11] Much cultural capital, he conceded, can indeed be attained
through formal schooling. But more is acquired in class-specific ways and
by living within an appropriate "cultivated habitus." Knowledge can be
learned in school and university – but refined taste, familiarity with the
arts, and the right language of discussing it – these are properties of a
distinct, exclusive elite. This originally caused great difficulties for Jews
and non-Jews alike. However, once the cultural monopoly of the aristocracy was broken, the European bourgeoisie, not only the German,
operated on two fronts: On one hand, it continued to seek – and preach –
openness, and on the other, it worked to delineate the limits of this very
openness. In an effort to exclude certain elements, it was always possible to lash out against *Bildung* as a kind of *Verbildung* (fraudulent
Bildung), *Überbildung* (exaggerated *Bildung*), and, worst of all,
undeutsche Bildung, namely, *Bildung* that was not genuinely German.

Illuminating examples of the difficulties of truly crossing the lines into
German culture may be found in the personal histories of two prominent figures in the first half of the nineteenth century. Felix Mendelsshon-
Bartholdy and Heinrich Heine acquired early on in life the basic scaffold-
ing of *Bildung*. Few Germans mastered the German language like Heine,
and few traveled the vast labyrinth of German culture as effortlessly as
Mendelssohn. And yet, even despite the fact that Mendelssohn's father
had already been baptized and Heine too opted for baptism at a rather
early stage in his career, they were both attacked as "un-German." It was
argued that theirs was not real culture; they lacked proper *Bildung*. This
line of argument, as Jacob Katz has shown, was first applied publicly by an
obscure teacher from Hamburg, one Eduard Meyer, who accused Heinrich Heine and Ludwig Börne, his contemporary and rival, a renowned
publicist and a staunch German patriot of Jewish descent, as being neither Germans nor Jews.[12] They were of a unique species, ran the argument, that was characterized above all by its lack of authenticity. Their art
could never be true, because nothing could properly erase the fact of their
foreign, oriental origin. There was no way for them to become genuine

---

[11] The relevant collection in English is Pierre Bourdieu, *The Field of Cultural Production*,
Cambridge, Polity Press, 1993, but see especially his *Distinction: A Social Critique of the
Judgment of Taste*, London, Routledge & Kegan Paul, 1984 (originally in French, 1979),
and his *Questions de sociologie*, Paris, Les Editions de Minuit, 1980. A useful summary
can be found in Richard K. Harker, Cheleen Mahar, and Chris Wilkes (eds.), *Introduction
to the Work of Pierre Bourdieu*, New York, St. Martin's Press, 1990, especially chaps. 4, 6.
[12] Jacob Katz, *From Prejudice to Destruction: Anti-Semitism, 1700–1933*, Cambridge, MA,
Harvard University Press, 1980, chap. 14 (on Wagner).

German artists. They may have had it all, but their style gave them away, as did their language and, most of all, their faulty intonation. It is indeed astonishing to observe how deeply Heine himself internalized the rules of this anti-Jewish discourse. In a review sent from Paris in April 1842, he compared Mendelssohn's oratorio *Paulus* with Rossini's *Stabat Mater*, both of which he must have heard in the concert halls of the French capital. Mendelssohn's failing sense of true Christianity cannot be ignored, Heine thought. A genuine approach, he claimed, "can neither be learned nor acquired through baptism."[13] Heine knew of course that precisely this type of criticism could be, and indeed was, directed against his own work, too. Within this discourse, the true German tongue as well as the authentic German musical modus were available only to purely German artists. It was the right "tone" that was repeatedly demanded of those of Jewish descent, and it was that which they presumably lacked.

The quest for proper style occupied Jewish-German intellectuals incessantly. They never despaired of fully internalizing it. As a rule, they made every effort never to deviate from it. Only a handful dared to cultivate their uniqueness, and these were always members of the uppermost elite. Ordinary Jews, who had come a tremendously long way in such a short time and could rightfully boast of substantial success, usually had other things to worry about. These little people, the rank and file of German Jewry, did not aspire for full recognition by the Germans, but for passive acceptance that would allow them a quiet, peaceful life. They did not wish to disguise and erase their distinctness; they only wanted to find a way to preserve it without provoking animosity. It was only all too human that they were searching for a social and cultural compromise that would allow them to enjoy their successes and ignore their failures as much as possible.

[13] Quoted in Siegbert S. Prawer, "Heine's Portraits of German and French Jews on the Eve of the 1848 Revolution," in Werner E. Mosse, Arnold Paucker, and Reinhard Rürup (eds.), *Revolution and Evolution: 1848 in German-Jewish History*, Tübingen, J.C.B. Mohr, 1981, pp. 352–83. The relevant passage is on 359–66, and the quote is from 360.

13

Forces of Dissimilation

a. The Limits of Assimilation

In the historical literature about German Jews, especially in writings from the Zionist perspective, it is common to look for a dividing line between the "Era of assimilation" and the "Era of renewed self-consciousness."[1] Such a turning point can indeed be easily identified in the aftermath of the dream of perfect national solidarity during World War I. The daily encounter with antisemitism on the front; the "Jewish census" of 1916, which was allegedly designed to refute the accusation that Jews were dodging military service on the front while accumulating wealth at the rear; and the direct encounter with Eastern European Jews along the Eastern front – all of these, so the argument runs, enhanced Jewish self-consciousness and brought an end to the period of their unreserved assimilation.

Yet the enhancement of self-awareness among German Jews actually began before the war. By the later part of the nineteenth century, the yearned-for dream of full membership in Germany's civil society seemed to have lost much of its credibility. The earlier years, beginning in the late eighteenth century, were a time of struggle for full legal emancipation, prior to which assimilation would be inconceivable. Then, in the middle of the nineteenth century, it seemed for a while that there was a real chance for Jews to "enter." But with the resurgence of antisemitism in the late 1870s, the enmity towards them and consequently their own doubts and alienation intensified. It was not only the antisemites who bashed the

---

[1] This is to be expected in works related to Zionism, but see also Eve G. Reichmann, "Der Bewußtseinswandel der deutschen Juden," in Werner Mosse (ed.), *Deutsches Judentum im Krieg und Revolution, 1916–1923*, Tübingen, J.C.B. Mohr, 1971, pp. 511–612.

Jews, and it was not only the conservatives who repeatedly hammered on their inevitable distinction as permanent foreigners. Even steadfast liberals sometimes refused to accept them. Liberalism in Germany, particularly in its Prussian version, was based on the call for constitutional liberty enhanced by uniformity and on civil equality enhanced by the eradication of any hint of difference. In the new Germany there was no place for pluralism, and those who attempted to uphold it were quickly labeled "enemies of the state" – the Catholics, for example, or the Social Democrats. From this point of view, any ethnic diversity, as well as any religious or class pluralism, was suspect. The call was for total blurring into the one and only German national community.

Originally, the typical reaction of most Jews to the demands of their liberal allies, as we saw, was based on a reassertion of shared assumptions. Jewish public figures and scholars of various disciplines argued for patience and tolerance until complete "Germanization" was attained. It was, however, Moritz Lazarus, who came from a remote town in the province of Posen, from an Orthodox and Yiddish-speaking environment, who first formulated what later became the principles of Jewish existence in Germany. Lazarus argued for the full authenticity of the Jews' sense of German nationalism: "We do not want to be, and cannot but be anything other than German," he preached, "not merely by our language, but also because we live in this country, we serve it and obey its laws. German *Bildung* is our guiding light, and German art fires our imagination. This is our cradle, and this is where our fathers have been buried for generations."[2] Contrary to Harry Bresslau and Hermann Cohen, at about the same time,[3] Lazarus insisted on the Jews' right to remain Jewish. He also made this right the cornerstone of both his academic career, as a pioneer of *Völkerpsychologie* and his general, social-political thought. Hermann Cohen, too, overcoming the effects of the new antisemitism of the late seventies, soon recaptured both his enthusiasm for German patriotism and his faith in the uniqueness of Judaism. In his later years he was preoccupied with the search for the true content of Judaism, a Judaism that could be integrated in German culture without relinquishing its essence.

The change of consciousness occurred in parallel with the consolidation of a new social context in which the German Jews now lived and operated.

[2] From a speech by Lazarus on December 2, 1879, "Was heißt National," Quoted in: Ismar Schorsch, *Jewish Reactions to German Anti-Semitism 1870–1914*, New York, Columbia University Press, 1972, pp. 59–60.
[3] On Bresslau and Cohen, see also Chapter 1, b.

Despite their almost full integration in Germany's public life, their private,
intimate affairs were more often than not experienced within the confines
of a Jewish environment. Gershom Scholem, for example, clearly stressed
in his memoirs that, despite the abandonment of most Jewish customs in
his parents' home, an exclusively Jewish company was preserved there.
Non-Jews rarely visited the house; when they did, it was primarily on
semi-formal occasions and usually without their wives. It was common
in those circles, he added, to maintain complete social exclusivity and
even look down on those who overtly sought the company of non-Jews.[4]
Similar descriptions can be found in other contemporary accounts. Jakob
Wassermann recalled how he found himself on arriving in Vienna in the
company of Jews only. In Prague, as Max Brod re-tells, an almost total
Jewish exclusivity was preserved on all intimate occasions.[5] In addition to
what I found with regard to the Jewish community in Altona, a number of
other studies also show that Jews still tended to reside in close proximity
to each other even in large, modern cities, and outside the public sphere
they usually preferred the company of their Jewish relatives and friends.[6]

There were plenty of signs, to be sure, of advanced assimilation. Usually, these were recorded in the rates of conversion or the withdrawals
from the community, which were legally allowed since 1873, as well as in
the rate of intermarriage between Jews and non-Jews. A recent summary
reaffirms that, between 1800 and 1870, there were approximately 11,000
converts to Christianity and this number was doubled by the end of the
century.[7] Mixed marriages were apparently one of the main reasons for
baptism, especially among women, and the habit of baptizing children,
while the parents remained Jewish, even members of the Jewish community, was also relatively widespread. Now, endogamy was a powerful
force in Jewish history for generations. In the discourse on the presumably

[4] See Gershom Scholem, "On the Social Psychology of the Jews in Germany," in David Bron-
sen (ed.), *Jews and Germans from 1862 to 1933: The Problematic Symbiosis*, Heidelberg,
C. Winter, 1979, pp. 9–32, especially 19. See also his memoirs, *From Berlin to Jerusalem:
Memories of my Youth*, New York, Schocken Books, 1980 (originally in German, 1977),
especially chap. 2.

[5] See Jakob Wassermann, *Mein Weg als Deutscher und Jude*, Berlin, S. Fischer, 1921, p. 102
(also available in English: *My Life as German and Jew*, New York, Coward-McCann,
1933); Max Brod, *Streitbares Leben 1884–1968*, München, F.A. Herbig,1969, pp. 153–4.

[6] For a detailed and complex picture, but in the end not unlike mine, see Marion Kaplan,
"Friendship on the Margin: Jewish Social Relations in Imperial Germany," *Central European History* 34, 2001, 471–502.

[7] See Monika Richarz' chapter on demography in Michael A. Meyer (ed.), *German-
Jewish History in Modern Times*, Vol. 3: *Integration and Dispute 1871–1919*, New York,
Columbia University Press, 1997, pp. 7–34.

approaching end of Judaism that developed in the immediate pre–World
War I years, it was, indeed, the collapse of endogamy and the widespread
tendency to marry non-Jews that played the main role. The data on this
matter are interesting, indeed.[8] Accordingly, figures reached the double
digits sometime after 1900; by 1920 they were as high as 20 percent, and
continued to rise during the years of the Weimar Republic. But here, it
is also well worth remembering that by the late nineteenth century, Jews
constituted less than 1 percent of the population in Germany. At the same
time, they were moving freely – geographically and socially – in German
society, so that the chances of intermarriage were very high indeed. If the
rates were kept below 10 percent as late as 1900, this can only be considered a substantial achievement. It surely reflects the continued strength of
the endogamic instinct among Jews rather than its disappearance. Still,
the trends were apparent and a cause for alarm among the leadership.
Less apparent were the countervailing forces working at the same time,
the forces of "dissimilation."

It is within that context that the story of Walther Rathenau becomes
paradigmatic. We encountered earlier his *Shema Israel* ("Hear, O Israel"),
the article in which he appealed to his fellow Jews to cooperate more
wholeheartedly in the assimilationist project.[9] These were also the years
in which his own father's meteoric success as an industrialist seemed to
him most unworthy. It was, after all, success devoid of genuine Germanization, so he felt, or success without integration. Gradually, however,
Rathenau found his way back to mainstream German Jewry, and he was
then able to recapture their ears and even their hearts. As early as 1911
he claimed that he did no longer understand what he himself had written in those earlier "difficult years," in that notorious article.[10] His new
book, *Staat und Judaismus*, contained a forceful attack on contemporary Germany and its rampant antisemitism. "In the life of every young
German Jew," he recounted, "there comes a moment he shall never forget.

---

[8] Data on mixed marriage are available in *ZSDJ*: for Berlin, in the volumes for 1906 and
1907, 79–80 and 107–108, respectively; for Munich: 1909, 95; 1911, 28; general figures:
1915, 181; 1924, 25. Compare also David Tachauer, "Statistische Untersuchung über die
Neigung zu Mischehen," *Zeitschrift für die gesammte Staatswissenschaft* 71, 1915, 399–
419, 614–43. Most comprehensive in the new research literature: Kerstin Meiring, *Die
christlich-jüdische Mischehe in Deutschland, 1840–1933*, Hamburg, Dölling und Galitz
Verlag, 1998. Compare part I, chap. 2.
[9] The article was first published on March 6, 1897 in Maximilian Harden's journal, *Die
Zukunft*.
[10] See Rathenau in a letter to his friend Willem Schwaner, from July 17, 1914, in Walther
Rathenau, *Briefe*, 2 vols., Dresden, C. Reissner, 1927.

It is the moment in which he first becomes aware of the fact that he has come into this world a second-class citizen, and that no talent or accomplishment could ever change this fact."[11] Yet, like many of his coreligionists, Rathenau never fully internalized this painful reality. If there was indeed such a moment in their lives, it was a fleeting moment. Trust in the power of their talent and the effect of their accomplishments had been vital for their stubborn optimism throughout the Wilhelmine era. Despite his stressful relationship with his father and the lethal criticism he directed at Germany's new industrial culture, which was epitomized indeed by his own family's concern, the Allgemeine Elektricitäts-Gesellschaft (AEG), Rathenau eventually remained a part of his father's milieu almost all his life. In his most taxing hours, he would always crave his father's sympathy and esteem. He was apparently never confident enough in his own gifts as a thinker and writer, so that he was never ready to give up the position that practically fell into his lap, so to speak, as an heir to his father. It was under the shadow of that success that Rathenau also finally relinquished the ideal of total assimilation. He rejected the option of conversion and was taking special care to present himself as a Jew in that strange combination of condescension and awkwardness that was so typical of him. Bernard von Bülow, the German Chancellor in the years between 1900 and 1909, recounted his first encounter with Rathenau: "He was about forty at the time, but looked old, extremely attractive and most elegantly attired. He approached me with a deep bow and said in a resounding voice, with one hand resting on his chest: 'Your Highness, before I am granted the honor of speaking with you, I wish to make a statement that is also a confession: Your Highness, I am a Jew. . . .'"[12]

Since the last decade of the nineteenth century, then, a number of trends seem to suggest that German Jews were finally seeking to cross the limits of the delicate compromise between inclusion and exclusion that they had learned to live with, rather comfortably, in previous years. Clearly, even assimilation-seeking Jews were now taking part in a process of dissimilation; quantitatively, perhaps, it was not a strong enough process to upset assimilation altogether, but qualitatively it was of great social and cultural significance.

[11] Walther Rathenau, *Schriften*, Arnold Harttung et al., (eds.), Berlin, Berlin Verlag, 1965, 108.

[12] Quoted in Walther Rathenau, *Gesamtausgabe*, Hans D. Hellige and Ernst Schulin (eds.), Munich and Heidelberg, G. Müller, 1987, vol. 2: *Gespräche*, 654. For a further discussion of Rathenau's fate see the Epilogue.

Two main forces nurtured dissimilation: the exclusiveness and recurrent hostility of the host society, on the one hand, and the inner dynamics of assimilation itself, on the other. Clearly, any attempt to explain it must begin with Jewish response to the outside barriers, both ideational and practical, placed by non-Jews on their path to full integration. Under the circumstances of Imperial Germany, antisemitism must have been the single most important factor in the collapse of Jewish faith in emancipation and in reviving Jewish self-consciousness. Individual biographies recounting the pain and disappointment caused by antisemitic encounters and a consequent return to some form of Jewishness in response to them are many and familiar enough. More interesting, perhaps, are the collective dissimilatory responses of German Jewry on the organizational and communal levels. From the middle of the century onward, as we saw, restrictions on Jewish membership in a variety of social clubs and local associations caused the establishment of parallel Jewish bodies. The *Bnei Brith*, for example, was a Jewish counterpart to the Masonic lodges, and the various Jewish student bodies, reading societies, and so on, all were in fact substitutes for membership in general German associations.[13] But by the late nineteenth century, the new Jewish organizations began to carry another message. Clearly, the emergence of the Zionist movement was an expression of a new Jewish consciousness, and in 1893, the establishment of the *Centralverein deutscher Staatsbürger jüdischen Glaubens* (The Central Association of German Citizens of the Jewish Faith), commonly known as the CV, in 1893, carried similar connotations. Concurrently, a considerable increase in public Jewish activity seemed to have taken place, much of it outside these two main bodies. That same year, the *Verein für jüdische Geschichte und Literatur* (The Association for Jewish History and Literature) began its activities, soon to be followed by the *Kartell Jüdischen Studentenverbindungen* (The Umbrella Organization of Jewish students in Germany) and a few years later by the *Hilfsverein der deutschen Juden* (The Aid Society of German Jews), mainly designed for helping immigrants from the East.

The story of the CV is particularly relevant in the present context. Although it was intended to provide a forum for the joint work of *Abwehr* (defense against Antisemitism), it, too, gradually became yet another center for an organized *Rückkehr* (return to Judaism). Paradoxically, the CV, while repeatedly proclaiming its commitment to assimilation, eventually

---

[13] On the role of Jewish organizations such as Bnei B'rith, see also Chapter 9, c and footnote 38.

became an agent of dissimilation.[14] After all, by the late nineteenth century it was no longer the defiantly traditional, Orthodox Jews, keen on stressing their distinctiveness, that were the target of antisemitism, but the liberals, the Reform Jews, the ones willing to adapt and to change; not the still half-segregated Jewish communities in villages and small towns, but the urbanized, bourgeois Jews in the large urban centers. They were the ones who were now forced to reassess their personal and public positions in the face of antisemitism, and it was they who flocked to the CV. Likewise, it was not only professional qualifications that made highly successful lawyers take up the leadership of this organization, but also the fact that it was they and their kind for whom public prejudice now often posed insurmountable obstacles. Antisemitism seemed less threatening to the striving, upward-climbing Jews characteristic of the first and second generations of emancipation than for those who had apparently made it later on in the century. These distinctly German Jews were most badly hit by the murky waves of the "new" antisemitism, and they set out to defend themselves. A half-century earlier, Jewish men – and women – had often been brought to conversion as a last resort in their efforts to overcome the hurdles of antisemitism. This was the context of the conversion of Eduard Ganz, for instance, Hegel's pupil and the unofficial head of the *Verein für Cultur und Wissenschaft der Juden* (The Association for Jewish Culture and Science) in Berlin of the 1820s. But by the end of the nineteenth century, while some continued to choose this route, others regarded it with contempt, as a kind of betrayal.[15] They felt confident enough now to respond to antisemitism as a group and in public.

However, antisemitism was by no means the only force working for dissimilation. At that time, traditional Judaism,based on complete obedience to religious laws and full loyalty to old customs, was almost entirely replaced by another type of Judaism in Germany, one ready and willing

[14] For the history of the CV, see mainly Arnold Paucker, "The Jewish Defense against Antisemitism in Germany," in Jehuda Reinharz (ed.), *Living with Antisemitism: Modern Jewish Responses*, Hanover, NH, University Press of New England, 1987, pp. 104–32; Jehuda Reinharz, *Fatherland or Promised Land: The Dilemma of the German Jew 1893– 1914*, Ann Arbor, MI, University of Michigan Press, 1975. More recently, using the discovered archive of the organization in Moscow, see Avraham Barkai, *Wehr Dich! Der Central verein deutscher Staatsbürger jüdischen Glaubens, 1893–1938*, Munich, C.H. Beck, 2002.

[15] The contributors to the official organ of the CV addressed this issue repeatedly. See *Im deutschen Reich*: 1897, No. 12; 1898, No. 4; 1900, No. 11; 1904, No. 7, 8, 10, and compare Alan Levenson, "The conversionary Impulse in Fin de Siècle Germany," *Leo Baeck Institute Yearbook* XL, 1995, 107–22.

to accept modernity. As a result, I argued, Jews did not become simply like other Germans but developed a new kind of uniqueness and were often drawn together in new and unexpected ways. Jewish demography and the Jews' vocational and social peculiarities, as we have seen, helped to reassert the ties among them and consolidated their identity in new and different terms. It was precisely those elements that made for their spectacular social climbing and far-reaching assimilation that also worked to sabotage that same assimilation. Many Jews, concentrating in the large towns and in a limited number of occupations, were reaching similar levels of education and developing similar attitudes to family life, the upbringing of children, the lifestyle they ought to lead, and the careers they should choose. They shared a common passion for German theater, literature, and the arts; they often had a knack for Wagner and an outspoken taste for modernism. They naturally moved within the same social circles and were brought into new kinds of contacts with each other. Surely they were protecting themselves against insults and rebuffs coming from the outside world, but they were also positively attracted to their own milieu by a multitude of common experiences, life strategies, hopes, and aspirations. Theirs was not a community of social exclusiveness but of the social attraction among likes. Finally, the community of the successful, talented, educated, and influential became an object of identification even for the poor and ordinary Jews. They were *drawn* together, indeed, as a result of shared domestic culture but also by common pride in their collective achievement and common belief in its promise. Thus, both antisemitism and the process of assimilation helped to set in motion a complex dialectical process of dissimilation.

b. Reassessing the Jews from the East

Here we encounter yet another paradox. For this dissimilatory trend to become more than a marginal phenomenon, the entire process had to be recognized and appreciated for what it was. And indeed, at this point, several elements in the history of German Jewry combined to enhance not only the dissimilatory trends themselves, but also the need to perceive, recognize, and eventually also to accept them. Among these, the so-called *Ostjudenfrage*, the problem of the Jews from the east, was particularly important. This was perhaps the issue that, more than anything else, forced German Jews into a constant process of reassessment, making dissimilation a conscious process, its denial almost impossible, and its acceptance increasingly inevitable. The *Ostjuden* issue is particularly

clouded by mutually derogatory "folklore." But in two outstanding studies, historians Steven Aschheim and Jack Wertheimer helped to clear up
much of the confusion, provided a wealth of new facts and figures, and
called for a renewed interpretation.[16]

The influx of Jewish immigrants from Eastern Europe, which took on
new proportions during the 1880s, found German Jews confused and
apprehensive. Jewish organizations, such as the *Deutsch-Israelitischer
Gemeindebund* (DIGB), and Jewish newspapers, such as the *Allgemeine
Zeitung des Judentums*, were seriously alarmed. In fact, the overall unity
of Jewish communities that the DIGB strove to achieve was now believed
to be particularly urgent considering the new social and cultural dangers
from the east. The organization even tried to appeal to the authorities to
control and limit the scope of this immigration, and it continued to pursue
this matter as a high priority as long as it existed. Every Jew in Germany
would be implicated in the deeds and misdeeds of these uninvited guests,
ran the argument. The hard-won respectability and solid citizenship of
the local German Jews was in serious danger of discredit. Heinrich von
Treitschke's comments on the filth brought into Germany by eastern Jews
received an ambivalent response from German Jews. Indeed, many of
them found it necessary to reiterate the distinction between themselves and
the "backward" newcomers. Some pleaded for more time and patience
for the full integration process of all Jews into the superior culture of
Germany, arguing that, because local Jews had proved their adeptness,
there was no reason to think their brethren from the east would not be as
quick to do the same. Even twenty years later, the newly established *Hilfsverein*, impressive as its charity work among Jewish immigrants from the
east had really been, clearly operated on the assumption of a deep cultural gap between *Ost-* and *Westjuden*, and the absolute superiority of
the latter. As an umbrella organization for extensive social work among
the needy immigrants, it nevertheless preferred to see them as transient
elements that were to be speedily dispatched to distant shores.[17] In a
CV meeting in Hanover in 1904, James Simon openly argued the need for
vocational training of Russian and Galician Jews, to make them eventually

---

[16] Steven E. Aschheim, *Brothers and Strangers: The East European Jew in German and
German-Jewish Consciousness 1800–1923*, Madison, WI, University of Wisconsin Press,
1982; Jack L. Wertheimer, *Unwelcome Strangers: East European Jews in Imperial
Germany*, New York, Oxford University Press, 1987. Unless otherwise indicated, statistics about eastern Jews are cited from Wertheimer's book.

[17] For the history of the *Hilfsverein*, see Moshe Rinott, *The Help Society for German Jews*
[Hebrew], Jerusalem, School of Education, the Hebrew University, 1963.

exportfähig ("exportable").[18] The attitude of this organization to Ostjuden was the ultimate expression of active and engaged solidarity combined with fear that was so characteristic of the majority of German Jews. While the constant flow of Jews from the east kept alive the old stereotype of the religiously orthodox Jew, a small speculator and a *Schnorrer*, it also strengthened the need of the assimilated to dissociate themselves from the newcomers, so as to avoid being identified with these "questionable" types.

But like antisemitism in general, its anti-*Ostjuden* version also had a dialectical, dissimilatory effect. Aschheim has convincingly shown the intermingling of old and new Jewish images, the "Caftan" and the "Cravat," as he had fittingly called them.[19] From Treitschke's onslaught in the late 1870s to the National-Socialist *Der Stürmer*, he explains, the link between these two images has always been constitutive for both the theory and the practice of German antisemitism. Gradually German Jews were made to perceive this fact as well. As time passed, and with the continuing stream of Jews from the east, it became increasingly clear that antisemitism was not only, or even primarily, directed against the old-type, unassimilated, ghetto Jews personified by the *Ostjuden*. It was even unlikely that some of the hostility would be deflected against them. The actual presence of the Caftan Jew in the streets of urban Germany was immaterial for the antisemitic message. His image could be easily conjured up in his absence, too, and there was more than sufficient popular material for this purpose. The main brunt of the attack was in any case to be borne by the local, Cravat-type Jews, who had relinquished the external Jewish marks more than a generation before. As the antisemitic campaigning continued, its real nature was made increasingly clear, and German Jews also learned to appreciate it.

Central to this process of recognition was the main fact about the *Ostjudenfrage*, namely, that it really never existed – or rather that it never existed in isolation and was intrinsically inseparable from the greater issues of assimilation. From this perspective, it becomes essential to look at a few relevant figures with greater care and precision.[20] By 1910, about

---

[18] James Simon, "Die Erziehung zur Bodenkultur und zum Handwerke: Eine soziale Frage," *Im Deutschen Reich* 10(3), 1904.

[19] I owe much of this discussion to Aschheim, *Brothers and Strangers*, chap. 3, 58–79.

[20] The data are based on Wertheimer, *Unwelcome Strangers*, and on data in the *ZDSJ*, June 1905, 10; December 1905, 4–8. See also Bruno Blau, *Die Entwicklung der jüdischen Bevölkerung in Deutschland*, Berlin, 1950 (a manuscript, a copy of which is held at the Leo Baeck Institute's Library in Jerusalem), 58–9.

12 percent of all Jews in Germany – that is about 70,000 men, women, and children – mostly from the so-called east, did not possess German citizenship and were legally considered resident aliens. Most of them settled in a few of the larger German cities and constituted a highly urbanized group. Some, to be sure, came from big cities in the east, but the majority combined the movement from one country to another with a transition from rural or semi-rural living to an urban, even metropolitan, environment, a feat that was normally achieved by other populations gradually and under less traumatic circumstances. On the eve of World War I, 57 percent of all foreign Jews came from Galicia, and between 8 and 10 percent came from Hungary. Thus, for about two-thirds of these immigrants, the German language was a mother tongue, and they had grown up, prior to immigration, into a German or Germanized environment. These men and women often had more than a touch of Yiddish in their German speech, and they normally carried with them a discernible foreign intonation, the remnants of Talmudic colloquialism, and a dash of Galician wit. They were, however, often surprisingly well versed in Schiller, for example, or at least well trained and comfortable in the German lower middle-class milieu with its prose and poetry treasures.[21] The wealthier among them may have indeed been "children of two cultures" but only rarely were they complete strangers in Germany. The better educated – and and this was not necessarily always the better situation – usually received some German Gymnasium instruction before they left for Germany.[22] Others were at least fluent in the language and had a typically large measure of spiritual openness to absorb new cultural contents. Among the *Galizianer*, many were energetic, adaptable, and open-minded, though of course some very poor and very ignorant were among them too.

My demographic study of the Jews in Altona provides illuminating information on this population.[23] The city of Altona was a powerful magnet for immigrants from the east. Its geographic location near the port of Hamburg, the main point of origin from Germany to the United States; the relatively low housing prices compared to those in Hamburg itself; and its reputation as an energetic Jewish community that was famous for its rabbis and scholars made Altona a natural center of immigration. In the last decade of the nineteenth century, Altona hosted not only Jews

---

[21] For an example of this kind of cultural background, see the autobiography of Marcus Ehrenpreis, *Between East and West* [Hebrew], Tel Aviv, Am Oved, 1953.

[22] This is how Ernst Simon saw Martin Buber (born in Vienna but educated in Brody). See his "Martin Buber and German Jewry," *Leo Baeck Institute Yearbook* III, 1958, 3–39.

[23] See Part III, Chapter 10, and the relevant footnotes there.

TABLE 13.1. *Social Division of the Jews in Altona, 1890, by Place of Birth (Percent)*

Born in	Upper Class	Middle Class	Lower Class
Altona	3.0	63.5	33.5
Hamburg/Wandsbek	2.9	59.4	37.7
Nearby migration (in Germany	5.4	55.1	39.5
Long-range migration (in Germany)	8.7	63.0	28.3
Russia and Galicia	2.0	77.6	20.4
Other countries	1.8	63.0	35.2

from fourteen different foreign countries, but also immigrants from every Prussian province and from every state in the *Reich*. By 1890, one-eighth of the entire Jewish population in Altona resided there for 5 years or less; one-fifth – 10 years or less, and more than one-quarter – 20 years or less. Out of the 2,005 Jewish persons for whom we have information concerning their place of birth, just under one-half were actually born in town. An additional one-eighth came from the neighboring communities of Hamburg and Wandsbek, and 15 percent came from the rest of Schleswig-Holstein. An additional 10 percent were born elsewhere in the *Kaiserreich*, and a little more than 10 percent came from abroad, mostly from Eastern Europe. Contrary to common assumptions concerning the familial character of *Ostjuden* migration, the data suggest that men were notably more numerous than women, and they were mostly a young and dynamic type of immigrant. Again, in contrast with the common view, by 1890 many Jewish immigrants from the east were notably among the better-situated residents in town. While quite a large number of them were industrial wage-laborers, some were independent artisans or salaried employees in trade, and none peddlers or paupers on welfare. In addition, whereas about 63 percent of Altona's natives were members of the middle class, about 78 percent of the immigrants born in Russia and Galicia were members of this class, considerably more than immigrants from the town's vicinity and other regions of the *Reich*. The full picture is presented in Table 13.1.

The residence patterns of the immigrants from the east also suggest their relatively high social standing. While many of them resided in the outskirts of town, as was common among newly arrived immigrants, and were less dispersed in the municipal space of Altona than its native Jews, they usually did not reside in the poorer quarters of town. Overall, the immigrants improved the average standard of living of the town's Jewish community.

They did not manage to fully integrate themselves within the local community. Only a small minority married native Altona residents, and those were usually members of the lower classes. Penetrating the Jewish-German society, even for these energetic and skillful immigrants, was clearly not an easy task, but legal compulsions brought them at least into the fold of the established German-Jewish congregations. Significantly, many of the newly arrived joined the central liberal synagogue communities in the larger cities, rather than establish their own separate synagogues, thus clearly indicating their wish to become part of the respectable, upward-moving, outwardly oriented Jewish social milieu. Their willingness to integrate made their eventual absorption into the existing local communities virtually inevitable. From a local perspective, the continuous immigration made the communities ever more heterogeneous. The local establishment was continually confronted with the need to absorb new elements. But willingly or reluctantly, this had to be done, though rarely was it done without complaint and inner conflict.

There was, in fact, nothing new in this situation. Looking back some sixty to eighty years, we cannot but observe a very similar picture. The large-scale immigration from across the Prussian borders had not yet begun, but the *Ostjudenfrage* was certainly there. Between 1824 and 1871, about 50,000 Jews from the newly acquired Polish province of Posen migrated into the older Prussian regions.[24] Another 50,000 traveled the same route between 1877 and 1905. They, too, were mainly moving into the large urban centers, especially in and around Breslau and Berlin. They were also often proficient German speakers, ready and eager for acculturation. And they also sought rapid entry into the established Jewish community, whether the locals liked it or not. Those Polish *Hosenverkäufer* ("trouser sellers") who threw Treitschke into such a rage were energetic Jewish immigrants coming from Posen. The model *Ostjude* that was described by Georg Hermann for posterity in the character of the presuming nephew Julius Jacobi, who sent the cultivated Jettchen Gebert into fits of sheer physical nausea, came from Posen.[25] The story takes

---

[24] Data for the following discussion on migration from Posen are from the *ZDSJ* 6 (May 1910), 65–7; Jacob Segall, *Die beruflichen und sozialen Verhältnisse der Juden in Deutschland*, Berlin, M. Schildberger, 1912, pp. 7–8; Jakob Lestschinsky, *Das wirtschaftliche Schicksal des deutschen Judentums*, Berlin, Zentralwohlfahrtsstelle der Deutschen Juden, 1932, chap. 2. Specifically for Posen, most significant is Bernard Breslauer, *Die Abwanderung der Juden aus der Provinz Posen*, Berlin, B. Levy, 1909.

[25] Georg Hermann, *Jettchen Gebert*, Munich, Herbig, 1971 [1906].

place in the early nineteenth century, but it was, of course, written in the early twentieth century and the situation it depicts is familiar. Bear in mind that those of Gershom Scholem's forefathers who did not come from the previously Polish province of Silesia in the second half of the century had come from Posen a few years earlier. Salman Schoken, Rudolf Mosse, Heinrich Graetz, Eduard Lasker, and Arthur Ruppin were all born in the province of Posen. While in the early nineteenth century more than 40 percent of all Prussian Jews lived in that province, by 1910 they constituted just over 7 percent. Their massive westward migration continued almost uninterrupted from 1833 onward, spurred by new legislation that slightly eased their movement. When the first study of the Jewish mass immigration from the east was published in 1881, one could speak of large-scale Jewish migration only with reference to Posen.[26] Even during the 1880s, the decade of the Russian pogroms, migration from Posen was still numerically larger than that of Jews from Russia. And despite the fact that they had lived in Germany for a generation or two, Posen Jews were still widely considered *Ostjuden*. Vis-à-vis the new Galician masses, they were finally beginning to be accepted as bona fide German Jews. As is the case in immigrant societies everywhere, the pressure was off them and directed instead at the newcomers. Foreignness is a highly relative matter.

The story of German Jewry during the century of emancipation is indeed above all a story of migration, from one culture to another, from village to town, from small town to metropolis, from east to west.[27] These elements of mobility were overlapped and amplified for most Jews in Germany, but immigrants from the east combined them most immediately. They personified the essence of the assimilation process, with their lives presenting its difficulties and reflecting its absurdities. Watching them struggle through turned out to be an educational experience for many local Jews, and watching them was becoming increasingly more common.

Jews from the east immediately joined the main effort of German Jews at the time – namely, the effort of social climbing. German Jews were by then turned into a segment of the German bourgeoisie, leaning on their private and communal achievements in acquiring its two indispensable marks, *Besitz* and *Bildung*. The *Ostjuden* were from the very beginning part and parcel of this development. In fact, they made it appear all the

[26] Salomon Neumann, *Die Fabel von der jüdischen Massenwanderung*, Berlin, L. Simion, 1881.
[27] On the scope of Jewish migration, see Usiel O. Schmelz, "Die demographische Entwicklung der Juden in Deutschland von der Mitte des 19. Jahrhunderts bis 1933," *Zeitschrift für Bevölkerungswissenschaft* 8(1), 1982, 31–72, especially 46–52.

more spectacular. After all, their geographic and cultural starting point was particularly distant. The Posen Jews, who settled in the former Polish lands, were deeply steeped in an Orthodox, Yiddish culture until well into the 1830s. Both inside the province and everywhere they went as they moved westward, these Jews managed a feat of acculturation and upward social mobility – often within one generation. In their original places of residence, too, they energetically took part in the economic development of the province and repeatedly overtaxed its education facilities. The percentage of Jewish boys and girls who received better than an elementary education in Posen was the highest in Prussia.[28] Jewish families from Posen seemed to be sending at least one outstanding physician each generation into the wealthy, and sometimes into the poorer, suburbs of Berlin. Those who moved to Berlin on the strength of their business connections and entrepreneurship were sure to eventually contribute their share of doctors, lawyers, and scholars to the Prussian capital. Within the context of a large community in which social success was a primary goal, these striving, industrious, ambitious men were bound to become well integrated. They may have not been entirely welcome while they were still the incoming parvenus, but they could no longer be left out once they had made it.

The list of Jewish contributors to German cultural and scientific life is full of individuals whose parents, or even they, came from Posen. A brief review of those who made the pages of the first twenty years of the *Leo Baeck Institute Yearbook*, when it was mainly devoted to preserving the memory of these outstanding people, reveals one-third born in Posen and Galicia, not counting those whose parents had made the move shortly before their birth. Some of the most distinguished German Jews were, after all, nothing but *Osjuden*. Among the easterners, the Moravian and Bohemian Jews were the first to be accepted as Germans. Posen-born immigrants were then slowly drawn in as a respectable part of the community. The Galicians arriving at the turn of the century merely continued a process that had started much earlier, and on the eve of World War I they were well on their way in, or better yet, on their way up.

The best description of the position of the Galician Jew in prewar Germany is to be found in Shmuel Yosef Agnon's prose. Having been himself born in the Galician town of Buczacz, Agnon was naturally free of group prejudices regarding the different elements comprising German

---

[28] See especially Jakob Thon, *Der Anteil der Juden am Unterrichtswesen in Preußen*, Brelin, Verlag des Bureaus für Statistik der Juden, 1905, pp. 26–8.

Jewry, as he was free of the tyranny of archetypes in general. He perceived and exposed the dichotomy of *Ost-* and *Westjuden* in all its
complexities and absurdities, with its occasional tragedy and hilarity.[29]
Herr Lublin, in whose warehouse Agnon was apparently forced to spend
an idle Saturday night, came to Leipzig from his Galician *Shtetl* as an
eleven-year-old runaway.[30] He was first employed – if such a respectable
term might describe the situation – by a female relative as a "peddler's
assistant." He then quickly made his way up by displaying a unique tenacity and outstanding business acumen. By the eve of World War I, Lublin
had already considered himself, like other German Jews in town, a loyal,
patriotic German citizen of the Jewish faith. Of his faith, Agnon dryly
comments, little was left by then; he was a German patriot in body and
soul. Lublin married his former boss's daughter and established with her
a model German home, bringing up his three children, Heinz, Thomas,
and Gerde, to be as fully bourgeois and as fully German as he himself had
learned to be. To the astonishment of his local relatives, even the non-
Jewish city elite, who found him always ready with clever, original, and
useful advice, respected Lublin. With unfailing insight Agnon describes
the paradoxes of this man's social existence, alluding to the buried relics
that disclosed his Galician origins – his unease at the theater, his special
family sensibilities, and above all his peculiar *Galizianer* wit and humor.
These hidden remnants of a Jewish origin repeatedly surfaced not only
in his contacts with his non-Jewish associates, but also, most embarrass-
ingly, in the company of the local Jews, and most of all at the home of his
assimilating in-laws, making for particularly sarcastic passages.

After all, Lublin was merely one or two generations away from acquiring the benefits of the German culture of his *Schwiegereltern* ("parents-in-
law"). His neighbors, for instance, who were among the famous Leipzig
fur merchants, had come into town – from Russia, Lithuania, or Posen –
only slightly earlier.[31] Now it was the Galicians' turn. By the end of the
nineteenth century they seemed to be on the move everywhere. Sigmund
Freud was the son of an immigrant who had just arrived in the Habsburg
capital from a small town in Moravia. The famous actor Fritz Kortner's

---

[29] See Baruch Kurzweil, "The Image of the Western Jew in Modern Hebrew Literature,"
Leo Baeck Institute Yearbook VI, 1961, 170–89; Dan Miron, "German Jews in Agnon's
Work," *Leo Baeck Institute Yearbook* XXII, 1978, 265–80.
[30] This and the following discussion are based on Shmuel Yosef Agnon, *In Mr. Lublin's
Shop* [Hebrew], Jerusalem, 1974.
[31] Wilhelm Harmelin, "Jews in the Leipzig Fur Industry," *Leo Baeck Institute Yearbook*
IX, 1964, 239–66.

father, a small street-corner watchmaker, was one such Hebrew-reading, Yiddish-speaking Galician-born Jew. Victor Adler was born in a small Moravian town on the Galician border. And the list goes on.[32]

In contrast with the Posen immigrants, however, the absorption of the Galician Jews was complicated by a number of factors. First, the wave of East European immigrants that began in the 1880s included a fairly large segment of Russian Jews. Following the pogroms, many were trying to flee the Tsarist lands, and by 1890 about 10,000 of them were more or less permanent residents in Germany. Unlike the *Posener* and the *Galizianer*, and even unlike the Hungarian immigrants, these men and women were easily distinguishable as foreigners. Their language, habits, discourse, and spheres of interest all disclosed their origin, and, again unlike others, they rarely tried to hide it. Their share in the wave of immigration, however, was quickly diminishing, and in comparison with the Galician and the Posen contingent, the Russian element was gradually becoming negligible. In addition, the eastern Jewish immigrants in the latter part of the nineteenth century were presumably characterized by a lower social profile than their Posen predecessors in the middle of the century, though precise data are not available. Despite their energy and ambition, *Ostjuden* were still usually seen as crowding the Jewish houses of charity and "significantly expanding the occupational spectrum" of the Jewish community.[33]

Finally, and perhaps most significant, the new immigrants, primarily the Galicians, coming into Germany in the late nineteenth and early twentieth centuries confronted obstacles that their predecessors never experienced; they had to deal with a local Jewish community that had left behind the early stages of emancipation and assimilation and was entering a new phase. While time was cut short by the approaching war, entrance into the established Jewish milieu was becoming ever more difficult. The barriers were growing higher. By the time Agnon's Lublin was making his way up within the German-Jewish and the general German society in Leipzig, a relatively large number of previously Germanized Jews were already at the top of their social climb – either because there was simply nowhere further to go or because the obstacles piled up by a bigoted society were found to be insurmountable. These second-, third-, and occasionally even

---

[32] For Fritz Kortner, see his autobiography, *Aller Tage Abend*, Munich, Kindler, 1959. On Victor Adler, see "The Jewish Background of Victor and Friedrich Adler: Selected Biographical Notes" (by R. W.), *Leo Baeck Institute Yearbook* X, 1965, 266–76.

[33] Jacob Toury, "Ostjüdische Handarbeiter in Deutschland vor 1914," *Bulletin des Leo Baeck Instituts* 6(21), 1963, 81–91.

fourth-generation social climbers were now gradually losing interest in the route up. To the efforts of social climbing was now added the struggle for recognition by both their immediate Jewish environment and especially the non-Jewish society. They were busy protecting what they had achieved so far and sought to add status to class and prestige to prosperity. They struggled not merely to become properly acculturated but also to be known as such. Under the circumstances they were forced to make special efforts to do slightly better than the non-Jewish German bourgeoisie on all counts. Above all, they strove to excel in performing the rituals of middle-class lifestyle and civility. At this stage, newcomers from the east were posing an acute problem: They were sometimes truly insufferable.

Norbert Elias, while laboring to describe the transformation of the old war aristocracy into a civilized court-nobility, also incidentally commented on the history of German Jewry.[34] His distinction between the early stages of social mobility and assimilation on the one hand, and a phase of consolidation and a new self-awareness, first personal and later collective, on the other, is central for this discussion. Thus at the early stages of emancipation, *Ostjuden* aroused some unease and irritation, mingled with a measure of familiarity and sympathy, and were eventually absorbed into the community on the strength of their economic, social, and cultural achievements. Later, however, when status became the central issue, *Ostjuden* began to be conceived as a major source of embarrassment that haunted the better-situated, better-acculturated, and better-assimilated Jews for the entire period of massive immigration in the late nineteenth and early twentieth centuries. According to Elias's analysis, *Sham und Peinlichkiet* ("shame and embarrassment") were indeed the two main emotional poles of this generation. Shame was experienced when one forgot or neglected, even for a moment, the strict rules of the civilization game; embarrassment was aroused by the inappropriate behavior of others. Because of the strict rules of behavior that German Jews imposed on themselves, shame became an integral part of their life experience. Concurrently, their peculiar sense of responsibly and solidarity kept them almost continuously in a state of embarrassment, with which they had to learn to live. Galician Jews, like other Jews before them, had penetrated bourgeois society against all odds, and in particular, despite their questionable customs and manners. But they remained a constant

---

[34] Norbert Elias, *The Civilizing Process*, Oxford, Blackwell, 1994 (originally in German, 1937), especially vol. 2, chaps. 6, 7 in the concluding section.

reminder of the hardships of such penetration and were a perpetual source of embarrassment for those wishing to forget and erase those hardships.

At this stage of assimilation the antisemitic idiom helped some Jews to finalize their break from Jewish culture. Others, however, were beginning to face and appreciate the depth of that final break. They now began to see that it often had to amount to a complete break with their closest relatives, which in a sense meant a break within themselves; it was an inevitable self-negation that they were now rejecting. In addition, in confronting the ever-continuing flow of *Ostjuden*, they were forced to reflect on their own lives and seek new definitions for their existence and self-understanding. It was a modest beginning in an effort to rethink their identity and gradually to reach out beyond the limits of their own complacent, solid, bourgeois German identity. In a slightly different context, in a letter to his parents in June 1916, Franz Rosenzweig wrote:[35]

> One does not write more illogically about the *Ostjuden* than about the *Westjuden*; it is only that in the case of the *Ostjuden* it all seems to come at once, but if one could conceive of the whole literature about the *Westjuden* written, let's say, in the last twenty years, as condensed into one single year, so that literature too would turn out to be, as our Eastern-Jewish grand- and great-grandfathers would have called it, "a nice *Bilbul*" [Hebrew for "confusion, perplexity"]. There is no *Ostjudenfrage*, there is only a *Judenfrage* – and even that does not really exist. By the way, just imagine that all that German fear of the *Ostjuden* was to be directed not at the *Ostjuden* as such, but at these same people as future *Westjuden* (well, your kind).

A generation of Jews who were relatively free from the anxieties of constantly trying to improve their living standards and securing their entry into and position in non-Jewish society could now afford, so to speak, to look inward. These were Freud's most intellectually productive years; it was the time of the great Jewish cultural critics, of an inflow of Jews into the membership and leadership of the Social Democratic party, and of the emergence of both organized liberal Judaism in the CV and Zionism. The constant contacts with the *Ostjuden* and the confrontation with the parvenus served the purpose of this reassessment well. Recognizing the foreigners as a reflection of oneself was essential for the entire process. It is not by chance that the Viennese Jews took such an important part in it. After all, Vienna was the real capital of Galicia, being constantly filled and refilled with new waves of eastern immigrants. As an aspect

---

[35] Franz Rosenzweig to his parents [June 7, 1916] in Edith Rosenzweig (ed.), *Briefe*, in cooperation with Ernst Simon, Berlin, Schocken, 1935, p. 95.

of this reassessment process, *Ostjuden* were beginning to be looked on with a different eye – not by everyone, not everywhere, but surely by a significant, articulate, and outspoken minority. Gershom Scholem wrote about it in his memoirs:[36]

I was particularly interested in the members [of "Jung Juda"] from Eastern Europe, and this interest was shared by others. The more we encountered the not at all infrequent rejection of Eastern European Jewry in our own families, a rejection that sometimes assumed flagrant forms, the more strongly we were attracted to this very kind of Jewishness.

This was to a large measure, no doubt, a matter of a generational conflict, as Scholem indeed hastens to add, but it may have also been something else: an expression of a new sense of self and a search for an old-new identity. Jews were beginning to accept the heterogeneity of their communality and to acknowledge the positive potential of this pluralism. For many of them it was a matter of reaching the limits of assimilation; the process had come to the end of the line. From that point on, one could either continue to lose any trace of Jewish distinction or turn backward and inward, seeking a new definition for one's identity, and often also a new self-respect.

[36] Scholem, *From Berlin to Jerusalem*, 43–4.

14

Inventing Tradition

Jews, then, were seeking to preserve their identity while continuing their efforts to be integrated into Germany's social life and embrace its culture. Much has been written about the process of integration, its relative success, and the frustrations associated with it. Much less has been written about the project of preserving tradition or, better yet, of inventing one, which equally preoccupied German Jewry at that time. "Tradition" is such a common concept that it seems self-explanatory. Nevertheless, it has become the focus of much research and controversy in a wide range of academic disciplines during the last two or three decades. The momentum was given by anthropology and folklore studies, but nowadays we can likewise use a host of other approaches to tradition as well as to its conceptual opposites, such as modernity or innovation. These are major themes in the fields of art history, literary research, and history.[1] From a prevalent term in everyday discourse, "tradition" has become a focus of scholarly attention; it requires analysis and definition now, because it has become an object for deconstruction and reconstruction – a promising subject matter in contemporary historiography.

Let us define tradition in terms that are as close as possible to its conventional, everyday meaning. Thus considered, it is the complex of textual, symbolic, and institutional tools by which a certain society seeks to preserve the memory of its past, its values, ethos, and particular genius. As

[1] On the anthropological context, see Dan Ben Amos, "The Seven Strands of Tradition: Varieties in its Meaning in American Folklore Studies," *Journal of Folklore Research* 21, 1984, 97–131; Eric J. Hobsbawm and Terence Ranger (eds.), *The Invention of Tradition*, Cambridge, Cambridge University Press, 1983.

such, tradition operates through a collective memory that is responsible for passing its components from one generation to the next, acting in an arguably similar manner to private, personal memory. Despite the problems inherent in this analogy, it allows us to rely on the characteristics of memory known to us almost intuitively. First, memory begins to function, by its very definition, only when its objects are no longer present, when they turn into our "past" – recent or remote. Second, it always contains more, but often less than a mere reflection of this past. While it all seems rather self-evident in personal terms, we rarely apply such insights to collective memory. We tend to respect and trust its offerings rather more readily, often disregarding our own experience and neglecting the fact that tradition, like memory, is often misguided and misleading. While every tradition assumes a certain level of historical consciousness or even only some kind of vague awareness of change occurring in time, it is, like memory, indifferent to accuracy. Unlike modern historiography, it has no pretension of reconstructing the past "*Wie es eigentlich gewesen*" (as it really was), following Ranke. Tradition plays an entirely different role in our overall cultural fabric. Its claim of authenticity is in fact no more than a selective combination of elements from the past that are adjusted and adapted to meet our present needs. It is designed, as it were, to meet these needs.

Religious traditions, more specifically, are also substitutes for experiences that are no longer extant substitutes for a true, transcendental experience. They are, among other things, a symptom of the deterioration of a religious lifestyle, neither a reflection of past experiences nor a genuine return to these. Like other traditions, they too seek to deny this very fact. Only thus can they win the degree of cultural authority to which they aspire. Such traditions, which command authority and respect, did not exist in Judaism, at least until late in the eighteenth century.[2] Sacred texts, holiday customs, and numerous religious laws have been passed on through the ages and undergone changes in the process, of course. But the ultimate source of legitimacy in Judaism has always been the *Halacha* (Jewish Law), posited as both nontemporal and supertemporal. Only practices incorporated through time and accepted as part of the written Halachic code were legally binding. And while the Halacha has always been open to interpretation, it alone served as the basis for

---

[2] See, e.g., Nathan Rotenstreich, *Tradition and Reality: The Impact of History on Modern Jewish Thought*, New York: Random House, 1972; Raphael J. Z. Werblowsky, *Beyond Tradition and Modernity*, London, University of London, Athlone Press, 1976, chap. 3.

a Jewish lifestyle. Halachic scholars through the ages often made use of "our forefathers' tradition," to be sure, but their authority relied above all on their scholarly expertise. As a dynamic and changing religion, Judaism had at its disposal a reservoir of more or less binding traditions to fall back on as an alternative source of legitimacy. But it was only in the modern age, in the midst of secularization and the assimilation processes, that a Jewish tradition of sorts acquired a critical weight. "Inventing tradition" as a deliberate and conscious activity is a modern phenomenon.

Moreover, the invention of tradition may be regarded as Judaisms' most comprehensive and arguably most important "project of modernity." The term itself, borrowed from contemporary German sociologist and philosopher Jürgen Habermas, seems particularly fitting in our context.[3] In contrast to other aspects of modernization in Judaism, which were largely inadvertent and unplanned, this was a real "project" that was usually deliberate and carried out self-consciously. Paradoxically, it was a project that was designed to rejuvenate Judaism, transform it, and adapt it to the demands of the modern world. Because denying this purpose had been an eminent part of the entire affair, its innovative aspects tended to be ignored. The "inventors of tradition" sought to offer a renewed Judaism as the genuine, old product. The novelty was conceived, as is often the case, as a return to the sources, a rediscovery of the real essence, revitalizing an ancient nucleus within an empty shell. Focusing on this project of "inventing tradition," we may discover a wholly neglected zone. Beyond the interest it holds per se, it also enables us to reassess the overall cultural process that German Jews underwent during the nineteenth century, setting us free from contemporary debates and the usual categories employed at the time, allowing us a fresh perspective.

The new tradition that gradually emerged among German Jews from the late eighteenth century was, like most traditions, double-tiered. In anthropological jargon, it contained a "great" and a "small" tradition analogous in many ways to the dichotomy between low and high culture or elite versus popular mores.[4] The links between these two "tiers" are always complex, but in our case, they are particularly close. Despite its abstract and highbrow concerns, the "great" Jewish tradition always had distinctly educational and apologetic objectives, and these could only be

---

[3] See Jürgen Habermas, "Die Moderene – ein unvollendetes Projekt?" – a speech reprinted in his *Kleine politische Schriften I-IV*, Frankfurt a. M., Suhrkamp, 1981, pp. 444–64. See also Chapter 8.

[4] See, e.g., Robert Redfield, *Peasant Society and Culture*, Chicago, Univeristy of Chicago Press, 1956.

achieved through a constant process of dissemination, through an ongoing insertion of its products into more popular levels, working in the direction of a "small" tradition. The "small tradition," in turn, was always particularly attentive to messages from "above," persistently and consciously reproducing them. Nevertheless, the two never entirely intermingled, and in what follows I will comment on each: a little less on the more familiar "great" tradition and a bit more on the lesser known "small" tradition.

Max Weber characterized modernization with regard to high culture as the process through which human insight, traditionally expressed in religion and metaphysical thought, was split into three separate and autonomous spheres: science, ethics, and art.[5] Indeed, as the basic unity of Jewish religious life had been lost, it was now possible to build in its stead an alternative, using other components. The aim was to rearticulate these new components within a single, harmonic framework, albeit one that was often artificial and even somewhat forced. The "project of Jewish tradition" is marked by an attempt to replace religion, first by science, then by a philosophical discourse about ethics, and, finally, by moving in the direction of a new kind of art, primarily a new form of literature. Such efforts were meant to infuse Jewish intellectual life in the modern world with a new, more suitable, relevant, and dynamic content.

Typical of the "project of modernity" in the sphere of the "great tradition" were the activities of the *Verein für Cultur und Wissenschaft der Juden* (The Association for Jewish Culture and Science), which was established in Berlin in the summer of 1819 and remained active until the mid-1820s.[6] Its members began by systematically addressing Jewish history or, perhaps more precisely, the history of Judaism, seeking to delineate the principles of a new Jewish ethos and augmenting it with modern backing – in poetry and prose alike. The attempt to develop a new type of Jewish history was not something to be trifled with in this context. After all, the world of Judaism, despite its historical symbolism and its rich, central narrative, was principally ahistorical. The emphasis on the

[5] This summary is borrowed from Habermas, "Die Moderene – ein unvollendetes Projekt?." Compare also Max Weber, *Gesammelte Aufsätze zur Religionssoziologie*, Tübingen, J.C.B. Mohr, 1922/3, vol. 1, pp. 15–25, or Weber's introduction to his *The Protestant Ethic and the Spirit of Capitalism*, New York, Scribner's, 1958 (originally in German, 1920).

[6] On the Verein, see Siegfried Ucko, "Geistesgeschichtliche Grundlagen der Wissenschaft des Judentums," *Zeitschrift für die Geschichte der Juden in Deutschland* 5, 1935, 1–34, and Isamr Schorsch, "Breakthrough into the Past: The *Verein für Cultur und Wissenschaft der Juden*," now in his *From Text to Context. The Turn to History in Modern Judaism*, Hanover and London, University Press of New England, 1994, pp. 205–32.

exegesis of an ancient and fixed textual corpus and the reliance on a highly developed national mythology preempted the possibility of a genuine historical discourse within Judasim. A modern, "scientific" Jewish historiography thus emerged only in the early nineteenth century, influenced by the world outside Judaism and interdependent on its contemporary trends. The *Verein* was clearly based on the emerging "professional" historiography in Germany of that time, relying on a kind of romantic historicism and applying its new research methods to the study of Judaism.[7]

But the impetus did not come only from the outside. A historical approach to Judaism that would stress its potential for change and renewal was vital for any kind of reform movement among contemporary Jews. Custom and ritual reform, as well as the reformulation of essence and text, have all won their legitimacy primarily from a new, historical presentation of Judaism as a perpetually changing religion. Soon enough the historical discourse ceased to be the narrow interest of outstanding scholars and grew into a fad among Germany's Jews: an intellectual substitute for the previous study of sacred texts that functioned simultaneously as justification for alteration and an integral part thereof.[8] Thus, to regard Heinrich Graetz's multivolume *History of The Jewish People* as the most momentous intellectual event of the time is, indeed, no exaggeration. Graetz's popularity was enormous, but his colossal endeavor, admirable no doubt in its own right, was but the tip of the iceberg. By the turn of the nineteenth century, it seemed that every educated German Jew was somehow involved in historical research. The sorting and selection process that is so pivotal to the shaping of any historiography, was wide-ranging and twofold. In terms of content, selection meant privileging certain periods at the expense of others; in terms of method, it meant selecting the manner of presentation, the interpretive mode, and the appropriate narrative style.

In his reviews of the entire *Wissenschaft des Judentum* in nineteenth-century Germany, Gershom Scholem was particularly outraged by the

---

[7] See Yosef Hayim Yerushalmi, *Zakhor: Jewish History and Jewish Memory*, Seattle, WA, University of Washington Press, 1982. Compare Amos Funkenstein's criticism in "Collective Memory and Historical Consciousness," in his *Perceptions of Jewish History*, Berkeley, University of California Press, 1993, pp. 3–21, as well as Ismar Schorsch, "The Emergence of Historical Consciousness in Modern Judaism," in his *From Text to Context*, 177–204.

[8] See mainly Michael A. Meyer, *Response to Modernity: A History of the Reform Movement in Judaism*, New York, Oxford University Press, 1988, chap. 2, and the introduction to the book he edited: Michael A. Meyer (ed.), *Ideas of Jewish History*, New York, Behrman House, 1974, pp. 1–42.

choice of material.[9] In fact, Scholem regarded Leopold Zunz's, Moritz Steinschneider's, and Abraham Geiger's scholarly project as "diabolical," an attempt to extinguish, indeed "bury Judaism." He sarcastically viewed their selection of materials from Jewish history and writings and fiercely opposed what he considered their intellectualization of Judaism. They were turning it all into a phenomenon devoid of mythical and irrational elements, cleansed of any sign of crisis or internal strife, he argued. Selection, however, was a principal aspect of any project intent on reshaping a modern Jewish identity. A few decades later, Zionist historians who were seeking to reconstruct their own version of this identity were forced to make their own choices. Interestingly enough, their preferences were not very different from those of their ideological rivals. Abraham Geiger, who was considered the leading light of Reform Judaism, took a special interest in the history of the period of the Second Temple and medieval Jewry in his scholarly work. But it was the word of the prophets that he repeatedly stressed in his sermons, turning it into the embodiment of the fundamental principles of his modernized religion.[10] For Zionists, the prophets, who expounded a universal ethic, also were of paramount importance. Reformers in general regarded with skepticism ancient rituals and the multitude of practical, daily commandments imposed by the Halacha. But these were of even lesser significance to Zionists, who were mostly secular in outlook. Thus, although the Zionists' treatment of the Biblical narrative was undoubtedly different from that of the various Reform scholars, they too preferred to skip the parts dealing with formal legal matters and instead stressed the general conceptual and moral issues. Much has been written and said about the near-missionary idealism of liberal Judaism.[11] Surely, that abstract, ethical-philosophical interpretation of Judaism was a modern invention. Prominent thinkers, such as Moritz Lazarus, Hermann Cohen, and Leo Baeck, sought to make Judaism more

---

[9] The acerbic formulation of Scholem's position first appeared in Hebrew in an article from 1945. See in Gershom Scholem, *Explications and Implications: Writings on Jewish Heritage and Renaissance* [Hebrew], Tel Aviv, Am Oved, 1975, pp. 385–404.

[10] See Meyer, *Response to Modernity*, chap. 2, sec. 4. See also, with emphasis on Geiger's scholarly work, Susannah Heschel, *Abraham Geiger and the Jewish Jesus*, Chicago, University of Chicago Press, 1998.

[11] See mainly Uriel Tal, "German-Jewish Social Thought in the Mid-Nineteenth Century," in Werner E. Mosse, Arnold Paucker, and Reinhard Rürup (eds.), *Revolution and Evolution: 1848 in German-Jewish History*, Tübingen, J.C.B. Mohr, 1981, pp. 238–69. A useful summary is found in Heinz M. Graupe, *The Rise of Modern Judaism: An Intellectual History of German Jewry, 1650–1942*, Huntington, NY, R. E. Krieger, 1979 (originally in German, 1969), chaps. 18, 19.

appealing as a religion for modern men and to infuse it with meaning
that was relevant in the context of nineteenth-century bourgeois society.
But behind, or shall we say beneath, this level of historians and philosophers, all of whom were busy formulating a "great" tradition for their
purposes, the realm of the "small" tradition was bustling with activity,
too. An entire army of tradition-inventors worked to popularize the findings of the greater tradition and add their own special contributions at
the same time.

More than 200 Jewish newspapers and periodicals were published
during the years of the *Kaiserreich*. The majority naturally remained
marginal, yet some continued to appear regularly for decades and accumulated a loyal readership. To be sure, distribution rates were generally low
even for the surviving publications. The *Allgemeine Zeitung des Judentums* (*AZJ*), clearly the most important Jewish weekly of the nineteenth
century, reached a subscription rate of 3,000 in the late 1890s. On the
eve of World War I, the Orthodox *Jüdische Presse* achieved similar numbers, and at that time, the distribution of the *Hamburger Israelitisches
Familienblatt* was almost four times as high, while the organ of the CV,
Im Deutschen Reich, apparently reached the majority of its members,
approximately 40,000 readers. In addition, many who never regarded
themselves as Zionists read the Zionist press, which was famed for its
quality. Thus, bearing in mind the relatively small readership of all newspapers at the time and the fact that we are dealing here with a population
of only about a half-million people, the data suggest a genuine spree of
paper reading – and writing, of course.

Even more intriguing is the fact that the content of these various publications was almost exclusively Jewish. The press regularly reported on
the life of Jewish communities around the world; discussed relevant current affairs; and ran stories in installments about ghetto life, the Jews
in medieval Spain, and other topics enjoying high demand. The *Judaica*
catalog of the Frankfurt municipal library contains thousands of titles,
mostly published prior to 1914.[12] It obviously includes materials associated with the "great tradition" project of German Jewry, such as Bible
criticism, comprehensive treatments of canonic Jewish texts; theological, medical, and scientific texts; literary treatises; and so on. But no
less impressive are its lists of publications associated with the "small"
tradition: more than twenty collections of sermons and hundreds of titles

---

[12] Stadtbibliothek Frankfurt a. Main, *Katalog der Judaica und Hebraica*, Vol. 1: *Judaica*,
Frankfurt a.M., 1932.

in the *Erbauungsliteratur* category – a term borrowed from the Protestant-Pietistic world that was here applied to a somewhat lighter literature on religious topics. While these lists cannot inform us of the actual content of the relevant publications, they do give us an idea of the scope of the collective effort involved and the intellectual investment in it. Modern historiography, which is usually preoccupied with the contribution of Jews to the general German culture, and is so impressed by the accomplishments of a small elite among them, is rather oblivious to this persistent activity within the Jewish sphere, despite its vast scope and its powerful influence.

Because this entire issue has been so neglected, it is perhaps useful to point out once again that, although German Jewry did include an impressive upper class of the rich and the educated, and although the genuine lower class element within it was, indeed, very small, it was, as we saw, primarily comprised of men and women of the lower middle classes. During much of the nineteenth century and well into the twentieth century, German Jews usually opted for independent employment in commerce and the possession of small, even tiny businesses. Their massive entry into the free professions occurred only from the late 1890s, and the percentage of doctors, lawyers, journalists, and academicians among them has never peaked beyond 10 percent of the entire Jewish workforce, even in Berlin. The percentage of Jewish enrollment, both boys and girls, in the humanistic Gymnasia and German institutes of higher education was conspicuously higher than that of the rest of the population, but more than half of the Jewish children in Germany received only elementary education at that time.[13] Many of them remained for the rest of their lives avid consumers of popular Jewish culture of the "small tradition" type, and this was energetically manufactured for them by numerous writers and publishers. They were the readers of the thriving recreational press and the bearers of the typical Bar-Mitzvah presents. They thrived on that new, Jewish "instant culture."

The trend was indeed very similar to the one that occurred in the general German popular literature. The emphasis in Jewish literature may have been more educational, stressing history, philosophy, and various kinds of didactic literature, whereas the regular, German *Trivialliteratur* concentrated on fiction. But nevertheless it was a parallel phenomenon, a Jewish version of the German lower middle-class literature. In both cases,

---

[13] Jakob Thon, *Der Anteil der Juden am Unterrichtswesen in Preußen*, Brelin, Verlag des Büros für Statistik der Juden, 1905, pp. 23–5.

such literature was directly affiliated with the elite culture, often bearing its broader cultural and ideological messages. Yet it seemed that the Jewish version was fulfilling its role more openly, perhaps even more aggressively. Every Jewish almanac from the mid-nineteenth century onward (and such almanacs were published regularly at least in Berlin, Leipzig, Vienna, and Budapest) listed information about Jewish holidays next to the dates of scheduled trade fairs across Germany. Every such yearbook contained a mixture of popular historical essays, usually on antiquity, portraits of prominent Jewish figures throughout the ages, and obituaries of recently deceased notables. They would often contain histories of Jewish communities, usually in the nearby European sphere; some poems in verse, primarily in Hebrew but always with a German translation; a chapter from a historical novel, frequently in the context of the illustrious history of the Jews in medieval Spain; or a picturesque scene from the life of the eastern European ghetto. It was a more or less fixed format that was designed to convey to as large as possible an audience the contents and values of a newfound Jewish tradition, a tradition that not only sought to exist alongside institutionalized religion but even meant to replace it.

The most well-known and most productive collector and creator of the elements of this tradition was Ludwig Philippson, the untiring editor of the *AZJ*.[14] From the 1830s to his death in 1889, Philippson produced a constant stream of articles and essays, stories and poems, historical novellas, and even guidebooks for Jewish adolescents. "Do you feel yourself happy being a Jew?" he opens one such guidebook, and to attain happiness, he offers an assortment of chapters on Jewish history, discussions of the moral and spiritual significance of religious rituals, holidays, the Sabbath, and so on, and concludes with a "useful" section on Judaism as a guide for everyday bourgeois life in Germany.[15] Philippson was a prominent representative of liberal Judaism, but the message in his writings is surprisingly similar to that developed by the "domesticated Judaism," which was preached by Orthodox leaders, too. Despite the rivalry between the factions, Philippson was a kindred spirit to Rabbi Simon Raphael Hirsch, the leader of German Neo-Orthodoxy. Both emphasized the values of the

---

[14] Unfortunately, a worthy contemporary biography of Philippson is not available, but see Meyer Kayserling, *Ludwig Philippson: Eine Biographie*, Leipzig, Hermann Mendelssohn, 1898; Johanna Philippson, "The Philippsons: A German-Jewish Family 1775–1933," *Leo Baeck Institute Yearbook* VII, 1962, 95–118.

[15] See Ludwig Philippson, *Eine Mitgabe für das ganze Leben an den israelitischen Konfirmanden (Barmitzva) und die Konfirmandin oder beim Austritt aus der Schule*, Leipzig, 1870.

Jewish family and the significance of communal solidarity; both shared a broad though unsystematic interest in Jewish history, and a moralist, didactic approach to it. In short, they both offered their readers a cultural blend suitable for law-abiding citizens, loyal German patriots, and faithful Jews, all at the same time.

This fabricated tradition was tailored to suit the needs of the times. But despite the plethora of publications disseminating it, and despite the Jewish reading societies, popular lecture series, clubs, and so on, the "project" itself remained paltry and inadequate in many ways. The main difficulty grew probably from the fact that this entire tradition, both "great" and "small," has never strayed far enough from its German background. It ended up, in fact, as an appendix to German culture, a marginal and not quite respectable addition. A comparison with its Russian counterpart immediately exposes the inherent shortcomings of the German-Jewish project. An alternative Jewish tradition was also being developed in Russia, albeit belatedly. To be sure, Hayim Nachman Bialik and Scholem Aleichem also worked under the influence of their Russian environment, but under the circumstances, they were obliged to remain within the more or less isolated Jewish milieu. They wrote in Hebrew or Yiddish (occasionally in both) only for a Jewish audience. Their reception depended on this audience alone. This, no doubt, has had its drawbacks, but it also had some considerable advantages. First, the need for apologetics was much less pressing within the lingual-cultural framework of eastern European Jewry, and, second, the new Jewish tradition that emerged there could hold on to its best minds, at least intil 1917. It prospered because it could allow for the development of an entire cultural hierarchy while still maintaining internal mobility, flexibility, and openness. In contrast, the new Jewish tradition in Germany had none of these advantages. Written entirely in German, it was always in danger of losing its best and brightest over to the non-Jewish culture. Poets such as Heine and writers such as Wassermann, for instance, searched for their way "out," hoping to cross over, join the general cultural sphere, and communicate with its greater public. The best among them did indeed manage this feat. Whether they converted or not, they have become German artists by virtue of their talent, subject matter, and approach; and the separate, co-existent Jewish culture as such lost them, one by one. Only a handful of the Jewish thinkers operating within that separate Jewish culture were truly exceptional. The intellectual framework provided by the new "great" tradition of German Jews in the late nineteenth century was comparatively too narrow and far from measuring up to the best that contemporary German culture had to offer. The new "small" tradition lacked even the entertainment value that marked German popular culture. In any event, it was perpetually losing its most successful personnel to the surrounding culture.

Gershom Scholem movingly describes the need he and other Zionist youngsters in early 1900s Germany felt to break through the intellectual barriers of that domesticated tradition.[16] But it seems that Germany's Zionists also failed to offer a true alternative. They too remained chained to the same framework. The Zionists were no less hampered by the powerful shadow of the dominant German culture. Martin Buber's version of Hassidic stories about *Haba'al Shem Tov*, for instance, is unmistakably Germanized, and Gershom Scholem's Jewish mysticism is ultimately as heady and as intellectual as the endeavors of his rivals in the camp of the *Wissenschaft des Judentums*.

---

[16] See Gershom Scholem, *From Berlin to Jerusalem: Memories of my Youth*, New York, Schocken Books, 1980 (originally in German, 1977), especially chap. 3.

Epilogue

Closing the Circle

Two general works on the Jews during the Weimar Republic have been
published during the last decade of the twentieth century. One is Michael
Brenner's book, *The Renaissance of Jewish Culture in Weimar Germany*,
and the other – a history of German Jewry from the eve of World War
I to 1945, written by Moshe Zimmermann.[1] They clearly represent two
diametrically opposed views. Zimmermann looks at German Jews on the
eve of the Nazis' rise to power and sees a disintegrating community whose
members are losing interest in being associated with it and instead opt for
secular life that is undistinguished from the rest of Germany's new civil
society. In Zimmermann's book, German Jewry thus continued the process
of radical assimilation that had characterized it for generations, increasingly neglecting old identities while fully adopting new ones. If conversion
never became a mass movement, most Jews showed no more interest in
their religious and communal ties now, becoming "ordinary Germans." In
addition, a variety of demographic indicators pointed out to the process
of their disappearance. They were now marrying non-Jews in growing
numbers, their birth and death rates had plummeted, they were becoming a smaller and an increasing elderly community. Contemporaries, too,
runs the argument, were engaged in describing the "Decline of German
Jewry," arguing its pro and cons. Despite the massive immigration from
the east following World War I, the German Jewish community seemed
to be shrinking – both physically and spiritually. "Even without Hitler,"

---

[1] Michael Brenner, *The Renaissance of Jewish Culture in Weimar Germany*, New Haven,
CT, and London, Yale University Press, 1996; Moshe Zimmermann, *Die Deutsche Juden
1914–1945*, Munich, R. Oldenbourg, 1997.

according to Zimmermann, this Jewry was steadily losing its "weight, significance and uniqueness."[2]

Michael Brenner looks at the same data and sees a completely different picture. In some ways he is probably closer to the line suggested in this book. Accordingly, the process of *dissimilation* that began in late nineteenth century had been ever more noticeable during the Republic. In terms of ideology, the crisis of liberalism led to a process of "constructing a new Jewish identity,"[3] while in terms of organization it brought about the emergence of a community based more on culture than on religion, building up its self-confidence, and manifesting itself in a multifaceted and lively Jewish public life.

Both Zimmermann and Brenner are right, in some respects, no doubt. Both admit, albeit somewhat feebly, that we are faced here with a dialectical situation, or at least with a complex, polarized reality. From today's perspective, the Jews' full integration in the general German culture of the Weimar Republic can hardly be disputed. Their cultural prominence, especially in the academic world and in literature and most particularly as part of the republican, leftwing intellectual milieu, has widely been acknowledged. But the individuals usually discussed under these rubrics were not representatives of the group as a whole. The Jewish community in Weimar Germany was not comprised only of expressionist artists, champions of modern drama, leftwing journalists, or revolutionary activists. Nor were all Jews in Germany owners of large marketing chains, department stores, or shipping companies. Not all of them were medical doctors and successful lawyers. Just as before the war, the majority of German Jews were usually small- or medium-sized traders. During the short republican era, they usually continued to give their political support to moderate liberalism or to the less radical flanks of Social Democracy.[4] Indeed, with the rise of extreme nationalism and the strengthening of the Right even within the liberal camp, and with the establishment of Social Democracy as a legitimate, even a ruling, party, increasingly more Jews tended to abandon the depleted liberal parties and support the socialists. At the same time, however, they continued to benefit from Germany's high culture, each according to their own level of education and the means left for

[2] Zimmermann, *Die Deutsche Juden*, 1.
[3] Brenner, *The Renaissance of Jewish Culture*, 39.
[4] In addition to Jacob Toury's older work, *Die politische Orientierung der Juden in Deutschland: von Jena bis Weimar*, Tübingen, J.C.B. Mohr, 1966, see also Peter G. J. Pulzer, *Jews and the German State: The Political History of a Minority, 1848–1933*, Oxford, Blackwell, 1992.

such pleasures in those turbulent days. They continued to delight in the achievements of that time's musical scene, in the opera and the operetta, the theater and the cinema. They spoke standard German, often with special care, read and wrote German literature, and breathed the free air of German cultural life under the new regime. Some of them did indeed lose touch with their Jewishness and often made conscious efforts to wipe out the last signs of their previous identity. But the majority retained daily contact with other Jews, visited the synagogue on special occasions, and enjoyed the "folkloristic" aspects of their ethnic distinction – on the culinary level, in inner-group witticisms and jokes, in the sometimes peculiar and idiosyncratic use of language, and so on. There were also those who, disillusioned by the surging antisemitism during the war years and its ugly manifestations throughout the Weimar years, were now attempting to reassert their Judaism, infuse it with a new content, and revive it for their own needs.[5] Zionists still remained a minority among them, but non-Zionists were also often seeking a Jewish "authenticity" in which they could share. The efforts to create a new and more appropriate tradition, which I earlier described with respect to the nineteenth century, continued unabated. Brenner shows that the emphasis shifted from philosophy and history to the various spheres of the arts. Even Yiddish and Hebrew enjoyed a certain revival. Thus, 150 years after they began penetrating into German society, the Jews still had not disappeared. In many ways they were even more self-conscious and also perhaps more vulnerable than ever.

In historical memory, the Weimar Republic as a whole is perceived as a political entity fraught with tension and conflict, and despite all its achievements, it is still mainly seen as a prelude to Nazism. The history of this fragile republic, even in current political discourse, provides a precautionary tale; it is an example of what might happen to a regime that is incapable of defending itself. The Weimar Republic is any democrat's nightmare. It was a state born out of struggle and sacrifice that was gloriously built on the basis of a progressive and enlightened constitution and fortified with a remarkably professional legal system that finally caved in to the insurmountable social and political tensions raging within it. The Weimar Republic seems to have exposed all the potential weaknesses of a democratic regime, and in Israel it has often been used as a warning

---

[5] On antisemitism during the Weimar years, see especially Dirk Walter, *Antisemitische Kriminalität und Gewalt. Judenfeindschaft in der Weimarer Republik*, Bonn, J. H. W. Dietz, 1999.

sign. There, too, after all, a new democracy was established and forced to work for its preservation without relying on long-standing tradition; it was unable to draw on past memories or an accumulated political experience. Just like the Germans after World War I, we too regard ourselves as being constantly under siege, surrounded by enemies, and depending on our ability to unite and persevere, to make the best of things under great pressures. The rampant inflation period during the late 1970s and early 1980s has inevitably evoked memories of Weimar. There, too, the young republic fought for its life under circumstances of ongoing economic crisis. The combination of political frailty and repeated economic catastrophes, as the Weimar example seems to suggest, may prove to be fatal in our case, too. As much as Israelis sought to avoid any analogies with Germany, it was difficult to ignore the experience of the first German republic. It is still occasionally brought up as a case in point.

I now come back to my point of departure. Once again, the context in which I write seems to overwhelm me. In the wake of Yitzhak Rabin's assassination on November 4, 1995, fears for the fate of Israel's democracy were intensified. The comparison with Weimar seemed all the more relevant, although it was now, of course, mostly a matter discussed by historians. Most of those who actually experienced the fall of the first German Republic were no longer with us, and the collective historical memory of its failure had lost much of its vitality. But an impersonal memory often proves just as effective. In any case, a comparison between the assassinations of Walther Rathenau, Germany's minister of foreign affairs in the summer of 1922, with that of Yitzhak Rabin seemed relevant to me. Rathenau also was assassinated during his attempts to find a compromise on controversial issues between Germany and the surrounding states; he too was murdered by rightwing fanatics who wished to prevent Germany from taking a step in that direction, and, in both cases, despite the initial trauma and promises never to let the murder change the course of events, the system was gravely jeopardized by the affair.

In addition, of course, Rathenau's Jewish origin was clearly of major significance in the tale of his assassination. His death was a landmark not only in German history but also in the history of its Jews. Rathenau was unquestionably the most illustrious Jew in Weimar Germany. A young industrialist and the son of the founder of the AEG corporation, he was a man of many virtues. In addition to being a renowned businessman and a skillful manager and organizer, he was also a prominent intellectual and the author of books on modern life in general and on German social conditions in particular. He was connected by many ties to the various elites in Germany – economic, cultural, and political, first in the context of imperial society and then during the early Weimar years. He tried his hand at many projects and always proved innovative and original. He was a man who continuously sought to lead and excel.

Rathenau's career in government had been particularly eventful. When World War I broke out, he was appointed head of the Raw Materials Department in the German Ministry of War. A few months later, however, this energetic bureaucrat was forced to resign in frustration, fed up with the entire German leadership – military and civil. Apparently, even his fervent patriotism could not help him overcome his rising resentment of that leadership and its adventurous policies. Moreover, Rathenau was apparently unwelcome by the top bureaucrats and the army generals with whom he was expected to work. It was likewise difficult for him to cooperate with his colleagues in the industrial sector, who kept questioning his motives and refused to believe he was devoid of self-interest. For his part, Rathenau predicted rather early the approaching defeat of the German army, and all in all, he welcomed, albeit not without fear, the revolution that had brought forth the Republic. Along with the rest of the top echelons of the Imperial era, Rathenau initially had no real influence on the affairs of the new democracy. While he enjoyed the reputation of a capitalist who fought against capitalism and a patriot who warned against the war's disastrous end, it was only when the revolutionary and social-democratic phases of the new republic had been exhausted that conditions for his re-incorporation in the leadership had ripened. Having been dispatched earlier on a series of unofficial diplomatic assignments and serving as an "external" consultant on matters of de-mobilization and reparations, Rathenau was finally appointed to the post of minister of foreign affairs in the short-lived cabinet of Joseph Wirth of the Catholic Center party on January 31, 1922. In his few months in office, until he was assassinated on June 24 of the same year, he initiated a policy of economic collaboration with the victorious western nations, but he also took the entire international diplomatic scene by surprise when he signed the special treaty with Soviet Russia at Rapallo on April 16.

In those days Rathenau had been the focus of national and international attention, and as had so often occurred in his career before, his course of action provoked resentment on both the right and the left. Nevertheless, the choice of the radical "Consul Organization," an extreme rightwing underground group, to assassinate him seemed at first sight rather strange. After all, Rathenau was neither the only nor the most outspoken supporter of a policy of collaboration that was so fiercely rejected by the Right. On the contrary, he at first made every possible effort, even prior to his appointment as cabinet minister, to ease the (mostly economic) pressure on Germany. Despite the unrestrained attacks against him in a parliament speech by Karl Helfferich, leader of the *Deutschnationale Volkspartei*, just a day before the assassination, the conservative *Deutsche Tageszeitung* was quick to stress that Rathenau's recent pronouncements in the Reichstag had in fact won wide approval on the right, too, and his relationships with the leaders of that camp throughout his tenure as minister for foreign affairs were "quite reasonable."

What the alarmed journalists did not know, and could not have possibly known, was that on the night before the murder, after Helfferich's speech, Rathenau had held a long meeting with none other than Hugo Stinnes, one of Germany's leading industrialists and a staunch supporter of the right. The Republic's economic leadership could in fact be nothing short of grateful to Rathenau, especially for his achievements prior to his official appointment, in the secret negotiations with the English and the French in the matter of reparations. In this last conversation, which lasted until dawn, Stinnes reasserted his basic agreement with Rathenau's policy moves.[6] At this stage he was probably more optimistic than Rathenau regarding the possibility of shirking some of Germany's financial obligations. In any event, the message he conveyed was no less authentic than the one implied by Helfferich's vitriolic speech a few hours earlier. Certain sympathy for Rathenau in rightist circles was not a rare sentiment. He had proven his patriotism more than once in the past, and his obvious personal interests and social position made him a natural ally of the conservative circles, certainly more so than of the socialists, who were always suspicious of the motivations of this capitalist tycoon.

It has often been claimed that Rathenau's assassination was intended as a provocation. The right expected an uprising of rank-and-file Socialists as a result, compelling "the forces of law and order" to repress the revolutionary elements in Germany once and for all. If indeed this was the plan, then the choice of Rathenau seems inappropriate again. It is difficult to imagine a popular revolt resulting from the murder of an elitist figure such as Rathenau. He was loved by nobody and always represented none other than himself. No political group in the Republic felt particularly threatened by his murder. He had always been attacked from all sides and no one had ever been openly or consistently committed to his

---

[6] See Gerald D. Feldman, *The Great Disorder: Politics, Economics and Society in the German Inflation 1914–1924*, Oxdord, Oxford University Press, 1993, pp. 446–49.

defense. Rathenau's murder had undoubtedly come as a shock to many democrats. However, it should be noted that political assassinations were not uncommon during the early years of the Republic. After all, it was established in a revolutionary act and political violence had been a routine practice since its inception. The first political assassinations were those of Karl Liebknecht and Rosa Luxemburg, on January 15, 1919 – the two outstanding leaders of the *Spartacus* movement. But political violence continued to characterize the Republic even after the early days of the revolution. Kurt Eisner, the leader of the Independent Social Democratic Party in Munich was assassinated as early as June 1921. In August it was the turn of Mathias Ertzberger, a key figure in German politics since 1916 and the single most influential man in the Catholic Center party. Like Rathenau in the days ahead, Ertzberger was incessantly defamed and attacked by the right for having been among the signatories of the Peace of Versailles. His assassins were never caught. "I may be the next," Rathenau told Ertzberger's widow on a condolence visit.[7]

Nevertheless, Rathenau's murder seemed to have shaken the system. The pro-republican forces reacted emphatically and the public seemed agitated and troubled. In this atmosphere, it was no longer possible to ignore the country's crisis, and the "Law for the Defense of the Republic" was quickly passed by parliament. Meanwhile, the presidential elections were temporarily postponed, and the two socialist parties initiated a process that soon resulted in their reunification. The murder had no doubt been a turning point in the history of the Republic. It was regarded as a symbolic act, a manifestation of the hate harbored by certain circles towards the Republic. The assault on Rathenau was an assault on the new state as such.

In addition, the murder turned Rathenau into a "political martyr," as his biographer Ernst Schulin wrote, imbuing his life with "an unequivocal content that he himself, despite all his efforts, was never able to give it."[8] Indeed, nothing in his life had ever prepared Rathenau for his role as sacrificial lamb on the altar of a regime he accepted but never really

---

7 Martin Sabrow, "Märtyrer der Republik: Zu den Hintergründen des Mordanschlags vom 24. Juni 1922," in Hans Wilderotter (ed.), *Walther Rathenau 1867–1922: Die Extreme berühren sich*, Berlin, Argon, Deutsches Historisches Museum, 1994, pp. 221–36, here 223.
8 Ernst Schulin, *Walther Rathenau: Repräsentant, Kritiker und Opfer seiner Zeit*, Göttingen, Musterschmidt, 1979, p. 138, and see also among his articles on this topic: "Walther Rathenau und sein Integrationsversuch als 'Deutscher Jüdischen Stammes,'" *Jarhbuch des Instituts für Deutsche Geschichte*, Beiheft 6, Tel Aviv University, 1984, pp. 13–38.

propagated. He was never affiliated for long with any one political camp. He was a Jew and an intellectual, the "other" per se. Because of his Jewish origins and his social position, he was bound to remain aloof and be regarded as an arch-capitalist by the workers and a dangerous reformer, even a revolutionary, by the capitalists. Rathenau was a sensitive, eccentric person, a sworn bachelor in a principally patriarchal society, and a maverick in every possible sense. Most importantly in our context, neither was he ever a representative of German Jewry in any sense of the word.

Even so, the murder had its inner logic. The assassins saw Rathenau as the planning mind and throbbing heart of the detested Republic. He clearly personified for them all its failures. Rathenau was never able to hold on to one and the same position for long. He always remained an observer. As an industrialist, he was forever toying with the idea of a "corporative economy." Despite his affinity for the world of industrial tycoons and the goals of Germany's imperialism, Rathenau's central interest lay elsewhere, namely, in his country's traditional highbrow culture. Despite being a technocrat and an avid "system builder," he was primarily an intellectual of a highly individual mind. His temperament always obliged him to examine and re-examine any subject and from every possible angle. He was always ready to rethink matters that appeared closed and settled. His constant fluctuations, skepticism, and hesitation could be construed as a fault or a weakness, but they also constituted a relative advantage. Rathenau's vision was complex and multifaceted. He never grew dogmatic and was always able to adjust to new conditions. Above all, Rathenau could tolerate a high level of ambiguity and ambivalence on a constant basis, as a given that must be faced. That is, no doubt, a rare quality among leaders of any kind; indeed, it is a rare quality at any time or place. And it was in great demand during the early years of the Weimar Republic.

As early as the 1890s, I argued previously, Germany was already split into a number of warring factions.[9] Rathenau did not fit into any of them. Despite his German patriotism, he could not accept the existing order with its fierce nationalism, unrelenting monarchism, and animosity toward anything socialist or egalitarian. All in all, Rathenau was an anti-modernist of a very peculiar shade – he was an anti-modern modernist. Even in his father's days, AEG, the family company, had been the first enterprise to ever install electric street lighting in Germany's larger cities. And that was no coincidence. Young Rathenau, like his father before him,

---

[9] Compare Chapter 5, c.

was an ardent supporter of organizational and practical innovations. He was excited by the new possibilities opened up by modernity in every facet of life. But at the same time he was constantly preoccupied with the cultural implications of that same modernity. Unlike many conservatives in his circles, Rathenau was not afflicted with the "cultural pessimism" that characterized most of them. He did not feel obliged to defend the Prussian nobility's lost privileges and was not deterred by what his nationalist acquaintances perceived as the dangers of cosmopolitanism and democratization. What concerned him was the impact of modernity on higher culture, particularly on the single, creative individual.

All of that made him suspicious in the eyes of the German Right, while his utopian propensity and his theoretical and practical experimentations with "state socialism" did not suffice to brand him a genuine left-winger. His critical view of the German government's policy since the beginning of World War I was exceptional among his industrialist colleagues and in the rightwing camp, no doubt. Finally, despite his doubts and criticism, it was Rathenau who volunteered to help the war effort in its early stages, and while he did toy with pacifism on occasion, he had always maintained contact with the *Reich*'s military leadership. Although he strongly objected to the German leadership's war goals, it was Rathenau who just days before Germany's final collapse, when even Ludendorff could not see any point in continuing the fighting, addressed the exhausted population with a moving plea to stand united against the approaching enemy. In the early days of the Republic, this wealthy capitalist publicly supported a broad social reform, including even a large-scale nationalization policy. He was quick to switch his loyalty from king to republic. From the beginning, he was more than a mere *Vernunftrepublikaner*, that is, a supporter out of pragmatism. He was now ready to defend the new order from its enemies within and without. While each of his position shifts may be plausibly explained, Rathenau did manage to upset everyone by what some saw as his creative flexibility and others as a basic instability.

Rathenau thrived on paradoxes. He cultivated ambivalence and knew how to appreciate complex situations. As such, he finally did become, indeed, an appropriate icon of the Republic. In the new democratic era nothing was as clear and obvious as it was in the old regime. The whole system was now based on tensions and conflicts. Thus a cabinet minister in the Social Democratic government could find himself cooperating with monarchist generals in an effort to repress workers' revolts. A staunch nationalist could decide to adopt a compromising course in addressing the enemies' demands. Veteran republicans criticized "the system" while monarchists were suddenly willing to contribute to its defense. The Weimar democracy, like any other, had to constantly grapple with social schisms; it had to adjust to a routine of incessant ideological debates, to an open conflict of interests, and to a public life that was incontrollable from the top down. Such tensions were difficult to manage. Yet Rathenau felt comfortable in this atmosphere and it seemed easy, indeed, to identify the problematic Republic with his personality. Its defenders and enemies both sensed these hidden relationships. In the eyes of the Republic's supporters, Rathenau epitomized everything that was good about it. He was a cosmopolitan German who was accepted by diplomats as well as by cultural figures everywhere on the European continent; he was an industrialist who was willing to make economic sacrifices and reach agreement with the working class; he was an intellectual who managed to survive in politics; and he was a Jew with a record of unprecedented achievements in the German state. For the Republic's opponents, Rathenau came to represent everything they detested – a symbol of the new situations' ambivalence, divisiveness, and internal strife and the overall sense of weakness and alienation that emanated, so they felt, from this regime. Rathenau seemed to be its perfect symbol: open to talent yet lacking in self-confidence, patriotic yet ready to compromise, modern yet conservative, egalitarian yet fraught with social fears, seemingly free of prejudice yet brimming with hate, and threatening to erupt time and again from under the surface. His assassination was an expression of the discomfort the Weimar Republic stirred up in widespread circles. When the emotional turbulence and rage evoked by his murder had subsided, the Republic went ahead in the same old route. Despite the legislation enacted to protect democracy and its supporters' ardent devotion, the anti-democratic poison continued to pollute it. Rathenau's murder, finally, did not serve to exorcise the evil spirits; it merely served as a foreboding.

Despite the fact that Rathenau was no more a typical Jew than a typical German, a typical industrialist, or a typical statesman, his unique life story sheds light on this chapter in the history of German Jews. His is the tale of success, indeed an astonishing success, in various spheres. It is also the tale of the dangers brought about by this very success. But above all, it underlines the internal conflict, the tension, and the dialectic that characterized the situation of German Jewry at that time, too. Ludwig Börne's motto in the beginning of this book, his desperate reference to the "magical Jewish circle" from which no one could escape, is relevant even in Rathenau's case. Some blamed him for being a Jew while others forgave him that fact, and there were even those who praised him for it. No one could forget his Jewishness.

Jewish integration in modern German society has after all been comprehensive and deep-rooted. In its own way, Germany was no less sincere than France, England, or the United States in its efforts to overcome prejudice and allow its Jews to live as equals within a society aspiring to be just and eventually even egalitarian. Moreover, the achievements of Jews in Germany were particularly impressive. Their role in that country has often been compared to the one Jews fulfilled during the so-called Golden Age in medieval Spain. No current example aptly parallels their flourishing in the years prior to the Nazis' rise to power, yet this blossoming took place while other forces within Germany were pushing for a radical change of direction. For years these forces seemed marginal. The antisemitism that occasionally raised its head could be construed as a relic from ancient times; it could be mistaken for an expression of a general anti-modern sentiment, and it was easy to underestimate. The quick and impressive success of Germany's Jews, their ambition, flexibility, and openness, all seem to have found creative outlets, despite the obstacles and even as a result of the conscious and unconscious efforts to overcome them. It was a blossoming on the edge of the abyss. Hence, from our perspective, it appears truly tragic. As my father wrote in one of his letters, at the last moment it became clear that Jews were living on the deck of a ship destined to sink. Although they did not notice the impending disaster, although they could be seen as fools ignoring the danger ahead, there was something heroic in their existence under the volcano. Jews and Germans, at least some Jews and some Germans, dreamt of a different kind of world. That dream turned out to be an illusion, but it never lost its value: the dream of men and women of different backgrounds and cultures living together, and a democracy that is capable of providing the range of prerequisites for a genuine cooperation among them. It is a worthy dream; many of us still hold on to it.

Index

Marxist, 122
National-liberal, 252
of master artisans', 104
of students, 109
of the *Mittelstand*, 106
popular, 22, 84
Socialist, 121, 124, 126, 128, 129,
150
cooperative, 123
Munich, 38, 44, 48, 212, 213, 214,
235, 242, 293
University of, 242, 246

Napoleon, 92, 93, 250, 252
Napoleonic wars, 172, 195, 198
National Socialism, ix, 49, 58, 68, 69,
70, 71, 72, 73, 74, 75, 80, 81,
154, 289
nationalism, 17, 19, 23, 30, 35, 91, 93,
94, 95, 96, 98, 99, 100, 101, 107,
108, 109, 113, 115, 137, 142,
143, 144, 148, 149, 162, 166,
169, 194, 196, 249, 250, 252,
253, 257, 288, 294
French, 94
integral, 149
Jewish, 21
Nationalzeitung, 100
nation-state, xi, 71, 91, 92, 100, 111,
161, 162, 163, 165, 166, 167, 168
Nazi
antisemitism, 58, 67, 69, 70, 71, 72,
74, 80, 81, 155
ideology, 78
leadership, 1
party, 74
regime, 79, 80
rise to power, 49, 160, 236
students, 3
see National socialism
Nazis, i, 1, 2, 5, 13, 19, 31, 37, 44, 47,
48, 49, 53, 54, 56, 67, 70, 71, 72,
80, 81, 155, 166, 170, 242, 287,
297
and Jews, 54, 55, 56, 155
neo-Romanticism, 249, 251
Nernst, walther, 247

Neustettin, 151
New York, 52, 212
Nietzsche, Friedrich, 3, 42, 252
Nipperdey, Thomas, 51, 94, 95
Nobel, laureates, 225, 230, 233
Nordau, Max, 27, 28, 29, 30
numerus clausus, 2, 53
Nuremberg, 48
Nuremberg, Laws, 2

Odessa, 16, 19, 33
Organization *Consul*, 291
Orient, 50
Orthodoxy, 191, 284
Oslo, University of, 241
Ostjuden, 263, 264, 265, 267, 269,
272, 273, 275
Ostjudenfrage, 263, 265, 268, 274
Ostwald, Wilhelm, 240, 246

pacifism, 136, 295
Palatinate, 173
Palestine Post, 56
Paneth, Friedrich, 234
Pan-German League, 112, 113
Pan-Germanic movement
in Austria, 109
Pankhurst, Emmeline and Christabel,
143
Paris, v, 25, 54, 55, 147, 150, 226, 255
patriotism, 73, 136, 137, 143, 150,
169, 194, 195, 197, 250, 252,
291, 292, 294
patriots, 118, 204, 296
Jews, 117, 251, 254, 257, 271, 285,
291
pauperism, 85
peace movement, 135, 136
peddlers, 88, 208
Peel Commission, 60
Perrot, Frank, 103, 106
Philippson, Ludwig, 50, 284
Philippson, Martin, 50
philosemitism, 118, 127, 139
Pinsker, Leo, 14, 15, 16, 17
Planck, Max, 244, 246
Podolya, 52

For EU product safety concerns, contact us at Calle de José Abascal, 56–1°,
28003 Madrid, Spain or eugpsr@cambridge.org.

www.ingramcontent.com/pod-product-compliance
Ingram Content Group UK Ltd.
Pitfield, Milton Keynes, MK11 3LW, UK
UKHW020339140625
459647UK00018B/2220